Anticipatory Grief

Anticipatory Grief

Edited by
Bernard Schoenberg
Arthur C. Carr
Austin H. Kutscher
David Peretz
Ivan K. Goldberg

With the editorial assistance of
Lillian G. Kutscher

Columbia University Press
New York and London 1974

Library of Congress Cataloging in Publication Data
Main entry under title:

Anticipatory grief.

  Includes bibliographies.
  1. Terminal care. 2. Death. I. Schoenberg,
Bernard, ed. [DNLM: 1. Attitude to death. 2. Grief.
3. Terminal care. BF789.D4 A629 1974]
R726.8A57 616   74-1252
ISBN 0-231-03770-8

Acknowledgment

The editors wish to acknowledge the support and encouragement of the Foundation of Thanatology in the preparation of this volume.

Thanatology, as a new subspecialty of medicine, is involved in scientific and humanistic inquiries and the application of the knowledge derived therefrom to the subjects of the psychological aspects of dying; reactions to loss, death and grief; and recovery from bereavement.

The Foundation of Thanatology, a tax exempt public foundation, is dedicated to advancing the cause of enlightened health care for the terminally ill patient and his family. The Foundation's orientation is a positive one based on the philosophy of fostering a more mature acceptance and understanding of death and the problems of grief and the more effective and humane management and treatment of the dying patient and his bereaved family members.

Contributors

C. Knight Aldrich, M.D., Professor of Community Psychiatry, University of Virginia Medical School, Charlottesville, Virginia; Director of Blue Ridge Mental Health Center, Charlottesville, Virginia

Arthur M. Arkin, M.D., Adjunct Attending Psychiatrist, Psychiatry Division, Montefiore Hospital and Medical Center, Bronx, New York

Martha W. Atchley, Department of Social Work, Memorial Hospital for Cancer and Allied Diseases, New York, New York

Jeanne Quint Benoliel, D.N.S., Professor and Chairman, Comparative Nursing Care Systems Department, School of Nursing, University of Washington, Seattle, Washington

H. Robert Blank, M.D., Associate Editor, *Psychoanalytic Quarterly;* Associate Professor of Psychiatry, Albert Einstein College of Medicine, Bronx, New York

Irwin M. Blank, D.D., Rabbi, Temple Ohabei Shalom, Brookline, Massachusetts

Myra Honore Bluebond-Langner, Ph.D., Department of Anthropology, University of Illinois, Urbana, Illinois

Irving J. Borstein, Ph.D., Director, Family Systems Program, Institute for Juvenile Research, Chicago, Illinois; Assistant Professor, University of Illinois Medical School, Chicago, Illinois

Irene G. Buckley, Executive Director, Cancer Care, Inc. of the National Cancer Foundation, New York, New York

Stanley Budner, Ph.D., Associate Professor (Sociomedical Sciences), School of Public Health and Administrative Medicine, Columbia University, New York, New York

Phyllis Caroff, D.S.W., Associate Professor, The Hunter College School of Social Work, City University of New York, New York

James O. Carpenter, Ph.D., Assistant Professor of Public Health Administration and Associate Director, Program in Health Gerontology, School of Public Health, University of Michigan, Ann Arbor, Michigan

Arthur C. Carr, Ph.D., Professor (Medical Psychology), Department of Psychiatry, College of Physicians and Surgeons, Columbia University, New York, New York; Chairman of the Professional Advisory Board, The Foundation of Thanatology

Daniel J. Cherico, Ph.D., Director, Group Therapy, Day Hospital, Burke Rehabilitation Institute, New York Hospital-Cornell Medical Center, White Plains, New York

Lois K. Christopherson, M.S.W., Chief Social Worker, Department of Surgery, Stanford University, Palo Alto, California

Susan Blecker Cohen, Department of Social Work, Memorial Hospital for Cancer and Allied Diseases, New York, New York

Brenda Comerford, Palo Alto, California

Charles Clay Dahlberg, M.D., Research Psychiatrist, Supervisory and Training Analyst, The William Alanson White Institute; Clinical Associate Professor of Psychiatry, New York University Medical Center; Assistant Visiting Neuro-psychiatrist, Bellevue Hospital Center, New York, New York

Bruce L. Danto, M.D., Director, Suicide Prevention and Drug Information Center, Herman Keiffer Hospital, Detroit, Michigan; Associate Professor, Department of Psychiatry, Wayne State University, Detroit, Michigan

Rose Dobrof, Assistant Professor, The Hunter College School of Social Work, City University of New York, New York

Irwin Gerber, Ph.D., Head, Social Research Unit, Montefiore Hospital and Medical Center, Bronx, New York

Ivan K. Goldberg, M.D., Associate, Department of Psychiatry, College of Physicians and Surgeons, Columbia University, New York, New York

Eda G. Goldstein, M.A., C.S.W., Ph.D., Senior Psychiatric Social Worker, New York State Psychiatric Institute; Assistant in Clinical Psychiatry, College of Physicians and Surgeons, Columbia University, New York, New York

Thomas A. Gonda, M.D., Associate Dean and Professor of Psychiatry, School of Medicine, Stanford University, Palo Alto, California; Director, Stanford University Hospital

Milton Graub, M.D., Professor of Pediatrics, Hahnemann Medical College and Hospital, Philadelphia, Pennsylvania; Past President, National Cystic Fibrosis Research Foundation

Stephen V. Gullo, Ph.D., Instructor (Psychology), School of Education, Brooklyn College, City University of New York; Staff Associate, Institute of Cancer Research, College of Physicians and Surgeons, Columbia University, New York, New York

Georgia Hall, M.P.H., Consultant, Navaho Tribe, Program for the Aged, Navaho Nation, Arizona

Jimmie Holland, M.D., Associate Clinical Professor of Psychiatry, School of Medicine, State University of New York, Buffalo, New York

Chaplain LeRoy G. Kerney, Chief, Department of Spiritual Ministry, Clinical Center, National Institutes of Health, Bethesda, Maryland

Annette Klein, A.C.S.W., Assistant Director, Child Psychiatry Division, University of Illinois; Associate Professor, University of Illinois, Chicago, Illinois

Austin H. Kutscher, D.D.S., President, Foundation of Thanatology; Associate Professor, Director, New York State Psychiatric Institute Dental Service, School of Dental and Oral Surgery, Columbia University, New York, New York

Austin H. Kutscher, Jr., Class of 1977, College of Physicians and Surgeons, Columbia University, New York, New York

Lillian Kutscher, Publications Editor, Foundation of Thanatology, New York, New York

Martin I. Lorin, M.D., Babies Hospital, Columbia-Presbyterian Medical Center, New York, New York

Sidney Malitz, M.D., Associate Director, New York State Psychiatric Institute, New York, New York; Professor of Psychiatry, College of Physicians and Surgeons, Columbia University; Chief, Department of Biological Psychiatry, New York State Psychiatric Institute, New York, New York

Joseph H. Meyerowitz, Ph.D., Director, Research Division, Ministry of Welfare, State of Israel, Jerusalem, Israel

Ruth Michaels, Director of Social Service, Cancer Care, Inc. of the National Cancer Foundation, New York, New York

Robert E. Neale, Th.D. Professor, Program in Psychiatry and Religion, Union Theological Seminary, New York, New York

Carl A. Nighswonger, Ph.D., Chaplain, The University of Chicago Hospitals and Clinics, Chicago, Illinois (deceased)

Reverend Thomas Nolan, R.N., Church of St. Benedict, Bronx, New York

David Peretz, M.D., Assistant Clinical Professor, Department of Psychiatry, College of Physicians and Surgeons, Columbia University; Chairman, Research Committee of the Foundation of Thanatology

Vanderlyn R. Pine, Ph.D., Assistant Professor of Sociology, State University College, New Paltz, New York

Marjorie M. Plumb, Ph.D., Assistant Clinical Professor, Department of Psychiatry, School of Medicine, State University of New York, Buffalo, New York

Elsa Poslusny, R.N., M.S., Associate Professor, Department of Nursing, College of Physicians and Surgeons, Columbia University, New York, New York

Elizabeth R. Prichard, Director of Social Service, The Presbyterian Hospital in the City of New York; Assistant Professor, Department of Medicine (Medical Social Work), College of Physicians and Surgeons, Columbia University, New York, New York

Mary T. Ramshorn, R.N., Ed.D., Assistant Professor, Department of Nursing Education, Teachers College, Columbia University, New York, New York

Allan W. Reed, Protestant Chaplain and Supervisor of Clinical Pastoral Education, Massachusetts General Hospital, Boston, Massachusetts; Clinical Associate, Episcopal Theological School and Boston University, Boston, Massachusetts

Reverend Robert B. Reeves, Jr., Chaplain, The Presbyterian Hospital in the City of New York, Columbia-Presbyterian Medical Center, New York, New York

Guy F. Robbins, M.D., Director of Extramural Education and Acting Chief, Breast Service, Memorial Hospital for Cancer and Allied Diseases, New York, New York

Benjamin F. Rush, Jr., M.D., Johnson and Johnson Professor of Surgery; Chairman, Department of Surgery, College of Medicine and Dentistry, New Jersey Medical School, Martland Hospital Unit, Newark, New Jersey

Bernard Schoenberg, M.D., Associate Dean for Allied Health Sciences, College of Physicians and Surgeons, Columbia University; Associate Professor of Clinical Psychiatry, Department of Psychiatry, College of Physicians and Surgeons, Columbia University, New York, New York; Chairman, Executive Committee, Foundation of Thanatology

John E. Schowalter, M.D., Associate Professor of Psychiatry and Pediatrics, Yale University School of Medicine; Director of Training, Yale Child Study Center, New Haven, Connecticut

Robert Shadick, Ed.D., Associate Professor and Chairman, Division of Elementary and Middle Schools, School of Education, Brooklyn College, City University of New York, Brooklyn, New York

Phyllis R. Silverman, Ph.D., Lecturer in Social Welfare, Department of Psychiatry, Harvard Medical School; Laboratory of Community Psychiatry, Department of Psychiatry, Harvard Medical School, Boston, Massachusetts

Margot Tallmer, Ph.D., Assistant Professor, Hunter College, City University of New York, New York

Rudolf Toch, M.D., Instructor, Department of Pediatrics, Harvard Medical School, Boston, Massachusetts

Richard J. Torpie, M.D., Assistant Professor of Radiation Therapy, Department of Radiation Therapy and Nuclear Medicine, Hahnemann Medical College and Hospital, Philadelphia, Pennsylvania

Lois Weinstein, Department of Social Work, Memorial Hospital for Cancer and Allied Diseases, New York, New York

Avery D. Weisman, M.D., Project Omega, Department of Psychiatry, Harvard Medical School, Boston, Massachusetts

Contents

Anticipatory Grief

PART *1*
INTRODUCTORY CONCEPTS

1

Some Dynamics of Anticipatory Grief
C. Knight Aldrich

I began to think about anticipatory grief almost twenty-five years ago, soon after beginning liaison teaching of psychiatry to junior medical students on their medical clerkships at the University of Minnesota Hospital. At that time, many of the referrals to the University Hospital were made as a last resort, and so resulted in a high proportion of patients without possibility of recovery. The students often discussed their distress at seeing how helpless medicine was in its efforts to cure these patients. They also reported how uneasy they were made by talking with the dying, and by the prospect of someday being responsible for deciding whether and how to tell the patient that he or she was going to die (Aldrich, 1953). They indicated how little help they received from their teachers in understanding these problems.

Most of the students did not think it was appropriate for a physician to deceive his patients. On the other hand, they believed that to tell a dying patient the truth about his prognosis would probably precipitate a depression, and might even lead to suicide. Since a discussion of this dilemma developed with almost every student group, it was necessary to try to understand more about the psychology of dying.

Much of the psychology of dying is concerned with the fear of death, which includes fear of the pain and disability attendant upon dying, the fear of an afterlife—or of oblivion, and the fear or anxiety at the prospect of separation from loved ones. Along with the fear, or instead of fear, there are usually symptoms of depression, either overt or covert. This paper is concerned primarily with the depressive rather than the anxious component of the psychology of dying.

WHAT IS ANTICIPATORY GRIEF?

The symptoms of acute grief, dramatically described by Erich Lindemann (1944) in survivors of the disastrous Cocoanut Grove fire who had lost a loved one, have much in common with the grief of the dying patient at the prospective, or anticipatory, loss of all of his loved ones (Aldrich, 1963). Although Lindemann used the term "Anticipatory Grief Reactions" to refer specifically to grief responses to possible death, as in the case of relatives' reactions to a member of the armed services entering a combat zone, it seems reasonable to apply the same term to grief expressed in advance when the loss is perceived as inevitable. The term "anticipatory grief," therefore, is used here to mean any grief occurring prior to a loss, as distinguished from the grief which occurs at or after the loss (Aldrich, 1955). Any grief that the dying patient experiences must occur before his losses, or in anticipation of loss, while the survivors' grief usually occurs both before and after the loss. Thus, as Parkes (1970) has reported, most widows have known about their impending widowhood in advance, and so experience both anticipatory and conventional grief in sequence. Furthermore, anticipatory grief is usually experienced (or denied) simultaneously by both the patient and his family, while conventional grief is experienced only by the survivors.

My early impression was that the dynamics of anticipatory grief simply paralleled those of conventional grief. It seemed to me that grief work could be carried out, losses could be denied, grief could be disguised, feelings could be repressed, displaced, converted, and so on, in much the same way, whether before or after the fact. Although the parallels are still apparent, as time has passed, several important differences have been conceptualized.

ENDPOINTS AND ACCELERATION

One difference is in the *endpoints* of the two types of grief. Conventional grief can be indefinitely prolonged; it can continue, as in the famous example of Queen Victoria's grief for Prince Albert, for many years and its duration seems to depend as much or more on the mourner's psychology as on the nature of the loss. Anticipatory grief, on the other hand, has a finite endpoint dependent on the external circumstance of the physical occurrence of the anticipated loss. Grief may continue after that point, but is no longer anticipatory grief.

Another, and perhaps more important, difference is in *acceleration*. Under ordinary circumstances, conventional grief decelerates or diminishes in degree as time passes, while anticipatory grief theoretically should accelerate, or increase in degree as the anticipated loss becomes more imminent. After all, the insecure mother whose only child is going to school for the first time is usually perceived to be more upset about it on Labor Day than on the Fourth of July, although she had known for a long time that the separation was coming.

But despite qualitative similarities, the quantitative impact of permanent loss through death differs tremendously from that of a loss that ends when the afternoon schoolbell rings. A major loss or its anticipation can be too devastating for the individual to face directly, and so it may mobilize the individual's spectrum of ego defenses, in a manner related to the extent and significance of the particular loss, and to his past patterns of defense, as well as to external circumstances. Denial of the reality of the anticipated loss is probably the most common defense. Perhaps the balance between denial (presumably forestalling anticipatory grief work) and acceptance (presumably facilitating anticipatory grief work) can help to explain the discrepancy between the theoretical expectation that grief will increase in degree as the loss approaches and clinical observations that overt grief in anticipation of loss does not accelerate consistently in degree as the loss approaches. Both the direction and rate of change in the extent of grief are affected by individual factors. For example, the reduction in ego boundaries (in the William James sense) as death approaches may reduce the impact of anticipated loss and so decelerate grief in the dying patient (Aldrich, 1963). If the potential survivors' period of anticipation is unusually long, their grief work may be accomplished to some extent in advance, with the result that the manifestations of anticipatory grief may decelerate as the time of the loss approaches.

AMBIVALENCE

Ambivalence has a special impact on anticipatory grief that differs in some respects from its impact on conventional grief. Conventional grief tends to be prolonged when for any of several reasons ambivalent feelings about the lost object are so unacceptable to the mourner that they are repressed or in other ways disguised, thus becoming inaccessible to conscious resolution. Ambivalent feelings may be unacceptable because of early training forbidding the acknowledgment of hostility, because of a persistent equation of hostile wish with hostile act, because of an unusually high component of hostility in the ambivalence, because of the extent of dependency in the ambivalent relationship, or because of any combination of these reasons. Some mourners who cannot accept their ambivalence may persist in their grief almost as if they feel that to stop grieving would be equivalent to an acknowledgment that they are glad that the loved ones are dead. In other mourners with unacceptable ambivalence toward lost objects, the guilt about (or fear of the consequences of) the hostile component stirs up too much conflict to permit any direct expression of grief at or about the time of the loss. In these cases the expression of grief is either delayed or disguised.

The difference in the impact of ambivalence on the anticipatory grief of family members is that the target of the ambivalent feelings is not only still alive but also particularly vulnerable, balanced between life and death. This vulnerability makes a death wish appear particularly potent and dangerous. This factor may contribute to the clinical impression that anticipatory grief appears to be more readily denied than conventional grief, to a degree greater than that which might be expected from the apparently more tangible (and so less easily deniable) nature of the loss in conventional grief. (On the other hand, one might argue that anticipated loss can be more tangible than actual loss; grandmother in the process of dying at home is constantly there to break down denial, while grandmother in her grave is out of sight.)

While there is life, there's hope, as the saying goes, and hope therefore can accompany anticipatory grief, while it does not, at least in the same realistic or short-term sense, accompany conventional grief. Thus, in anticipatory grief the mourner can take action that might conceivably delay the loss or prevent it from happening. He can or he cannot negotiate for a change of physicians, seeking a miracle cure; he can overprotect—or underprotect—the patient; he can increase—or decrease—the amount of time he spends in encouraging the patient to eat and keep up his strength, and so on. The anticipatory mourner with unacceptable ambivalence, therefore, can increase his guilt about his death wish by committing what he may interpret as errors of omission or commission in patient care. By contrast, in conventional grief whatever measures the mourner takes cannot affect the timing or extent of the loss. He may or may not expiate any guilt that intensifies or distorts his grief; he may or may not bring back the loss in fantasy. But nothing he does can change the irrevocable fact that the loss has occurred.

Since objective evidence for what might lengthen or shorten a patient's life is often absent or obscure, those grieving in anticipation can seldom be sure that a decision they make is best for the dying patient. Even without appreciable quantities of unacceptable ambivalence, they are made anxious by the need to decide. Richmond (1955) says,

Because of the considerable anxiety which parents of a child with a malignant disorder faced, we believed it undesirable to add to this anxiety by leaving decisions concerning treatment to them. We are aware of the fact that it is not uncommon for physicians to leave a decision to parents as to whether an attempt at treatment is to be instituted, with potential prolongation of life. We believe that the feelings of guilt which every parent has to some extent are too great to permit the intensification which may occur when the parent is placed in a position of making a decision which may or may not alter the course of the disease.

A period of anticipation, therefore, may provide a mourner with an opportunity to carry out grief work in advance of loss, but at the same time it complicates the working-through process by giving the hostile component of ambivalence a more realistically destructive potential. A long period of anticipation increases both the duration of the destructive potential and the opportunity for working through. This balance between factors increasing and factors decreasing the intensity of the conventional, post-loss grief reaction may account for such contradictory findings as those of Parkes (1970), Maddison (1968), and Clayton (1968), who observed that the duration of the period of anticipation is not significantly related to the severity of the grief reaction, and Parkes' 1972 study, which found more emotional disturbance in widows following deaths for which they had had little time to prepare.

Parkes (1970) points out that Lindemann's observations of the relatively short duration of grief reactions has "caused several workers, including the writer, to underestimate the probable duration of uncomplicated grief" (p. 464). In all of Parkes' cases, "there has been some evidence of illness before death occurred; nineteen of twenty-two wives had been told of the seriousness of their husbands' illnesses, thirteen of them at least a month before the death," (p. 447), whereas the "normal grief reactions" reported by Lindemann included a high proportion of relatives of Cocoanut

Grove victims, who had had no period of anticipation. If it can be confirmed that a period of anticipation, however brief, does indeed tend to prolong conventional grief, particular attention should be given to preventive intervention during the anticipatory grief phase. However, in a disaster such as the Cocoanut Grove Fire there may be group factors—shared mourning, evidence of nationwide sympathy—that facilitate early working through of grief.

DENIAL

Originally, I attributed the high prevalence of *denial* among dying patients to the extent of their anticipated losses. I now suspect that the special impact of ambivalence on anticipatory grief may also be a contributor. A dying patient grieves in anticipation for the loss of his loved ones. He must be very tolerant indeed of his ambivalence if he can cope without denial with feelings which, translated into words, say, "I don't want to die; I wish instead that it were he (or she or they)." Or, "I can't bear to leave them all; I want them (or some of them anyway) to come with me." In this way, ambivalence may increase the likelihood of denial, at least until such time as the dying patient's disengagement from his loved ones and his narcissistic withdrawal have progressed to a point from which he can face death and loss with relative equanimity.

SUMMARY

The dynamics of anticipatory grief have much in common with those of conventional grief. There are differences, however, in such aspects as endpoint, acceleration, hope, and vulnerability of the object of ambivalence that may affect the duration of conventional grief when it follows a period of anticipatory grief.

REFERENCES

Aldrich, C. K., "The Dying Patient's Grief," *Journal of the American Medical Association,* *184:*329, 1963.
——— "Psychiatric Teaching on an Inpatient Medical Service," *Journal of Medical Education,* *28:*36, 1953.
——— *Psychiatry for the Family Physician.* New York: Blakiston-McGraw-Hill, 1955.

Clayton, P., L. Desmarais, and G. Winokur, "A Study of Normal Bereavement," *American Journal of Psychiatry, 125:*168, 1968.

Lindemann, E., "Symptomatology and Management of Acute Grief," *American Journal of Psychiatry, 101:*141, 1944.

Maddison, D., and A. Viola, "The Health of Widows in the Year Following Bereavement," *Journal of Psychosomatic Research, 12:*297, 1968.

Parkes, C. M., "The First Year of Bereavement," *Psychiatry, 33:*444, 1970.

Parkes, C. M., and R. Brown, "Health After Bereavement—A Controlled Study of Young Boston Widows and Widowers," *Psychosomatic Medicine, 34:*449, 1972.

Richmond, J. B., and H. A. Waisman, "Psychologic Aspects of Management of Children with Malignant Diseases, *American Journal of Diseases of Children, 89:*42, 1955.

2

Notes on Anticipatory Grief *
Arthur M. Arkin

The phenomenon of grief before the fact of actual bereavement has been the subject of increasing attention in recent times. From one point of view, one might consider that the anlage of this phenomenon may be found in early development. For example, after the establishment of the infant's emotional attachment to a specific mothering person, the infant often shows signs of what appears to be anticipation of possible abandonment. Furthermore, somewhere around the age of five, children begin to notice that living things have the capability of dying. The occasion of this awareness is often the observation of a dead animal, or of dead leaves falling from trees. At the same time, children tend to express concern about whether people in the family will die. Perhaps the famous Buddhist legend of the "Four Passing Sights" provides a relevant lesson about the importance of these precursors of anticipatory grief.

Gautama Buddha's father, a chieftain of a tribe in India, was warned at the time of Gautama's birth that the child might someday give up his birth-

* The material for this paper was obtained from the work and workers on a research grant from the National Institute of Mental Health, #MH-14490, Center for Studies of Suicide Prevention, entitled "Brief Psychotherapy to Bereaved Families," on which project the following personnel from the Departments of Psychiatry and/or Social Medicine of Montefiore Hospital and Medical Center, Bronx, New York, were also involved: Irwin Gerber, Ph.D., Alfred Wiener, M.D., Arthur M. Arkin, M.D., Ernest Koller, B.A., Delia Battin, M.S.W., Alice Harrell, R.N., B.S., Elinor Lawless, and Paula Herz.

right and become a homeless monk, but that, if prevented from this choice, he might become Emperor of India. Believing that awareness of death and the sorrows and sufferings of life turn many people to religion, the father was determined to shield his growing son from any hint of knowledge that human life is terminated by old age, disease, and death, and he went to elaborate lengths to accomplish this. But the gods decided that it would not be so, and when Gautama was a young, married prince they descended to earth in the form of apparitions of old age, disease, and death, each appearing before Gautama as he traveled along a road. The apparitions caused the young prince to reflect that this, too, was his own fate, and he became deeply depressed. Only the Fourth Passing Sight restored peace of soul—a calm, ascetic monk who gave him religious instruction. In short, Gautama was prevented by his father from living through the precursors of anticipatory grief and acquiring serviceable defenses against it. As a result, he was vulnerable to a severe depression which bore the earmarks of anticipatory grief in its content—a mourning for the fact that life was all too transitory. He was grief-stricken in *advance* that someday all would come to an end.

During adult life, the cognitive-emotional needs of diverse types are gratified in relationships to other persons, to pets, institutions of employment, one's dwelling, and so on. Not only do these provide us with something to love dearly, but also with something from which we receive love and sustenance. In addition, the components of such relationships become familiar units of individual cognitive maps by which we navigate through our separate worlds and which impart a predictable stability to our lives. Any threat to the integrity of such relationships arouses earlier anxieties which the adult continues to harbor but has managed to assuage by means of these instrumentalities. Death robs us of these familiar and stabilizing relationships. What human beings dread most is being taken by a frightening surprise which they feel unprepared and unable to master. Death is such a frightening shock, against which one can never be totally intellectually fortified.

How might these considerations apply to the question of anticipatory grief? It is a commonplace clinical observation that patients will often experience unbearable agitation when someone close to them becomes ill. This agitation is frequently accompanied by vivid fantasies of the ill individual inexorably getting sicker and eventually dying. This may be further amplified by expressions such as, "Now he too will go down the drain," or "I have to find a way of writing her off," or "Will I be able to bear the loss of this treasured person (thing)? Will I be able to find someone new as a replacement?"

Efforts to defend against such anxieties by denial and reversal may take the following form: "I *won't* be destroyed by the death; I didn't need him (her); he (she) was quite a burden anyway—good riddance!" That is, patients give evidence at such times of wanting to detach themselves emotionally from the ill relative or friend and to form a new attachment to someone or something else in order to quell the anxiety occasioned by the loss of the emotionally invested object. They feel compelled to "line up" someone in advance, to have someone immediately available to slip into the breach. Such fantasies in themselves arouse considerable shame, guilt, and self-reproach. These, in turn, increase the need to find another person on whom one can depend for absolution. In addition, patients having such fantasies are prone to feel that, as they are ready to discard an ill relative because he is useless and a burden, so the same thing must happen, and indeed should justly happen, to them. The phenomenon of anticipatory grief is made more understandable if one ascribes to it the function of rehearsal to better withstand the dreaded event. That is, the person, rather than being taken by surprise by the sudden loss of the emotionally important object, rehearses the loss in fantasies again and again in an effort to gird his loins, the better to endure the final moment of actual death and the accompanying anxiety. (The above description is certainly incomplete because it omits essential psychodynamic elements, such as guilt occasioned by unconscious death wishes being evaluated as the cause of the illness itself.)

The question arises as to whether anticipatory grief possesses adaptational value; that is, is it possible that the person who experiences intense grief in anticipation is more likely to have a less distressful and disabling period of bereavement? To the best of the author's knowledge, this has not been adequately researched. Studies have been made on analogous situations which may throw some light upon this question. For example, Janis (1958), in his study on preoperative anxiety in relation to postoperative psychiatric morbidity, concluded that an optimum amount of preoperative "worry work" is associated with less postoperative morbidity than either the absence or unconscious repression of preoperative anxiety or overwhelming conscious preoperative anxiety. Other studies, such as those of Titchener *et al.* (1957) are not consistent with Janis' conclusions. In addition, it has been observed that soldiers who have been afflicted with anxiety neuroses in civilian life often do better in battle than many who have never experienced anxiety before, and for whom it comes as a frightening surprise. To the former group, anxiety is a familiar experience and, therefore, often apt to be less overwhelming.

A definitive clinical research project would be of some practical importance because it might indicate that the relatives of a fatally ill patient should be encouraged *in a psychotherapeutically appropriate manner* to carry out an optimum amount of anticipatory grief work as a prophylaxis against later disabling pathological grief and bereavement syndromes.

REFERENCES

Janis, S. L., *Psychological Stress*. New York: Wiley, 1958.

Switzer, D. K., *The Dynamics of Grief*. Nashville, Tenn.: Abingdon Press, 1970.

Titchener, J. L., *et al.*, "Consequences of Surgical Illness and Treatment," *Archives of Neurology and Psychiatry, 77:*623, 1957.

3

Is Mourning Necessary?

Avery D. Weisman

Bereavement results from loss, but not every loss results in bereavement. We can undergo many individual griefs, without mourning, sadness, or feeling bereft. It is probably correct to surmise that behind each separate grief and painful separation is the image of death itself, our common fate and ultimate fact.

The word "Grief" does not necessarily signify grieving or being in a state of mourning. Its more precise meaning is conveyed by the phrase "coming to grief," which carries the sense that we are overtaken or seized by misfortune. The term "bereavement," better designates the *entire process* of accommodation to specific loss. It is not the same as grief, grieving, sadness, mourning, depression, or estrangement. Moreover, we should also distinguish the process of bereavement from both its most conspicuous symptoms and from the social customs and ceremonials that have grown up around the loss of a loved one.

Anticipatory grief is the first stage of bereavement. In its broadest outline, the stages of bereavement consist of (a) anticipatory grief, (b) mourning, (c) resolution, and (d) restitution. There is a wide spectrum of symptomatic responses at each stage. In general, however, anticipatory grief is followed by more serious problems of disorganization and depletion, of crying and craving, perceptual aberrations, and then, gradually, coping, return of effective behavior, and closure. The process is completed when the factual loss becomes a significant memory. We continue to care, but the loss is no longer devastating.

It is not merely loss with which we contend in anticipatory grief, but certain kinds of loss. When does it begin? For whom do we start to grieve? And why do we grieve? The deprivation in death is because a human life has reached zero potential and a part of one's self is dead. The unique characteristic of anticipatory grief is that we mourn for a loss that has not yet happened. The future is seen in terms of an irretrievable past.

We grieve only for someone whose absence would create the most significant disruption in our life. We may rue the death of a contemporary or of someone who was once very important. But we rarely undergo anticipatory grief, imagining what life will be like without that person's presence. The degree of anticipatory grief is in direct proportion to the love we feel. If we imagine the death of someone we love, it is fair to say that anticipatory grief begins just as soon as love is implanted. This bittersweet flower carries the seeds of remorse, regret, dread, and separation. It is nurtured by our image of death, loneliness, deprivation, and potential destruction of a salient part of our own life.

It is essential that we see grief and love as mirrored images. Consequently, in order to discuss anticipatory grief we should also recognize a state of anticipatory love. This does not mean that love ends when grief begins, but rather that love and grief enhance each other. Just as being in love inflates our sense of reality, anticipatory grief diminishes us. Anyone who has ever been in love recalls the anguish of anticipatory grief, which is as vivid as the immediate satisfactions and frustrations. To have, but not to hold . . . to hold, but not to have—these are the torments shared by those who anticipate both love and death. It is natural to deny the reality of death, and say, "Never!" Then, when the shadow of death comes closer, to say with equal force, "Not yet!" Finally, after the actual loss occurs, part of the pain comes out when we cry, "Nevermore!" In psychological terms, premonitory denial has gradually given way to confrontation with extinction.

"Never." "Not yet." "Nevermore." These are sentiments which are characteristic of an irrational timelessness. The process of bereavement brings both love and death back into time, subjecting them to the sharp discriminations of reality testing. Just as conflict requires resolution, profound loss must find a new version of itself, so that restitution can be followed by closure. Anticipatory grief is a significant part of this process because it permits us to cope in advance with a loss that hasn't yet happened. The transition point is located between the never and the not yet. The threat becomes apparent, and the incipient separation and loss re-enter time.

Some people start anticipatory grief with symptoms typical of mourning, as if the loss had already occurred. They feel and act disorganized, weep and crave some relic of the loved one. Sometimes they detach themselves prematurely, even while the person is still alive. Lindemann discusses young women who married just before their husbands went overseas during World War II. They grieved, behaving as if they were already widows. Then, after their husbands returned, nothing was left. In some cases, not even memories remained; their husbands were strangers. Resolution and closure had taken place. Love vanished along with mourning, so that the bereavement process was completed.

Death represents everything we learn to deplore in life. In a general sense, the meaning of death is that it systematizes all our suffering. This is why mankind fears death so much, and why bereavement inflicts so much anguish. We deny death because we have no other way, it seems, to deal with it. Anticipatory grief, in some instances, is fear of bereavement. The fear of death becomes the fact of death. When this happens, the bereavement process may be accelerated or delayed. Some cases of pathological grief and mourning can be traced to aberrant timing between psychological preparation and the fact of death. Delayed or accelerated bereavements are frequently found in survivors of patients who have had long, drawn-out fatal illnesses.

Diluted forms of pathological or, indeed, normal bereavement are regularly found among professionals who tend the dying and bereaved. They are exposed to two hazards: caring too much, and caring too little. When the first occurs, the "worker" (what a sad term!) becomes a surrogate mourner. Because he loses a piece of himself whenever someone he cares about dies, he is not much use to the genuine survivors. When the second occurs, the professional worker becomes a brisk technician, presiding over the passage of still another statistic.

Despite these hazards, study of how "death workers" manage to maintain their equilibrium may help us to understand more about the bereavement process, and thereby reduce the anguish that comes with actual, unprepared-for mourning. It is something like learning more about what goes on inside a blast furnace by measuring the temperature with sensitive instruments and observing the molten material through a protective shield.

There are some people who have a natural immunity to many kinds of stress. They can be repeatedly exposed to various pathogenic conditions without overt damage or development of symptoms. On the other hand, we can acquire a degree of immunity to certain diseases by becoming its victims. It is possible to "learn from experience," and to accept the reality of significant losses for ourselves, and for others, without overidentification or exacerbation of old griefs.

A third form of immunity can be acquired when we deliberately expose ourselves to a diluted strain of a pathogenic organism, and actively undergo a slight case of that disease. All three forms of immunity can be found among death workers. Deliberately excluded from this discussion are people who seek self-treatment through working with the dying and bereaved, or those who choose this specialty as a counterphobic vocation. One of the encouraging aspects of working in thanatology is that repeated slight cases of bereavement permit us to face each new encounter with lessened fear. Thus we are able to offer more constructive help to the bereaved and the dying. Part of the effectiveness, such as it is, is the result of eliminating self-pity, remorse, and mourning. Painless bereavement requires that we facilitate anticipatory grief, recognize the elements in suitable resolution and restitution, and take steps to encourage closure.

Let us imagine that we were suddenly given two powers: to postpone death for, say, another twenty years, and to be immune to sadness, suffering, and mourning. There would be two consequences: survival would be extended long enough to relieve anticipatory grief and even to restore our innate belief that death might never come. The second consequence is that our immunity to suffering, with all of its guilt, shame, anger, and hopelessness, would enable us to deal more effectively and compassionately with the important issues surrounding life and death.

Immunity to suffering, which means minimal mourning, would be equivalent to compassion, sensitive regard for someone else. It would be quite different from what we often find now: premature closure, protective indifference, or exaggerated pity. Extended survival would almost certainly postpone actual mourning and, as indicated, relieve anticipatory grief. But the certainty of death might remove it from the "never, never" of futile hope to the "not yet" of anticipatory grief. Whenever we experience anticipatory grief, of necessity we extend the domain of love. In short, these two imaginary powers might mean a heightened capacity for being mindful of what really matters—for me, from you, from me, for you—for our mutual reality.

But, one might and should say, we cannot extend survival another twenty years. At best, medicine can extend life only by hours, days, and weeks. Sometimes this is even worse than dying. The quality of life may suffer as we attenuate it. However, what is meant by citing this imaginary power is that it would permit us to familiarize ourselves with death before it is at the door. Anticipation might mean preparation, and even creative recognition of what it means to be alive. Of course, were the first power granted, we might even bargain for another extension. Longevity is seldom long enough, and does not consist of a fixed number of years. Endless survival cannot be our goal. We do not need an imaginary extension of time if we can sustain the sense of being alive as a significant person. Hope depends not on endless survival, but on the sense of worthiness. This is expressed in how we anticipate grieving for those who mean the most to us. This does not mean professional impersonality or emotional isolation. Rather, we should examine our fear of bereavement during anticipatory grief. By doing so, we come closer to the second imagined power: to be compassionate through immunizing ourselves to the painful aspects of bereavement.

We can use anticipatory grief. Compassionate survival for all of us means that this is the substance of hope, without deception. In caring for the dying and bereaved we often find guilt, remorse, and vanity intertwined. Largely, this results from an unwarranted belief in a state of being exempt from death and from a fear of living in vain. The illusion that death can be prevented or at least postponed indefinitely is equivalent to feeling that we have or can seek the imaginary power of extending survival beyond the reach of grief. To be surrounded by reminders of mortality is by no means a gloomy prospect. The phrase "memento mori" should not be pessimistically construed. Awareness of our limited life span can, with compassion, awaken us to the necessity and obligation of individual death within finite time. In one sense, we are living on borrowed time—and would like to extend our indebtedness. But in another sense, we have not borrowed time; we are living within an undetermined allotment. Hence, anticipatory grief is part of our anticipated reality. Practically enough, compassion can generate a fusion of death and love which is the basis for finding a death we can live with.

4

A Societal Response

Margot Tallmer

It is a curious and patently significant fact that there is a notable exclusion of the topic of death from current gerontological literature. Two social scientists, Elaine Cumming and William Henry, explain this puzzling phenomenon as a reflection of the widely accepted "activity theory" of aging. This theory holds that the aging individual who manages to maintain social and nonsocial activities as long as possible, or to find suitable replacements for those he is obliged to abandon, is considered psychologically better adjusted and more satisfied than persons unable to withstand constriction. If constant expansion and prolonged engagement with life are the desiderata, it would hardly be fitting within such a framework to elaborate on disengagement or death. The activity theory of aging has not been scientifically promulgated but has been accepted as a moralistic position.

Cumming and Henry (1961) question this implicit assumption of the value of extended activity into old age and suggest, contrariwise, that a social and psychological withdrawal may be a necessary condition for optimal aging. As functional theorists, they argue that a certain homeostatic balance is necessary for both the individual and the group, and since this equilibrium must not be disrupted by the death of a human being, both society and the individual prepare in advance to avoid the break. It would be difficult for society to have its current work, such as economic production, child rearing, and the like, impeded by the leave-taking of those deeply involved in societal functions. And the older person himself can accept death more comfortably when he no longer has any social ties.

"Accept death more comfortably" is a key phrase because a major premise of this theory is that withdrawal is mutually satisfying for the individual and for society—that, indeed, the process is initiated by the individual and by others in his social system, enabling both the individual and society to preadjust to death. The authors speculate that at some point around the age of forty, one becomes aware of the remaining time alloted to him, perceives his social space as decreasing, with a concomitant diminution of ego energy, and commences voluntarily to disengage. Disengagement, as here defined, is the opposite of engagement or the interpenetration of the person and his society, and may be measured by the potential disruption to society a person's death would occasion. Death would be total disengagement by definition, but living persons can also be fully disengaged.

The aging person is thus seen by Cumming and Henry not as a victim of societal pressures but rather a willing and eager confederate. For, coincidental with the individual's realization of the shortness of life, is society's awareness of this and its consequent permission to disengage. One is no longer required to be involved and can adapt reasonably to an intense interest with inner concerns, a simultaneous growth in passivity, less control of impulse life, and detachment from the mastery of the external world. With social participation at a minimum, the geront person feels ready to die and is given license to do so by a permissive, accepting society. Disengagement is considered to be a biologically determined, universal, self-perpetuating, and inevitable process. The theory, as propounded and inductively developed from a cross-sectional study of an urban population, attempts to explain within a functional framework the patent observation that many of our elderly are socially and psychologically withdrawn from the society in which they live.

Disengagement theory attempts to explain this fact in the way that functionalists traditionally view social progress. If a partially true observation about our social system is made, the event has a purpose and a meaning, and its existence precludes a necessity to search either for causative factors or for possibilities for change. The functionalist, noting the withdrawal of old people, would not then examine underlying causes or interaction between the elderly person and his environment (Rose, 1964).

Because man is mortal and death a universal fact, disengagement is considered to be worldwide. It is apparent today in America that a greater value is placed on youth, its standards, achievements, and competitive values, than upon merits commensurate with old age. Additionally, our economic structure helps to accelerate the disengagement of the elderly. But there are present trends which may positively affect the lamentable position of the aged, including recent medical discoveries with implications for a longer and healthier life, increased economic security via pensions, Medicare, and the like, and social movements of the elderly themselves. This was witnessed clearly in the White House Conference on Aging. Reports from other countries suggest further that the concept of universality is not valid for all countries, nor are the same criteria of worth exhibited. For example, Talmon (1963) has indicated that older persons are functioning well in Israel, showing a shift and rearrangement of role relationship rather than a linear decrement. Current accounts from Abkhasia, in the U.S.S.R., delineate a nearly full participation by an unusually large group of aged, ranging in age from eighty to 119, "who are still very much a part of the collective life they helped to organize."

We have noted that disengagement is considered to be an intrinsic rather than a receptive process, natural rather than imposed. The process is preceded or accompanied by an individual's self-preoccupation and by a withdrawal of emotional involvement with surroundings and people. This ego alteration is seen as physiologically determined, so that biological and societal aging become equated with each other, both proceeding in one direction. As a deteriorative process, once begun, it becomes self-perpetuating.

To suggest that disengagement is a gradual linear process is to deny information that we have about development. The latter is not a smooth, gradual process, advancing step-by-step toward a goal, but rather is characterized by qualitative shifts, by forward and backward maneuvers.

Cumming and Henry have not considered other forces in the social environment that may explain withdrawal. As such, it is not a theory of the process of aging but more a description of the sociopsychological changes experienced by some geronts, a description of possible events. Society does not act in a passive manner toward the elderly, but rather intercedes with strong, negative forces, removing many possibilities and then proffering only dull or inadequate substitutes for that which is taken away (Kleemeier, 1964). But a minimal quantity of excitation is necessary if behavior and activity are not to deteriorate (Hebb, 1955; Heron, 1957). "A certain amount of arousal is necessary to keep the organism functioning. There is a kind of psychological tonus, not too different from the concept of physical tonus, which is maintained by arousal stimuli. When these drop below a certain level, all activities are affected" (Anderson, 1959). Anderson's proposal leads to the idea of a vicious cycle operating: lack of stimulation leads to a decrement of activity, which results in still less stimulation and ultimately to deterioration of behavior.

Because society has interfered, we must question if the process is natural, as stated by the theory. We are concerned over the meaning of the word natural—"according to nature"—as it is applied here. Withdrawal is occasioned by events. It is not a result of a natural process, a result of growth and development. There is distinct, valid, and definitive empirical evidence that disengagement can be predicted to occur as a concomitant of social and physical assaults such as retirement, widowhood, and ill health, and that the effect of these insults is as great and usually greater than the effect of age (Tallmer and Kutner, 1969). The word "natural" implies an evolutionary state, and the assumption is made that it is better to acquiesce to what is "natural," and not to interfere with a process that makes the individual more comfortable.

The concept of increased comfort and higher morale is a central issue of the disengagement theory, and one that is of most interest in our concern with anticipatory grief. Although societal happiness is a concept that borders on the metaphysical, it is used repeatedly to justify this theory. One questions whether it is possible to ascertain society's idea of Elysium, since it is such an amorphous, abstract idea that does not lend itself readily to empirical confirmation. It is equally or more conceivable that the relationship between society and the individual is based on endogenous change and society's well-being might be better served if its members were able to reintegrate their lives at various crucial times rather than be able only to submit passively and withdraw. Such a reintegration may be an essential contribution to society's ongoingness.

It is possible, unfortunately, that society's increased distance from its elderly population may be "satisfying" because an unavoidable problem is thereby eliminated; society's disinclination to deal with death or old people is repeatedly evidenced by tendencies to segregate them in nursing homes or homes for the aged. Thus, disengagement must be considered not solely within a functional orientation, but as a modal process governed also by conscious and unconscious motivation, interaction effects, intrapsychic needs, and the like. For, in spite of contradictory evidence, we witness the continued interest in disengagement theory, with scant attention paid to the reasons for societal intervention. Thus, in a later article, Cumming (1964) reasserts the causes of society's withdrawal: the competition for power roles based on achievement, the newer knowledge of youth, the inability to expand indefinitely the top jobs so that the oldsters are thus forced out, the futility of assigning crucial roles to a group with high mortality rates, and the gap between generations resulting in youth approaching the elderly, if at all, with condescension. These are all possible but insufficient explanations.

In contradistinction to group satisfaction measurements, we can attempt to assess individual morale. Later studies do not corroborate the findings of higher satisfaction and greater disengagement (Tallmer and Kutner, 1970; Lowenthal and Boler, 1965), although this is not the most damaging criticism of the theory. It is the reliance on quantification and the straying from data, terminating in unsupported speculation, that is so troubling. We have mentioned the belief that the individual and society collaborate to meet the fate of ultimate death. But the process of preparation is not directly investigated, and no linkage is demonstrated between increasing disengagement and the alleged readiness for death.

Indeed, this is not therapeutic, responsible insight into death for the individual but represents rather the working out of ego-alien pre-death grief by society, according to its own idiosyncratic time schedule, rather than being geared to the individual's need. One way for groups to deal with anticipatory grief is to project needs on to the person. Thus, the paradigm may be explicated—we are going to be upset by death and we wish this to be at as convenient a time for us as possible. One way to handle this is for the dying person to withdraw in advance, a possible projection of our own wish to withdraw from him. Not only is the dying person to exclude himself, but he will be happier doing so. (The imposition of the societal time schedule is clearly evidenced by the assertion that the recognition of immortality occurs for the first time at midlife.) Further, we are able to massively deny the problem, because the dying will be segregated physically.

Self-fulfilling prophecy is also applicable here, and it is interesting to speculate on the effects of enforced retirement and/or exclusion. We have mentioned studies elucidating the need for continued stimulation. Additionally, social interaction theory may be pertinent. We develop, retain, and validate our self-appraisals through interaction with others. Since activity is so highly valued in our society, inactive people receive negative reflected appraisals, thus causing a crisis in one's self-esteem (Maddox and Eisdorfer, 1962) that leads to further decline, contraction, and uncertainty. It is certainly true that with enforced isolation thinking may become less reality-oriented and inner events more salient. But to deem this as biologically determined constitutes an error of the post hoc, ergo propter hoc, type that merely justifies exclusion.

Finally, the assertion that disengagement is beneficial to all because it circumvents the problem of wrenching an involved person away from life's network is not borne out by current reports from Abkhasia (Benet, 1971) where deaths, considered irrational, even at the advanced age of 120, are reacted to violently by the population. Here too, we witness the desirability of the continuity of the life cycle whereby the elderly are usefully effective until death. Surely, there must be more enlightened and positive means for dealing with our impending self-grief than by displacing it on to the senescent or denying the problem by forcing the elderly into a slow, steady passage of withdrawal, deemed beneficial. The activity theory, in its extreme, may also be regarded as a counterphobic solution. The Cumming and Henry (1961) statistics that after age sixty-five, the thought of death is least frightening and seldom thought of may be an unfortunate reflection of both our own reluctance to discuss death and the pejorative nature with which we endow such speculation.

REFERENCES

Anderson, J. E., "The Use of Time and Energy," in J. E. Birren, ed., *Handbook of Aging and the Individual*. Chicago: University of Chicago Press, 1959.

Benet, S. "Why They Live to Be 100, or Even Older, in Abkhasis," *The New York Times Magazine*, 1971.

Cumming, E. M., "New Thoughts on the Theory of Disengagement," in R. Kestenbaum, ed., *New Thoughts on Old Age*. New York: Springer, 1964.

Cumming, E. M., and W. Henry, *Growing Old*. New York: Basic Books, 1961.

Hebb, D. O., "The Mammal and His Environment," *American Journal of Psychiatry, 3*:826, 1955.

Heron, W., "Pathology of Boredom," *Scientific American, 196*:52, 1957.

Kleemeier, R. W., "Leisure and Disengagement in Retirement," *Gerontologist, 4*:180, 1964.

Lowenthal, M. F., and D. Boler, "Voluntary vs. Involuntary Social Withdrawal," *Journal of Gerontology, 20*:363, 1965.

Maddox, G., and C. Eisdorfer, "Some Correlates of Activity and Morale Among the Elderly," *Social Forces, 40*:254, 1962.

Rose, A., "A Current Issue in Social Gerontology," *Gerontologist, 4*:45, 1964.

Tallmer, M., and B. Kutner, "Disengagement and Morale," *Gerontologist, 10*:317, 1970.

—— "Disengagement and the Stress of Aging," *Journal of Gerontology, 24*:70, 1969.

Talmon, Y., "Dimensions of Disengagement—Aging in Collective Settlements," Paper presented at the International Social Science Seminar on Social Gerontology, Sweden, 1963.

5

Anticipatory Bereavement *

Irwin Gerber

Anticipatory grief (Lindemann, 1944) is alleged to possess natural adaptional value. It is a "rehearsal" of what to expect after an impending loss. An individual will partially work through emotional reactions, normally observed after the loss. It is akin to what Janis (Janis, 1958) called "worry work" in his study of surgical patients. Inherent in any discussion of anticipatory grief is the temporal period between knowledge of the impending loss and the actual event. If the time span is minimal then the potential influence of anticipatory grief may be negligible and even detrimental to the individual. It is assumed that early knowledge of a potential loss will elicit the highest rate of adjustment. On the other hand, how effective this phenomenon will be is contingent on many factors such as the *type* of loss one expects, the degree of *emotional* attachment to the object, and whether or not the bereaved-to-be accepts the inevitable. In general, clinicians agree that the future survivor will show signs of emotional grief work that are similar

* The observations for this paper were obtained from an investigation entitled, "The Aged in Crisis: A Study of Bereavement." This program was supported in part by U.S.P.H.S. Grant MH-14490 and Grant 93-P-57454/2-01 from the Administration on Aging, Social and Rehabilitation Service, Department of Health, Education and Welfare. The author wishes to thank Drs. Arthur Arkin and Alfred Wiener, Mrs. Roslyn Rusalem, Mrs. Delia Battin, and Mrs. Natalie Hannon for their dedicated work on the program and their critical suggestions during the preparation of this paper.

to those observed after a sudden or unexpected death (Peretz, 1970, Ross, 1969). In varying degrees shock, denial, anger, depression, anxiety, and guilt are present. The only outstanding emotional manifestions of anticipatory grief which cannot possibly be noted during bereavement after a sudden death are hope and memories of the "death watch." As a general statement of agreement, where there is an impending death the process of grief, or "grief work," begins well before the actual death.

Most observers of this phenomenon are of the opinion that survivors of a chronic illness death will be less susceptible to various types of maladjustments than survivors of a sudden death. This phenomenon is pictured as offering the bereaved-to-be time to work through a large portion of the emotional trauma normally associated with bereavement. The anguish of watching a slow debilitating death, associated with an illness such as cancer, and the realization that a fatal episode of angina could occur at any time, is supposed to serve an extended function of softening the event of death. Emotional preparation will reduce the intensity of grief after the death, and therefore the survivor should be less vulnerable to untoward medical, psychological, and social reactions. Survivors of a chronic illness death will do better than survivors of a sudden death.

What is generally missing in various descriptions of anticipatory grief is the consideration that this phenomenon has a social component. To prepare for, or anticipate, the death of a loved one brings forth deliberation about role functioning after the death. The proper disposition of the body; handling financial matters; taking care of children, if there are dependent offspring; where to reside; role transformation such as cooking and cleaning chores for a widower; and thoughts about remarriage are all practical social considerations the bereaved-to-be have to face. Although health professionals, relatives, and friends may follow the general societal value of viewing these thoughts as improper, for most future survivors these are realistic considerations. For example, it is not uncommon during some phase of the terminal illness that the future survivor will ask, "What will I do without him?" "What will become of the children?" The use of the concept anticipatory grief represents one professional orientation and therefore may be too restrictive in application. Switzer (1970), in his excellent work on grief, illustrates this orientation when he differentiates between *bereavement* as the state of loss and *grief* as the response of emotional pain. However, grief as an emotional state cannot be considered the only aspect of preparing for the death of a loved one. In order to more fully understand the impact of the preparatory stage on the survivors' adjustment, the concept of "anticipatory bereavement" will be introduced in this paper. Anticipatory bereavement is less restrictive because it takes into account both the emotional and social characteristics of preparing for a death.

Anticipatory bereavement is akin to what sociologists and social psychologists have labeled anticipatory socialization (Brim, 1966). Anticipatory socialization is a social process because it is a learning experience based on informal exchange with others in the immediate environment. The mechanics of anticipatory socialization serve a needed personal and societal function of preparing an individual for specific and expected behaviors related to a social role. Of importance, is that the existing role an individual is anticipating or preparing for provides clues and directions for the recruit. Because of these existing blueprints one can prepare for the new role. Anticipatory bereavement can be looked upon as a period of socialization into the "bereaved role."

By defining anticipatory bereavement as a period of socialization into the bereaved role one must take into account certain social arrangements for a new life-style after the death. These designs for living are not always stabilized as neat packages, but they do exist, at least, in thought. Plans for the future are not formed by the bereaved-to-be in an independent manner. The initial thoughts about taking care of children, resolving expected financial problems, relocation, going on an extended trip, moving in with relatives, and remarriage are lightly considered until significant others are approached. This is a most critical stage in planning for the bereavement period. How relatives and friends respond to the initial plans determine for the survivor how appropriate are such thoughts. In effect, a sensitive positive response from others makes anticipated social plans an acceptable and legitimate part of anticipatory bereavement. If the future survivor's preparations are considered by significant others as in "bad taste," or too premature, this may signal for both parties an uncertain period after the death.

ADJUSTMENT PROBLEMS

The luxury of time to prepare future social plans can leave the bereaved-to-be in a state of false comfort. Too much time to think and plan under the expectation of permanent loss may be self-defeating. Although some designs for social adjustment are realistic, many are not because they are thought-out under the stress of waiting for the death to occur and without professional objective advice. Promises made by others, such as "Don't worry, Dad, we'll take care of you, you can live with us," are sincere in most cases. However, they are generated from an emotional attempt to relieve the bereaved-to-be of the anguish of watching a spouse die, and the expected hurt after the death. We must not forget that the future survivor is extremely susceptible to advice from others and to his own assessment of the future, which is a reflection of this advice. Anticipatory bereavement can very easily present false promises based on unrealistic assessments of what lies ahead. When the time comes for the survivor to rely on promises of help, support, and security, a period of fulfillment may ensue. However, this may be short-lived, and all the unanticipated problems either hidden by the stress of anticipatory bereavement or suppressed in order to protect the future survivor erupt simultaneously. The incongruency between what one expects and what actually occurs is difficult to adjust to for lesser crises. A crisis such as loss through death may be compounded to a point of weakening the individual and making adjustment extremely difficult. The destruction of an anticipated new life following the destruction of the old is not the ingredient for proper adjustment to a loss.

The concept of anticipatory bereavement is presented as a period of socialization into the bereaved role, a time before an impending loss when the survivor-to-be prepares socially as well as emotionally for this position. Anticipatory bereavement has a wider analytical scope than anticipatory grief because the former takes into account preparations for a new social role as well as the more traditional emotional factors. In contrast to other socialization periods the present one is highly sensitive, directed toward a unique role. Because of the emotional strain of waiting for a death to occur, the poorly defined set of bereaved role expectations, and the drastic change in life style caused by a permanent loss, anticipatory bereavement may contain the seeds for future problems.

REFERENCES

Brim, O. G., and S. Wheeler, *Socialization After Childhood*. New York: Wiley, 1966.
Janis, I. L., *Psychological Stress*. New York: Wiley, 1958.

Lindemann, E., "Symptomatology and Management of Acute Grief," *American Journal of Psychiatry, 101:*141–148, 1944.

Peretz, D., "Reaction to Loss," in B. Schoenberg *et al.,* eds., *Loss and Grief.* New York: Columbia University Press, 1970, pp. 20–35.

Ross, E., *On Death and Dying.* New York: Macmillan, 1969.

Switzer, D. K., *The Dynamics of Grief.* New York: Abingdon Press, 1970.

6

Dying, Death, and
Social Behavior *
Vanderlyn R. Pine

꙳꙳꙳꙳꙳

The goals of this paper are: (1) to differentiate between the social conceptions of dying and death; (2) to discuss the practical consequences on social behavior of either and/or both; and (3) to distinguish grief as an overall social process through which people pass. To a certain extent the differentiation between dying and death presents a conceptual problem. However, the actual influence of either has different practical ramifications on the social behavior of those people involved. It is in view of this influence that we treat grief as an overall process. Specifically, we contend that grief, as do all processes, occurs in a temporal setting. Moreover, we argue that the grief process has several stages which operate to link the state of ''no grief'' at the start to the state of ''resolved grief'' at the end. Each of these topics will be treated separately, moving from dying to death, to social behavior to grief.

The empirical evidence which led to many of the theoretical arguments presented and developed in this paper are the result of fifteen years spent working with the bereaved relatives and friends of recently deceased people. During this period, the author worked with and observed some 3,500 grieving individuals, members of over 1,000 families. These people were ob-

* The preparation of this paper was facilitated by a National Institute of Health Fellowship, No. 1 F01 MH 38124-01A1, from the National Institute of Mental Health.

served in a nonexperimental setting (the first seven years of which the author did not even think of as a research setting). However, the last eight years of observations were guided by a research orientation, even though the grieving families were not told that they were research subjects. Most of the observations took place in funeral homes, although some did occur in hospitals or private homes. Interviews with the bereaved families focused on information essential for carrying out funeral arrangements. However, additional questions were asked concerning communication about dying and death, the dissemination of news about death, and the attitudes of the bereaved toward institutionalization of the dying and the process of grief. (For a fuller treatment of the communications about dying and death, see Pine, 1972.)

DYING

Dying is a process through which all of us must pass, and which may be described as having a trajectory over time and space (Glaser and Strauss, 1968). Such a description conforms to common sense and focuses largely on the way in which, and length of time during which, the dying process affects the dying person. The trajectory of dying lies on a continuum, from a very brief period of time to a rather protracted period of time, with different locations along this continuum engendering different forms of behavior. For example, at the long-period extreme are patients dying slowly from a terminal illness such as cancer. They and their families learn to behave in constant expectation of death. At the other extreme, when death occurs suddenly, such as in an automobile or airplane crash, the dying process may be almost instantaneous. Thus, there may be a short period of time or none at all in which to anticipate death.

Patients dying from a terminal illness often experience periods of remission during which the disease is said to be retarded, controlled, or reversed. At these periods there tends to be hope that the dying process can be stopped permanently, although such reversals are rare in the medical literature. It is noteworthy that even sudden death often engenders a hope for remission, in that those dead from instant causes are closely scrutinized to ascertain whether they are in a coma, have fluttering eyelids, a chance of breathing, or other life signs that would indicate that the dying process is remitting.

In this sense, then, dying may be seen as a process whose end result is death, but a process from which there is the possibility of "escape." Therefore, dying does not present a totally "hopeless" picture. It allows the dying patient himself and those close to him a chance to construct reality so as to make death, the eventual outcome of the process, less distressing. Thus, people allow themselves to anticipate the death and at least some of its consequences, that is, they go through anticipatory grief. Fulton and Fulton (1972) put it this way:

Over an extended period of time, therefore, the family members may (1) experience depression, (2) feel a heightened concern for the ill member, (3) rehearse his death, and (4) attempt to adjust to the various consequences of it. By the time the death occurs the family will, to the extent that they have anticipated the death or dissipated their grief, display little or no emotion.

DEATH

Death occurs at the conclusion of the dying process, and it represents and defines the ultimate loss from which there is no chance to regain what is lost. Although there is no remission from death, there are certain residuals after death occurs. For example, the dead person "lives on" in people's memories, and his personality, actions, and other traits and characteristics are not easily or quickly forgotten by those surviving him. Also, there is the residual of the dead body, which represents the last tangible evidence of the dead person. As an artifact of human life, the body plays an important part in the process of grieving.

Even though death is a biologically determined consequence of life, it is a special problem today because (among other things) it is not seen as the rational conclusion of life, and humans think of themselves as basically rational. The contemporary pattern of scientific rationality includes efforts to "eliminate" death. Parsons (1963) observes that:

The attitude conspicuous in the United States is one of bringing to bear every possible resource to prolong active and healthy life. It would seem then, that a clue to the development of some aspects of our attitudes toward death might be found in the whole complex of health and the tendency to prolong life in good health.

It is not unusual, at least occasionally, to wish that our life might go on forever, but presently this is not possible, even though current medical advancements aim at extending life and improving chances for survival. In fact, as Parsons notes, medicine has created a culture-set of health-conscious people in which disease is being obliterated and the thoughts for the future are for greater expansion of life-enhancing developments.

Although man may survive relatively free from disease, he cannot as yet live beyond a certain length of time. However, "old age" is not a sufficient cause of death, and present laws require that all deaths be "caused" by something specific, that is, either natural causes (cancer, pneumonia, cardiovascular failure, etc.); accidental causes (drowning, automobile accident, etc.); or unnatural causes (murder, suicide, etc.). Moreover, to a great extent we believe the world to be "controllable," and generally our efforts are purposive and based on predictability. Death creates a problem at this point, for as Glaser and Strauss (1965a) point out, even though death's certainty can often be established, its time of occurrence can seldom be accurately predicted.

Death poses a serious social threat because it separates individuals from the group, thereby demonstrating society's vulnerability to it. Thus, the imminence and occurrence of death give rise to a wide variety of beliefs and practices which exist in different societies. Furthermore, as Durkheim (1951) long ago pointed out, man faces death with culturally defined emotional reactions ranging from resignation to hysteria; and the occurrence of death provides an occasion for socially conditioned grief reactions and mourning practices.

SOCIAL BEHAVIOR

Beginning with the initial psychological impact of potential or actual separation, there are social and psychological forces that affect the bereaved and condition their responses to death. However, death involves not just the bereaved family but also the significant others of the dead and their relatives. As Blauner (1966) observes: "Since mortality tends to disrupt the ongoing life of social groups and relationships, all societies must develop some forms of containing the impact." For many people, the ultimate crisis is loss by death of a loved person; and dying, death, and bereavement present a complex situation common to all men. Moreover, the resolution of grief remains an intricate yet imprecisely understood reaction to dying and death.

Dying and death give rise to a specific problem which has important social-psychological, grief-related consequences. Bereaved people must drastically revise their conception of self, especially so since prior to dying and death, the bereaved and the deceased usually interact extensively and form (in one sense) a complete social unit, a dyad. From this relationship stems the reflexive elements of self. After death, however, there can only be a retrospective notion of that aspect of self. As one moves from the status of wife to widow or child to orphan, the status transition is so ill-defined and noncontinuous that the transition may bring about disapproval (Glaser and Strauss, 1965b).

There are further problems because in modern, industrialized society the handling of illness and death are increasingly the responsibility of institutions other than the family. Simultaneously, death is commonest in the ranks of the elderly. This has happened because of the general elimination of infant mortality and considerably greater control over the illnesses of adolescence and middle age. It has been estimated that most people attend only one or two funerals a decade during the first fifty years of life (Blauner, 1966). Clearly, the average American has very little "to do" with death and its consequences. Thus, part of the "taboo" of death is likely to be a matter of widespread inexperience and general lack of contact with it.

Besides, there are less ritualized observances for the dead, and religious and ceremonial responses to death have generally become less important in American society. Even though death is less important on a societal level, its prospects and consequences are far more serious for the bereaved individual. Blauner (1966) explains that man "experiences grief less frequently, but more intensely since his emotional involvements are not diffused over an entire community, but are usually concentrated on one or a few people." In this sense, then, death may not just be disapproved of and embarrassing, but also it may be personally isolating and socially disruptive for the individual. Moreover, the orientations that most Americans hold toward death have created an aura around the subject that makes it difficult to face and/or accept. Fulton (1965) claims that "death, like a noxious disease, has become a taboo subject, and as such it is both the subject of much disguise and denial as well as raucous and macabre humor."

Disguise and denial foster the development of more serious problems. Grief caused by loss, separation, and death has been shown to contribute to psychosomatic disease (for a summary of some psychological studies of this topic, see Fulton, 1965, pp. 181–332). Unsatisfactory resolution of grief may lead to acute problems in later life, and one important step in preventing these is to encourage the resolving of grief. The processes commonly called "anticipatory grief" and "normal grief" help foster this resolution.

THE STAGES OF GRIEF

Implicit (if not explicit) in most treatments of anticipatory grief is the assumption that anticipation takes place in advance of or instead of normal grief. Thus, anticipatory grief refers to the changes which those close to the dying patient undergo during a terminal illness. Moreover, anticipatory grief is supposed to occur before the onset of the "normal" grief which results from the loss by death of an individual. In this context, normal grief is thought to occur only after an actual loss, while anticipatory grief is thought of in terms of potential rather than actual loss. Furthermore, grieving occurs only after it is triggered by a specific communication of some kind or another.

Our observations suggest that anticipatory grief may occur as a post-death activity which results from a reconstruction of reality by the grieving person. This conceptualization grows out of the logical framework developed by George Herbert Mead, who maintained that the human mind is capable of reconstructing social reality over and over again to fit the needs of the moment. (For further and more detailed discussions, see Mead, 1934; Strauss, 1934; Berger and Luckmann, 1966; Holzner, 1968.) An example of such reconstruction makes the point clearer. Many of us select from memory those incidents which are most pleasant. Thus, the pleasant aspects of a summer vacation may be recalled, while to a great extent unpleasant aspects of the vacation are disregarded or at least reduced in importance. In this way, "the mind's eye" reconstructs reality in such a fashion that we "see" past events and occurrences differently. In this way, we are better able to cope with the tension and strain of displeasure or pain by recalling "most clearly" that which is most pleasing. Of course, we can not always remember just the pleasantries of life. One of the most common ways in which people confront some of life's cruelties, threats, and displeasures is through dreams (Freud, 1952). The idea of the reconstruction of reality makes common sense, and although the way in which it occurs may be elaborate and complex, most of us are not only capable of such reconstruction but actually practice it regularly.

Research shows that in order for a person to anticipate or experience grief some communication must trigger it. Death itself may be such a trigger. For example, the surviving next-of-kin and close friends of those who had died suddenly often reconstructed mentally the dying process so as to take it out of the "instant" category and put it in a temporally ordered historical perspective. This is evidenced also by the way in which physicians and other institutional personnel responsible for dying patients deal with sudden or unexpected deaths. In this setting, dying is almost always placed in a historical perspective (Sudnow, 1967; Glaser and Strauss, 1965a and 1968). This enables the surviving relatives and friends to conceive of dying as a process through which the deceased has passed.

The way reality is reconstructed after a death message is received usually goes something like this. After death occurs, and the communication about its occurrence is received, the grief process is initiated. The first stage of grief is disbelief. The disbelief stage of grief is quite similar to the denial stage of dying. (For a fuller discussion, see Kübler-Ross, 1969.) The main difference is that the disbelief stage of grief occurs after the fact, when the mind must come to terms with the loss. During the disbelief stage, it is common for people to talk to themselves, saying such things as "It can't be. I just saw him a few minutes ago"; "It's not possible. You must be wrong, she couldn't be dead." People seem to try to convince themselves that their disbelief is legitimate and that there really has not been a death. It is common to observe disbelieving grievers mumbling and shaking their heads in a negative way, as if to say, "No. No. No."

The second stage of grief is the questioning stage. It is at this time that the grieving person begins to look for reasons why the death occurred. It is common to hear such comments as "What happened? How on earth did he die?" It seems that the etiology of the death is important in making death believable. The questioning stage is often a pathetic one. The grieving person fruitlessly searches for an answer that will satisfy his conception of the causative agents of death.

Questioning is commonly followed by the third stage of grief, anger. Anger is often expressed in such terms as "Why did this have to happen to him?" "I can think of a number of people who deserve to die more than she did," or "You can't love a God who lets somebody like him die." It is common for people during the anger stage of grief to kick at immovable objects, such as curbstones or porch posts, or to bang their fists against a table or desk-top. Usually, anger is accompanied by desperation.

The fourth stage, anger combined with desperation, seems to overwhelm the grieving persons with resignation, dismay, and despair. The grieving person avoids eye contact with those around him, looks upward and downward rapidly. The utter hopelessness and despair that accompanies being resigned to the fact that a death has occurred shows through the staring eyes of the sufferer, who often looks upon his surroundings with unseeing eyes.

The fifth stage of grief, resolution, does not always follow, but when it does it seems to grow out of the others. It may be argued that there is seldom, if ever, complete resolution of grief, in the same fashion that it may be argued that seldom is the imminence of death accepted by the dying patient or his family. However, observations indicate that most people to a lesser or greater extent do resolve their grief.

Our notions about anticipatory grief suggest that people who work through the grief of loss while it is still potential are better able to cope with death because, in effect, they have resolved their grief in advance. Similarly, those who do not expect a death pass through stages similar to those of people who have experienced anticipatory grief through the potential loss period of dying. After death, however, the mind is temporally retrospective, and it reconstructs circumstances and situations appropriate and suitable for anticipation. It is common to hear people say soon after a death, "You know, he never was very careful about such things"; or, "I just didn't think she was herself recently"; or, "I've always been afraid this would happen."

The question cannot help but arise, at what time does this process of grief begin, and how long does it last? The theory of anticipatory grief posits that the grieving process begins with the realization that an individual has an illness from which there is no chance of recovery and that he is therefore a dying patient. The contention is that over a period of time and through the stages of dying the patient and his family come to terms with death and accept its occurrence. In theory, this process makes a great deal of sense. In practice, however, it is not so clear that it works exactly this way. To be specific, the author's observations of 3,500 bereaved people indicate that the clinical notion of "resolved anticipatory grief" glosses over a great deal of grief that continues to exist. Moreover, observations of grieving people over many years lead to the belief that anticipatory grief may reduce the intensity of normal grief, but it does not necessarily eliminate it.

To a large extent, many of the studies about grieving people have been carried out during the period of someone's terminal illness and have stopped soon after news of the death has been communicated. It is at this point, just following the death, that most anticipatory grief studies cease. When the bereaved leave the confines of the hospital, they are no longer available for easy scrutiny or observation. However, it is not only possible to have observational access to grieving people in a confined setting after death has occurred. It is necessary for funeral directors to work actively with them exactly at that time.

NORMAL GRIEF AS THE POST-STIMULUS RECONSTRUCTION OF ANTICIPATION

Of the 3,500 people observed during the post-death grief period, the vast majority moved through the process of grief with a historical perspective. More specifically, for those who had anticipated the death for a long time, some of the stages of grief had already been accomplished to some extent, while other stages remained to be resolved by post-death activities. For example, the mother of eight children, all of whom had been healthy throughout childhood, tearfully commented following the death of her second youngest son after a six-month battle with cancer, "Don't let anybody kid you. It doesn't help very much to know that someone is going to die. Bobby was as important a human being to me as any of the other kids, and just because he and we and the doctors knew that this was going to happen, now that it has happened everything about Bobby is different. Just between you and me, I miss him terribly no matter how much I knew this was coming."

When death occurs suddenly, with little or no forewarning, the survivors of the deceased are generally told about the death in a historical perspective. For example, a thirty-five-year-old man whose father had dropped dead very suddenly was reported having been told the following by "some doctor" at the hospital. "Your father has been taken very ill. He had a massive heart attack." At this point the son asked whether it was serious or not. "Any heart attack is serious," the doctor said, "and the one your father had was especially so. As a matter of fact, as a result of the attack the heart was irreparably damaged. Damaged so much that not even a miracle could keep him alive." At this point the son asked, "Is he going to die?" (Notice the use of the future tense.) In his mind his father was now a "seriously ill" patient; so seriously ill that he *himself* could imagine that his father might die. The doctor was fully aware of this, and now that he had brought the man through the period of anticipation, he delivered the final blow. "Yes, you could expect anyone having a heart attack such as this to die. Even though your father was a very strong man, he just couldn't survive. Just about an hour after his attack he died."

What often happens following a sudden death is not nearly as smooth

as the case just described. It is far more common for the survivors to learn
of the death rather bluntly and not in an anticipatory and historical perspective. Thus, in many instances it is left up to the survivors themselves to
translate knowledge of death into their own terms, which they can interpret
in an ongoing fashion. Observations lead to the conclusion that the process
of grief is assisted considerably by the period following death, usually called
the funeral. How and why this happens depends on many factors. There are
a number of problems which have been observed, and some of them will be
described and discussed.

Grief and mourning serve to implement man's acceptance of death, and
many traditional funeral customs attempt to provide a recognizable societal
support mechanism upon which the bereaved may lean. Gorer (1965) emphasizes the connection between ritual and mourning:

I call attention to the potentially important roles played by ritual and by those
members of society with whom the mourner comes in contact in giving help to the
mourner in the period of shock and the stage of violent grief and assisting him in giving expression to and working through his distress; and to the maladaptations which
may result if this help is not forthcoming.

It may well be that the elimination of social grief and mourning results
from an unwillingness to accept death and the social separation of individuals. The contemporary emphasis on life and living adds further restrictions
to ''sentimental,'' that is, nonutilitarian, approaches to death. There appears
to be a growing tendency to omit from the usual mourning practices the
custom of viewing the dead body. The elimination of this practice may
mean that maintaining reality is more difficult. Jackson (1957) explains
that:

When a family has spent three days, as is the case in most Christian communities, or
seven days as is the general Jewish practice, in accepted mourning procedures, the
reality of the death of the body is impressed on the mind and emotions in a way that
cannot be easily denied.

An unwillingness to accept death suggests a refusal to accept the ensuing separation as real. Herein is a secular adaptation of the sacred concept
of immortality. This present-day attitude may point to a basic human need
to conceptualize life as nonterminous and to believe that death is only a
temporal indicator. Moreover, contemporary Americans often seem to act

as if death did not exist. This form of death-denial may represent an effort to rationalize that the dead are not really gone. Such an unrealistic view can create a fantasy around the entire death process. This fantasy implies a hope that not only will death not be painful, but also that it will not happen. (Of course, it can be argued that some people accept death as inevitable and consequently give it little thought, thereby *seeming* to deny it.)

Death is the loss of something individual which also creates a problem for society, threatening it as a nonrational phenomenon. Furthermore, it may be that some people believe that by getting rid of the rituals of death, and thus the ambiguity of celebrating "nonculture," they hope to affect an extension of life for the culture as well as for themselves.

The possibility of mass death and species destruction compounds the problem for many contemporary Americans. It seems that this threat makes funeral rituals meaningless. If we all die there would be no reason to have funerals. Thus, by eliminating any commemoration of death, some perhaps aim at preventing its occurrence. To handle death by utilizing a social mechanism, such as the funeral, implies that we realize and admit that we, too, must die.

In the past, man has attempted to treat this admission with the attitude that by providing a ritual for the dead he commemorates an amorphous kind of continuity. Today, some people seem to be turning toward the total rejection of this by not admitting that anyone need die, thus implying that death does not exist.

With such questions that probe into the very meaning of man, consciousness, and death, it may well be that some of the answers may be found in the notion of awareness. If it is accepted that there is value in being aware of death on a conscious level, it may be that the reification of death by death itself, as when confronted with funeral rituals, increases human awareness. This follows the reasoning of Jackson (1957) and Irion (1954), both of whom suggest that one of the values of funeral and mourning practices as traditionally followed is to "gradually bring the consciousness of death to all levels of being, and make it difficult for fantasies or illusions to develop in the thoughts or feelings of the individual" (Jackson, 1957). This clarifies some of the usefulness of death ritual as a social reminder of the pains and pleasures of life.

Hertz (1960) contends that among tribes organized around physical agricultural activities, very old people are mourned differently once they have died, and that when they are in the process of dying they are largely excluded from social activities as well. Therefore, when their deaths do occur, they are considerably less disruptive to the overall society. Glaser and Strauss (1965a) claim that in America, where organization is around institutions other than the family, for example, hospitals, treatment of dying patients is largely institutionalized. Thus, dying patients are to a great extent eliminated from active society. Sudnow (1967) recognizes this same point in his discussion of "social death." Social death occurs when the "social organization of dying" effectively isolates a biologically living human so that he may be considered "dead and gone" by the members of his social group and by society at large.

Hertz (1960), Malinowski (1948), and Firth (1964) all argue that when death occurs to relatively young individuals still important to the workings of society, their loss is considered important and "shakes the solidarity" of the group. Because of this shakeup of the social order, beliefs and practices surrounding death are intended to reintegrate the group's sense of cohesiveness.

Hertz's (1960) description of the practice of provisional burial emphasizes that the dead actually may be part of the living organization of society, influencing people's behavior until the finality of burial. This situation is diametrically opposed to the one described by Sudnow (1967), in which social death often occurs in hospitals. In the former situation, biological death precedes the social death, while in the latter, biological death follows social death.

The handling of death is influenced considerably by the way in which a society is organized. For example, among the provisional burial tribes, the highest age specific death rate is among the young, and the loss of an individual is important to the entire society. Thus, many beliefs and practices continue to include the deceased in social activities. Put differently, among societies in which the age specific death rate is highest among those who are an important part of the community social organization, that is, the young, there is an unwillingness to release the dead from their obligations to society. At the opposite extreme, in societies where the age specific death rate is highest among the old, who have lost their value to the community, it is common to exclude the still living but inert and socially dead human organism. Clearly, it is not so much the value of life which is at question; instead, it is the importance that individuals have for a given social organization. (For a fuller discussion, see Pine, 1972.)

Another societal characteristic influencing the beliefs and practices surrounding death is the extent to which the society is formally organized. Specifically, in those societies which are organized around bureaucratic structures and highly formal institutions, the death of an individual is considerably less important to the system, no matter how much that loss might mean to those individuals with whom the deceased has interacted on an interpersonal level.

This is the case in the United States, where the handling of illness and death is increasingly institutionalized—and there are a number of problems arising because of the nature of American social organization. Parsons (1963) points to the fact that this is largely because of the "demographic revolution [which has been] characterized by passage from a high-birth-rate, high-death-rate balance to one of vastly lower death rates, and where something of a balance is maintained, necessarily much lower birth rates."

This means that Americans face death much less often than previously. As with any experience, less contact with it means less familiarity with how to cope with it. Parsons (1963) points out that an important reason for this change is the advances of medical science. He contends that the institutionalized structural arrangement of America is such that science and medicine are elevated to a very high level. Furthermore, the demographic changes, which are largely the result of technological advancements, are accompanied by vast organizational changes in the arrangement and configuration of those institutions which influence death-related behavior.

There are culturally prescribed social obligations of individuals to society at the time of death. Through funeral rites, the bereaved become the center of attention for group support, and the extension of sympathy tends to give rise to a sense of comfort and social acceptability. Firth (1964: 224) remarks that "Rituals reflect and express structural arrangements of the society and of component though divergent elements in it. They provide occasion for group assembly, and reaffirm social values." Acceptance is important if we are to live meaningfully after the loss of some key life figure, but to do so is a universal problem. Society has certain established mechanisms which afford man a measure of support through the period of bereavement. These mechanisms depend largely on projection by others, and are geared to provide help both to individuals and to the society at large. They are supposed to help us accept loss, not necessarily by scientific reasoning, but by socially reactive empathy. Clearly, one of the values of any culture is to provide certain channels for the expression of common human needs and to assist us through depressing circumstances.

In spite of the differences found in numerous societies, it may be contended that the post-death period is commonly used for the reconstruction of anticipation. This reasoning makes common sense. Moreover, not only matters of grievous consequences elicit the reconstruction of anticipation, but also there are other practical phenomena involving social conceptualization.

People begin the process of grief only after having received the stimulus which triggers it. When an actual death has occurred and people become aware of it, they almost always initiate funerary activities. Our observations indicate that the funeral period provides an opportunity for people to reconstruct reality, not only for themselves as individuals but also for the social groups of which they are a part. This means that by carrying out funerary activities the bereaved are able to implement their reconstructed anticipation with others. For example, the immediate next-of-kin usually explain over and over again to each new visitor how the death occurred and what they were told about the individual's passing. The repetition to many of their friends of how they learned of the death and how it occurred enables all involved to experience a community response to the anticipation which they failed to receive in advance of the death.

This social reconstruction of reality is extremely important. Of the few families who did not experience the "social gathering" of the funeral, most later reported that they experienced difficulty with friends, who seemed to be unwilling or afraid to communicate with them about the death. Such unwillingness to communicate is not hard to understand. The following poignant case exemplifies many of the problems that arise because of the hesitancy to communicate.

Billy, an eighteen-year-old college freshman who had been his high school's most outstanding graduate in years, was stricken with cancer and died twelve months later. Theoretically, his family had passed through the stages of dying and had gone through anticipatory grief. Upon his death, his parents decided that no commemorative service was necessary, saying "We've suffered all we need to." As time passed, the author observed them to be only partially able to face Billy's death. Specifically, they seemed as grievously upset as others who had not passed through the stages of dying.

A major problem in this approach to Billy's death was not apparent immediately. In the few days that followed his death, literally hundreds of telephone calls were received by the funeral home. All the callers asked the same question: "As friends, what can we do?" Since the family wanted nothing done, everyone was told that nothing need be done. Without consulting the family, Billy's former high-school class planned and conducted a rock concert to honor his memory. His former fellow students set up the program, handling all of the arrangements. They carried off the rock concert in a serious and well-intentioned manner.

The introductory speech by one of the student organizers helps make clear what they were trying to do. He told the story of Billy's illness, explaining that the minor surgery which he had undergone while in high school was the beginning of his problems. As he described the ensuing months and Billy's declining health, many of those present wept openly and unashamedly. These students were expressing their anticipatory grief at hearing how the formerly robust captain of last year's football team had declined in health and become a gaunt, cancer-ridden, almost dead person. Finally, the speaker concluded with a description of the death itself.

As is so common, Billy's death had been placed in historical perspective for all those attending the rock concert. In this way, the students helped themselves through the anticipatory process, and the rock concert became a socially acceptable, community-oriented funeral. It enabled these friends, many of whom had lost contact with Billy and his family because of graduating, to reconstruct reality after death, thereby enabling them to anticipate it in a community way.

Another example of community reaction to sudden loss followed the deaths of four students at Kent State University in the spring of 1970. The day after the Kent State deaths, seemingly simultaneously, students across the country held marches, went on strike, occupied buildings, and in general participated in community-directed social activities which commemorated the deaths of the students. An examination of the texts of most of the student orations and public eulogies shows how the process of reconstruction of anticipation operates. Almost unanimously, the talks described the activities at Kent State leading up to and concluding with the shootings. Each of the dead students, then, was individually singled out, his characteristics and attributes made explicit so as to connect the individuals with the acts which had killed them. Newspaper stories about the students also fostered the reconstruction of anticipation. Throughout the period following the Kent State deaths large groups of people personalized the deaths of the four students and actually grieved for them.

In the events following the assassination of President John F. Kennedy, the same phenomena are evident. An entire nation somehow had to cope with his death. The sudden assassination came with no warning or chance for anticipation. The reconstruction of anticipation, however, was no less real and followed the same general pattern.

The organizational problems of death and the way in which anticipation is reconstructed are related on a very practical level. The ability and willingness of any of us to reconstruct anticipation depends upon the individual who dies, his social and organizational role, and the way in which death occurs. It is through a combination of all these that grieving is seen as a process which depends upon social as well as psychological factors.

SUMMARY

The purpose of this paper has been to differentiate between the social conceptions of dying and death, to discuss the practical consequences on social behavior of death as a social event, and to treat grief as an overall social process. These are important concerns because the customary behavior patterns of grieving people are to a great extent influenced by the overall social and psychological orientations in American society. Furthermore, the general theoretical concerns raised by the preceding discussion should help to emphasize why death is an occurrence which so greatly modifies usual human behavior.

It seems important to point out once again that when death occurs a crisis arises that modifies considerably all aspects of human behavior. Clearly, the critical nature of death, both theoretically and practically, brings about many strains on interpersonal relations. Furthermore, such strains become most clear-cut when death is seen in terms of the held attitudes and beliefs of grieving people.

REFERENCES

Berger, P. L., and T. Luckmann, *The Social Construction of Reality*. New York: Doubleday, 1966.

Blauner, R., "Death and Social Structure," *Psychiatry, 25:*378, 1966.

Durkheim, E., *Suicide*. New York: The Free Press, 1951.

Firth, R., *Elements of Social Organization*. Boston: Beacon Press, 1964.

Freud, S., *On Dreams*. New York: W. W. North, 1952.

Fulton, R., ed., *Death and Identity*. New York: Wiley, 1965.

Fulton, R., and J. Fulton, "Anticipatory Grief: A Psychosocial Aspect of Terminal Care," in B. Schoenberg *et al.*, eds., *Psychosocial Aspects of Terminal Care*. New York: Columbia University Press, 1972.

Glaser, B. G., and A. Strauss, *Awareness of Dying*. Chicago: Aldine Press, 1965.

—— "Temporal Aspects of Dying as a Non-Scheduled Status Passage," *American Journal of Sociology,* July 1965b:48–59.

—— *Time for Dying*. Chicago: Aldine Press, 1968.

Gorer, G., *Death, Grief and Mourning*. New York: Doubleday, 1965.

Hertz, R., *Death and the Right Hand*. Glencoe, Ill.: The Free Press, 1960.

Holzner, B., *Reality Construction in Society*. Cambridge, Mass.: Schenkman, 1968.

Irion, P. E., *The Funeral and the Mourners*. New York: Abingdon Press, 1954.

Jackson, E. M., *Understanding Grief*. New York: Abingdon Press, 1957.

Kübler-Ross, E., *On Death and Dying*. New York: Macmillan, 1969.

Malinowski, B., *Magic, Science and Religion*. New York: Doubleday, 1948.

Mead, G. H., *Mind, Self and Society from the Standpoint of a Social Behaviorist*. Chicago: University of Chicago Press, 1934.

Parsons, T., "Death in American Society—A Brief Working Paper," *The American Behavioral Scientist, 6:*61, 1963.

Pine, V. R., "Institutionalized Communication About Dying and Death," *Journal of Thanatology* (in press).

—— "Social Organization and Death," *Omega,* 3:2, May 1972.

Strauss, A., *George Herbert Mead on Social Psychology*. Chicago: University of Chicago Press, 1934.

Sudnow, D., *Passing On*. Englewood Cliffs, N.J.: Prentice-Hall, 1967.

7

The Concept of Anticipatory Grief from a Research Perspective

Stanley Budner

Concepts are tools. In fact they are the basic tools we use for understanding and dealing with reality, and how they are defined often determines how useful a particular concept will be as a tool. What follows is an attempt to conceptualize or define the concept of anticipatory grief. It includes a comparison of the clinical and research approaches to conceptualization, a preliminary definition of anticipatory grief, and suggestions for future efforts.

THE CLINICAL AND RESEARCH APPROACHES

Clinicians are concerned with and focus upon individuals. While people live in a world of events, it is not so much the objective event as their subjective reaction to that event which appears to be critical to the texture of life. Thus, the immediate and personal experience for most individuals may not be the achievement of goals, the denial of their wishes, or the reality of death and dying, but the satisfaction of achieving, the anger because of frustration, and the pain caused by bereavement.

Hence, the concern of the clinician in our society, as he helps an individual patient with what he defines as the problem, usually translates itself into an approach which starts off with the immediate and the personal, with the subjective element in the patient's interactions with life. This does not mean that the clinician avoids dealing with reality, but that he realizes that there are at least three levels of reality: the subjective reactions of the patient to a situation; the gross behavioral responses to that situation; and the situation itself. Sooner or later in the course of work with a patient, the clinician probably deals with all three realities. But the starting point, and possibly the major emphasis, is on what is perceived as critical by the patient—the immediate and personal reaction.

Which of these three possible focuses of intervention should be the model for clinical work is not the concern here. However, it should be obvious that the choice of focus has significant ramifications. For example, a focus upon subjective reactions reflects an implicit affirmation of individualism; a focus upon behavioral responses, an assertion of the need for social control; and a focus upon the situation brings out the need for social reform. The choice of approach also has consequences for research. The clinician does not function in a vacuum; nor are his responsibilities limited solely to patient care. Thus, the actions taken by the clinician in patient care are supposed to be based as much as possible upon scientific research. Further, the clinician is not just a one-way conduit from research to patient care. The ideal and quite often the reality of clinical work is the development of definitions, concepts, and hypotheses which can be incorporated into ongoing research activity. And the subject of this chapter, anticipatory grief, falls into that category, a phenomenon initially identified by clinicians as a potentially significant one.

Because of the elaborate technology involved in research, it is easy to lose sight of the fact that ideas for understanding and coping with reality are the currency of research. Men, not techniques, are the sources of ideas, and the nature and structure of ideas which particular individuals will come up with are likely to reflect their general concerns and commitments. Thus, a clinician's definitions of reality tend to focus upon subjective responses, the phenomenology of human experience. Although the importance of this experience cannot be questioned, whether research should begin with a focus upon it is questionable.

Research concepts must be measurable by some agreed-upon standard. In the nature of things, the range of phenomenological experiences (our moods, our feelings, etc.) are difficult to classify, much less measure. The fact that something is difficult to classify and measure does not mean that it is unimportant or to be ignored. But it may be best to begin exploring the unknown where guides are more rather than less easily come by.

Approaching the concept of anticipatory grief can be somewhat like approaching a jigsaw puzzle. First, the perimeter pieces, which are the easiest to identify and locate, are put together. The counterpart of these perimeter pieces would be the objective situation, that in which the anticipatory grief response presumably occurs. The second step in putting the puzzle together is to move from the perimeter inward, and so progressively surround the unknown center. The counterpart of these pieces is the individual's overt behavior in the situation. Finally, there is the attempt to fill in the center, that internal, subjective state which has been labeled anticipatory grief. In short, focusing upon the externals of anticipatory grief is solely a tactical decision to obtain a reasonably objective context for viewing the personal experience involved.

Another possible advantage to this approach should be noted. Human beings are adaptive creatures, and adaptation implies varying responses by different individuals to the same as well as different situations. Thus, a focus upon the situational context rather than the specific response to that situation may contribute more to our understanding of the total grief experience.

THE CONCEPT OF THE ANTICIPATORY
GRIEF SITUATION

Given these general considerations, it is proposed that the starting point in this area should be the perimeter of the jigsaw puzzle. Thus, the concept of the "anticipatory grief situation" may be substituted for the more common one of "anticipatory grief" as both conceptually clearer and operationally more practicable.

This concept of the anticipatory grief situation has a limited referent—the impending death of a person who is part of a nexus of primary (familial) role relationships. The concept of anticipatory grief would appear to include more: the impending death of a person who is part of a nexus of primary role relationships; an awareness of that impending death by the others in the nexus of relationships; and, finally, a subjective state paralleling the subjective state associated with bereavement. All things equal, in this area a simpler definition is preferable to a more complex one. First, simplicity is neater. Second, the more variables that are included in the definition, the fewer are open to study. (For example, the degree of awareness of impending death appears to be a variable deserving of investigation in its own right to see how awareness affects the treatment of the dying patient as well as the reactions of those close to him.)

There are also the criteria of measurability to be considered. The concept of the anticipatory grief situation includes three elements requiring measurement: impending death; primary role relationships; and anticipatory emotions. Although these elements cannot be measured as objectively and precisely as might appear possible at first consideration, reasonably adequate objective measures can still be developed: medical diagnosis for impending death; family relationship, quasi-family relationship (fiancé, lover, etc.), and living in the same household for primary role relationships; and any arbitrarily chosen time period prior to death for anticipatory grief. On the other hand, the concept of anticipatory grief not only includes more elements which require measurement but also ones which pose greater problems in that respect, particularly where subjective states are concerned.

Aside from the criteria of simplicity and measurability, there is the impact of the concept of anticipatory grief upon the breadth of our perceptions. This concept focuses attention upon one hypothesized reaction to a grief situation. From a research point of view, such an a priori limitation of our view of a phenomenon may stultify our investigation of reality. And from a clinical perspective, it may tend to distract attention from the fact that all people caught in an anticipatory grief situation may need help, whether or not they have an anticipatory grief reaction.

POSSIBLE FUTURE EFFORTS

Given the definition, what steps should be taken next, at least in terms of research? The approach might be the one described earlier—that of the jigsaw puzzle. Thus, if a research program in anticipatory grief were to be established, it might be most profitable to begin with the gross, more objective reactions. This could include studies of the impact upon the health of individuals in an anticipatory grief situation, effects upon work performance, organizational contacts and activities, and on personal and familial relations. The same general approach can be taken with the psychological reactions to the anticipatory grief situation by a focus upon the more objective and measurable aspects in that area, for example, cognitive functioning (set maintenance, new learning, etc.), perceptual discrimination, frustration tolerance, and so on.

Once some data on the physical, social, and psychological effects of the anticipatory grief situation are obtained, and some hypothetical models developed, then the more difficult area of investigating the qualitative phenomenology can be undertaken. Such studies are always difficult, but it is to be hoped that they will be less difficult within a framework of objective data and explicit hypotheses.

Finally, there is the question of the relationship between the anticipatory grief reaction and the actual grief reaction. If this question is to be answered, comparable data on reactions to both situations must be obtained. One way of obtaining these data is by developing a research approach for studying bereavement which parallels the one suggested for studying the anticipatory grief situation.

CONCLUSION

This has been an attempt to define the concept of anticipatory grief from a research perspective and in terms of objective or measurable dimensions. The focus upon a research orientation was not for the purposes of asserting the primacy of research over other activities. Rather, it reflects the fact that scientific research is the technique adopted here because of its effectiveness in adding to our understanding of and ability to cope with problems. The focus upon the objective and the measurable was not solely because they are the sine qua non of research. Clinical intervention involves the manipulation of elements in a situation, and it is only that which can be grasped which is susceptible to effective manipulation. Neither death nor grief can be prevented, but those who grieve are still helped most by tangible social support, the gathering round of family and friends.

8

Suggested Stages and Response Styles in Life-Threatening Illness: A Focus on the Cancer Patient

Stephen V. Gullo, Daniel J. Cherico, and Robert Shadick

While Kübler-Ross (1969) and her associates have pioneered studies on the psychological effects of the process of dying, only limited attention has been given to the psychological effects of the prospect of dying. This distinction between "process" and "prospect" implies that the prospect of death may entail a type of behavioral experience and response different from that of dying. One situation involves a threat to life, the other demands a confrontation with the certainty of death. Specifically, in a life-threatening illness, death is often perceived as one of several possible outcomes; in the aware terminal patient, death is recognized as the probable outcome. Life-threatening illness, therefore, normally involves a reduced physical and psychological threat. In addition, the patient has (and needs) a greater latitude of behavioral response since the outcome of his illness remains unclear for an indeterminate period of time. Experience has indicated that it is often in the patient's best interests to plan for any one of several consequences.

The reduced threat, the requirements for a broader spectrum of adaptive behavior, and the overall uncertainty of the situation suggest that responses to life-threatening illness may differ significantly from the experience and

behavior characteristic of truly terminal patients. The nature of these differences, and whether they are qualitative or quantitative or an interaction of
these two factors, remain an empirical question. The primary objective of
this exploratory study, then, will be:

1) To investigate the experience of and the response to life-threatening
illness in the adult cancer patient.

2) To investigate whether response to life-threatening illness can be
described in terms of a continuum or stage theory.

3) To find if stages exist in the response to life-threatening illness; and
if so: (a) Do they differ from the stages experienced by the dying patient as
described by Kübler-Ross? (b) If they differ, what is the nature of the apparent differences and similarities?

4) To investigate the issue of generalized or predominant response
styles which endure throughout the illness.

Subjects

While the idea for this study evolved from interviews with physicians,
nurses, ministers, and others who care for the dying and seriously ill, the
data presented are based on extensive interviews with five patients and
members of their immediate families—usually a parent or a spouse.

All subjects had been operated on for cancer. They were aware of the
nature of their illness and the guarded prognosis for recovery. Although the
individuals tended to be somewhat overly optimistic, all reported a recognition of the life-threat and the possibility of dying from the disease.

Patient A. A twenty-one-year-old male, unmarried. Patient was operated on for removal of malignant melanoma of skin and possible metastases
to lymph nodes.

Patient B. A sixty-three-year-old widow with two married children. Patient was operated on for cancer of the uterus.

Patient C. A sixty-two-year-old married housewife with four grown
children. Patient underwent a radical mastectomy.

Patient D. A fifty-two-year-old married male with two children in
college. Patient operated on for lymphosarcoma.

Patient E. A twenty-three-year-old married male. Patient underwent
removal of spleen as part of treatment for Hodgkin's disease.*

* Patient reported there was some confusion as to the specific type of cancer.

All patients were members of the Caucasian race and represented middle to upper levels in socioeconomic status.

Methods and Procedure

Data for patients A, B, C, and D were gathered through a series of interviews with the patients and family members. Patients were interviewed during early hospitalization or immediately prior to it, again after surgery, and a third time—usually coinciding with release from the hospital. Depending on the availability of the patients, two to three interviews were conducted with each patient in the six months subsequent to hospitalization. Family members were interviewed in the beginning stages of the illness, shortly after the patient's release from the hospital, and during the four months subsequent to the hospitalization.

Patient E entered the study two months after his release from the hospital. He had compiled comprehensive diary notes during the course of the illness and these notes were used in lieu of the traditional interviews. The patient's wife, however, was interviewed for the purpose of securing her current and retrospective views.

All interviews were open-ended and focused exclusively on the patient's response to the illness and the life-threat it presented. While the interviews varied somewhat depending on considerations of time, patient, condition, stage of illness, etc., the specific topics covered normally included the following:

Patient's initial reaction to illness.

Patient's feelings about having cancer: (a) when first given diagnosis; (b) during hospitalization; (c) after hospitalization.

How patient is coping with illness.

His most important concerns at present time.

Future expectations—how does patient deal with life-threat?

Has patient made any promises to self, family, God, etc. which he hopes to carry out if he recovers?

Has patient noticed any changes in his attitudes, response to illness, and so on?

Patient's reactions to surgery and its effects on him.

Has this experience significantly changed him, his relations with others, or his life goals?

Comments on interactions with medical personnel and family members.

Is there anything patient wants to add or feels it is important to mention?

The interviewers were two advanced graduate psychology students trained in interviewing techniques. The interview reports were analyzed for significant trends, shifts in patient attitudes, family evaluations of patient, recurrent themes, manner of dealing with life-threat, and so forth.

THE CONCEPT OF STAGES IN RESPONSE TO LIFE-THREATENING ILLNESS

While recognizing that each person's manner of adjustment will effect uniquely the individual's experience of and response to life-threatening illness, it is nevertheless possible to identify response patterns which are common to all individuals in this study. In addition, these patterns of response appear to emerge through a series of successive stages which can be characterized as follows:

STAGE I: SHOCK

While many patients harbor suspicions about the nature of their illness or are sensitive to a "sense of impending doom," they are still shocked when their suspicions are confirmed. It is not so much a feeling of surprise as a sense of what patient A describes as "totally overwhelmed" and "incredulous that this could happen to me! Me!" There is very little obvious denial of the illness, and the patients emerge from shock to a recognition of the gravity of their situation and the hope that they will be cured. On the other hand, they tend to avoid or deny the question of dying from this disease. Patient D reports, "I've always gambled and I'm usually the fellow who wins, so I'm sure my luck will hold up now." Patient E is somewhat more adamant: "This——disease is not going to do me in. I didn't go through 'Nam' to lose now."

The patients' attitudes, however, extend beyond a mere defense strategy such as denial. The optimism and avoidance of the death issue are often supported by the medical staff and family members, who reassure the patient and highlight the positive. In this respect, the patient's behavior may be quite appropriate since it reflects the "realities" he perceives in his environment.

STAGE II: ANGER

The "How could it happen to me?" of Stage I quickly changes to "Why me?" in most patients. Patients B and E were particularly bitter and irritable. Patient E recalled feeling, "I've already gone through enough." Patient B repeated again and again, "Why me? The good always suffer. I've never gotten any breaks and now this." All patients did not, however, experience this stage fully. Patient A stated simply, "It's a bad break," and even patient E explained bitterly, "That's life! I don't try to figure it out. I fight it!"

STAGE III: GRIEF AND ANTICIPATORY GRIEF

In the patients interviewed, grief and, to a lesser degree, some depression were present from the point of diagnosis. Now, however, grief becomes the predominant experience of the patient. This period very often sets in as the patient makes plans to enter the hospital. The reality of cancer and cancer surgery take on a very personal meaning and sense of threat. Those who have previously avoided or denied the possibility of death must now confront the requirements of their situation. Either in relation to death during surgery or possible death from cancer, all patients report considering, at least, the prospect of death. One patient, nevertheless, was fairly consistent in denying that the possibility could ever become a reality in his particular case (patient D).

In addition to grief over things already lost, anticipatory grief assumes a role of major significance in an individual's behavior. The patient mourns for the losses which are projected to lie ahead. He mourns not only for the possible loss of life, but also for the active, committed life-style he may no longer be able to maintain. He mourns over the possible disfigurement and aftereffects of surgery, the possible separation from those he loves, the uncertainty of the future, the relinquishing of cherished roles (for example, family provider or protector), and, often, for the crumbling of the illusion that cancer and death are only nightmares that happen to others. Concurrent with the experience of grief and anticipatory grief, there very often develops a sense of profound loneliness and vulnerability. The patient recognizes that while others can be supportive, he and he alone must undergo the trauma of this experience. There is "no exit" from this dilemma, nor will the trappings of personal wealth, influence, or public prominence protect him. It is the dawning of reality for those who have nourished dreams of invincibility and for those who have traditionally relied on personal power or "special connections" to ease life's burdens. At this moment, perhaps for the first time in their lives, they are "just" men or women facing a serious threat to life.

The statements of patients poignantly illustrate the psychological strain of this stage:

Patient A: "It suddenly hit me: that I was alone now. My parents, my friends, no one could be with me. I had never been in a hospital before and I was really terrified about whether I could still live—not just exist—when this was over. I hope I will still want to live!''

Patient B: "I don't know what's going to happen to me. I know I don't want to die or lose my children or grandchildren. You just can't talk about how it feels, you cry!''

Patient D: "How will my wife and children manage? There's so much left to be done. My children need me still. It can't be my time yet!''

Patient E: "All that matters to me is my wife. I want to live for her . . . except I wouldn't want to live if I have to be a vegetable. I'm a man . . . not some freak to be pushed around in a wheelchair.''

STAGE IV: BARGAINING OR "PROMISSORY NOTE" BEHAVIOR

The recognition of the gravity of the situation and the suffering of grief and anticipatory grief very often overwhelm the person, and he feels that his own inner strength is inadequate. He has been "brought to his knees" and must now turn to a source of strength greater than himself. This external source of strength very often is God. All patients reported praying to God for strength, even those who did not consider themselves "religious" or members of any formal religion. In addition, patients A, B, and E promised certain life changes if God would help to cure them. Patients C and D made promises, but not to the Creator. Patient D made a promise to himself which he declined to reveal.* Patient C promised her husband and her children that she would "slow down" and "begin enjoying life . . . if I get through this in one piece.''

The day and particularly the night before actual surgery were the times when most patients felt the need to turn to outside sources of strength and

---

* Patient D continued to insist that he would surely recover and all he would add was that his promise had to do with "enjoying life more.''

inspiration. At these times, their fears and anxieties about living and the quality of life they would live in the future were most intense.

In these difficult and lonely hours filled with grief and anxiety, it appears that all human consolation is inadequate and that the patients feel impelled to offer major changes in life-styles. One can only speculate whether these promised alterations arise from a sense of guilt, a magical hope of swaying divine providence, a genuine re-evaluation of one's life, or a combination of these factors.

STAGE V: THE PERIOD OF UNCERTAINTY

It is at this point in the course of the illness that a major external intervention takes place—the patient is operated on and now begins the process of recovery from surgery. The nature of his psychological experience is very much tied to the extent of any disfigurement, the degree of discomfort, present and projected disabilities, and whether or not the operation has been successful.

In the five cases studied for this report, the patients reported tolerable levels of discomfort, and relief that the operation was over. While they were concerned about scarring and disfigurements, the principal concern was "getting well." This prospect was felt to be sufficient to justify the trauma and loss they had undergone—even in the case of patient C, who had the radical mastectomy.

The days immediately following surgery are characterized by a sense of relief that the operation is over. Patient A commented, "Well, at least I'm still here." The anxiety about the operation, however, is soon replaced by anxiety about what the operation revealed and whether or not it was successful. As the wait for pathology reports began, the patients experienced heightened anxiety and uncertainty about the outcome. "Promissory note" behavior, or bargaining, also continued. The duration of the period is generally dependent on the time required to receive the medical reports. Two patients, C and E, compared this wait to the night before the operation. In both cases, they reported, there is an "overwhelming uncertainty," a feeling that "the control of your life has passed from your own hands" and "you are facing impending doom." During this time, patients desperately seek information—each nurse's and doctor's remarks and gestures are carefully studied for any clue to the patient's condition, and the patient may often suspect that the staff is concealing information from him. Patients D and B also reported the experience of depression and a loss of hope, but this situation rapidly improved as discomfort lessened and strength returned.

Each of the patients in this study reported that the surgeons and pathologists had given a prognosis which indicated guarded optimism for a successful recovery of health. Upon receiving the "good news," a renewed desire (determination) to live was apparent in their comments—with the exception of patient B, who doubted the veracity of the report.

Two final points appear relevant within the context of this period of uncertainty. First, the authors are undecided about whether the period of uncertainty is truly a stage. That is, this overwhelming feeling of uncertainty is not so much a spontaneous feeling as it is an artifact of the waiting period between the operation and the receipt of medical reports indicating the overall prognosis. It appears that if the waiting period did not exist neither would Stage V. It has been included as a stage because uncertainty and a corresponding suspension of life expectations are the predominant psychological experiences of this period. It is important, however, that the stage is artificially generated by an environmental circumstance unrelated to the patient's illness.

The final point of discussion centers on the fact that the behavior of patients A, C, D, and E was strongly influenced by the favorable prognosis for their recoveries. It is interesting to speculate what the response would have been if the individuals were told that the metastases were so extensive that there was little hope for survival. Based on some very preliminary work undertaken, the authors would hypothesize that this situation would confront the patient with a new reality: he is dying and medical science has done all it can. His death is no longer a prospect, it is a certainty. The patient is no longer life-threatened; he is in the process of dying. The empirical question can now be raised: Will this patient experience the five stages of denial, anger, bargaining, depression, and acceptance that Kübler-Ross (1969) has associated with dying? If the patient has cherished the hope that he will survive the life-threatening illness, then he is not prepared to accept death, and the realization of imminent death would be a shattering reality. In adjusting to this new set of circumstances, his behavior might well reflect the stages outlined by Kübler-Ross.

STAGE VI: RENEWAL AND REBUILDING

This stage is characterized by a renewal of life aspirations. As the recovery continues and the patient can resume caring for himself and the other functions of a normal life, he returns to the plans and goals that had been set aside due to illness. He has not forgotten the possibility of death or further treatment but has made his own adjustment to these risks. A recurrent theme in the thoughts of most of the patients was articulated by patient D: "I've got to go on living . . . I will!"

A period of rebuilding accompanies the renewal of life aspirations. The rebuilding actually represents the behavioral manifestations of the motivational forces set in motion by the resumption of life goals. About this time the person also begins planning for a return to work, and gradually resumes social life and other commitments.

The patient interviews are particularly indicative of the renewal and rebuilding phenomena:

Patient A: "I'm daring to hope and plan again. I want to return to school immediately. That'll be better than any medication for me."

Patient C: "It looks like my house will have someone to love it again. I have some pain in my right arm but it's not an obstacle. Anyway, my legs are perfect, so I can go where I want . . . and there are a lot of places to go."

Patient D: "When the swelling goes down, I hope to go back to my company. I really don't have any serious aftereffects so I'm looking forward to resuming my job."

Patient E: "I guess I need to rest for a while. I'm just collecting my strength again. I don't mind the time off because I'll have to go for further treatments. When they are finished, I plan to be back in circulation."

Of the five patients in this study, only patient B did not fit the mode of behavior characteristic of this stage. While she did gradually resume her daily activities, she did not indicate any renewal of life aspirations. In fact, it appears that she had regressed to Stage III, the period of grief and depression. She continued to grieve over having cancer and her continuing misfortune. She commented: "How can you be happy when you've gone through something like this? I've been through so much. It's been an ordeal and it still is. These things happen only to the good people. I don't know! I just don't care any more. What is there to live for when you have to live like this?"

STAGE VII: INTEGRATION OF THE EXPERIENCE

All subjects were interviewed during the six months after their hospitalization to determine if and how they had integrated the confrontation with serious illness into their lives. Certainly to have faced death from cancer does not leave a life untouched. It is the type of experience which alters one's sense of the past and present and one's approach to the future. The researchers were particularly anxious to know whether the "brush with death" had resulted in changes of life-style and new life goals, and whether the individuals were able to integrate the experience by profiting from it in some way.

All patients, except B, reported some positive benefits from the confrontation with life-threatening illness:

Patient A: "I felt that I had proven several things to myself. First, that I was a man, not a weakling who crumbled in the face of death. Another thing I discovered is that death, my greatest fear, was not so scary and that I could face it. I also realized how much I was loved by my family and friends and this gave me a stronger will to live. I settled a lot of personal issues with myself as a result of that crisis."

Patient C: "I think I have already told you that I believe each person's life is part of God's plan. This doesn't mean that we just sit back; it takes courage to face up to the will of God and to live with it. I am grateful that I was able to do this. I am grateful that I am getting better and I am grateful for sixty-two years of a wonderfully happy and complete life. I hope I will have a long life but during those long days and nights in the hospital I made my peace with God, my family and myself and I am ready for whatever the future holds. I am no longer afraid of cancer, or heart disease or even death. This is as much a part of life as birth and everyone must die of something. I think I've grown a little wiser and more accepting about life."

Patient D: "I've always sensed I would make it . . . I'm not the ordinary guy. I had to live for my wife and to see my kids grow and now I am more certain than ever that I'm safely home. A year ago I thought 'there would always be time' . . . now I know time is limited and precious and there are times when it's more important to be with my family than behind my desk."

Patient E: "You learn never to give up. That you've got to be strong. I also realized that my head is put together very well and that my wife is the most important thing in life to me. I'm OK now but it's still 'touch and go.' The life I do have, I appreciate it more!"

Of the five, only patient B could not identify any positive developments or personal changes that had come about as a result of her illness. She was still concerned about "Why me?" and grieving for her accumulated misfortunes. She had apparently settled into a morbid pattern of grief which has been described clinically as "chronic grief."

The ability to integrate the experience appears to be the last stage in a patient who recovers from life-threatening illness. It appears to enable the individual to profit from the experience and, in some cases, to enrich the quality of his life. Just as grief must be endured, experienced and expressed in all its distress and pain (Lindemann, 1944), the grief and trauma of life-threatening illness must follow a similar path. The patient who failed to develop these modes of expression encountered severe problems of adjustment.

It is hoped that the seven stages outlined herein will serve as a step in identifying behavior in response to a life-threat and provide a framework for investigations into broader issues, such as why some individuals are able to advance from shock and grief to a renewed life and why others are not.

Perspective

The preceding section has outlined a stage model for describing the individual's response to the prospect of death in a life-threatening illness. Kübler-Ross has undertaken pioneering studies in a parallel area of research—the response to the actual process of dying. It appears that several notable differences are evident in the patterns of response, depending on whether one is faced with death or just the possibility of death (see Table 1). The different patterns of response stages may be related to the following:

1) A life-threat constitutes a far less severe challenge to the individual's integrity of functioning than does dying. Hence, the response behavior will tend to be different.

2) In the life-threatening illness, the initial presentation of the negative information, cancer diagnosis, was followed quickly by positive information: "There's so much that can be done." "It's one of the most highly treatable cancers." And so on. Hence, while one may be shocked to learn of his cancer, he is also given hope (very often realistic), and this appears to counteract the compulsion to deny the threat. In addition, the person is forced to confront the reality of the situation since he must enter the hospital for immediate surgery. There is very little hope or "good news" that can ease the experience of dying. Death constitutes a threat of enormous magnitude and, very often, the only way to cope is to deny. Hence, one finds denial com-

TABLE 1. STAGES IN LIFE-THREATENING AND
TERMINAL ILLNESS

Life-Threatened States	Death and Dying Stages (Kübler-Ross, 1969)
1. Shock	1. Denial
2. Anger	2. Anger
3. Grief and anticipatory grief	3. Bargaining
4. Bargaining	4. Depression
5. Uncertainty	5. Acceptance
If Diagnosis Favorable	*If Diagnosis Unfavorable* ↓
6. Renewal and rebuilding	Denial ↓
7. Integration of experience	Renewed anger ↓
	Renewed bargaining ↓
	Depression ↓
	Acceptance

↓ = Projected sequence

monplace as an initial response to the recognition that one is dying, while the need for this defense is not as acute in the case of a life-threat.

3) In the life-threatening illness, anger gives way to grief and bargaining. In the process of dying, anger gives way to bargaining and depression. For the life-threatened person, grief, not depression, is the primary experience since he is mourning for the loss of his health and the possible loss of such things as his life-style, cherished role relations, and finances. Yet, he is still able to maintain a sense of optimism and hope since these losses may be restored through medical treatment. Second, as patient A reported, "I was in the hospital a day after being diagnosed, and I was operated on the day after that. There was no time to get depressed." In fact, the patient was not only occupied, but the very things that kept him occupied—entering the hospital, surgery, and its aftermath—also gave him hope that something could be done to preserve his life. The terminal patient cannot, realistically, long maintain such a hope. Furthermore, the withdrawal of attention and disengagement by medical and family members can hasten any sense of doom and depression. Lastly, the terminal person's depression is quite ap-

propriate since he is about to lose everything and everyone he has ever loved, as well as his own life. For the life-threatened patient, there may be a significant chance of escaping any confrontation with death.

While bargaining occurs in both life-threatening and terminal illness, its onset appears to be somewhat earlier in the terminal situation. To explain this event, it is first necessary to discuss bargaining and the conditions which give rise to it.

As applied to the case of illness, bargaining represents an act of magical thinking wherein the individual hopes to sway some unknown or divine force through the act of making a deal with it. The individual will undertake a certain promise if he is "cured" or restored to health. Bargaining usually occurs in response to a severe threat which is not alleviated by the traditional forms of human intervention. It is, in a manner of speaking, the last refuge of desperate men. The terminal patient is very often driven to such behavior since his situation is desperate. The best medical efforts have been exhausted and have proven unsuccessful. His remaining options are very few. This situation is not analogous in life-threatening illness, in which medical treatments are often quite successful and there is a realistic basis for hope. More importantly, the life-threatened individual is often encouraged by the results, and he retains confidence in human efforts and in his doctors.

When the perceived threat to life increases, however, during the period immediately before surgery, some bargaining behavior will be evident in the life-threatened. This phenomenon is usually of very short duration, and arises out of uncertainty and lack of information rather than desperation.

Since the threat to life is significantly greater when the patient is dying, and since desperation and loss of faith in human efforts are common to such situations, it is reasonable to assume that terminal patients will resort to bargaining at an earlier stage than the life-threatened. In addition, their need for bargaining should be far greater, as it often provides the only ray of hope in a hopeless situation.

Another relevant consideration is that the gravity and inescapable reality of cancer seems to "hit hardest" when the patient enters the hospital and is being prepared for surgery. Prior to this time, the patient has been grieving for loss of health and the possible consequences of cancer. Now it becomes apparent that nothing can save him from this experience and that he may not be the "same" person once the surgery is over. This recognition and the uncertainty of the situation often bring about a heightening of anxiety and threat-perception. The result may be bargaining behavior. The important dimension, however, is to note the sequence of events experienced by the cancer patient. This has a significant effect on the psychological stages he will experience. It may also explain why grief, anticipatory grief, and some depression precede bargaining in life-threatening illness.

The different circumstances surrounding the bargaining of the life-threatened and the terminally ill should not obscure the fact that bargaining serves the same function in both cases—the reduction of anxiety.

A final consideration arises from the limited sample size of the present study. Five subjects constitute a highly limited sample of the life-threatened population, and the differences in stages between life-threatened and terminal behavior may have been influenced by this or other design variations.

In brief, this study has presented evidence for stages in life-threatening illness. The evidence is only suggestive, however, and additional research is needed to explore the life-threatened person's experience. A second area of study is a comparison of response behavior in life-threatening and terminal illness. The researchers believe that the differences noted result from the fact that the life-threatened person is confronting only a possibility of death, while the terminal patient is actually dying. It is also possible that, when one theoretical model is compared with another, variations will appear due to design and experimenter differences. This factor has been noted and, if possible, control for it should be injected into future research. In the authors' opinion, its influence will probably be insignificant—but that has yet to be demonstrated.

PREDOMINANT RESPONSE STYLE (PRS) TO LIFE-THREATENING ILLNESS

Discussion of findings on life-threatening illness would be incomplete if it concluded with the presentation of a stage model for describing the response to such illnesses. There remains one finding of possible significance which has not been reported previously here or in the research literature.

Four of the patients interviewed experienced all the outlined stages of life-threatening illness, and patient B experienced the first five. If one reviews the statements of all patients experiencing a particular stage (for example, stage of shock), there are obvious communalities of experience, and these common experiences have formed the basis for that stage. Yet, a more careful analysis of each patient's comments indicates an underlying diversity, and this diversity is one of attitude. It indicates that although the individual reported specific feelings and concerns common to others experiencing this stage of life-threatening illness, he retained a unique attitude about the illness and the possibility of death reflective of his own way of coping with crisis. If one examines the development and path of this attitude in each of the stages experienced by the individual, it appears that this phenomenon is indicative of what can be described as the individual's predominant response style to a life-threatening illness (PRS). The PRS may not be the most obvious element in the individual's responses and comments, but it is the underlying behavioral theme which seems to endure through the different stages. It exists concurrently with the successive response stages of shock, anger, grief, bargaining, uncertainty, rebuilding, and others. In essence, the PRS is the sum total of the individual's responses gleaned from an analysis of his response stages to the life-threatening illness.

The data in this study and numerous other interviews and observations conducted by the researchers suggest a tentative identification of five different types of PRS. Not coincidentally, each patient in this study was selected initially because he or she appeared to illustrate clearly a particular PRS.

In analyzing patient interviews, differentiation was made between recurrent themes appearing throughout the course of the illness (PRS) and phase-specific themes characteristic of a certain period in the illness. Five predominant response styles have been tentatively identified by the authors, and each of the patients in this study is representative of one of the different PRS's. The five styles will be described, and the statements of the patient typifying a particular style will be included under the appropriate rubric. In addition, the statements of the patient will be drawn from several stages in the course of life-threatening illness to demonstrate the enduring nature of a PRS. Lastly, the classification of an individual as a specific type of PRS is based on an analysis of recurrent themes. Hence, the continuity of a theme from stage to stage is of essential importance. The statements made by the patient in one stage of illness are of little significance per se; it is the overall evaluation of the stages taken together with the "feeling tone" expressed by the patient that determines the PRS.

Type I: The Death-Accepter

The patient tends to be a realist.

He confronts the reality and gravity of the illness and acknowledges that his life is in danger.

He will fight to get well but, if death becomes inevitable, he will find the strength to accept it.

He makes plans to deal with continued illness and even death. Yet, he vigorously follows all medical procedures required of him.

He wishes, hopes for, and anticipates a long life but he is aware of the cancer statistics.

He grieves for the loss of health and the suffering endured and he experiences anticipatory grief about changes in his life which may result from the operation.

Case example: Patient A

Stage I. Comments: "I cannot believe this is happening. I think I will wake up tomorrow and find it was just a nightmare. Yet, of course, I know with my mind what Dr. B. is talking about. I'm just too numb to feel it or try to figure life out. I suppose there's really no reason."

Stage III. Comments: "I don't really know what lies ahead. I try not to ask why either. I've been really quite sad because I don't know what I'll look like after this is over. It's OK but I'm pretty strong; I will be able to accept it. I said before, 'I hope I will still want to live.' Of course, I will still want to live . . . the alternative is worse." And a little later: "I said I don't look for reasons. Life is an odds game—and I was unlucky in this respect. Now it's up to me to make the best of this situation and to face it."

Stage V. Comments: "It is foolish to struggle against death. That's the way it is—you fight when it will help. You don't fight when it serves no purpose but to prolong suffering. If I have to die—and I don't know that I will—then I'll hope to be courageous—and also realistic about my own strength."

Stage VII. Comments: "I may not like being sick and I certainly wish I could change it. I know it 'ain't much fun' being sick. Unfortunately, I cannot do very much about the situation except to realize this is the way it is. I was never one of those people who always have to ask 'why?' I'm happy to be healthy now but I realize that someday I will still have to face sickness. This nightmare has helped me to realize that and to value these happy, 'ordinary' days." On further questioning, the patient told of a prayer which best expressed his life philosophy: "Dear God, give me the courage to change the things I can in life, the patience to accept the things I cannot change, and the wisdom to know the difference."

Type II: The Death-Denier

The patient acknowledges the nature and gravity of his illness.

He may even acknowledge that the prognosis is poor in *most* cases.

The patient insists, however, that he will definitely be one of the "lucky" ones who survive all obstacles and odds.

While acknowledging illness and even the possibility of his own death, the patient cannot come to terms with death on a personal, nonintellectual level. He cannot accept the fact that death could conceivably happen to him. He is even angered at the inconvenience illness causes.

Often the patient claims, "I just know I'll be the one in a hundred. I just know it."

Since he is "certain" he will not die and that he will recover, he reports minimal anticipatory grief.

Case example: Patient D

Stage I. Comments: "I've always gambled and I'm usually the fellow who wins, so I'm sure my luck will hold up now."

Stage II. Comments: "I've got so much to do at the office and with the business and now I have to take time off for this——thing. There are 200 million other people in this country and it picks on me. Well, I'm the wrong person, because this time cancer loses." It is only in the extreme anxiety of Stage III that patient D seems to show a weakening of the denial.

Stage III. Comments: "I can't afford for anything to happen to me. How will my wife and children manage? There's so much left to be done. My children need me still." But later in the interview, he adds: "I know I'll make it. It's not my time yet to go."

Stage VI. Comments: "I just knew I would make it. You see I even told you. What would they do with me upstairs anyway? My strength is coming back already and you can chalk up one for me and zero for cancer."

Stage VII. Comments: "I've always sensed that I would make it . . . I'm not the ordinary guy."

Type III: The Death-Submitter

The patient confronts the fact that he has a life-threatening illness and this realization leads to a feeling of being overwhelmed, abandoned, and completely helpless.

The patient tends to be a pessimist. While noting that death is only a possibility, he is convinced he will die.

Although the patient acknowledges the illness and its gravity, he cannot accept death as a reality which is (an unfortunate) part of life. He can only express resignation or submission. He feels so totally overwhelmed and helpless that it is impossible to cope with the prospect of death.

The patient feels he is "fated for doom," that it is inescapable.

The patient tends to become unmanageable and uncooperative at times—even refusing necessary medication.

The patient tends to reject any favorable information as "lies" told just to provide consolation.

Anticipatory grief tends to be overshadowed by depression.

The patient shows a weakening of the will to live and to recover from the illness.

The death-submitter PRS appears to entail the opposite reaction to the death-denier PRS. The death-submitter is convinced he will surely die; the death-denier is convinced he will surely survive—no matter what the odds may be.

The patient is unable to integrate the experience or profit from it in any way.

Case example: Patient B

Stage II. Comments: "Why me? The good always suffer. I've never gotten any breaks and now this. It should have happened to someone like_____."

Stage V. Comments: "I don't need to wait for the reports. I know the results. I can see it in their faces. There's no hope. God, what am I going to do? The way children are these days, there's no one around to take care of you." Later in the interview, she adds: "I can tell why they're treating me this way. Don't you think I know? There's no hope when it's cancer. That's a death sentence. What's the use of taking medicines that don't help. They just annoy me and make me depressed. I have enough problems without these pills and the nurses."

Stage VI. Comments: "I have to take care of things still but it's different now. Once you have cancer you're on the way out. There's no more fun in life. You're like a machine. I just keep busy while I still can. Otherwise, I just sit around and cry my heart out. It's unbearable." The patient was reminded of her favorable prognosis, and commented: "Oh, they tell that to everybody. You should know that! I'm not easily fooled . . . they give themselves away by the way they act. I've seen too many people die of cancer among my family and friends to believe those things anymore."

Stage VII. Comments: "There's no justice in fate. The good people are always the ones to suffer. You're ruined with something like this. You just sit around waiting for your time to be up. Sometimes you feel better but that won't last long. I don't know!"

Type IV: The Death-Defier

The patient acknowledges illness and the possibility of death. The patient seeks and welcomes favorable information, but he is a "cold realist." He recognizes that even with a favorable prognosis recovery at this stage of the illness may be questionable.

The patient hopes that his intense will to live, his intense fight to recover and his refusal to accept or to be overwhelmed by death, may "turn the tide."

While the patient anticipates and perhaps even looks forward to the struggle for survival vs. death, he realizes that medical treatment may ultimately prove futile. At such a point, he purports he would still continue to fight, not so much to recover as to preserve his "dignity and freedom to act."

The patient experiences grief and anticipatory grief but does not "allow" himself to become depressed.

The patient is filled with anger and rage, which he directs at conquering the illness and death.

The death-defier PRS, unlike the death-denier, does not have any exaggerated hopes of being the "one in a hundred" who survives. He is realistic and can confront the prospect of death on an intellectual and personal level, while the death-denier can deal with death only as an intellectual entity that happens to others. In addition, the death-defier, even when aware of the futility of further struggle, refuses to accept death peacefully, as does the death-accepter. Of these individuals, Dylan Thomas has written, "Do not go gentle into that good night [death]. Rage, rage against the dying of the light."

*Case example: Patient E ***

Stage I. Comments: "This disease is not going to do me in. I didn't go through 'Nam' to lose now."

Stage II. Comments: "That's life! I don't try to figure it out. I fight it."

Stage V. Comments: "This [the encouraging prognosis] is the first good news in a long time. It gives me hope and strength to face the future. No matter what lies ahead."

Stage VI. Comments: ". . . I need to rest for a while. I'm just collecting my strength again. I don't mind the time off because I'll have to go for further treatments. When they are finished, I plan to be back in circulation." Additional diary comments read: "You can't relax yet . . . particularly not now. This adjustment makes the difference whether you live as a 'real person' or a 'sick person.' "

Stage VII. Comments: "You learn never to give up; that you've got to be strong." He adds at another point: "During my hospitalization, I kept on thinking of *The Myth of Sisyphus* by Camus, in which a guy keeps on rolling a rock up a hill although the rock continues to roll back again. The guy knows his efforts are doomed but he continues and in so doing he affirms his own existence and freedom in the face of the absurdity of life. This is the way I felt I would want to die if anything goes wrong. Of course, my efforts may not help and they may even prolong the ordeal, but they would matter to me, and that's the one thing I would have left in the face of death."

Type V: The Death-Transcender

The patient acknowledges illness and the possibility of death.

The patient can confront the prospect of death, which all people must face at one time or another.

The patient views death as an integral link in the plan of creation. An individual life may end but that person's "life force" continues to live through offspring and family. In addition, the patient may also explain (or substitute for the first explanation) death in terms of the religious concept of immortal-

* E's comments represent edited diary notes, as indicated previously.

ity. He believes that death cannot really destroy life since the soul is immortal.

The patient grieves for the loss of health and the anticipated changes in lifestyle. Grief connected with death is centered on death as a force which separates one from loved persons—not the fear of death.

The death-transcender PRS is not just an acceptance of death, although this is part of the response. The individual goes beyond acceptance to a point where death is viewed in terms of a broader concept of life. In addition, the patient sees death as the logical completion of his efforts in this life.

Case example: Patient C

Stage III. Comments: "At times like this it is very hard to face life. You've lost a lot and you may still lose everything else you have. I have to keep on reminding myself that in God's plan this experience has some meaning."

Stage V. Comments: "Breast surgery is not a pleasant experience. Fortunately, at my age nobody will be stopping to notice. I don't know what to say about the future although I try to be optimistic. Everything is part of God's plan and I'll try my best to carry out that plan."

Stage VI. Comments: "I'm glad the hospital experience is behind me now. What a relief to be able to take care of things for myself . . . almost like before. I've always tried to find the positive in a situation and now it has come true. Of course, I can't be certain what comes next, but I have strong faith, and confidence in myself, and that's more important than knowing the future."

Stage VII. Comments: "I think I have already told you that I believe each person's life is part of God's plan. This doesn't mean that we just sit back; it takes courage to face up to the will of God and to live it. I am grateful that I was able to do this. I am grateful that I am getting better and I am grateful for sixty-two years of a wonderfully happy and complete life. I hope I will have a long life but during those long days and nights in the hospital I made my peace with God, my family, and myself, and I am ready for whatever the future holds. I am no longer afraid of cancer, of heart disease, or even death. This is as much a part of life as birth and everyone must die of something. I think I've grown a little wiser. . . ." At the end of the interview, the patient added: "I saw my daughter and grandchildren this morning. There is so much of my husband and me in them that I was kind of reassured that I had left some small mark on this world that will live on after I've gone. It gives you a special sense of trust that death is not an end . . . just as Christ taught, 'Life is changed, not taken away!' ''

Perspective

This section has presented a description of the predominant response styles to life-threatening illness (PRS) encountered by the researchers in the patients studied. Of course, human behavior cannot be compartmentalized so deftly, and patterns of behavior in a serious illness may often reflect a combination of acceptance, denial, submission, and transcendence. There is no succinct equation that can be drawn to express such complex behavioral interactions. The essential element remains, however, the issue of endurance or recurrence. The predominant response styles were not determined on the basis of a single stage or period of time; they evolved from an exhaustive analysis of the recurrent themes expressed by the patients throughout the entire course of the illness. The stage descriptions, on the other hand, arose from an analysis of behavior and expressed concerns dominant during a specific period of the illness but which did not endure to any significant degree.

It is noteworthy that although individuals usually experienced the same sequence of stages in their response to life-threatening illness, the predominant response style often differed markedly from one individual to another. The researchers believe that the uniformity of the stage responses is in many ways related to environmental circumstances. If one examines the series of events encountered by the typical cancer patient, these would include:

1) Receives diagnosis
2) Enters hospital
3) Surgery or medical intervention
4) Receives report on the success or failure of operation
5) Recovery
6) Release from hospital
7) Begins rebuilding life—if possible.

The seven stages appear to be highly predictable psychological responses to these occasions. For example, it is to be expected that a person who has been told he has a life-threatening illness, such as cancer, will initially be shocked. It is also predictable that he will experience difficulty accepting that "it is really happening to me!" (Stage I). Since there is usually no answer to the "Why me?" question, one can expect a temporary period of bitterness—often directed at "Fate," those who are well, or even the self (Stage II). In addition, grieving for lost health, the alteration of life-styles, possible disability, and even death is totally appropriate under such conditions (Stage II). A similar line of reasoning can be applied to explain many of the dimensions of the other stages. The central issue which emerges from such a discussion is this: To what extent are the stages triggered or influenced by environmental events? The answer appears to be that environmental events do exercise a significant, if not causal, influence.

The PRS, however, is an overall response style for dealing with the crisis of illness and the life-threat. It continues to evolve during the entire course of the illness, and while its path is certainly influenced by environmental events and the long-term readjustments they require, a primary role must be given to the past history of the individual, his internal equilibrium, and his resources for dealing with conflict. In the case of the individual about to receive a diagnosis of cancer, the range of predictable behavior is quite limited, and is usually covered by such terms as shock, disbelief, denial. The behavioral repertoire and style for handling crises is as broad and varied as one individual's life differs from another. The situation not only allows for a wider range of appropriate behaviors, but it also demands it since individuals have different needs and resources. Hinton (1968) has investigated the role of life-history in the development of response styles to serious illness, and he points out:

Death can be very distressing if viewed as the final disillusionment, and this can well occur in those who have seen their lives as a sequence of blighted hopes. If a person has always been self-doubting or guilt-laden, the coming of death and its taking away all remaining hopes of expiation during life can cause profound depression. Among the observations of dying patients made by a psychiatrist, Cappon, he describes how he found that a patient's distress when facing death grew out of his manner of coping with life. A person may manage to present a stable front to the world throughout his lifetime only by a series of complex psychological maneuvers. These ways of compensating for inward strife, these defenses of the ego are also likely to determine the sort of response made to approaching death. Sometimes the prospect of death is so overwhelming that the usual methods of coping with an emotionally disturbing situation break down. If a dying person can no longer use effectively his usual psychological tricks that prevent too outrageous uncertainty, if defensive tactics such as denying the unpleasant, or blaming others are no longer effective, then he may experience distress to the full.

Jerome Bruner (1966), in one of his rare ventures into the realm of personality development, differentiates three phenomena which are central to the behavior of the life-threatened individual: coping, denial, and integrity of functioning. A fourth term of relevance, dysfunctional behavior, was employed by the researchers. Most of these terms have recurred throughout this report, and all of them are defined in the appendix to it.

The primary objective of defense, to avoid or escape a problem without violating one's integrity, coincides with the primary objectives of the death-denier. Denying the fact that his life is threatened in a very real sense, he insists he has a "special sense" that he will definitely survive.

The death-accepter accepts the reality and possibility of death on a personal level, and in so doing respects the reality of the situation. This behavior style appears to be primarily coping in its objective.

The death-defier and the death-transcender accept the possibility of death on the personal level but tend to avoid the pain of this reality through intellectualization in the case of the death-transcender, and overcompensation in that of the death-defier. These behavior styles entail primarily a combination of coping and defense.

Predominant in the experience of the death-submitter is a sense of being overwhelmed and hopeless. This behavior style is essentially passive in that the individual just submits and does not attempt to develop coping or defense behaviors. In the case reported by the present authors, the sense of hopelessness and being overwhelmed appears to have interfered with the prescribed course of medical treatment, relationships with medical personnel and family, and ultimately the patient's recovery. It does not respect the realities of the situation, even when they are favorable, and violates the individual's integrity of functioning. Hence, the death-submitter PRS can be classified as dysfunctional behavior. At the very least, it certainly violates the behaviorist's edict that "the purpose of life is to function."

In considering the above classifications, it is important to keep in mind a factor mentioned previously: the condition of the patients in this study did not deteriorate to a point where any one of them was actually dying. (Even though patient B maintained she was "ruined," she was able to take care of herself at home with little difficulty and eventually had a favorable prognosis and returned to work.) If they had been dying, then those behavioral styles developed for the life-threat may have proven inappropriate or unsupportable.

The previous warning against interpreting data in light of five case studies remains relevant for the PRS. In addition, it must be emphasized, whether one speaks of stages in response to life-threatening illness or predominant response styles, that some of the findings may be disease-specific. Since all patients in the study were cancer patients, it remains an empirical question whether cardiac, kidney, or other patients would encounter the same or similar phenomena. Dovenmuehle (1965) provides guidelines for an eventual clarification of this issue. Lastly, the possible influences of such variables as sex, age, socioeconomic status, and cultural background on life-threatening and terminal behavior have yet to be explored.

CONCLUDING NOTE

When dealing with a relatively uncharted research domain, a time-honored tradition is to end a study with the observation that more questions have been raised than answered. This traditional ending also happens to be accurate here. Yet, one must go one step further and ask, "Are these the right questions?"

The authors have attempted to identify two principal ways of analyzing the individual's response to life-threatening illness: the response stage and the predominant response style. The limitations of design and population have been discussed, and possible interpretations of the data collected have been suggested. While this work has been described as an exploratory study, it is not so much a study in its own right as a first report of an ongoing project. It is hoped that the preliminary data will provide an embryonic model within which one can begin the painstaking analysis of life-threatened behavior. As for the issue of raising the "right questions," that judgment must await the outcome of further investigations and, ultimately, it must rest with the patients who may benefit from this research. For the present, the authors can offer a tentative mapping of the experience and evolving path of life-threatened behavior and can only note—"to be continued!"

APPENDIX

DEFINITIONS

Coping (Bruner, 1966): Behavior which respects the realities of the problem(s) encountered while still respecting the individual's integrity of functioning. Hence, the person continues to function through dealing directly with the requirements of his situation.

Defending: A strategy whose principal objective is avoiding or escaping from problems for which there is no solution. It does not, however, violate the integrity of functioning

(Bruner, 1966). In defense, the person avoids confronting an unpleasant reality which cannot be altered. Yet, the strategic behaviors he develops to achieve this end do not interfere with the requirements of his life-style.

Dysfunctional Behavior: Behavior which violates the individual's integrity of functioning. Of course, human behavior cannot be compartmentalized so deftly, and patterns of behavior often reflect a mixture (or, perhaps, admixture) of coping, defending, and dysfunctional behavior. Nevertheless, for the purposes of research it is important to recognize the different behavioral processes which may be operating in any behavioral situation.

Integrity of Functioning (Bruner, 1966): A required level of self-consistency or style, the need to solve problems in a manner consistent with the most valued life enterprises.

Response Style—Predominant: Describes the patient's predominant and enduring mode of response to life-threatening illness as evaluated by the three researchers in the study. Response style often includes coping, denial, or both.

REFERENCES

Bruner, J., *Toward a Theory of Instruction.* Cambridge: Harvard University Press, 1966.

Dovenmuehle, R. H., "Affective Response to Life-Threatening Cardiovascular Disease," in *Death and Dying: Attitudes of Patient and Doctor,* Symposium No. 11, Vol. 5. New York, Group for the Advancement of Psychiatry, 1965.

Hinton, J., *Dying.* Baltimore: Penguin Books, 1968.

Kübler-Ross, E., *On Death and Dying.* New York: Macmillan, 1969.

Lindemann, E., "Symptomatology and Management of Acute Grief," *American Journal of Psychiatry, 101:*141, 1944.

9

Dying: Dromenon Versus Drama

Joseph H. Meyerowitz

The essential distinction between dromenon and drama is that the former is a participant rite and the latter an observer's show: *hoc est corpus* versus hocus-pocus (Harrison, 1913). Neither the process of death education for student-physicians and physician-residents nor the doctor-patient relationship can successfully achieve their goals as a drama. It is only through the therapist's participation in the terminal sequence that learning can take place; and only through the therapist's acceptance of the role of actor (and not of observer) that a measure of comprehensive treatment can be provided the patient.

For the purposes of this chapter, dying will be considered in terms of the terminally ill in hospitals. We will focus on the patient, his immediate family and physician, and understand that the meaning of these parties' functioning is determined in larger social and medical institutional contexts. The author takes the position, with Fulton (1972), that a primary problem for patient, family, and physician is anticipatory grief.

Anticipatory grief will be used as a subclass of patterned desocialization. These culturally peculiar ways of undoing interdependency networks reduce the cognitive and/or affective aspects of previously established relationships. They minimize the assumed disruptive effects of dissolution.

In the psychoanalytic tradition, the management of libidinal energy requires grief for emotional liberation from the lost object until the individual can successfully test reality, become aware of object loss, and invest in new objects (Wretmark, 1959). This chapter explores those phases of grief which begin before the loss.

With separate consideration being given to the physician, family, and patient, it may be useful to recognize that in their anticipatory grief each is attempting "maintenance of control." Every individual wishes to feel that he can, at least partially, control his situation and that others are seeking not to usurp, but rather to augment his management. The dying patient threatens the physician; the family and physician may be seen as controlling the patient; the family's guilt (where no unconscious hostility toward the patient can be elaborated) may be a defense to handle existential anxiety, an attempt to control the uncontrollable (Gardner, 1969).

THE PHYSICIAN

Feifel (1967), on the basis of a series of studies, concluded that:

above-average fear of death is a relevant variable in the choice of a medical career. Physicians utilize the medical professions, through which the individual secures prominent mastery over disease, to help control personal concerns about death. . . . in encounter with the fatally ill—his reawakened anxieties . . . lead him to . . . disinherit his patient psychologically at the very time he enhances attention to his physiological needs.

The dying patient represents a threat to the physician's omnipotence—the patient has no right to die. Feelings of omnipotence lead to ambivalence and subsequently to rejection of the patient. As the physician's wish becomes equated with impending death, retaliation (according to the *lex talionis*, the law of reciprocal punishment) is feared from the patient. The physician who fears closeness (that is, emotional vulnerability) finds that the patient has moved their relationship from peripheral to central. The physician who needs love from his patients finds he is elaborating, overexplaining in an attempt to control his mounting anxiety as the patient's life wanes. Both types use anger in the service of projection, and the result is rejection of the patient (Schnaper, 1969).

Out of his own concern, the physician focuses on triumph over death, forgetting that neglected anticipatory grief and bereavement may also become pathologic. First to the patient and then to the family, "nonpersonhood" is bestowed, and then confirmed through sedation. In absenting himself, the physician obscures the positive aspects of grieving and allows the development of pathologic dependency in the bereaved and, with respect to their grieving, sustains a lie.

By promoting the processes of preparation for dying—facilitating grieving, assessing loss, nurturing manifestations of strength—the physician can surpass the negative goal of controlling suffering and enhance life for both patient and family. While it is not in the purview of this evaluation, evidence continues to build as to the harmful effects and catastrophic decisions which result from incomplete or uncontrolled mourning (Marshall *et al.,* 1969).

Not only the physician but also the entire staff become remote and progressively isolate the patient, both psychologically and physically. All are fearful of contributing to the death and have awakening feelings of inadequacy and worthlessness manifested as inability to function and hostility directed toward the patient. But the primary physician is the most shielded from overt criticism because the patient, or family, "chose" him. The staff finds itself in a "double bind" as it wants the patient to be reassured that he isn't dying (that the staff is potent), but at the same time reward (with solicitous behavior due to anxiety) his impotence (Binger *et al.,* 1969; Quint and Strauss, 1964).

One special problem of working with the terminally ill is, in part, that well individuals leading productive lives and not continually confronted with object-loss seldom need shift from dealing with the existence of death (nonpersonal) to the presence of death (awareness of one's own mortality, not imminent) or presentiment of death (imminent personal death). Here the staff becomes a participant in the presentiment of death and the resultant interaction (bind) reduces therapeutic effectiveness and intensifies the process of dying (Chandler, 1965).

Identification with the "brave" patient allows the physician to suppress his emotions. But as anxiety breaks through the patient's defenses, his demands for physician involvement increase. The physician's response of chemical tranquilization may dampen the patient's fear, allowing a semblance of equilibrium, but it does not deal with the cause of anxiety (Cramond, 1970).

Teaching goals, in physician training, are aimed at the physician's optimal participation in the dromenon. These goals are on a continuum including: (a) helping him to deal with his own feelings; (b) balancing attention previously given the sequence of dying toward the quality of life; (c) developing comfort, within one's specialities, in dealing with the aspects of dying; and (d) training specialists who will work with dying patients and their families and the medical staff around them in facilitating anticipatory grief and productive bereavement. Specifically:

1) The physician must be aware of his own cultural position, attitudes toward death, and defense modes. These influences will affect his response to each patient in terms of "social worth" and ease of separation (Lasagna, 1969). It is through the complex filter of countertransference that the patient and his needs are seen. The physician must learn to make the distinctions involved in fear of dying versus death, fear of others dying, and personal extinction (Collett and Lester, 1969).

2) The physician must be aware of the patient's cultural position and the nature of his familial relationships. While he must understand the patient's neurotic defenses, he should not hasten to analyze them.

3) The physician must be aware of the institutional setting into which he has placed the patient in terms of its therapeutic and countertherapeutic aspects for this person.

4) The physician must be sensitive to the patient's crisis, his increasing fear of loneliness and abandonment, and be able to distinguish between appropriate depression (anticipatory grief) and unnecessary physical suffering.

5) The physician must resist the temptation to take advantage of the patient's kindness or his own denial through the fantasy of "having done all he could," and thereby justify separation. The patient's greatest "need" is a continuing relationship (Ellard, 1968). There is a two-way transference of affect. These attitudes were originally ascribed to family members. Identification leads to expectations. Because of the transference relationship, the patient is able to recreate the early child-parent trust situation. Continuity of care is essential; and the patient must not lose this primal tie by accident or design.

6) The physician should be available to listen, to cope with the patient's silence or anger, as a reliable empathic object able to respond appropriately to patient needs. Once reassured, the patient makes fewer demands for extra time. Reassurance and calm concern will usually allay patient shame. The physician must be available to re-establish, in part, the object-loss continually being experienced, available *not* to be manipulated, yet stubbornly

persistent in being present. He is demonstrating indestructibility, strength to withstand terror, fright, and the assault of the patient.

With the terminal patient, the nonpsychiatric physician can aid in the ventilation of early memories and safely inquire about dreams without interpreting them. Through reassurance and sadness (as at the parting with a friend) combined with hope, the physician can allow the continuity of the "I" (implied in "When *I* am dead") through children (friends) and memory (Chandler, 1965; Cramond, 1970).

Although few will choose to assume major responsibility for psychotherapy with the terminally ill, it is a desired goal. Norton, in a detailed account of one such case, speaks of how the patient finally expressed her envy of the therapist's health. In the final phases of the relationship, the patient was comforted by being able to take the therapist "along" even into death. The dying patient specifically confronts the therapist with guilt and with an injury to his narcissism. That the patient is actually dying inevitably mobilizes the therapist's childhood death wishes and serves as a painful reminder of his own mortality. Countertransference responses are inevitably provoked, and their acceptance and utilization can be most therapeutic (Norton, 1963).

In the Freudian tradition, Eissler writes ". . . through the establishment of transference—[which] reawakens the primordial feelings of being protected by a mother, the suffering of the dying can be reduced to a minimum" (Eissler, 1955). All this the physician should know and be able to choose in order to utilize.

THE FAMILY

Although 80 percent of physicians expect families to manifest anticipatory grief, and an even higher percentage expect families to feel "unfaithful" to the dying patient, few doctors include care for the family within their role definition (Schoenberg *et al.*, 1969).

If physicians recognize that object-loss is a potential stress leading to illness, then object-maintenance and replacement must be considered important variables in sustaining health and adjustment. The doctor and hospital come to be experienced as supporting psychic objects for the patient. Family members experience grief as a disease fulfilling all the criteria of a discrete, separate syndrome. They suffer, consecutively: shock/disbelief leading to awareness/somatization; crying/emptiness leading to somatic impairment; and then restitution/recovery (Engel, 1961).

While the phases overlap, their number is variously described. There is agreement that before restitution/recovery comes hostility/guilt for having been spared, and often projected as resentment toward the initial diagnosing and primary physicians. If professionals are prepared for this, they can become a source of help, instead of becoming enmeshed in a pattern of mutual recrimination (Schnaper, 1969; Binger *et al.,* 1969).

The acute phase of grief work is normally completed six to twelve weeks after the death, and entirely within two years (Hodge, 1971). But this pattern is changing. The bulk of grieving may be completed before the patient's death, with both positive and negative consequences (Fulton and Fulton, 1972).

In a study of chronic childhood illness, the first stages of anticipatory grief were found to set in almost with diagnosis of the child's condition. (Indeed, in cases were the fetus is not expected to survive the first neonatal days, parental separation behaviors [avoidance of emotional investment] may be said to precede the object.) This material—specifically, familial response to stress—is reviewed elsewhere. A few comments here may indicate the facets of the problem (Meyerowitz and Kaplan, 1967; Patterson *et al.,* 1973).

The initial responses of the parents to the knowledge that they will lose their child are of denial. As they begin to deal in terms of accepting the reality, they also begin to perceive negative attitudes (anticipatory grief is seen as equaling defeatism) on the part of the larger society, which create a self-fulfilling cycle of isolation. The nuclear family finds itself called upon to give support to the extended family just when it is itself most vulnerable. A frequent observation in cases of serious childhood illness is that relatives, especially grandparents, display severe denial and avoidance responses, and often prove to be even more vulnerable to the anticipated loss of the child than the parents. For these relatives, as for the parents, the effect of delayed diagnosis is to intensify the "feeling of frustration regarding aspirations for the child." Unlike the parents, the relatives have a greater social distance from the child which permits them to maintain, and even intensify, their avoidance and denial defenses rather than deal directly with the reality of the diagnosis. Such avoidance and denial by relatives would certainly appear to the mother as a lack of familial understanding and support. Both patient and family suffer from the lack of closure of completed fantasy tasks; giving up "what might have been" is part of the grief work. How any specific family fares under stress is a result of the foregoing as well as pre-existing family integration, perception of crisis, and previous experience (which may lead to overreaction rather than improved coping). Hospitalization of the patient may be more a response to familial than patient need, and somatic complaints of family members are often a response to the patient's attempt to talk about prognosis. In bereavement, the focus is as often on the initial diagnosis as upon the final death.

Although anticipatory grief "may well form a safeguard against the impact of a sudden death notice, it can turn out to be a severe disadvantage at the occasion of reunion" (Lindemann, 1944). While sudden death is exceedingly traumatic, prolonged grieving produces resentment and, in turn, guilt (Lasagna, 1969). While it is possible for a family to be so decathected that it cannot help or be helped, this is very rare (Norton, 1963).

An effective, integrated therapeutic program does not aim to remove the pain and feeling of loss caused by death, but rather to relieve the patient's anxiety, bring comfort to his family, and allow the staff to confront an emotionally complicated situation. Terminal illness frequently causes role inversions as parents are cast in a dependent status in relation to their children. As important as coordination of community services may be to the patient, priority should be given to early assessment of the family system (Sheldon et al., 1970). The larger families of the past provided for role continuity. The nuclear family unit, often with separate "worlds" for each member, leaves each member isolated in coping with stress and vulnerable to repercussions as each seeks to "help" another. Children, especially, are protected from experiencing anticipatory grief when what they need is help in mobilizing it (Ellard, 1968).

As has been noted previously with regard to the terminally ill child, the diagnosis is often recalled as the hardest blow to the family. Often parents have begun anticipatory grief while the grandparents and friends may continue complete denial. Remission and relapse become equal threats to tenuous adjustment. Parental fantasy of the child's psychic condition is frequently worse than fact. Fathers suddenly in need of—and unable to obtain or accept—support absent themselves, leaving the mother to cope. About half of the families studied reported significant negative behavior shifts in siblings of the terminally ill child. When the child is in a disease treatment center and many families are in contact with each other, inappropriate sorrow becomes a problem. While some parents can express a sense of relief at the time of the child's death, more express grief in the form of anger (Binger *et al.,* 1969). The physician could "give permission" for acceptance with histrionics, or often acceptance without emotional ventilation, and thereby allay the guilt feelings of years which are now flooding the defensive dikes (Annis, 1969).

Chronically ill patients experience withdrawal by family more frequently than do acutely ill terminal patients. "Extinction is less feared than the prospect of progressive dissolution." To overcome the family's aversion to the impending death, rites such as drawing the shades, hushed voices, and unnatural attitudes are used. These indicate, to the patient, capitulation, abandonment, and premortem burial (Weisman and Hackett, 1961). Feeling the ambivalence of their own helplessness, many families begin withdrawal by reducing the frequency and duration of their visits (Chandler, 1965). "Perhaps it's because of the defense against countertransference that so many patients are left alone to die" (Norton, 1963). Other families, attempting to obviate guilt and loss, move too close to the patient and try to take over, telling him (and the physician) what to do (Schnaper, 1969).

To help the family manage anticipatory grief, the physician must (1) intervene in the acute phase (that is, at or near diagnosis) and initiate movement; (2) provide support, both psychic and pharmacologic; (3) orient to the total family—the dependency initially manifest will recede with the crisis; (4) promote grief work; and (5) maintain hope while overcoming social pressures to be stoic.

Many of the problems for the family relate to the unstructured nature of anticipatory grieving and to the unsatisfactory, for many, nature of our bereavement ceremonies. Crosscultural studies impress further our own situation. As compared to "Western" families, Shinto and Buddhist families were found to suffer less somatic distress following the loss of a family member. They consistently felt the deceased as "present" and saw no threat, therein, to their own sanity (Yamamoto *et al.,* 1969).

THE PATIENT

Studies have shown that intelligence and social status seem to play no role in the amount of distress suffered by the dying patient (Osler, 1906; Exton-Smith, 1961; Hinton, 1963). While variable by illness, distress was consistently high. Anxiety was especially high where dyspnea was an aspect. Patients who were under fifty years of age, or had dependent children, a "tepid" religious faith, or hastened to tell the interviewer that they *knew* they were dying, tended to be the most depressed. Their depression does not obtrude and may not be recognized by the medical staff, seen only as physical discomfort or exhaustion. C. C. Herbert suggests that an alteration in mood (such as might result from the intervention of a helping person) may be a causative or contributive agent in the timing of death (Hinton, 1966).

Studies of chronically and terminally ill children note that there can be no doubt that by the time these children are four years old they are aware of their prognosis and concerned about separation, disfigurement, and pain. They are preoccupied with bodily changes and eager to talk, but the institutional environment defeats them, resulting in melancholia and deep depression on the wards. Psychological damage is greatest to children who "know" but can't tell their parents. The physician must find a way to let the child know that his concerns are shared and understood; that he is willing to listen and to talk. The child needs reassurance that all will be done to alleviate his discomfort. But communication and hope are impossible without recognizing with the child what he already "knows." Until then, the child cannot voice his sadness, fear, helplessness, and feelings of loss and anxiety. If he is lied to, he is being deserted (Binger *et al.,* 1969).

Studies of the general public serve to reinforce points previously made. First, the psychic significance of death independent of illness (the GSR responses to "death" and "sex" word-stimuli imply an affective similarity significantly different from the response to "basal" words); second, the cultural dependence of death's meaning, and, third, the hierarchy of concerns—loss of family and friends, then broken plans, pain, concern about the existence of a hereafter, loss of body. Older people worry more about their dependents; Catholics more about a hereafter; lower-status individuals worry first about pain; atheists are perturbed about plans and loss of experience. Everyone fears death because it eliminates, in special ways relevant to him, the opportunity to pursue self-esteem (Ellard, 1968).

There is not unanimity in the way the terminal patient is viewed and how the physician should relate to him and his family. One authority advises that: ". . . [the] wife or nearest relative should always be told . . . if she plays her part . . . and does not let him guess, by word or gesture, . . . she will be bearing her husband's burden for him. . . ." (If the patient is told, ". . . soften, manipulate and present truth . . . [so] that it does not demand the humiliation of open acknowledgment. . . . As a rule, however, patients do not ask, or if they do they do not want the truth. . . .'') "He realizes, too, that it is far better for both of them that his wife should not know that he knows, or that he knows that she knows, and that the last few weeks will be intolerable unless he continues to play the part we have allotted to him" (Ogilvie, 1957). There is scant evidence to support this approach.

Although couched in a language of death, the problems of anticipatory grief are those of living. The fear of death represents a specific attitude toward the process of dying, usually a sense of imminent disintegration. This is more closely allied to primary anxiety or panic than to any transfiguration that death is assumed to entail.

Bluestone and McGahee (1962) studied persons in the death house and, surprisingly, found them not to be anxious and depressed. While several explanations might be hypothesized to explain this difference from the patient population, two need special attention. First, prisoners know that until a scheduled date they are more protected from deadly danger than are others. Second, prisoners may be sustained by rescue fantasies (Ganser Syndrome). Some physicians attempt to divert the patient's attention from the terminal prognosis, which the physician is impotent to change, to the secondary complications from which there can be "rescue." The consequence for these patients is often increased physical pain.

Feelings about the "existence" of death are at the impersonal level— unilateral, an "I-it" relationship to specimens whose unique existence does not matter. This approach is developed as a defense in medical training. The "presence" of death is at the interpersonal level—"other one-I; so far I've been spared." This is the result of early diagnosis. The "presentiment" of death is intrapersonal—"soon *I* will be gone." This is the state of the fearful patient, and does not necessarily correspond with the physician's evaluation. The withdrawn person with heightened preoccupation with visceral sensations and diminished concern with the world, and who interprets internal events as portents of fatal illness—the patient whom the physician calls "hypochondriacal"—is manifesting fear of dying and death.

The anxious terminal patient fears for his sanity if it seems to him that the world is no longer connected by familiar ties, that it is "falling away." The world, which is normally at one with our perceptions, becomes alien, disjointed when the terminal patient tries to think of it running along without him. Whether or not unconscious narcissism permits us to think of subjective death (and in death fantasy there is a continuity and successful resolution of life problems) is irrelevant to the immediacy of the patient's anxiety.

It frequently appears in the terminal phase that the sharp antithesis of living and dying gradually becomes modulated into a dampened harmonic line. But the physician's and patient's grief work go on by dealing with the awareness of progressive erosion of body and mind, depletion of resources, accumulation of regrets. The patient experiences perseveration of the past, obtuseness in the present, and a blunted appetite for the future.

When death comes to be seen as "appropriate," it is robbed of its sting. Such a state is attained if death is a "solution" to life's problems or there are few remaining problems; super-ego demands are reduced; optimal interpersonal relations are maintained; the ego is functioning at as high a level as physical condition permits (Weisman and Hackett, 1961).

The patient wants to, can, *needs* to discuss his feelings and fears—but needs a respondent. Fear of the process of dying is basically a fear of abandonment—a re-enactment of early real or fantasied separation from the mother figure. The patient is having a normative (not "a normal") mourning reaction, commonly labeled "depression," to the loss of the prime love object (self). He is about to lose all that marks him as "him" and provides status. His normative depression may take the form of insomnia, *pavor nocturnus,* anorexia, irritability, fearfulness, apathy. It may become pathologic, leading to a suicidal preoccupation in an attempt to regain control of the timetable and quality of life. The physician can help the patient find a basis of validating his life as having worth. The patient will, if conventionality doesn't interfere, be angry. "Mother" figures are being lost and the "omnipotent father," here the physician, can't save the "child in the patient" from loss and hurt. As the patient weakens, he will regress further toward a childlike dependency, awakening shame and guilt. Terminally, there will be constriction of interest and a loosening of social ties (Cramond, 1970).

Strong, well-integrated personalities may do better than others at concealing their depression, but they are the more vulnerable in anticipatory grief. Persons with depression antedating the fatal illness, who have lost interest in living, are seen as accepting death with equanimity. The amount of grief work to be done is related to the number and meaning of interpersonal losses. If a measure of the person's strength of personality is his capacity for relating to others, the strongest will suffer most!

For many patients, denial is an important defense. Without belief in survival, a patient may be incapable of settling his affairs. Each step of "depossession" may be seen as "forcing" death. As the illness progresses, the patient begins to retract his ego boundaries. (This process is accelerated if there is physical pain.) He "undoes" ties with others as he becomes more concerned with himself. Consequently, the extent of anticipated loss and grief is reduced until denial and depression are unnecessary and the patient is capable of "accepting" death. Until the patient is spontaneously prepared to give up denial as a defense, this should not be the goal of any psychotherapeutic attempts.

The patient's "working through," with or without the physician-therapist's help, follows a predictable sequence: (1) denial (spontaneous ego reaction to the threat of nonbeing); (2) anger and/or resentment—"Why me? Why not you?"; (3) bargaining (magical thinking); (4) depression, when the unconscious resolution of emotional conflict may occur; and (5) acceptance, resolution (Kübler-Ross, 1969).

The process of resolution requires the expansion of the patient's libidinal field into the domain of death. Dreams of life gradually insinuate themselves into the image of death. If the personality is not to die before the person, identity must be disassociated from the disease itself. Janis (1958) speaks of "unrepression" in surgical patients. This eagerness to work through should be utilized to rectify wrongs, reaffirm objectives, discuss matters not previously discussed. Human exchanges between those who live and those who will shortly die are the way (Eissler, 1955; Weisman and Hackett, 1961).

It is not clear how much help psychotherapy can offer. Some contend that, as no personality changes occur in terminal illness, even if neglect leads to hardship on those left behind it is not justifiable to disturb the tenuous balance of the dying, whom one cannot help, for the sake of the living who may help themselves. These therapists place the roots of a fear of death in the destructive death drive, suggesting that it is an ego defense against the wish to die, binding self to Id. They see the terminally ill person as hard to approach as ever, in need of all his old defenses and rapidly shutting out communication. In impending dissolution, the experience of dreaming is blanketed at waking. Reporting dreams is "giving" something to the therapist. The patient is seen as prepared to receive help to the extent to which he gives. Dreams begin to be shut off. With the advance of the dying process, libidinal ties are broken as a motivation toward death (*mortido*). The patient may yet deny the prognosis, but forebodings (the recurrence of dreams) are prevalent. Somatic perceptions in dreams, dream-lyses, are believed to be experienced long after the reporting ceases. The loose love-ties which hold life together dissolve until there remains only the narcissistic investment in the body-self (Cappon, 1959).

An alternate position, that of the value of facilitating the patient's anticipatory grief, holds that mourning eases the person's plight by decathexis of objects. Therefore, death can be accepted as a "natural consequence of an energic constellation in that moment [although] perception conveys the fact of the [continued] existence of the love objects." Treatment, in this view, is a "gift situation," "an unusual favor of destiny" (Eissler, 1955). The crucial gift is the therapist as an available object.

In the process of therapy, the patient is helped to defend against object-losses by facilitating the development of regressive relationships which preclude object-loss. The order of mourning (undoing of ties) begins with the more recent relationships, then spouse, then parents. Separation from self and children (a relationship which often tends to become a unity) is continuous and always incomplete. Libido detached from objects through mourning becomes transferred to the therapist until the sole relationship is the therapeutic one. In the final stages of resolution, there is regression to childlike wish fulfillment dreams as the super-ego and Id are externalized. Reunion fantasies of joining others who have died play an important part here, and offer a new form of status. As the ego is externalized, infantile separation anxiety is manifest. Introjection (of the therapist) leads to contentment and peace.

Audrey Evans (1968) has pointed out that the discussion, in therapy, of unreal fears may be an excellent way of dissipating them, but that the fear of death is by no means unreal. The physician, in his therapy, may be helping the patient to rationalize or he may be unloading responsibility for emotional defenses from his own onto the patient's shoulders. Despite the questionable incentive, the goal may be seen as desirable. The patient should be enabled to maintain responsibility for his emotional defenses, and this includes transferring, in his proper time and way, some measure of trust to the physician.

Whether the "therapist" is a physician, the spouse, or a friend, the goal of anticipatory grieving is for the patient to

reach a stage during which he is neither depressed nor angry about his fate. He will have to be able to express his previous feelings, his envy . . . , his anger. . . . He will have mourned the impending loss of so many meaningful people and places, and will contemplate his coming end with a certain degree of quiet expectation. . . . it is not a resigned and helpless "giving up". . . . Acceptance . . . is almost void of feelings. It is as if the pain had gone (Kübler-Ross, 1969).

REFERENCES

Aldrich, C. K., "The Dying Patient's Grief," *Journal of the American Medical Association, 184:*329, 1963.

Annis, J. W., "The Dying Patient," *Psychosomatics, 10:*289, 1969.

Binger, C. M., A. R. Ablin, M. D. Feuerstein, J. H. Kushner, S. Zoger, and C. Middelsen, "Childhood Leukemia," *New England Journal of Medicine, 280:*414, 1969.

Bluestone and McGahee, "Reaction to Extreme Stress: Impending Death by Execution," *American Journal of Psychiatry, 119:*393, 1962.

Caplan, G., "Crisis in the Family," *Medical Opinion and Review, 1:*21, 1966.

Cappon, D., "The Dying," *Psychiatric Quarterly, 33:*466, 1959.

Chandler, K. A., "Three Processes of Dying and Their Behavioral Effects," *Journal of Consulting Psychology, 29:*296, 1965.

Collett, L. J., and D. Lester, "The Fear of Death and the Fear of Dying," *Journal of Psychology, 72:*179, 1969.

Cramond, W. A., "Psychotherapy of the Dying Patient," *British Medical Journal, 3:*389, 1970.

Eissler, K. R., *The Psychiatrist and the Dying Patient,* New York: International Universities Press, 1955.

Ellard, J., "Emotional Reactions Associated with Death," *The Medical Journal of Australia, 1:980,* 1968.

Engel, G. L., "Is Grief a Disease?" *Psychosomatic Medicine, 23:*18, 1961.

Evans, A. "If a Child Must Die," *The New England Journal of Medicine, 278:*138, 1968.

Exton-Smith, "Terminal Illness in the Aged," *Lancet, 2:*305, 1961.

Feifel, H., S. Hanson, R. Jones, and L. Edwards, "Physicians Consider Death," Proceedings, 75th Annual Convention, American Psychological Association, 1967.

Fulton, R., and J. Fulton, "Anticipatory Grief: A Psychosocial Aspect of Terminal Care," in B. Schoenberg *et al.,* eds., *Psychosocial Aspects of Terminal Care.* New York: Columbia University Press, 1972.

Gardner, R. A., "Guilt Reaction of Parents with Child with Severe Physical Disease," *American Journal of Psychiatry, 126:*634, 1969.

Harrison, J., *Ancient Art and Ritual.* New York: Holt, 1913.

Hinton, J. M., "The Physical and Mental Distress of the Dying," *Quarterly Journal of Medicine, 32:*1, 1968.

Hinton, J. M., "Facing Death," *Journal of Psychosomatic Research, 10:*22, 1966.

Hodge, J. R., "Help Your Patients to Mourn Better," *Medical Times, 99:*53, 1971.

Janis, Irving L., *Psychological Stress*. New York: Wiley, 1958.

Kübler-Ross, E., *On Death and Dying*. New York: Macmillan, 1969.

Lasagna, L., "The Doctor and the Dying Patient," *Journal of Chronic Diseases, 22:*65, 1969.

Lindemann, E., "Symptomatology and Management of Acute Grief," *American Journal of Psychiatry, 101:*141, 1944.

Marshall, J. R., G. M. Abroms, and M. H. Miller, "The Doctor, the Dying Patient, and the Bereaved," *Annals of Internal Medicine, 70:*615, 1969.

Meyerowitz, J. H., and H. B. Kaplan, "Cystic Fibrosis and Family Functioning," in P. Patterson, C. Denning, and A. H. Kutscher, eds., *Psychosocial Aspects of Cystic Fibrosis: A Model for Chronic Lung Disease*. New York: Columbia University Press, 1973.

—— "Familial Responses to Stress: The Case of Cystic Fibrosis," *Social Science and Medicine, 1:*249, 1967.

Norton, J., "Treatment of a Dying Patient," *Psychoanalytic Study of the Child, 18:*541, 1963.

Ogilvie, H., "Journey's End," *The Practitioner, 179:*584, 1957.

W. Osler, *Science and Immortality*. London: Constable, 1906.

Quint, J., and A. Strauss, "Nursing Students, Assignments, and Dying Patients, *Nursing Outlook, 12:*24, 1964.

Patterson, P., C. R. Denning, and A. H. Kutscher, eds., *Psychosocial Aspects of Cystic Fibrosis: A Model for Chronic Lung Disease*. New York: Columbia University Press, 1973.

Schnaper, N., "Management of the Dying Patient," *Modern Treatment, 6:*746, 1969.

Schoenberg, B., A. C. Carr, D. Peretz, and A. H. Kutscher, "Physicians and the Bereaved," *GP, 40:*105, 1969.

Sheldon, A., C. P. Ryser, and M. J. Krant, "An Integrated Family Orientated Cancer Care Program: The Report of a Pilot Project in the Socio-Emotional Management of Chronic Disease," *Journal of Chronic Diseases, 22:*743, 1970.

Weisman, A. D., and T. P. Hackett, "Predilection to Death: Death and Dying as a Psychiatric Problem," *Psychosomatic Medicine, 23:*232, 1961.

Wretmark, G., "A Study in Grief Reactions," *Acta Psychiatrica et Neurologica Scandinavica, 34* (Supplement 136):292, 1959.

Yamamoto, J., K. Okonogi, and T. Iwasaki, "Object Loss Prior to Medical Admissions in Japan," *Psychosomatics, 10:*46, 1969.

PART 2
CLINICAL ASPECTS

10

A Surgical Oncologist's Observations
Benjamin F. Rush, Jr.

The surgeon who specializes in the treatment of patients with cancer is exposed to and must be prepared to recognize the multifaceted elements making up the syndrome of grief (Averill, 1968; Clayton *et al.*, 1968; Volkan,
1970). The initial diagnosis of cancer sets in motion powerful emotional
forces related to the patient's fear of loss. These may range from fear of loss
of life to fear of loss of vital parts or functions. In addition, all oncologists,
surgical and otherwise, distinguish as one of their major responsibilities the
careful follow-up of the patient beyond diagnosis and treatment since several
years must pass before one can be certain that the disease has been con-
quered. This careful follow-up exposes and re-exposes patient to physician
and vice versa. The emotional crisis of discovery of recurrent disease is unfortunately a familiar problem. The present discussion concerns itself with
the syndrome of anticipatory grief (Averill, 1968) and how it may be stimulated in such patients either before or after treatment.

PREOPERATIVE ANXIETIES

Anticipation of Death
BY THE PATIENT

Any patient who has been informed that he must have an operation for a
tumor must confront the possibility that he may not survive. The prospect of
operative death appears to be a relatively minor threat to most of today's pa-

tients. The faith in the physician's ability to carry the patient successfully through the operation itself is usually high, even when the patient has been informed of the mortality rate for the operation. It is usually not higher than 10 percent, and the patient finds it easy to assume that the one patient out of ten who will die will be someone else. There are exceptions, of course, relating to the patient's past experience. If there has been someone in the family who has died during an operation, or the patient is highly strung and suspicious, the threat of death may seem more imminent.

A far more important determinant is the patient's attitude toward cancer. There are still many patients who equate the diagnosis with a death sentence, and who assume that once cancer has been diagnosed death will most certainly follow in a short time, that is, between six months and a year after diagnosis. It can be safely assumed by the physician that, regardless of what he tells his patient about the tumor, there is enough information in today's society to suggest to the average patient that the tumor may be malignant. The basic policy for the physician is to tell the patient as much as he wants to be told. There are some patients in whom denial is such an important part of their response to the likelihood of cancer that they will carefully avoid any specific information as to their illness. A physician must be careful how he informs such patients of their diagnosis and not thrust details upon patients who do not want to receive them. At the same time, he must be honest in what he says so as not to destroy his credibility.

In summary, then, the role that anticipatory grief may play in the preoperative picture depends to a large degree upon the patient's attitudes, and perhaps to an equal degree on the manner in which the physician manages these attitudes. Certainly, the physician should be ready to diagnose the appearance of shock and despair which mark the first two phases of grief, and which may interfere substantially with preparing the patient for operative stress. Depression associated with anorexia and withdrawal during the preoperative period may well be a reflection of anticipatory grief, and must be dealt with accordingly. The responsible physician must know when help from psychiatric consultation is needed and be ready to call for it.

BY THE FAMILY

The family is usually in receipt of much more frank information than the patient. The physician has probably been most precise with the family as to the exact risk of the operation as well as to the chances for success. If his predictions are grim, they may set off a chain of anticipatory grief in the family which will be sensed by the patient. Since the patient is part of the family unit, and probably shares the same attitudes, the physician must be alert to family attitudes toward cancer since they will give an index of the patient's response. The physician's own attitudes toward cancer are reflected in his advice to the family. Most oncologists who have made it a part of their specialty to have a very precise knowledge of prognostic figures for the different types of cancers tend to be much more optimistic about various malignant lesions than many physicians outside this specialty. Some interesting surveys have indicated that many physicians consider almost any lesion of Hodgkin's disease, testicular cancer, or melanoma as almost certainly lethal, whereas actual figures indicate that patients treated in the early phase of any of these lesions have a better than 50 percent chance of permanent cure.

Anticipation of Incapacity

While denial of the risk of death and optimistic anticipation of cure may be successful patient mechanisms in averting grief patterns in the preoperative period, the operation itself may threaten varying degrees of incapacity which the physician has had to discuss quite frankly with the patient. It is possible for the patient to mourn the anticipated loss of functions which are particularly precious to him in the same way that he might mourn the possibility of death.

GENERALLY THREATENING INCAPACITY

Certain areas of loss from surgery are much more likely to stimulate anticipatory grief than others, depending on the patient's personality. Perhaps the most potent threat is a loss of sexual function, such as occurs in men with carcinoma of the penis, in which amputation is necessary, or in women with carcinoma of the breast. Perhaps the most commonly seen pattern is apparent in the woman with breast cancer when the loss of a breast is expected. This is usually complicated by the fact that until a biopsy of the lesion is done, no one is certain whether it is malignant or benign. Thus, most women undergoing biopsy, even of clearly benign lesions, may suffer a component of anticipatory grief in the preoperative period which can be resolved only by the final biopsy and outcome of the operation.

Loss of special senses or functions is also of special importance in promoting a grief reaction. Of all the special senses, the most threatening loss is that of sight, as might be required by bilateral retinal melanomas. Hearing loss is a lesser threat, and is encountered only rarely as a result of a cancer procedure. Prospective speech loss seems to disturb patients only modestly in the period prior to a total laryngectomy, but may be a major factor in the postoperative period when the patient actually begins to deal with the problem. It is possible that patients have great difficulty imagining what it is like to be unable to speak at all. The incidence of gastric ulcer and of suicide is said to be much higher in the laryngectomized patient than in the normal population. Most such patients, however, indicate that the realization that they are unable to utter a single sound does not affect them fully until the laryngectomy has been performed and they are actually experiencing the handicap. Nothing in their previous experience, no matter how carefully they have been prepared, has invoked a concept of this condition. This very lack of ability to appreciate the disability involved probably lies at the root of the apparent lack of concern which often seems to precede the operation.

Another cause for loss of speech is the operation which threatens partial loss, such as amputation of major portions of the tongue. Anticipatory grief prior to such an operation may be more acute than that prior to laryngectomy. Loss of the tongue was a part of ancient punishment and is enshrined in popular legend. Popular film depictions of individuals who are mute because of such mutilation exist in our culture, and the patient can draw an unhappy parallel between this often overdramatized situation and his own fate. The fact is that speech does not become too distorted for communication until more than two-thirds of the tongue has been removed, and even with more extensive removal the majority of these patients can make themselves fairly readily understood, although their speech may be distorted. The postoperative state is actually a far happier one than for the patient who has undergone a laryngectomy.

Locomotion. Anticipation of amputation of one or more extremities may also cause considerable prior grief depending on the feeling of dependence that the patient may have on the part to be lost and the extent of the amputation. Perhaps the most dramatic and threatening loss is hemicorporectomy, in which the entire lower half of the body is removed. This operation, of course, combines a number of major losses, including the loss of sexual function, the loss of both lower extremities, and the loss of normal orifices for defecation and urination. It is therefore not surprising that when patients are offered a choice, they frequently refuse this "hemideath," feeling that this much loss of their body substance is too much to bear and that they would rather die of their disease than undergo such a procedure. It is obvious that many physicians regard the procedure similarly and do not refer their patients for consideration of such an operation. Many surgeons capable of the operation are not convinced of the worth of performing it. Despite the overwhelming emotional antipathy, there are certainly a few very select patients who probably can tolerate the psychological trauma and who would benefit from such a procedure. Any patient awaiting the operation would undergo considerable emotional stress. His behavior patterns almost certainly would include many of the components of both pathological and physiological anticipatory grief.

Colostomy. Most patients who are anticipating an operation which involves loss of one or more of the normal excretory orifices identify the procedure as "colostomy." The lay public has gained considerable understanding of this. Many individuals have had a member of the family, a friend, or a relative who has undergone such a procedure. Still, there is deficient knowledge of what the procedure really means and what is involved in the care of the orifice. Management of colostomy, ileostomy, and of the various types of ureteral diversions has become quite acceptable with present-day techniques. Postoperatively, most patients tolerate the problems introduced by management rather well. Fear of odor and accident is usually managed quickly when the various forms of appliances and skin seals are found to work so well. Sometimes a patient may have special psychological problems because of prior anal attitudes, and these must be handled with special psychiatric help. However, the point is that grief for the loss of the excretory organ and for the problems that will be introduced by its new location is likely to be more intense and to cause more worry prior to the procedure than postoperatively.

Loss of Identity. Certain operations which involve the head and neck require major resections of a portion of the face which result in a total change of the patient's countenance. Regardless of how acceptable or unacceptable this change may be to the patient's family and the general public, even minor changes may be very hard for the patient to accept since he compares the image he sees in the mirror with the former image that he had of himself, and by this standard even modest changes in contour may completely distort the patient's own self-image. This is more likely to lead to postoperative rather than to preoperative grief, since it is difficult for an individual to conceive that he can lose his identity in this fashion. Moreover, he has no standard against which to measure or anticipate the alteration. Despite ample warning of what may be involved, the full implication is not apparent to the patient until the operation has been accomplished. This serves to protect the patient against anticipatory grief preoperatively but to intensify his response and reaction postoperatively.

Loss of Cerebral Function. Any operation which involves the brain is certain to arouse in the patient dread of loss of cerebral function. This is especially intense if the patient prizes his intellectual ability, and perhaps is best exemplified by Samuel Johnson's reaction to his stroke, as quoted by Boswell: "Oh God," Johnson prayed, "take from me whatever you will but preserve my brain."

SPECIALLY THREATENING INCAPACITY

The incapacities listed above are those most likely to stimulate in the patient a feeling of anticipation of loss which will lead to varying degrees of grief. It is rare for a patient to grieve for the possible loss of a portion of or all internal organs so that the possibility of a subtotal gastrectomy, a hemicolectomy, or a total pancreatectomy is unlikely to affect him in any way emotionally other than from the standpoint of the pain and risk of the procedure itself. Reaction to the potential loss of any one of the structures or functions cited above may be greatly intensified if it occupies a special place in the individual's life style. The loss of a leg to an athlete, loss of speech to a singer or orator, loss of sight to an artist—all these are obvious examples of situations which may intensify grief preceding the loss. While these are dramatic examples of such problems, an individual's regard for his abilities in certain areas may intensify the anticipation of loss in a way which is most apparent to the physician. A patient may not make his living by song but singing may be a talent which he treasures and which has played an important role in his past life. Even the most physically unattractive patient may pride himself on his appearance and may think of himself as handsome. The prospect of an altered countenance may mean something very special to him. It is unnecessary to illustrate the point further. It should be clear that the physician must understand his patient thoroughly in order to guard against and avoid situations in which anticipatory grief may become so intense as to be pathological.

RECURRENT CANCER

We have been examining the degree of anticipatory grief which may be stimulated by the fear of the loss of a body part intrinsic to an operation, by the fear of death that might be produced by the operation, and, finally, by the fear of death which may be induced by the diagnosis, that is, of cancer. The patient who has already been treated for cancer and who has a recurrence which requires a second operation may present a much more complex and difficult problem. The cancer patient who has had an operation performed with the hope of cure often places his surgeon on a pedestal. That is, if the surgeon is highly skillful, then certainly the operation will be successful and promise cure. When recurrence is diagnosed, the surgeon tumbles from his high place. It may require a considerable intellectual effort for the patient to accept the failure of his treatment as the natural consequence of the disease rather than the direct fault of the therapist. Grafted to his conscious or unconscious resentment is the threat offered by further treatment. This treatment may now involve loss which was avoided at the initial procedure. A partial laryngectomy which fails may now require total laryngectomy. An unsuccessful wide excision of a soft-tissue tumor may now require a major amputation. The patient approaches this second procedure with a much more acute realization that failure can occur a second time and that, in fact, the chance of failure is even higher after the second procedure than after the first. The pain and discomfort of the first treatment may still be fresh in his mind. The element of grief for his new loss, both the loss of a part and the increased likelihood of loss of life, may now be much more intense. Empathy on the part of the surgeon must be profound. He must understand the patient's position in regard to his disease, to the coming operation, and to his physician, the surgeon who has "failed" the first time.

THE ROLE OF THE SURGEON

While patients are being prepared for surgery, the profound physiological and psychological changes which may be introduced by intense grief must be recognized and managed by the surgeon, either directly or through appropriate consultation. If grief is truly pathological, the operation may have to be postponed and psychiatric consultation obtained. Under other circumstances, it may be preferable to end delay and proceed with the operation as rapidly as possible.

Grief is recognized as a state which may produce profound physiological changes. Changes in adrenocortical secretion and symptoms of sympathetic nervous system hyperactivity have been recognized (Averill, 1968; Volkan, 1970). It has been suggested that pathological grief may introduce a catabolic state with inhibition of gastrointestinal activity and anorexia. Patients with cancer are often in a moderate to advanced stage of malnutrition when first seen, and if the diagnosis and prospect of an operation intensify their anorexia and provoke inactivity, isolation, and withdrawal, the problems of preparing them to undergo the major stress of an operation are compounded. Moreover, dissecting the symptoms produced by grief and despair from those symptoms produced by the cancer itself may be difficult. At times, denial is an effective and useful emotional tool for the patient if the period between diagnosis and operative therapy is short and if denial is not so intense as to lead to rejection of any thought of treatment, that is, "I don't have the disease, therefore, I don't need the treatment." If, for any reason, the period between diagnosis and therapy is prolonged, as happens today when radiation and operation are sometimes used in combination to treat advanced tumors (three months may elapse between the initial diagnosis and the final operation), denial alone may not suffice. Faith in the prospective treatment may also be a useful tool and certainly not an irrational one, especially when the patient is aware of others who have had similar treatment and have been cured. On the other hand, knowledge of others who have had similar treatment and who have died may set off an intensified grief response.

The surgeon must cultivate a deep understanding of the patient and of his past experience in order to manage these problems adequately. If denial is obvious and the period between diagnosis and operation short, the surgeon must protect his credibility but, at the same time, not shatter entirely the patient's defense mechanisms. If the period between diagnosis and operation is long or the patient's faith in the possibility of cure seems tenuous, the surgeon can resort to various tools which have proved useful in the past. A routine maneuver in all patients about to undergo a laryngectomy is to introduce such a patient to someone who has had a total laryngectomy and has learned to use esophageal speech effectively. This demonstrates that useful speech can be regained. At the same time, if the former patient's operation was performed several years ago, it can serve as an example that cure is feasible.

Discussion with the family is also of great value in establishing the proper atmosphere at home. This is especially useful when prospects for cure are good and the surgeon can advise the family optimistically. Certain malignant diseases, regardless of success or failure of treatment, are very indolent in their course. Patients, therefore, may not die of a lesion for several years, regardless of the outcome of therapy. A family that initiates mourning while the patient is still alive and part of the family unit can destroy the patient's attitude toward his upcoming operation. By premature mourning, the family members can exhaust their own emotional resources long before terminal illness occurs and the cultural pattern of mourning will be required. The author recalls a young patient in whom carcinoma of the ovary was inoperable. The family was advised that the patient's outlook was hopeless and that death could be expected in six months. Carcinoma of the ovary is often characterized by a very indolent growth which may extend over several years. The patient's sister broke up her household and, bringing along her son and husband, moved in with the patient to care for her in her last six months of life. For two years the patient thrived while the family mourned. Any unnecessary noise made by the sister's young son provoked strict discipline, and while the various members of the family tiptoed about the house because of a supposedly dying patient, the patient herself continued to do remarkably well. By the time that she finally developed intestinal obstruction, almost thirty months later, the rest of the family members had reached a point where they obviously wished that this was indeed the final event. It was obvious that the patient had to die in order for them to return to a normal life. With her ultimate death, there was undoubtedly an enormous amount of guilt on the part of those who lived.

Many patients can tolerate the prospect of death if it is a distant one. We all do. If it seems likely that a disease is gradual enough so that the actual date of death is indeterminant, and that at worst it may occur two or three years or more in the future, the physician can be remarkably frank and yet threaten neither the patient nor the family as much as he may fear. The older the patient is the more likely this is to be true.

Available tools to counteract anticipatory grief are primarily empathy (Paul, 1967), understanding, and explanation. These may be supplemented by drug therapy, in terms of some of the mood-altering drugs; and if the patient is so depressed that nourishment is interfered with, it may be justifiable for a short period prior to the operation to resort to some of the techniques of forced alimentation, such as intravenous hyperalimentation or tube feeding. These last efforts must, of course, be reserved for the most severe cases, in which there is no time to handle the situation otherwise. This is especially true if it appears likely that the operation itself may bring the grieving process to a halt.

REFERENCES

Averill, J. R., "Grief: Its Nature and Significance," *Psychological Bulletin, 70:*721, 1968.

Clayton, P., L. Desmarais, and G. Winokur, "A Study of Normal Bereavement," *American Journal of Psychiatry, 125:*64, 1968.

Paul, N. L., "The Use of Empathy in the Resolution of Grief," *Perspectives in Biology and Medicine, 11:*153, 1967.

Volkan, V., "Typical Findings in Pathological Grief," *Psychiatric Quarterly, 44:*231, 1970.

11

Organ Transplantation

Lois K. Christopherson and
Thomas A. Gonda

A variety of excellent writings have been devoted to grief experienced by
the dying patient and members of his family. Elisabeth Kübler-Ross (1969),
for example, describes with great sensitivity the symptoms of denial, anger,
bargaining, and depression that often precede a patient's final acceptance of
his impending death. Erich Lindemann (1944), on the other hand, in his
classic Coconut Grove fire study, describes behaviors that are characteristic
of bereaved family members. Included are such symptoms as somatic distress, guilt, hostility, preoccupation with the image of the deceased, and alteration of previous patterns of conduct. Both of these works have obvious
relevance to anticipatory grief. Lindemann emphasizes that "grief work" of
the bereaved may occur not only after but also in anticipation of the death of
a loved one. In the Kübler-Ross studies the dying patient is in fact grieving
in anticipation of his own impending death.

Whereas the broader psychosocial issues in organ transplantation have
been described (Gonda, 1972), this chapter focuses more specifically on
some ways in which the processes of anticipatory grieving influence the involved patients and families. Cardiac transplantation, although uncommon,
and renal transplantation serve to illustrate clearly the impact of medical advances upon anticipatory grieving. The following observations, however,
would appear likely, as these procedures become more common, to apply

also to the transplantation of other organs, such as the liver, lungs, or pancreas.

CARDIAC TRANSPLANTATION

The potential heart recipient is, as a requirement of the team performing the transplant, a patient who is in imminent danger of death and for whom no other medical or surgical procedure offers any hope. It is for these two reasons practically inconceivable that the patient and his family are not in some way aware of the likelihood of an end to the patient's existence. The patient has probably experienced consultation with a number of physicians in addition to his family doctor. Each of these consultations has, in turn, raised his hopes of being cured and then dashed them down as the physician was unable to provide more than limited help. In several cases, the specialist was the person who first suggested cardiac transplantation as "the only hope." In one instance known to the authors the accidental reading by a patient and his wife of a specialist's letter describing cardiac transplantation as "the only available chance" led directly to their referral to Stanford University. The family doctor had not considered transplantation, but the family was able to convince him of their desire to proceed with more "heroic" forms of therapy.

Families of potential cardiac recipients have observed the increasing disability of the patient, which has progressed from slight restrictions on his activity to the virtually bedridden state usually present when the patient is accepted for cardiac transplantation. This disability has probably been accompanied by a variety of temporarily helpful medical and surgical procedures. Hope has often been engendered by use of drugs or by surgery, only to be shattered as the patient again exhibits a downhill course. Most families have reported being told previously that the patient "might not make it through the night" or through an operative procedure.

To say that a patient and his family are somehow "aware" of the possibility of death, however, is by no stretch of the imagination to say that they have accepted its inevitability. Nor should "acceptance" of death be considered as the desirable psychological state in which a patient is referred for transplantation. For most patients and their families feelings are mixed, although there is often evidence that prior predominance of denial shifts, before transplantation, to feelings associated with bargaining.

The Period of Candidacy

Referral for cardiac transplantation while a patient and his family are in a state of denial can be the most difficult for them—and can also result in refusal of the transplant opportunity. The authors have experienced at least one case in which a patient and family described their primary purpose in coming to the Medical Center as a way "to show that stupid M.D. back home that I don't need a transplant."

When the transplant team concurs with the judgment of the referring physician, the patient is then in the position either of moving from his stage of denial or of moving from the transplant team in order to leave his defenses intact. Particular stress is aroused at this time for those families wherein the patient and significant family members are "out of phase" with one another. Communication can all but cease if the patient accepts his illness while the spouse refuses to think or talk about it or, on the other hand, if the spouse is eager to proceed with transplant preparations while the patient denies that a transplant is needed.

The patient who presents for evaluation while in a stage of anger and resentment, although theoretically having made psychological progress from the denial phase, is in practice often the most difficult for the medical team to accept. The commonplace antipathy of medical personnel to a complaining, critical patient is complicated by the fact that the cardiac transplantation team knows it is offering a clinical trial and only a guarded chance for extended survival. The patient's anger at the results of being treated in traditionally accepted ways may be seen as potentially multiplied a hundredfold when the results of transplantation are at best highly uncertain. Nurses who experience the patient's anger in the relatively secure environment of a ward situation are often enormously distressed by the thought of caring for such a patient in the confines of the isolation room required after the transplant procedure.

The patient who has been accepted for cardiac transplantation and members of his family are often remarkably open in their discussion of and preparation for the patient's possible death. In one sense this should probably be seen as a function of self-selection: the patient and family who do not accept this reality will find some means to move away from transplantation prior to official acceptance. At the same time, however, one must evaluate the role which hope plays in enabling the patient and family to talk about death. Some of the pain and inevitability of death have been—at least temporarily—removed. Planning for what "may" happen is seen as good sense, and it becomes tolerable because "may" is not the same as "will." Referral for cardiac transplantation may have some effect in reducing feelings of guilt for family members. It is a confirmation that "even if he dies, I'll know we did everything we could." Keeping hope alive is also a happy role for the nursing staff in their relationships with both the patient and family members: "We don't want them to give up now." In only a couple of cases have there been indications, characterized primarily by anger on the part of family members, that the hope offered by the transplant came too late or disrupted their readiness to accept the patient's death. If the grief work is completed prior to the patient's death, or despite the patient's unexpected survival, family members may have emancipated themselves so effectively from the patient as to preclude further deep emotional involvement with him.

After Transplantation

The stage of bargaining, described by Ross as a brief and transient one, appears to be greatly expanded and developed when transplantation occurs. Christopherson and Lunde (1971) have described the frequency with which "having things left to do" not only enters the minds of heart recipients but also serves as an indicator of reasonably good post-transplant adjustment if the patient survives and leaves the hospital. The patient is aware of his limited life expectancy but hopes, understandably, that transplantation will extend his life long enough for him to see, for example, a daughter graduate from high school or a son get married. Holidays, especially Christmas, enter strongly into the bargaining process, and it can be a source of great disappointment for team members as well as the patient's family if a patient dies shortly before "another Christmas" or "another birthday."

The "good child" aspects of the bargaining stage may be pronounced for the cardiac transplant survivor because of the uncertainty surrounding the factors in long-term survival. While it is easily recognized that regular taking of immunosuppressant drugs is required to prevent rejection, other factors, such as adherence to a well-balanced, low-cholesterol diet and frequent vigorous exercise, are less specific in their relationship. In these factors, however, a patient may excel; he may exercise "more than anyone else," avoid "all saturated fats," or move toward a health food and vitamin E type diet to avoid "contaminating his body."

It can be hypothesized that the most difficult ongoing task for both the transplant recipient and his family is that of balancing hope for continued survival with recognition of the nearness of death. Prior to the transplant there is always the possibility that the patient will die before an appropriate donor becomes available or that he will become so critically ill that he can no longer survive transplant surgery. In the days and weeks following the transplant the rejection/infection battle is omnipresent. A rejection episode may be brief and easily controlled or it may signal the beginning of the end for the patient; an infection may have little impact on the patient's course or it may spread rapidly throughout his body. Even after the patient is discharged to return to a seemingly "normal," active life-style, he is often reminded of his tenuous hold on life by the publicly reported deaths of other "transplant survivors." In view of the combination of specific stresses involved in heart transplantation, the patient and his family have little alternative to ongoing bargaining if they are to cope successfully.

RENAL TRANSPLANTATION

Less than ten years ago, members of kidney transplant teams might well have observed the same stages of anticipatory grieving in patients for whom kidney transplants were recommended as are now observed in patients receiving new hearts: denial of impending death moving toward bargaining if the transplant appeared successful; toward acceptance of death if, as was likely, the transplant soon failed. The reader may remember that in the early 1960s there were press reports following kidney transplantation which bore a remarkable similarity to those that later followed the early heart transplants. The patient's survival was measured on a day-to-day basis, and there was little doubt that death might accompany renal failure.

In the past few years, however, there has been a sharp increase in public knowledge of and confidence in kidney transplantation. The patient in end-stage renal failure can be treated not only by transplantation but also by hemodialysis. As a result (if only in parts of the country where dialysis and transplant facilities are readily available) patients and their families may be more likely initially to mourn the patient's loss of independence and self-sufficiency than to anticipate a loss of life.

As treatment procedures have become more successful clinically, it is not surprising that anticipatory grief has taken on a different form and that its symptoms are not as unremitting. During a meeting of head nurses and social workers in dialysis/transplant units, an experienced nurse described her concern that patients and families are actually less prepared now than they were in the past for death while on dialysis or following transplantation. "It used to be that everyone expected the patient to die. They would be grieving when they came into the unit, and we would try to help them have hope that the patient could get some extra time from dialysis or a transplant. Now they expect things to be too good. We help them accept that the patient's kidneys won't work, but they usually don't mention any thought that the patient might die."

Responses to Renal Failure

The first response to a diagnosis of end-stage renal failure may well include a feeling of "I don't even know where the hell my kidneys are." While cardiac symptoms (palpitations, awareness of one's heartbeat) and anxieties are experienced by most persons, a patient is unlikely to be aware of his kidneys except in an abstract way during urination. To tell a patient that his kidneys are failing is to force him first to think about what he has rarely thought about at all.

A diagnosis of renal failure is usually followed by kaleidoscopic feelings of denial, anger, and bargaining—but in relationship to the patient's kidney function, not to his life. "I just can't believe my kidneys aren't going to work ever again. If they're diseased, some doctor must have discovered a way to treat the disease." Even patients who are on dialysis and eagerly awaiting a transplant often resist pretransplant removal of their kidneys. "Shouldn't we leave them in just in case I reject the transplanted kidney but the old ones start working again?" Difficulty in accepting end-stage renal failure is complicated by the fact that a patient's kidneys may continue to produce urine despite their increasing lack of effectiveness in maintaining the body's chemical balance.

A second set of responses characteristic of patients in renal failure and their families is related to the working through of feelings about dialysis and/or transplantation. For most people, life "tied to a machine" implies a severe loss of self-sufficiency and independence. Several factors enhance the feeling of helplessness: the extreme cost of chronic dialysis, especially if it is hospital-based; the loss of sexual potency secondary to uremia; and the inability of a patient to carry on full-time employment unless he can be dialyzed at night either at home or in a program that operates twenty-four hours a day. Unless the patient has unusually negative feelings about surgical procedures, he is likely to find transplantation his first choice or, in a few cases, "the only thing I could live with."

Effects of Awareness of Death

In rare instances the kidney transplant recipient may go through his entire transplantation experience with negligible awareness of the possibility of death. He has several dialyses to prepare him for surgery, family members may volunteer eagerly to serve as kidney donors, and the post-transplant hospitalization is brief and unmarred by any but the slightest hints of rejection. For these patients, especially if they live some distance from the transplant center and have active, meaningful life-styles, death continues to be remote and easily forgotten.

More commonly, however, kidney transplant patients and members of their families experience a number of events that lead them from awareness only of the loss of renal function to awareness of a potential loss of life. The search for a related donor is often the catalyst that brings them to this point. First it is likely that the surgeon will compare the results of related versus cadaver kidney transplants in terms of five-year survival. Whether the figures are given in terms of graft survival or patient survival, their impact is to introduce the idea that time is limited. Second, the donation of an organ, even one which is paired, is a considerable gift and potentially a marked sacrifice. Most people are willing to donate a kidney only to save the life of someone who is very close to them.

If a patient does not have a related donor, his wait for a cadaver kidney is likely to introduce the idea of death. This is partly because his transplant depends upon someone else's death. More important, it is because over a period of time he will become acquainted with other renal patients who die either after an extended period of dialysis or after an unsuccessful transplant attempt. In one case, a thirty-nine-year-old wife and mother, of average intelligence, comfortably underwent dialysis for several months while awaiting a cadaver kidney transplant. Then another dialysis patient with whom she had become friends died unexpectedly of a cerebral vascular accident. The woman began to experience fear of the dark, difficulty in sleeping, and dreams in which black-robed figures hovered over her. She gradually recognized her fear of death, and explained tearfully, "I just never thought before that I could die. I don't want to leave my family."

In another situation five young adults were successfully transplanted, mostly from related donors, over a period of a few months. All did well medically and psychologically, finding in each other a source of support and friendship. When one later died of pneumonia, probably related to the effects of immunosuppressant drugs, the others experienced depression, anxiety, and anger. As one patient described it, "I guess we just realized we all could die."

Bargaining is a characteristic we see less often in kidney recipients than in heart patients. The use of five years as a measure of survival tends to negate an immediate awareness of death. And the availability of dialysis means that "if something does go wrong, I can always go back on the machine." Within the conceptual framework of Glaser and Strauss (1968) the anticipated time of life remaining seems to play an important role in determining the nature of the grief process. Because life trajectory is longer in kidney than in heart transplantation, and in view of dialysis backup, anticipatory grieving is less clearly related to the transplant procedure. Rather, phases of anticipatory grieving occur sporadically and in various forms, such as depression, denial, or anger. This grieving is short-lived, repetitive, and often closely related to stressful events, such as the death of someone in the program. Because this type of grief reaction is frequently difficult to identify as such, it is especially important that those caring for the patient be sensitive to these grief episodes and able to provide prompt and appropriate support.

REFERENCES

Christopherson, L. K., and D. T. Lunde, "Selection of Cardiac Transplant Recipients and Their Subsequent Psychosocial Adjustment," *Seminars in Psychiatry, 3*(1):36, 1971.

Glaser, B. G., and A. S. Strauss, *Time for Dying.* Chicago: Aldine Press, 1968.

Gonda, T. A., "Organ Transplantation and the Psychosocial Aspects of Terminal Care," in B. Schoenberg *et al.,* eds., *Psychosocial Aspects of Terminal Care.* New York: Columbia University Press, 1972.

Kübler-Ross, E., *On Death and Dying,* New York: Macmillan, 1969.

Lindemann, E., "Symptomatology and Management of Acute Grief," *American Journal of Psychiatry, 101*:141, 1944.

12

Anticipatory Grief and Cancer
Guy F. Robbins

In this crisis-oriented world, those health care personnel involved with cancer patients must develop and implement realistic two-way communications between the family unit and health professionals. There is no formula that will minimize the fears associated with cancer. Anticipatory grief is inevitable regardless of the stage of the disease. However, it can be a unifying force when those involved are provided with a flexible blueprint of events to come, with the emphasis placed on looking at life as a half-full bottle of wine, not a half-empty one. As one who, for thirty years, has limited his professional activities to cancer-control programs, the author is convinced that early development and continued maintenance of meaningful two-way communications between health professionals and the family unit provide a structured means of tolerating, accepting, and utilizing anticipatory grief.

A program of this magnitude will be successful if the health professionals are well-trained, articulate, and have empathy. All too often patient and family become involved blindly in the diagnostic and primary therapy phases of coping with cancer.

Frequently health professionals do not level with patients and their families during the diagnostic and primary treatment phases of, say, breast cancer. They play games, sometimes suggested by well-meaning relatives, but all too often by the professionals themselves, who are too fearful or inadequate verbally to explain what must be done. The result of these games is mistrust by the patient. Once the patient observes the extent of the treatment and recalls how the professional had not prepared her for the total removal of a breast, the professional will always be suspected of untruths. A lack of communication with relatives may ignite the same chain reaction of disbelief. In order to minimize misunderstanding and develop a maximum awareness of what will happen to the patient who is to be hospitalized for diagnostic and therapeutic procedures relating to breast disease, the staff of the breast service at Memorial Hospital in New York City has developed a five-minute phonograph record which is given to breast patients at the time arrangements are being made for their hospital admission. Then the patient takes the record home and plays it, the husband and family often listening too. The mechanics of admission procedures have been explained while the patient was in the doctor's office. However, experience has shown that the potential patient frequently retains little of this information. Thus, repetition is essential, and the record serves this purpose. It contains several messages. First the patient is congratulated on making up her mind to do something about the breast problem. The explanation of advised consent is presented, eliminating the shock of receiving the information from a house officer while she is half nude in the entirely strange environment of the hospital. In addition, facts concerning insurance, the preoperative workup, including preoperative prepping of the breast and axilla, the recovery room, length of stay in the hospital, length of convalescence and time before return to work if benign tumor or a cancer is found—all are detailed. Several thousand patients have received this record and patients, husbands, and other relatives and friends have attested to its value.

Today, when a woman examines herself after surgery and finds that she has only one breast remaining, she knows for sure that she had cancer. The "games" that health professionals and relatives often try to play may well set the stage for real trouble if the disease subsequently recurs. Firmness, consideration, and structured efforts to assist the patient to readapt to society are as important as wound healing, and must be instigated within the immediate postoperative time period. These activities include visits by trained postmastectomy patients, physiotherapists, nurses, and social workers. Classes with multidisciplinary leadership are provided for the patients and their husbands. These activities give patients and husbands an opportunity to express their misgivings, grief, and doubts. In addition, practical advice which has proven to be helpful to the family unit is offered. Evaluation feed-back from the patients has been developed two weeks after hospital discharge and at the three-month level. Data reveal that patients are readapting to society more quickly and thoroughly than prior to the instigation of this program. In addition to rehabilitation classes, each patient is given another phonograph record to take home. This record presents three postmastectomy patients who discuss their postmastectomy experiences, which include their relationship with society and their outlook on life. Here again the family is involved. Evaluation of the reactions of several thousand of these women revealed an increased ability to cope in comparison with patients treated previously.

Once the patient has left the protective hospital environment she and her family will usually need some protection from well-meaning friends and relatives. Support is available if the hospital team has thoroughly prepared the patients for readaptation to family living. However, the physician, surgeon, visiting nurse, and office or clinic staff become their mainstays. Here again, communication is essential. The referring physician must know exactly what happened in the hospital and what to expect. Similarly, the hospital family, including the surgeon, must keep the others informed, including the employee, clergy and office staff. The office or clinic secretary and nurse, the visiting nurse, and immediate family members, as well as the patient herself, can funnel information to the primary physician which may well assist in alleviating the patient's fears and griefs. Health professionals must communicate, listen, investigate, and, at times, advise. Patients require reassurance; they need to be shown concern, and, above all, they cannot tolerate abandonment. Lack of sincerity will build up walls between those involved that will eventually destroy mutual faith.

Unfortunately, blunt statements regarding recurrence of cancer may destroy the relationship between the family unit and the health professionals. One must be realistic but must also individualize his presentation of situations which might eventually cause the death of the patient. Several patients with incurable breast cancer were observed attending the funeral of their surgeon, a dedicated man who had made a habit of postulating exact survival times for patients when specific recurrent breast cancer appeared. Such foolish and cruel prognostications create needless confusion and doubt in the family unit.

Krant and Sheldon (1971) have documented in depth the failures of communication between health professionals, incurable patients, and their families. Unlike many reports on dying patients, much of their data come from talking to the dying patient and not from theorists who are interested but not really involved in the process of dying. In addition, Krant and Sheldon have provided solid data on realistic means of assisting the family unit cope with problems attendant on cancer.

If the family, health professionals, and the patient have communicated and attempted to solve problems from the beginning of their contact with cancer, usually new problems are met in a more realistic and successful manner, provided the patient is not abandoned by his family and health professionals. In this structure, grief will not cease to exist but can be tolerated. Plans for the future can be discussed and initiated, and it is not uncommon for broken families to reunite during these trying times.

It is essential to consider the success of palliative treatment as to their degree of objective and subjective effects—not in terms of length of life. The maintenance of electrolytic balance and a pulsebeat are worthless if the economic status of the family is destroyed and the patient is allowed psychologically and spiritually to become a miserable shadow of her former self. Anticipatory grief will become intolerable and frequently quite difficult to accept in the future. Such situations can be minimized if there have been long-term, two-way, significant communications between those involved.

We live in a crisis-oriented world. If a noncrisis-oriented treatment plan is evolved and implemented by considerate, knowledgeable, communicating health professionals and the family unit, anticipatory grief will be structured so it can be a positive force.

REFERENCES

"Advice to a Breast Patient," Breast Service, Memorial Hospital for Cancer and Allied Diseases (New York, New York), New York: Americom Corp.

Krant, M. J., and A. Sheldon, "The Dying Patient—Medicine's Responsibility," *Journal of Thanatology, 1*:1, 1971.

"Panel Discussion of Postoperative Breast Problems," Breast Service, Department of Surgery, Memorial Hospital for Cancer and Allied Diseases (New York, New York), New York: Americom Corp.

13

The Patient and Prolonged Terminal Malignant Disease: Experiences from a Radiation Therapy Center

Richard J. Torpie

Cancer seems most frequently used as a model for terminal illness. It can be a slowly catastrophic disease whose challenge is often met by multiple attempts at cure and palliation, even when chances for success appear slight. It is the insidiousness of cancer that allows descriptions such as ''lingering'' and ''eaten-away''; it is its very capriciousness which makes it appear that the patient is making ''a fight against cancer.'' Most often the cancer patient arrives at a terminal situation after a series of lost battles, with little resemblance to his original brave self. He also usually possesses fewer allies to offer comfort and support in the one final battle which he knows he must lose. The conflict involves giving up all that is still important and all that is taken for granted, especially the remnant basic joy of living. This ''letting go'' unfortunately involves an immense sadness, the grieving of anticipation of death, those dreaded moments which are the most miserable, yet most necessary to the act of dying.

The threat of loss presumes an anticipatory sense of grief in many life situations. Most of this grief must be fantasied, as might be seen in the thoughts of a child bringing home a poor report card or in the comments of a patient anticipating the possibility of cosmetic mutilation from surgery.

Reactive grief following the loss may or may not bear any resemblance to the character or intensity of its anticipation.

The anticipatory grief of the dying patient is a total response to the realization of future total loss; it is characterized by absolute finality. It is felt before the actual fact of loss and yet may never be experienced since, in a philosophic sense, death presumes the end of all experience. It is inevitable and final since there can be no restitution of the loss, and only faith and imagination conceive of a substitute for nothingness, that is, an afterlife. Anticipatory grief must be composed, interpreted, and magnified by the patient's sense of past loss and grief and past premonition of threat of loss. This anticipation, therefore, consists of elements of fantasy which have a realistic basis, but which also may be colored quite unrealistically by weakness, fear, isolation, feelings of inadequacy, and loss of control. The key to comforting the patient lies in allowing him to work out realistic grief-loss situations and also in providing support to minimize unrealistic fantasies whose exaggeration would otherwise cause extremes of desolation and depression. This presumes that there has been an ideal amount of communication and recognition between the patient and those who care for him. Certain characteristics of this grief may help better define it.

SEPARATION

Disruption of interpersonal relationships may pose even a greater threat than dying itself. It has been suggested that persons with large family and many friends have more to lose and, therefore, experience greater grief. In the author's opinion, this is inaccurate; grief is proportional more to the intensity of invested ties felt for loved objects and persons as a collective whole. It may be fixated on those persons who are particularly close. It may be difficult to distinguish objectively between the grief felt by a lonely woman for a pet cat in comparison to that of a mother for her five children. The difference we perceive may reflect our own subjective sense of values.

At the time of terminal existence, the patient has regressed in terms of dependency needs and distortion of time. Each daily separation serves to point to the imminent final separation. It would be healthy for the dying patient and relatives and staff to share this grief, but too often the dying patient must witness the continuing well-meant denial of friends and relatives. A woman dying from lymphoma but still mentally alert wearily told the author, "Doctor, I know I'll never go home again. Please make my husband cry with me.'' How often must people fight back tears behind a false smile on the pretext of protecting the dying from pain? This creates a cruel kind of isolation in an experience that could be shared. It is the failure to say good-bye.

The saddest separation is that of parents from young children since a large element of guilt arises when the parents cannot function in the daily and immediate details of their children's lives or in their future. The modern large hospital manages to exclude young children by imposing visiting regulations. Conveniently, this arrangement spares the parent an immediate sense of obligation, but little else. The patient may quite adamantly indicate that he or she does not wish to be seen in a deteriorated state. This may also be a convenient excuse, and while initially respected it should be explored with the patient. Prior guilt regarding a child may further aggravate this refusal. In one situation, a woman dying of disseminated ovarian carcinoma with ascites steadfastly refused attempts to have her ten-year-old mongoloid daughter brought to the hospital. She lapsed into a coma, but when she had recovered sufficiently to call home and find that her daughter was being cared for elsewhere by relatives she was distressed. This was resolved by a tearful but gratifying reunion with the child at her bedside.

Every effort should be made to facilitate visits, even when there is painful resistance. There were few barriers from the home deathbed, which allowed meaningful ritualistic involvement of the entire family in a grief situation.

THE UNFULFILLED SELF

Death completes life, but dying leaves the task of living undone. This may be manifested in unfinished goals or the unresolved conflicts of the dying patient. As future time and energy become more limited, the patient may become preoccupied with a sense of incompleteness and insufficiency. Frustration may lead to resentful anger which challenges the support of the staff and family, but gentle persistence, kindness, and attention can remain comforting. There should be respect for privacy and silence (which is not the same as desertion) when these are indicated. Support should not emphasize the work ahead but rather the task completed.

One elderly man in terminal stages due to bone metastases from prostatic carcinoma lamented certain failures in his late life, failures which became more burdensome as he became more disabled. It was discovered that he once held the record for the longest home run in major league baseball. A campaign was mounted to encourage him to discuss his career. This relieved his psychic distress and physically he felt "improved," even ordering a steak on the day he died. Nostalgia can allow one more meaningful reunion with the pleasant past, thereby making all things past easier to give up.

Verbalization of fears and intense introspection may overcome the frustration of unresolved conflicts. These may never be fully overcome, but with discussion and conservative interpretation they may be minimized and a satisfactory truce effected, much to the patient's comfort. At times mourning may be bizarre, as in the case of a homely woman who felt incomplete because she had never realized her ambition "to be a fashion model." Inappropriate fixation such as this should serve to alert the physician to a deeper conflict, which in this instance was the woman's treasured virginity and the ambiguity she felt between being chaste and never having been loved. In certain circumstances, inappropriate grief may be a displacement defense against an object that has been mourned throughout the patient's life, or perhaps a last feeble defense against the fear of death itself.

DECATHEXIS

As grief becomes diminished and worked through, the narcissistic self becomes consumed. All complaints and expectations end; past and future are contracted into the moment; and the mind rests. Effort is no longer expended on diligently applied defenses. There is relative peace and a resistance against all unpleasantness. This condition is basic to the scheme of regression, a scheme which requires few words but rather a protective presence. Extension of any therapeutic effort at this time would only interfere with the final dignity and peace of death.

REFERENCES

Abrams, R. D., "The Patient with Cancer—His Changing Pattern of Communication," *New England Journal of Medicine, 274:*317, 1966.

Aldrich, C. K., "The Dying Patient's Grief," *Journal of the American Medical Association, 184:*329, 1963.

Chodoff, P., "A Psychiatric Approach to the Dying Patient," *CA, 10:*29, 1960.

Eissler, K. R., *The Psychiatrist and the Dying Patient.* New York: International Universities Press, 1955.

Hinton, J. M., "The Physical and Mental Distress of Dying," *Quarterly Journal of Medicine, 32:*1, 1963.

Nahum, L. H., "The Dying Patient's Grief," *Connecticut Medicine, 28:*241, 1964.

Norton, J., "Treatment of a Dying Patient," *Psychoanalytic Study of the Child, 18:*541, 1963.

Platt, R., "Reflections on Aging and Death," *Lancet,* Vol. 1, 1963.

Rosenthal, H., "Psychotherapy for the Dying," *American Journal of Psychotherapy, 11:*626, 1957.

Rosner, A. A., "Mourning Before the Fact," *Journal of the American Psychoanalytic Association, 10:*564, 1962.

Stehlin, J. S., and K. H. Beach, "Psychological Aspects of Cancer Therapy: A Surgeon's Viewpoint," *Journal of the American Medical Association, 197:*100, 1966.

Verwoerdt, A., *Communication with the Fatally Ill.* Springfield, Ill.: Charles C. Thomas, 1966.

14

Anticipatory Grief in a Cancer Hospital

Martha W. Atchley, Susan Blecker Cohen, and Lois Weinstein

Entering Memorial Hospital for Cancer and Allied Diseases (New York City) for the first time, a patient anticipates dying. "Cancer" still rings ominously of inevitable death. The word "Memorial" evokes thoughts of those who have already died. Even patients who cling to the possibility that theirs is an "allied disease" fear on a deeper level that all hope must be abandoned here.

Conversely, a Center such as this * does offer hope to the frightened and despairing who may have begun their grieving process before actual arrival at the hospital. It is seen often as a court of last resort by those whose disease has been diagnosed and treated elsewhere and whose local physician has referred them for more effective therapy. Here are the skilled surgeons, the cobalt machines, the latest chemotherapeutic drugs. Here are experts who can cure what was formerly incurable. This is a hospital committed to the principle that "patients will be optimistically and aggressively treated

* Other centers, similar in many aspects, include Columbia-Presbyterian Medical Center, (Institute of Cancer Research), New York, New York; Tufts Medical Cancer Unit, Boston, Massachusetts; Mayo Clinic, Rochester, Minnesota; Pack Medical Group, New York, New York; M. D. Anderson Hospital, Houston, Texas; National Cancer Institute, Bethesda, Maryland; University of New Mexico Medical Center, Albuquerque, New Mexico; Billings Memorial Hospital, Chicago, Illinois; and Ochsner Clinic, New Orleans, Louisiana.

whatever the phase of the disease" (Beattie, 1971), and this approach transmits confidence, no matter what the diagnosis or prognosis.

Social workers in such an institution dealing with life-threatening illness must have broad experience with the multiple and conflicting reactions engendered in patients, families, and staff. In this paper, case examples are presented which focus on one particular part of the feeling spectrum: anticipatory grief. This is understood to be a preparation for future loss: of life—one's own or that of a loved person; of health; of function or role; of a body part or parts. Like the grief which follows bereavement, anticipatory grief is a normal feeling and process, not an illness, and it has positive elements as an adaptive reaction. It is, of course, manifested in different ways, according to circumstances and pre-existing life patterns. It can be silent or exaggerated. When not released or not permitted by others, it may be displaced or immobilizing.

Evaluation of patients and families includes assessment of their readiness to discover and to express their feelings of anticipatory grief. They are encouraged to share these feelings with staff and with significant others when it is judged that to do so will be beneficial. "If we can help them express their grief and their mourning . . . their grief would be much less prolonged and much less deep, and they would not be ashamed of it or feel unmanly" (Kübler-Ross, 1971). Many people under stress need some help in sorting out their feelings, in determining which fears are reality-based and which imaginary, and in reordering their value systems. Then it is possible for life to retain meaning even as death approaches. Allowing the open communication of anticipatory grief feelings also helps patients avoid a sense of isolation and rejection. Although patients may gradually withdraw from personal bonds as they approach death, the staff here endeavors to maintain a meaningful relationship with each patient. Admittedly, it is not an easy task for any of us to face the inevitable questions: "Am I going to die?" "Why me?"

It has been said that the practice of medicine represents an attempt to master the fear of death (Feifel, 1965). In a cancer hospital, where death is confronted daily, all staff needs to protect itself with strong defenses. Since hope and diligence are key attitudes of the institution, open grieving and acceptance of dying may be discouraged. Nevertheless, feelings such as grief, frustration, fear, and anger persist in patients and their families, and they are mirrored in the staff despite their coping mechanisms. Although the role of helper may bestow a sense of power and immunity, everyone—staff and patients alike—is engaged in a latent or acknowledged struggle to deal with an erosion of the sense of immortality and to evolve a concept of death.

Toward that end, we can attempt to gain a clearer understanding of anticipatory grief, of the place it assumes in the continuum of feelings which accompany critical and terminal illness, of the ways in which it is susceptible to modification in order to enable patients, family, and staff to function more comfortably and effectively. It is hoped that the following impressions and interpretations of some of our experiences at Memorial Hospital will be enlightening and provocative.

PRODUCTIVE ANTICIPATORY GRIEF

Anticipatory grief can serve constructively during the period in which a patient is aware that life is finite. Mrs. P. had to struggle with pain and loneliness, but she successfully mobilized her strengths to put her house in order before dying.

Mrs. P. was an attractive and intelligent forty-five-year-old divorced woman, formerly a teacher, with widespread ovarian cancer. Her reactions combined depression and sorrow, denial and anger. After reaching the point where she could say, "I guess this is the last time I'll come into the hospital," she worked hard to strengthen her children's ties with her mother and former husband. The two older sons, nineteen and seventeen, were both at college and fairly independent, but the youngest, age fourteen, had a congenital deafness and needed attention and care. Mrs. P. was able to ask her own parents and her ex-husband to assume responsibility for this fourteen-year-old and make plans for him to attend a private school the following year. Mrs. P. showed a remarkable amount of strength in turning to her ex-husband once again, although she feared a repetition of past disappointments. Twelve years earlier he'd left her alone with this deaf child and dealt her a crushing blow by going off with her best friend. Because she realized that she might not have much longer to live, she felt an urgency to tell him exactly how she felt about their past difficulties and what she hoped he would do for the children in the future. She asked for the social worker's support in this and they rehearsed together what she wished to say to him prior to his visits.

Obviously Mrs. P. was not immobilized by her grief, nor did she use denial in a way that interfered with the sense of reality that was needed for planning. Although she was fairly comfortable and her pain was controlled, she was afraid of future suffering and depressed by the fact that she was probably going to die soon. What was striking was her *conscious* examination with the social worker of her own denial: she found herself thinking that the chemotherapy would work magically and pretended and daydreamed about going home, but had such a strong grasp of the reality of the situation that she constantly pulled herself back from dwelling on this.

Mrs. P. had enough strength to confront her panicky feeling that her world was disintegrating. During her last few days, she felt especially trapped and confined. She removed her IV tube in a gesture of independence—it was the only free choice she had left—and of surrender. Her struggle had brought her through the period of mourning to an acceptance of death. She met the challenge of a shortened life span by setting goals for herself. The difficulties had been mixed with wonderful moments of rediscovery as she worked out solutions to problems out of the past. Often angry that so much was required of her, she did not deny her anguish or the inevitable outcome. After all of her sadness and her regret that she could not finish her tasks as a mother, she saw death as a final relief.

Mr. R. was another patient who could grieve openly as he approached death, and he and his wife were able to share their anticipatory grief and to lend each other strength. Their demonstration of mutual support was deeply touching to the staff.

Mr. R., a thirty-seven-year-old engineer, was told his diagnosis of reticulum cell sarcoma in the presence of his wife. At first they were both hopeful that the prescribed therapy would cure him, but after it became evident that conventional treatment was ineffective, the R.'s agreed to an experimental protocol.

At the time of the above decision, the couple presented themselves to the caseworker for help with "financial problems." After receiving this assistance, they gradually came to use her support to express to each other their deep and positive feelings. Having known each other since they were fourteen, as friends before they were lovers, they had many moments of shared joy and work to recall. Although both mourned that the relationship would soon end, neither doubted that the depth of what they had known would have a lasting influence. Mrs. R. was able to tell the children at a turning point in Mr. R's. disease, "Daddy may not get well," and finally, "Daddy is dying." However, both Mr. and Mrs. R. continued to express hope, even while they were saying good-bye to each other. Half an hour before Mr. R. went into a final hepatic coma, he struggled to eat jello "for strength." (We often see such examples of Feifel's observation that "a realistic acceptance of death and its rejection co-exist in subtle, equilibristic balance" (Feifel, 1965). The productive effect of the R.'s joint efforts in their grief work was evident almost immediately upon his death. Mrs. R. expressed her recognition that the time of mourning was done and the task now was to learn to live without the physical presence of a man who had played such a significant part in her life that his influence would provide strength for building a new life.

This example corroborates Blacher's observation that "Anticipatory mourning is quite common and explains the frequent lack of a strong grief reaction in the survivors when death follows a prolonged illness'' (Blacher, 1970).

TO GRIEVE OR NOT TO GRIEVE

For many people, death ceases to be a distant end and becomes an immediate enemy when cancer is diagnosed. Even though an effective treatment program may be offered and expectation of survival may be good, the possibility of dying arouses a complex of feelings in which anticipatory grief is an element. This was observed in postmastectomy patients, where mourning over the loss of a significant body part is accompanied by frightened grieving over anticipated death. One woman put it succinctly: "How do we know it stops here?"

Where illness is chronic or slowly progressive, anticipatory grief may be seen not as a stage, clearly characterized by sadness or depression, but as a fluctuating, recurring thread in the pattern of responses which each patient exhibits. Personality factors, characteristic ways of coping with crises, age—all color these patterns. A younger person finds it more difficult to believe in the real possibility that his illness will be fatal, so anticipatory grief is usually diluted by other feelings or may be displaced altogether.

Two women in their early thirties reacted to hospital admission by anticipating their own deaths, but their feelings were displayed and handled in very different ways.

Miss B., a thirty-five-year-old unmarried Jewish woman, announced to the social worker with inappropriate laughter, "I may have two terminal illnesses!" Her symptoms, which included weight loss, severe diarrhea, difficulty in swallowing and eating, and reduced energy, were indeed threatening but still undiagnosed. A bright and delightful woman, she had been very active as an executive of a women's political pressure group. She began by relating to the social worker as one professional person to another, giving her an analysis of the floor culture. She commented that the nurses organized their tasks piecemeal and inefficiently in order "to distance themselves from this heavy scene."

She was fascinated by her doctor's search for a diagnosis and demanded full information about her work-up and findings, even managing to read her chart. In the words of one doctor, she was "a spectator at her own illness." No direct attempt was made to breach this defense of intellectualization, but gradually grief reactions appeared. She was depressed over possible loss of role function, saying "I am my work." Her unresolved feelings toward her parents, from whom she had become outwardly free years before, surfaced and aroused anxiety about renewed dependency; she was afraid that her mother and father would use their concern as an excuse to intrude into her life again, and she resented her need for their financial help. She became hysterical when she did not receive what she felt to be an adequate explanation of her radiation treatment, for she was apprehensive that damage to healthy tissues would outweigh the benefits. By the time a diagnosis (lymphoma and amyloid infiltration of the small bowel) and treatment plan were reached, she was more depressed than fascinated by her illness. However, when therapy began to prove beneficial, she was able to return to work and to postpone her grieving, which had been a realistic although early reaction to the possibility that her disease would become chronic, disabling, and eventually fatal.

In relation to other patients, Miss B. was a helper, not a spectator. She established friendly relationships, and was concerned about patient care on her floor. It happened that she and Mrs. A. shared a room and the same social worker, so Miss B. would notify the worker when Mrs. A. became particularly upset.

Mrs. A. is a thirty-one-year-old mother of six children whose local doctor had diagnosed cancer of the cervix, although there had been no pain or other symptoms. Admission to Memorial Hospital precipitated fear of dying, but because the illness was unreal to her, only a label attached by the doctors, and because she needed to continue to function as a mother, Mrs. A. employed denial and anger as defenses against her fears. She expressed her distrust of the doctor's diagnosis and her resentment of the program of radiation treatments and surgery to the social worker. Following radiation, she underwent an exploratory operation which revealed more extensive disease than had been suspected. The doctors informed her frankly that they had not been able to resect all of the tumor so had implanted radioactive iodine. Mrs. A.'s first reaction to this bitter news was again anger, and she inveighed against her doctors and God, saying she had lost all faith. Several days later she seemed to have reached a calm acceptance. Without tears, she talked quietly of dying. She and her husband had been able to share their feelings about this tragic situation, although Mrs. A. wished the doctors had not told him because it was so hard for him to bear. Since her children already knew that she had cancer (but had been told that the operation would cure her), she said she would tell them truthfully that she was dying. However, the tenuousness of Mrs. A.'s "acceptance" was revealed by her comment, "I am saying all this but I don't really believe it's true." A day later she was again expressing doubts about the validity of the doctors' diagnosis. She hopscotched from one reaction or stage to another—aggressive behavior, depressed withdrawal, determination to function independently, hopelessness—taxing the agility of the social worker, whose efforts were directed toward helping her live with the awareness that her life would be shortened and to make use of her remaining time with her family. Even when pain handicapped her in performing household tasks, she refused to accept help. Much work remains to be done in helping Mrs. A. and her husband use their knowledge of her prognosis constructively. She alternates between denial of the existence of her disease or of any need for help and a frightened grieving over her approaching death. Perhaps she will never reach acceptance of the fact that life can end at thirty-one, with so many tasks as a mother of six unfinished and so many needs unfulfilled.

IMMOBILIZING ANTICIPATORY GRIEF

Sometimes close family members of the patients are so overwhelmed by their feelings of impending loss that they become helpless. Then casework intervention is geared to helping the relative cope with his feelings and see the patient as still alive and dependent on him for support. This is illustrated in the case of the O.'s.

Mr. O. was a good-looking, husky, apparently healthy married man of forty-five whose malignant melanoma was diagnosed just four months before his death. After the sudden onset of the disease and the physician's blunt announcement of the grave prognosis, his wife became immobilized both psychologically and physically. Confined to her bed with low blood pressure, she was unable to visit her husband at first or to discuss discharge planning with the social worker. Gradually, she could share with the social worker her fears about her husband's illness and her doubts about her ability to care for him. She admitted to the anger she felt at him for becoming ill and leaving her with so many problems. As she regained her emotional and physical equilibrium, she was able to care for him at home, even providing him with loving support until he required readmission. Following Mr. O.'s death, her mourning was intense, but she proved capable of caring for herself and for their fourteen-year-old son. With follow-up help and encouragement from the social worker, she began to plan for a new way of life.

We have observed that patients who have experienced catastrophic losses prior to their illness may respond to the new crisis situation with reactivated feelings about their earlier losses. One senses that these patients and families are protecting themselves from the current threat by turning backward and, at the same time, trying to rework previous tasks in order to generate strength for meeting new demands. Until this is accomplished, grief may be partially paralyzing, as in the case of Mr. and Mrs. T.

Mr. and Mrs. T. are a couple in their fifties who came to the United States from Poland following World War II. Recently Mr. T. was diagnosed as having esophageal cancer. His prognosis is poor. Although the T.'s do not yet acknowledge that he has a fatal illness, both the patient and his wife are aware that his condition is worsening. The family was referred to the social worker when the floor nurses noticed that Mrs. T. was agitated and depressed. After an initial interview, the social worker felt that a good bit of the depression arose from Mrs. T.'s determination not to expose her fear or anxiety to her husband. Despite this intent, her overwhelming grief caused her to sigh and sob over him. In an attempt to allow Mrs. T. to share this burden, the social worker arranged daily interviews. Mrs. T. began to talk about the experiences she and her husband had shared during the war in Poland. Each had been married before, he to her sister and she to a different man. Both families shared the fate of most Polish Jews and were imprisoned in concentration camps. Following liberation, the T.'s met and found that they were the sole survivors of their families. Their mutual losses and grief evolved into caring for each other, and they married. After crying for her sister and her ex-husband and all the devastating experiences in the camp, Mrs. T. was able to make the transition to the present crisis, using the bridge "We felt we had our share, and now this—!" Now that her endurance is being tested again, Mrs. T. says that the only answer is prayer. Mr. T. in separate interviews (which in this initial stage he begins with a reminder that the contents are not to be shared with his wife), speaks of his worry over a malignancy he has been told does not often respond to treatment. He feels he cannot burden his wife with his feelings because he has caused her enough pain by his illness. He mourns his own impending death and expresses poignantly the sadness he anticipates for his wife who will come home to "empty ceilings and walls." The social worker is working toward helping Mr. and Mrs. T. talk *together* so they can be mutually supportive as long as possible.

ANTICIPATORY GRIEF REACTIONS IN STAFF

"The emotional responses of professional caretakers of the dying child parallel those of parents. Sorrow, guilt, apprehension, and anger may reflect anticipation of loss, identification with the suffering of child and family, feelings of professional ineffectiveness arising from inability to alter the outcome, and doubts about the capacity to master the psychic pain and remain supportive toward the patient" (McCollum and Schwartz, 1972). These observations of McCollum and Schwartz apply to work with all critically ill cancer patients, adults as well as children.

Staff can move toward patients with compassion and empathy until capacities are overtaxed and defenses become inefficient or inappropriate. If distance and objectivity are used to handle grief and anxiety, patients may perceive this as not caring. When false optimism is engendered in order to avoid mutual pain, the result may be future mistrust and bitterness. When the patient's high expectation of cure is not met, our goals may be the more realistic ones of life extension and the improvement of life quality. The staff must handle its own anger and disappointment as well as the patient's. As a patient's pain is shared and his loss anticipated, members of the treating staff experience grief which can prevent them from giving optimal care, particularly when professional feelings are not openly recognized and discussed.

One young doctor said, "I'm afraid to tell the patient he has cancer because he may cry and then I will too." He had received little preparation in medical school for losing battles against illness or for dealing with the patient's and his own anxiety about dying. He had not yet learned that it is all right to show feelings, that one cannot always hide behind laboratory data and scientific facts. To be a concerned human being as well as a doctor or nurse or social worker is a vital dimension of professional practice.

Staff as well as family members often fear that open expressions of grief or of awareness that death approaches will lead to the patient's demoralization and make caring for him more difficult. On the contrary, such verbalizations often tend to provide a catharsis, to strengthen defenses, and to free a patient to deal with the concerns of daily living. A patient who today acknowledges that his body is wasting away from cancer may tomorrow complain about meals. One woman who had faced up to her diagnosis with the doctors said, "They don't have to keep hitting me over the head with it."

Anticipatory grief is only one of the many dimensions of a patient's life, and the staff's work puts it in touch with the whole range of human qualities, many of them inspiring: love, courage, nobility, selflessness, humor, even joy.

There is the case of a young man with a most appealing personality who brought great pleasure as well as pain to the staff. Their overidentification with him and their grief over his predictable death compounded the problems of treating him as well as intensifying his own difficulties.

Mark was a bright, attractive, and humorous twenty-year-old college student with leukemia. Over the four and one-half years of his illness, he became deeply involved socially with the treatment staff and was granted special privileges on the hospital floor because of his status as a favorite. He used denial of his doubts and fears very effectively and was able to foster his image as something of a superman by making the All American soccer team during one of his remissions and by seemingly defying all medical odds and pulling through two critical relapses. The hospital was his surrogate and loving family, his territory where parents were not permitted to interfere with his special relationships. Staff was overinvolved and overidentified with Mark because most of them were also young, and to acknowledge the probability of his death was to admit the painful possibility of their own. They supported his denial because it was what he asked for and what they wanted to believe, and both patient and floor staff resented efforts of the psychiatrist and social worker to examine this situation more objectively and admit negatives as well as positives.

During Mark's second relapse, the pain and mourning of the staff were almost unbearable. Mark became somewhat paranoid and blamed his sickness on food contamination by the nurses. After he recovered from that episode he felt extremely guilty about acting badly and abusing those who helped him. He said he was relieved when one nurse who had been important to him left (for unrelated reasons); he commented that now she wouldn't have to suffer. He was able to express to the social worker the tremendous burden of being "special," of always having to act a certain way. However, he continued to seek out the same privileges.

After several months of remission, during which he jogged five miles a day, Mark relapsed and entered the hospital for what was to be his final period of treatment. Staff had been very drained by the last admission and adopted a more distant, objective approach. In order to protect themselves, they decided to call him by his last name. The inappropriateness of this gesture was not lost on Mark, who retaliated by ironically reintroducing himself and giving everyone permission to call him by his first name. Through interdisciplinary meetings, the staff was able to examine how their defenses against their grief were interfering with their ideal of professional care. They were able to permit themselves legitimate expression of what was warm and caring and human without feeling overwhelmed, guilty, and manipulated. They were able to drop their denial and face with Mark the fact that he was dying.

CAN WORDS HELP?

The wife of a dying man shared her grief with the social worker author of this chapter. With tears running down her face she described in vivid, intelligent language her desperation over the imminent loss. The social worker mentioned that she was writing a paper on this difficult subject, and the woman replied: "I'll tell you what to say, just hand in a blank piece of paper. *Words don't do any good.*" Nevertheless, in the two long interviews before she took her husband home to die, she revealed her need to talk about this experience, and demonstrated her ability to contend with death even though words could not forestall it.

We agree with Dovenmuehle (in Feifel, 1965) that "if the patient is encouraged to verbalize his hopelessness and helplessness, he may feel accepted and supported in a way that helps him to withstand the assault of illness with less trauma." Nonverbal communication also plays an important part, particularly when patients are inarticulate, withdrawn, or very ill.

There is a great deal of physical touching between staff and patients, a spontaneous reaching out which helps patients feel that they are not repugnant or rejected because of their illness.

One young man with Hodgkin's disease was not able to discuss his grief directly with either his wife or the social worker, but encouraged his wife to see the worker because of *her* problems. A free-lance writer, after he left the hospital he wrote poems, and the following prayer. He gave them to his wife, who saw this as his way of sharing his deep feelings of anticipatory grief.

What do you do when even your courage is gone? When prayer and faith are gone? When only death is the future—permanent irrevocable death? When death is here already in the joys no longer enjoyed? What do you do when being brave doesn't do anything for your vanity anymore? When life is unbearable and suicide is unthinkable and natural death is too fearsome to be able to ever come to terms with and you're too proud to cry and tears wouldn't do any good and no mother can make you feel better, no wife no child no prayer no friend—What to do when it's Spring in the world and no more Springs for you and you didn't relish the last one and what difference does it make? What do you do when you're stripped and gutless and afraid?

REFERENCES

Beattie, E. J., "Concepts of Cancer Control at Memorial Hospital: The Multidisciplinary Approach," *Clinical Bulletin, 1*:11, 1971.

Blacher, R. S., "Reaction to Chronic Illness," in B. Schoenberg *et al.*, eds., *Loss and Grief: Psychological Management in Medical Practice*. New York: Columbia University Press, 1970.

Feifel, H., "The Function of Attitudes Toward Death," in *Death and Dying: Attitudes of Patient and Doctor*, Symposium No. 11, Vol. 5. New York: Group for the Advancement of Psychiatry, 1965.

Kübler-Ross, E., "Coping Patterns of Patients Who Knew Their Diagnosis," in *Catastrophic Illness in the Seventies*. New York: Cancer Care, 1971.

McCollum, A. T., and A. H. Schwartz, "Social Work and the Mourning Parent," *Social Work, 17*:34, 1972.

15

Variations on a Theme:
Case Reports from Cancer Care *

Irene G. Buckley and
Ruth Michaels

Key functions of the community-based social service program of Cancer
Care are: 1) provision of services to help self-maintaining patients with advanced cancer to remain at home as long as possible; 2) provision of professional counseling to help both patient and family deal with the problems
arising from or exacerbated by the patient's illness. These services are given
by fully trained social workers in individual interviews and in counseling
groups. As an adjunct to the casework services given, financial assistance is
made available to those who need it. Each year, over 5,000 patients are
served and more than 17,000 people, mostly family members and relatives,
are reached. Although some patients improve with treatment or have remissions, every family includes at least one patient who is fatally ill. It is inevitable, therefore, that cancer care deals daily with anticipatory grief.

For the patient, anticipatory grief includes his sense of the imminent
and irreversible loss of his own life, loss of emotional investments, and loss
of people intertwined with his self-image. It also includes a weakened con-

* This chapter is based on the experiences of Cancer Care, Inc., the service arm of The
National Cancer Foundation, Inc. (All names disguised to insure confidentiality.)

cept of his own role and his deep regret for the unfinished business of his life.

Family members, to whose way of life the patient is central, experience parallel feelings of anticipatory grief. They may be facing the need to make painful adaptations in their own life-style. At the very least, they are facing the loss of a person who has been important in their lives. Although depression is often one feature of anticipatory grief, the grieving process can sometimes draw family members closer together against the reality of their imminent loss as they seek the comfort of mutual emotional support.

CASE REPORTS

Resolving Unfinished Business

Many of the patients (and families) aided by Cancer Care go through a painful period of anticipatory grief, sometimes articulated, sometimes covert and unspoken. Part of the caseworker's responsibility in these situations is to help bring out the patient's pent-up grief for his own relief and improved comfort. When this is possible, patients often come to some kind of terms with death, after resolving the "unfinished business" of their lives.

One such patient was Mrs. Alvarez, a financially comfortable thirty-six-year-old woman referred by her clergyman. Never in her adult life dependent on anyone, she accepted his offer to get her a licensed practical nurse, but almost immediately became very ambivalent about the nurse's presence, seeing it as a threat to her independence.

Already ill for two-and-a-half years, Mrs. Alvarez had a short life expectancy when she came to Cancer Care. Married for many years, she had been involved in a chronically stormy relationship with her husband, from whom she had not been able to separate, but with whom she could not live in peace. She described "knock-down, drag-out" fights. There were constant quarrels about his excessive drinking and what she considered his misuse of money. For her part, she threatened suicide. She was particularly upset because she felt that her husband interfered with her warm, close relationship with her sister. This kind of marital relationship was very different from what Mrs. Alvarez had always thought suitable for herself, and she was angry and ashamed that she had never been able to terminate it.

She was also filled with rage toward her doctor. She kept pushing him to talk with her about her illness and outlook. He kept insisting she was "doing fine," when she knew that she was dying.

Mrs. Alvarez told her social worker, "I'm not afraid of dying, I'm afraid of living the way I am now." Her big fear, like that of many other independent patients, was that she would lose control. In the last weeks of her life, she voiced her greatest hopes: that she could find the courage to make a final break with her husband, and that she would die quickly. She did both, and talked with her social worker during the final days of her life about her relief at disposing of an ongoing aggravation of many years, and her increased self-respect, now that she had ended what she "should never have put up with all these years."

In other situations, we have observed that there are some special circumstances which seem to intensify the depth and sometimes the length of anticipatory grieving of patients and family members.

Recurrent Nightmare

This term describes the situation of the patient or family member who lives with the illusion that he is reliving an earlier, hideous experience. For example:

Mrs. Heller, a woman in her forties, had six children between the ages of four and one half and fourteen. Her mother had died of cancer of the breast when Mrs. Heller was fourteen-years-old. Now she too had a widely metastasized breast cancer and was approaching death, and her oldest daughter, with whom she identified closely, was fourteen years old. This repetition of a most painful period in her life was particularly hard for Mrs. Heller to bear.

Like many other patients, Mrs. Heller had a great fear of pain. She was hospitalized for six months, and at times begged the doctors not to prolong her life. She was angry at their refusals, but later expressed her gratitude, because they enabled her to be home for a last Christmas with her children.

Mr. Roberts was another patient suffering repeated trauma, but his conviction of an afterlife enabled him to cope more constructively.

This sixty-one-year-old, very handsome, and well-groomed man had led a colorful life. His government position had required him to travel in many parts of the world, and he was writing a book.

Mr. Roberts' twin brother had been killed in World War II, and his three sisters had died of cancer. He had lived with, helped support, and given personal care to these sisters during their last illnesses. He talked readily of his anxiety about the horror of living through similar indignity and pain.

Until a few weeks before his death three months later, he had weekly interviews with his Cancer Care social worker. He spoke of his concerns, of all he had lost in his life, and of all that he was now losing. As the interviews continued, his anxiety was substantially reduced, and he took comfort in the caseworker's assurance that Cancer Care would be available to him for any help it could give in this critical period.

He voiced his worry that he might lose some of his faculties and his capacity to maintain control of himself; he feared he might not recognize his own deterioration.

He exacted a promise from his social worker that if she thought he could no longer manage his social life or his daily living, she would let him know it was time to consider a terminal facility. He also welcomed her recognition of his strengths, apparent in his past responsibility for his family and in his job, as well as in his own careful planning for what was ahead.

He maintained a vigorous social life until the very end. All his affairs were in order, and he confided that his only "unfinished business" now was his book. He hoped only to be spared intractable pain. He was, for he died peacefully in his sleep.

Mrs. Heller and Mr. Roberts were both patients reliving an experience of cancer and loss. A comparable group includes patients and families who were themselves caught in the life-threatening Nazi holocaust at the time of World War II, and who may have lost family members in the crematoria of the concentration camps. Having survived and painstakingly rebuilt their lives, they were highly vulnerable to having their hard-won security destroyed by fatal illness over a quarter of a century later.

Anger is mixed with grief among many clients with this background. This is particularly true of the elderly, who have experienced long, close marriages, and who face again the threat of disaster and still another loss.

Effects of Traumatic Childhood

Among Cancer Care patients are those who have felt cheated by life because of traumatic childhood experiences. As adults they have lived proudly and alone, often with considerable detachment and almost in isolation. Miss Graham is an example.

Miss Graham had lived alone most of her life. An only child, she lost her father when she was eight, her mother when she was seventeen. She was raised by aunts who did not want her, and had always felt unloved. After an adrenalectomy, she was referred by the hospital to Cancer Care for emotional support and planning for care at home. She knew that the social worker who visited her at home came from Cancer Care, and she said angrily: "What a terrible name! Why don't you call yourselves Cancer Cure?" She was intrigued by the worker's reply: "What's wrong with caring? We care very much about helping the people who need us."

Miss Graham said, with open anger, that nobody had ever really cared for her. In discussions, it gradually emerged that she had some friends, but not very close ones. She was angry at them for visiting less often than she thought they should, and angry at the doctors for their unwillingness to respond to her questions about her outlook.

She had mood swings, possibly related to her surgery, and developed unsightly and uncomfortable symptoms. Religious conviction was helpful in seeing this woman through her ordeal. Within a few days of her readmission to the hospital, she called the nurse, saying that "she wanted to say good-bye to the Cancer Care social worker," and shortly thereafter she died. The availability of the social worker and the use Miss Graham made of her service contributed to her ability to express her grief as well as her anger.

Patients like Miss Graham, who try to cope with their loneliness by isolating themselves even further, often effectively ward off the warmth and intimacy for which they may secretly long. In overt or covert ways, their relatives and friends tend to remove themselves from the dying patient, as professionals in the situation are also apt to do.

The social worker, certainly, can become a particularly important "stand-by person" if able to provide the double role of offering warmth, understanding, and support, and yet respecting the patient's sense of privacy and dignity.

The next example illustrates how a husband's alienation from close relationships intensified his problem. Alone and without help, he was not coping effectively with anticipatory grief.

Mr. Chase, husband of a thiry-eight-year-old patient who had been a speech therapist, was referred by a psychologist friend for counseling and guidance. Orphaned very young, he had been brought up in foster homes and a children's institution.

The Chases had three children, aged five, nine, and eleven. The doctor had given Mr. Chase his wife's diagnosis and prognosis, but had withheld this information from the patient herself. Now Mr. Chase, who had always depended heavily on his wife, saw only disaster ahead. What would the children do? Who would take care of them, and how could he afford to pay for this care, since his earnings as an Assistant Manager of a variety store were very modest?

He described himself as estranged from his few relatives, and admitted fear of close relationships. Yet he stressed the closeness of his own household. He had been willing to tell only one person, an aunt, about Mrs. Chase's illness. He could not bear the idea of telling the truth to his wife. He repeatedly said, "I'm afraid I'll burden her. If she asks if she has cancer, I'll deny it."

Focus here was on Mr. Chase and his fears. He tended to remove himself from the current scene, and to turn from every topic under discussion to the problem of the children.

Mrs. Chase became well enough for a time to return to work once a week. When she began to go downhill again, Cancer Care placed a once-a-week domestic in the home to keep the children's clothing in order, prepare meals, and clean house. Moving gradually out of his isolation into involvement with a source of help, Mr. Chase started and continued weekly counseling sessions with the Cancer Care social worker.

Grief and Immolation

Elsie Simons, the patient, was three years old. Her mother applied to Cancer Care for help in late September, having recently returned from Lourdes. In an open panic at the realization that no miracle cure had been effected, she contemplated suicide. Mrs. Simons also had a six-month-old son, whom she had sent away to her sister to care for in a distant part of the state. Mrs. Simons threw herself into caring for Elsie, with no energy or interest left for her husband, her baby, or anything else. She had invested herself totally in the sick child, to an extent destructive to family life. She kept saying to Elsie: "You don't want your little brother to come home, do you? You don't want him to cry all the time? You don't want me to be his mother, too, do you?"

Although her solicitude and intensive preoccupation with Elsie were to some degree appropriate, the caseworker soon recognized that much of Mrs. Simons' self-immolation for the child was not appropriate. Instead, it reflected a deep-seated problem which might well interfere with her ability to come through her grief and, finally, to pick up the strands of living. Counseling help was therefore directed toward supporting Mrs. Simons through the terminal phase of Elsie's life and the crisis of her death. The crisis intervention prepared Mrs. Simons for ultimately accepting psychiatric treatment which could more effectively free her to mourn and thus to survive.

After Elsie died, further discussions were held with the caseworker, and Mrs. Simons went into psychotherapy to help her regain her equilibrium.

Appointment in Samara

There is an old story about a young prince warned by a soothsayer that he would die. The prince harnessed his best horses to his fastest carriage and raced off to the distant city of Samara, only to find Death himself waiting there for him.

From time to time, there are "Appointment-in-Samara cases" at Cancer Care, cases of people running frantically to escape death. In common with other health professionals, Cancer Care workers can usually do very little to help them.

Mrs. Carter was an attractive woman who had been recently remarried. She had lost her first husband in the Nazi gas chambers. Mrs. Carter learned suddenly that she had advanced cancer of the face, and needed deforming surgery which might make her more comfortable but would be unlikely to save her life. She refused the various counseling and concrete services offered to help her get through this period, and wound up protesting, "You want to help me die! I don't want to die! I want to live! And I'll find a way!"

Both Mr. and Mrs. Carter proceeded to travel from doctor to doctor and from hospital to hospital around the country without changing the outcome of her illness. Family funds were seriously depleted, but despite the doctors' efforts and those of the Cancer Care, their flight ended with her death.

Mr. Burke, on learning his diagnosis of advanced cancer, called Cancer Care for help, but was never able to use it. He wanted relief from his panic, was extremely anxious, and could not concentrate. His business was failing, as he was. Only medication helped him to feel and sleep better, and helped him regain his concentration. He soon began to lose ground. He lost the use of one hand, then the other, but refused to believe the doctor's statement that there was nothing to be done. He persisted in frantic efforts to find a doctor who could do something, switching from doctor to doctor. Although he came to Cancer Care for several interviews, he found no lasting relief in talking with the social worker, the doctor, or anyone else. He was unwilling to have a Cancer Care professional talk with his wife or his son, who was in his late twenties. Both his wife and his son remained shadowy figures when he discussed them. He could not transcend his obsession with his own deterioration and how to stop it.

Fortunately, in many situations where professional people recognize the symptoms of vacillation between hope, despair, and apparent "acceptance," patients and their spouses find relief and easement in the availability of a listening ear, and feel less alone as death approaches.

Not Everyone Dies Hard

Some people, like the patient described below, come to some kind of terms with themselves and their lives. They maintain control of themselves, their destiny, and the way in which they will die.

Like many of these people, Miss Patterson was acting in accordance with a well-ingrained life-style. Miss Patterson, age seventy-six, was alone in the world when she entered the advanced phase of her illness. She had worked as a secretary, and had never married. She was an only child, as had been both her parents, and she had no "family."

Suffering from rectal cancer (and diabetes), she knew her diagnosis, and had come to Cancer Care. At first she carefully avoided discussing her illness. As she grew to know the social worker better, she talked about it, saying "I used to say I had lesions, but I knew they were the spreading cancer." Her euphemism was clearly symbolic of her own progression toward death.

She prepared herself for dying in careful steps. Her cat was her family, and the only living thing she loved. When she began to doubt that she would ever leave the hospital, she talked with the social worker about the alternative possibilities for the cat's care, including that of farming him out. Ultimately, she "had him put to sleep." It was the caseworker's philosophy, as it is the agency's, that any subject important enough for the patient to want to talk over in this final phase of life is worth consideration, time, and effort.

Miss Patterson did rally, however, and came home. Since she was very ill and living alone, she "allowed" Cancer Care to obtain a forty-hour-a-week medical homemaker to provide the personal care she needed. She has since established her eligibility for Social Service Disability and for Medicaid, after considering the alternatives with the agency. She made her will. After talking to her minister, she arranged for cremation. She sent the dress in which she wanted to be cremated to the cleaner, and is keeping it ready in a plastic bag in her closet. She had her good shoes polished, awaiting the day. She chose the possessions she planned to leave to her friends, and informed each friend what would be coming to her. Then she said, "Now I'm just waiting . . . *really* waiting." She commented that her mother had died of cancer at the age of ninety-three, without pain, and she hoped she would be free of pain, too.

As indicated, not all patients are as purposeful in their last days and weeks, and many more are apt to struggle against the inevitability of death. Their expectations and plans vary with their medical condition and sense of well-being, resulting in ups and downs of pessimism and optimism, or even denial. Consequently, many patients, having found relief and easement in the listening ear of the social worker, feel less anxious and isolated as death approaches.

As Hinton (1967) has reported, people usually die as they have lived, in their own life-style, meeting the ultimate crisis of death as they have met the earlier crises of their lives.

ROADBLOCKS TO HEALTHY EXPRESSION OF EARLY GRIEF

Although health professionals are concerned about help for the fatally ill patient, it must be admitted that sometimes they unwittingly contribute to roadblocks which prevent healthy expression of early grief. Among those unwittingly responsible are physicians who avoid discussions with the patient regarding his condition, and at times discourage the family from communicating with the patient and allowing him to convey his grief. Family members, too, are frequently "overprotective" out of concern for the patient or out of concern for their own limits of tolerance.

These attitudes lead to the situation seen all too frequently in our professional practice, where the family is involved in "game playing," destructive game playing unfortunately. There is the hushed conference outside the patient's room, at home or in the hospital; the aura of secrecy reinforcing the isolation of those who are grieving, and heightening their levels of anxiety and sense of impending doom. Worst of all, the lid settles inexorably on the patient's feelings, discouraging his ability to express them. More often than not, this leaves him in his own purgatory, a "nonperson."

Nurses and social workers are not immune either to the temptation to "smooth things over," give false reassurance, and presumably thereby "avoid upsetting the patient." It may be the better part of wisdom when the social worker is doing this to ask, "for whose benefit?" Is it for the patient's comfort, really, or for the comfort of the professional person who, perhaps, can do no more and is often faced with his own frustration and, perhaps, his sense of failure?

THE LISTENING EAR AND THE DIAGNOSTIC EYE

Different examples of various ways of coping with anticipatory grief have been illustrated here. The patients and families involved are coping with the same core problems; many present the same set of difficulties, but there is no common answer in providing help.

The effectiveness of the psychological help provided in various professional disciplines ultimately depends largely on the quality of the differential assessment of personality, character, and life-style. The diagnostic eye, a product of the viewer's own personality and training, is a vital factor in responsiveness to the patient, or for that matter to the involved relative. Both face the steady progression from anticipatory mourning to the actuality of death.

REFERENCES

Busse, E. W., "Stress, Deprivation, and Catastrophic Illness," *Catastrophic Illness in the Seventies: Critical Issues and Complex Decisions.* New York: Cancer Care, 1971.

Hinton, J., *Dying.* New York: Pelican Original, Penguin Books, 1967.

Schmale, A. H., "Coping Reactions of the Cancer Patient and His Family," *Catastrophic Illness in the Seventies: Critical Issues and Complex Decisions.* New York: Cancer Care, 1971.

PART 3

CHILDHOOD ILLNESS

16

Parental Anticipatory Grief and Guidelines for Caregivers

Brenda Comerford

In March 1968, I learned that our daughter had leukemia and that her life might end from one month to two years later. The easiest way for me to convey how we as a family anticipated her death is to recall the day we heard the tragic news and share the nineteen months we lived together before her death.

Karen had been hospitalized by our pediatrician for tests to determine why she had so many aches, pains, and bruises. Within three hours we were told she had leukemia. I will never forget the sinking feeling in my stomach as the doctor told my husband and me. A friend's child had been stricken with this disease a year previously, so I was aware of the implications of the diagnosis. I remembered also how awkward I had been with this friend, not knowing what to say or do to ease her suffering. (These remembered experiences proved to be helpful in the months ahead, for I knew what friends and relatives were feeling and I was able to say that I knew how they felt. This served to ease many tensions.)

When I left the hospital that evening, I cried bitter, angry tears for hours, wondering why this should happen to me. Something that belonged to me would be taken away; a beautiful, innocent child would have to suffer. Hours later the realization hit me that all the crying and all the anger would not change things, that I was not at the "helm," that Karen's life was completely out of my hands.

All my life I had believed that everything happened for a reason, so I asked myself, "What can I possibly learn from this tragic situation?" In the nineteen months that followed, my husband and I discovered the answer to this question.

My husband reacted to the doctor's diagnosis with overwhelming pain and anger. He cursed God, the world, everything. After days of torment, he realized that for everyone's sake, and especially Karen's, he had to pull himself together and face the tragedy effectively, no matter how much he was dying within himself. Consequently, in the weeks that followed, we managed to draw strength from each other and were able to endure our sorrow together. We let each other know when we needed a shoulder to cry on and were deeply thankful for each other's support. Together we worked out a plan for how we would behave with Karen and our other two children.

It is amazing how one's attitudes and priorities can change overnight. To buy a new couch, a color television set, or fashionable clothes was not very important anymore. We decided that our main focus would be to enjoy all three children to the fullest: doing the things we had planned to put off until the children were older, giving all three quality time, and appreciating what Karen (age five), Donna (age four) and Paul (age three) were saying and doing.

A human being always has hope and, deep in our hearts, our hope was that a cure for this disease would be just around the corner and that our child would be one of the lucky ones. Karen did respond to the first medication, and after days in the hospital and a few weeks at home she returned to school.

Because of the medication and the regular trips to the clinic for blood checkups, Karen knew that she was still sick. But she called it "bad blood." She did not know that "the sickness" was serious. Although she missed many weeks of classes during her illness, Karen was a bright child and did well in schoolwork. Because she was so aware, she would have noticed any preferential treatment and wondered about it. So my husband and I agreed to try as much as possible to treat Karen like our other two children. I remember the first time I spanked her after she had been home awhile from the hospital (after that first terrible visit). I could see that she was delighted, for the spanking meant she was not "different." I thought I would have tremendous feelings of guilt later for having spanked her, but I knew that if she did survive, we did not want a spoiled "brat" for a daughter and that she must learn that one does not always get one's own way in life. Also, she had to be disciplined in fairness to Donna and Paul.

Since our three children were so close in age, I had always treated them the same way, never giving to one without giving the other two the same amount—juice, cookies, anything. Karen required many pills daily, so Donna and Paul received vitamin pills regularly to assure them that they were not being left out!

I was most thankful to be only a twenty-minute ride from one of the four main hematology centers in the United States. Because the hospital was so close, I was able to make clinic days "fun days," taking the whole family for a picnic on the grass outside the hospital or eating in the cafeteria for a treat. This gave the younger ones an idea of where their sister went when they were not with her. (Later, when complications in Karen's illness appeared, I left the children with friends.)

The first thing that impressed us about our friends, and even some people we did not know very well, was that they were desperate to help. My faith in mankind was affirmed. People were constantly asking if they could take care of Donna and Paul. (Fortunately, they were very close, and as long as they were together they were happy. They knew of Karen's need for us to be with her when she was hospitalized, but usually one of us returned from the hospital to pick them up and bring them home to sleep.) Our friends asked if we needed food prepared, clothes ironed, housework done, and where they could donate blood. With that kind of support, and with the countless prayers being said, we could not help but be uplifted. Everyone feels the joy of giving, and while we were giving to Karen others were giving to us.

Just before school closed for that summer of 1968, Karen came home looking worried. I told her I sensed that she was brooding over something and she said, "Let's talk about dying, Mom!" I gulped and said, "Okay," and I talked about my faith and the human spirit and how I was not afraid to die and that everyone must die some day. After our talk she hugged me, and I could literally see the curtain of fear lifting from her. Then she said she knew she was going to die soon. An innocent little friend who had overheard her parents talking about Karen had told her.

I told my husband that evening what had occurred, and he wanted me to remember word for word what I had said, so that our stories would coincide. He realized then that children do not hear the words as much as the feeling with which they are said. He needed to share what he felt about death, and if he could come to terms with it, his strength and faith would be communicated to Karen. From that day on, she accepted her destiny with a faith and strength that were unbelievable to behold.

In November we learned that the medication was not preventing the leukemic cells from invading Karen's brain, so she required several spinal taps. These taps are tricky things to perform; sometimes the doctors would succeed quickly and other times they would seem to take forever. Karen went through them stoically. Her faith in the doctors and nurses was strong, for she knew she was loved and that the hospital was the best place for her. In fact, she would often ask to go to the hospital when she felt too uncomfortable at home.

The staff waived the rule of "Mothers out of the room during treatments," so I was present to encourage and comfort my daughter, giving her the knowledge that we were in this together, and that no matter what was to be done, her Daddy or I would be there with her day and night. I would find out ahead of time what the doctors' plans were and explain them to her step by step, as best I could, realizing that fear of the unknown is much worse than any knowing. Often she would cry, and I would cry with her, but by the time the treatment began we would be over the tears. The effects of injecting stronger medication into her spinal fluid would last almost two months to the day, and then we would return to the hospital for another series until her body built up an immunity to the drug. But even the spinal taps could not relieve Karen's headaches.

One day, after a number of unsuccessful taps, I felt Karen withdrawing psychologically. I think this was the most terrifying time for me, for I felt that as long as the lines of communication remained open between us we had a chance. The next day she resumed talking. When I told her how scared I was the day before, she said, "Do you know what I was thinking about? I was wishing I was dead 'cuz it's no fun being in so much pain." I told her I would probably feel exactly the same way if I had been through what she had, but that I did not want her to lose her will to live as we loved her very much, and that everyone was doing everything possible to make her well. She said, "You have two other children when I go!"

Another time, my husband and I had to rush her, convulsing, to the hospital. Donna and Paul witnessed this terrifying scene. We cried together, and I began preparing them for the fact that when children are too sick God takes them to be with Him. This time Karen was unconscious for three days and we did not expect her to pull through. But she did, and on the way home she turned to me and said, "You thought I was going to die this time, didn't you?" I honestly replied that I had, and she said, "Fooled you, eh?"

Now the doctors began giving her more toxic medication, a compound which had side effects of total hair loss and a bloating that made her look pregnant. She was used to the bloating from previous medication, but I felt I should warn her ahead of time that her hair would fall out and that, if she liked, we could get a wig for her. She wept, and I was worried that I had done the wrong thing in telling her in advance. But the next day, when she was having her blood checked, she announced to the technician, "My mom is going to buy me a wig." The technician replied, "Oh how ridiculous! Little girls don't wear wigs." Our six-year-old said, "I'm on strong drugs and so my hair will be falling out and I can have the wig instead of my own hair." Within twelve hours Karen had come to terms with something that I know I certainly would have agonized over much longer.

She did go completely bald, but said that she didn't need the wig, and that it was what the person was like inside that counted! It was remarkable to see this friendly, funny looking, bald child who felt so good about her inner self that she could confidently meet the stares of strangers and friends. She did so with such warmth and interest and a "here I am" attitude that she was beautiful. She demonstrated at such a young age what adults strive to grasp in a lifetime.

During our frequent visits to the hospital, we were able to establish close relationships with other parents of children who had terminal illnesses. Only those who have gone through something like this can say, "I understand." We met periodically to talk about our hopes and fears, about what to say to a sick child, or to the brothers and sisters. Generally, we were supportive to each other, people caring together during the joys and the suffering.

Karen died on October 11, 1969, after much suffering. Our feelings were mostly of relief that she was finally at peace. We felt privileged to have been her parents, for she had taught us so much. I had read somewhere that "suffering ceases to be suffering when it has meaning," and I feel that this is what happened inside me when I first heard that she would not be with us for long. I saw her as a teacher, as I saw all those terminal children. They were all exceptional human beings, and their lives did have meaning. We are constantly reminded of the lessons she taught us.

I had always wondered how I would react during a trauma, and I found that one can find positives in negative happenings, that good can come from bad, and that life is both joy and sorrow. Since Karen's death, we have continued our emotional support to the parents of other leukemic children, either by telephone conversations or by being available for baby-sitting or transportation to and from the hospital. Sometimes just sharing our own feelings with parents who cannot communicate is helpful. These shared experiences show parents other ways of handling trauma and instill a feeling that they are not alone with their grief.

Anticipatory grief tests the individual, the marriage, the siblings, the grandparents, other relatives, and one's faith. Where does the doctor fit in? Our experiences were very positive with most of the doctors, but there were a few who seemingly remained uncaring and aloof from the whole situation, adding to our pain and that of other parents. Some could not make eye contact with parents, others pretended that the child was fine when the child was actually dying. I am not suggesting that doctors should become too emotionally involved, but certainly there should be a reaching out, honest and caring, so that a most painful experience is lightened. The ultimate achievement during a tragedy is the doctor, the patient, and the parent working as a team with trust, understanding, and honest communication.

The following are some thoughts to guide both physicians and parents during the course of a child's terminal illness:

For Physicians

1) Lay out the course of the disease from start to finish, rather than allow the parents to be deluded into thinking that their child will be cured.

2) Be honest with the parents when they ask questions, and be honest about the prognosis. "I don't know" is refreshing to hear and more acceptable to the parents than vague hopes. There are some parents who want to be deceived by the doctors, but uncertainty can be harder to live with than knowledge of the facts. Our doctor told us the tragic news within three hours of our child's arrival at the hospital, and we preferred it that way.

3) Have someone with a positive attitude available, someone who has experienced what the new patient and parents will have to go through, and who can offer advice and guidance regarding the mechanics of the hospital setting and the necessary treatments.

4) Give the parents a list of questions that the patient will probably ask, according to his age. This can help the parent to prepare answers, or at least to think through things ahead of time. What counts is not what the parents say to the child, but how they say it. If they are fearful, their fear will be communicated.

5) Affirm the tremendous responsibility that the mother has from the beginning. She sets the atmosphere of the home. How the others cope is mostly dependent on her. But explain that the husband needs to be there to support. She will be "down" and need him to be up, and vice versa. An experience such as this, even though tragic, can strengthen a marriage and reorder priorities.

6) Help parents to be aware of how a child's illness affects healthy siblings. They have fears that are expressed in various ways, and parents must be aware and able to interpret what the sibling is really asking.

7) It would be valuable for parents to be told that when human beings are going through an emotional crisis their normal physical desires may change. It is important to know that this is only temporary.

8) Encourage the parents to talk with other parents in the clinic in order to give them a better idea about ways of acting that feel right for them. Also, only a person going through the same ordeal can say, "I understand."

9) Explain to the parents other people's reactions and their possible inability to communicate their feelings. Some truly care and are able to work through their fears of death; but others stay away and would rather not face the situation. Parents must accept this.

10) Reconsider the instructions concerning "not getting involved." The doctor *is* involved, and although this does not mean that he has to die each death, he should exhibit some feeling and concern.

11) The doctor diminishes trust both with the parents and the child when he does not become involved to some degree with the parents and patient and tries to put up a front that everything is going along nicely. The child knows when he is well and when he is sick. When a doctor says, "He's just fine," everyone doubts if that doctor is really being truthful.

12) Be very careful not to use the term "leukemia" in front of the child. Television is so explicit that the child may learn of his fatal illness in a traumatic way.

13) At all times parents should put the child first and not have to worry about catering to the doctors. Physicians are notorious for assuming—on purpose or not—a "Godlike" aura, and people who are insecure often feel

inferior to them. If the doctor cannot be a caring human being, and the parents feel that they cannot voice their fears and hopes, something crucial in their relationship is lacking. If the physician remains on a pedestal, the parents expect Godlike actions and miracles. More people need to know that doctors are people simply trying to do a good job but that the stakes are higher.

14) Consider and be sensitive to the needs and desires of the relationship between parents and patient. The trust which has been built up can be destroyed by an insensitive doctor. The mother and child may function well together, and the child will cooperate fully with the doctor if the mother is allowed to be present during treatments. The doctor imposes more fear on the child by insisting that the mother cannot be present. If a particular physician cannot perform the treatment with parents present, then he should step down and allow another physician to do it.

15) Parents must realize that the goals of the doctor are different from their own. The doctor tries to minimize stays in the hospital but also be sensitive to when the parents have reached the end of their endurance of looking after a child who is in pain at home. This requires frank communication to get parents to say, "We've had enough!"

16) Physicians should admit that they are worried or confused rather than have the parents leave still wondering. The doctor should be specific when the child goes on another drug and describe to the parents and the child some of the average reactions to this drug.

17) Realize that some parents panic easily. The honest doctor tells them if they are being overly anxious or if they have a right to be concerned. The doctors to be admired are those who level with the parents, and the ones who, when the parents are having a rough time with their child, come in and say, "Bad times." The parents then respond, for they know that the doctor knows where they are, both intellectually and emotionally.

18) While some parents do panic unnecessarily, others have an intuitive ability to sense significant changes in the child's condition. Doctors should be aware of this and listen when parents describe certain things. The mother is often the one who is around the child most of the time and who can spot changes most readily. It is most frustrating when the mother knows that something needs to be done and the doctor delays treatment. In the meantime the child is suffering needlessly.

19) Make it clear to parents that rushing to the emergency room will not always change things. Parents feel a tremendous responsibility with a

terminal child, and it would take some of the burden off them if doctors would tell them what some of the side effects of a particular drug may be, what to look for, and what should be and not be regarded as alarming.

20) As time passes, the child has been through various episodes and treatments. He knows which ones he loathes and is afraid of and which ones he can tolerate. Doctors do not need to tell a child at 8 A.M. that at 2 P.M. he or she will have thus and such a treatment. The parent can know ahead of time, but the child should be told only shortly before. It is cruel to let the child suffer longer than necessary.

21) Physicians must know when to step down or turn the performance of a treatment procedure over to another doctor who can perform it with greater skill. A doctor's inability to succeed in all of his efforts should not be regarded as failure.

22) The child should be aware that her doctors love her and are doing everything in their power to help her. This concept should be stressed constantly to children in order to maintain their trust, particularly as their doctors perform the necessary but often painful treatment procedures. Seeing the same doctor each visit can help children gain this trust.

23) Be sensitive to the fact that as the disease progresses and the parents know the end is near, they fear that the child will suffer an agonizing death.

For Parents

1) Answer the child's questions as honestly as possible, because children *do* compare notes in clinic. Let him know, for example, that puffiness and hair loss are due to a particular drug. If the child sees that his parents are not bothered by these things, he will not be either.

2) Remember that children are much more aware than they are often thought to be. If they feel that they are being lied to, the wool pulled over their eyes, they will play along with the game, and the parents will be denied some of the most beautiful and close moments of sharing both sadness and joy.

3) Keep a sense of humor and treat the child as normally as before. The sick child hates to be considered different, and his fears become greater if he sees a different pattern of behavior in his parents. Also, siblings will hate or resent "the monster" the parents create through spoiling. It is not "loving" to spoil any human being. A child must learn to give and take and that the world and society have laws to be obeyed.

4) Do not focus completely on the sick child. Parents must carry on

their responsibilities to each other and to the siblings so that there are relationships to return to after the child has gone.

5) Give siblings constant reassurance of love as well as explanations. Even young ones understand more than often given credit for.

6) Be aware that a sibling may worry that he also will become sick.

7) Clinic day can actually be made fun. Lunch out at the cafeteria or picnic on the lawn so that the child does not fear clinic visits so much.

8) Most people have plans for the future. When faced with the reality that for this child there is no future, it is good for parents to think of some things that they really want their child to do—and do them! *Realize that the quality of time spent with children is important and not the quantity.* Parents can be around their children twenty-four hours a day and yet not be present at all.

9) Recognize that it is only human to be angry and bitter about what has happened. One must release these feelings and then go on supporting and loving the sick child.

10) Parents must be very confident in their actions and motivations. Are we being "real" in handling the child or are we merely catering to everyone else's opinions? This requires constant communication between husband and wife about their management of the sick child. They must decide, and should not be swayed by what others feel they would do under the same circumstances. Others do not know for they are not going through it. Parents must remember what the main priority is during this time: it is the terminal child. Valuable energy cannot be wasted in worrying about "what people are thinking about us."

11) Some people may put you on a pedestal as being so much better than they are; others may call you a phony. If you cry, some will say you're not holding up under the strain; but usually people will feel more comfortable with you when you are crying, for that seems to be the most acceptable way to handle the situation. The phrase one hears most often is, "I know I'd never manage if my child got really sick—I'd fall apart."

12) Parents feel uncomfortable around others who are fearful of the situation. If the parents demonstrate a willingness to talk openly, this will free their friends and relatives.

13) If parents can cope as the end of the child's illness approaches, they can make final arrangements. This prevents a tremendous amount of emotional trauma at the actual time of death.

14) In any situation, fear can either free one to grow or it can immobilize. Working through fear is possible with faith, and one certainly needs faith during a terminal illness.

For Both Physicians and Parents

1) Assure the child that his illness is not a punishment for wrongdoing.

2) Be conscious of a child's withdrawal and encourage him to share his thoughts and voice his innermost fears.

3) Our society measures a man by his strength, and he is not expected to cry. Encourage fathers to show emotion. There is no shame in tears; it is much healthier to cry than to repress one's tears.

4) Contemplate the meaning of tears. Is it that, perhaps, something that is mine is being taken away from me, or is it a blow to the ego? If the parents are religious, the child may be regarded as having been loaned to the parents by God.

5) Parents need to know that they will be drawing on all aspects of their experience: their childhood, their relationships with their own parents, their marriage relationships, their relationship with the sick child and the siblings. If they know help is available from all these areas, they may be able to take advantage of it.

6) Having a seriously ill child prevents parents from doing what they would normally want to do—and the parents have feelings about this which should be frankly expressed. Their attitude can be one of resistance or response. The former causes inner torment; the latter gives joy, the joy of giving totally to another person without a thought about one's self.

17

The Thoughts of a Bereaved Father

Milton Graub

How can anyone relate how he really feels after the death of an eighteen-year-old daughter, a child so beautiful in soul, delicate in mind, and so loving to all? The task is almost unbearable.

I will never forget the night I spoke to Evelyn, my wife, who was with our ill daughter, Kathy, then age two. Evelyn informed me not only that the results of Kathy's duodenal drainage tests were positive but also that Kathy had cystic fibrosis. (Almost two years earlier the same diagnosis had been established for our infant son.) It was 1951. I was a young and optimistic pediatric resident just beginning to learn something about this "rare and fatal disease." My words to my wife were simple and straightforward: we must be strong and have faith; we would do all we could for our children, and beyond this we could do nothing more. This attempt to support Evelyn, and the support she gave me, became a way of life for both of us; without it I am not sure that we could have survived the following sixteen years.

My first real feelings of depression and despair occurred that night. I was alone and cried most of the night. The future seemed almost hopeless—to have had two children both with this dread disease was incomprehensible to me. Every other problem I had ever faced could be rationalized and, with persistence and work, some reasonable answer could be found. But I could see no positive outcome from my current plight, no matter where or how my thoughts turned.

My despair finally took the form of compromise: compromise in the knowledge that I had a wonderful wife and that we could still be a small, happy family. In my youth and innocence, I had not yet experienced how beautiful children, well *or* sick, can be. And I had not come to know that life is just a series of memories after all.

Kathy did fairly well until the age of eight, when she developed her first serious pulmonary infection. I had been fairly relaxed until then, enjoying her every experience with her. It was at this time that I was brought harshly back to reality. It had been my policy to leave all health decisions to Kathy's pediatrician, not even asking the results of her laboratory studies. However, when she was hospitalized with this infection, I saw her radiographs and for the first time realized that she was showing typical progressive changes of the disease. Prior to this, she had been attending school daily, enjoying vacations with us, and was well-nourished. I had shut out the true progressive nature of the disease, and when confronted by the objective evidence of the radiograph films I was shattered, and re-experienced the despair, depression, and hopelessness that I had felt when she was an infant and the initial diagnosis had been made.

Time and her presence again were my immediate salvation. The next ten years were years of great love, delight, and growth, both for Evelyn and for me. Kathy taught us so many things: how to be appreciative of each day; how, in spite of deficiencies, to adapt and make the best of a situation. She loved baseball, went out for her school softball team each year (though she didn't make it, since she couldn't even run to first base). But in trying she taught us how to be positive and look at life in a more humorous vein; and, above all, to be brave in the face of a life of medications, treatments, and the all-pervasive knowledge of cystic fibrosis.

The above qualities, together with a wonderful ability to show affection, made her a very special person to us; and so, when Kathy became critically ill, I initially could not accept the idea that she might die. She had been sick so many times before and had always responded to treatment. It was not until the day that her dedicated physician indicated to me that she was in cardiac failure and was not responding that I realized the truth. Even though I knew how little functioning lung tissue remained, and could see her peripheral edema, only upon being told by someone else did I fully realize that our Kathy was dying. Denial had been the only defense, and now it failed.

I could not control myself. I stayed with her all that day and wept continuously. I simply could not understand how we could bear not to have her with us. Her problems, her therapy, and her limitations had become an integral part of our daily existence. They had become normal focus and no burden on the family. How could this large part of our existence suddenly disappear and life remain whole?

Kathy spoke infrequently that day but continued to open her eyes to see if we were there. She seldom smiled and once, seeing my tears, asked why I was crying. I believe she had always maintained such a positive outlook that she actually didn't realize that she could be dying.

I couldn't find a comfortable place that day or night. I paced and wept, saying little. My mind was numb but groped for some basis upon which I might continue living without her. I believe my feelings added up to a total of "nothingness."

Kathy died the next morning. Although I did not feel that she had been relieved of her suffering and was, therefore, better off, I was consoled by the thought that she had lived a full, happy, and intellectually active life. It was also consoling to know that, as parents, we had loved her, that this love had been returned, and that we had done all that was humanly possible for her.

She knew how deeply involved our family was with the cystic fibrosis cause and I think she always believed that because of efforts such as ours, the "control" would come in time to help *her*. This thought supported her to the end.

We lived the "Impossible Dream."

18

Management of Parental Anticipatory Grief

Rudolf Toch

The achievement of as "normal" a life as possible for the whole family is the goal of all medical and related care of a fatally ill child. For the purposes of this discussion "anticipatory grief" is defined rather broadly as those aspects of parental adjustment to the knowledge that their child will die. Emotional support of all members of the stricken family in their coping with this knowledge is an integral part of the comprehensive medical care that families need and deserve. Only a smoothly functioning team of experts under the leadership of one primary physician can accomplish this.

Preparing parents for the loss of a child is an essential part of the initial discussion once a fatal diagnosis has been established. Often the physician responsible for communicating with the parents may assume that after this discussion the parents will be able to adjust to the tragedy in a rational and sensible manner. Unfortunately, this is often not so. Parents under stress are not rational, objective, or sensible. They are overwhelmed by grief, fear, and a sense of guilt. They may feel abandoned if no effort is made to help them with the many problems created when life with a dying child must be faced. The physician who is sensitive to the parents' needs spends as much time as may be necessary discussing all the facets of their problem. He also insures that all members of the medical team, particularly while the patient is hospitalized, avoid giving conflicting advice or information to the parents.

Furthermore, he mobilizes all other resources available, particularly social workers and members of the clergy, who can be relied upon to reinforce a desirable attitude within the parents.

Ideally this attitude should be a calm and controlled acceptance of the inevitable by the parents directed toward creating as normal and serene a life for the child and the whole family as the nature of the illness permits. To achieve even an approximation of this ideal depends on the physician's knowledge not only of what to suggest as a modus vivendi but also of what to be on guard against.

Some of the patterns that can defeat this goal are, in effect, efforts of the parents themselves to cope with their grief. These may be considered diversionary tactics that make possible a temporary avoidance of the ultimate tragedy by concentration on lesser and often artificially created or disproportionately exaggerated concerns. While far from exhaustive, the following list includes some of these concerns and attitudes of grief-stricken and frustrated parents. Many more could be added.

1) Protracted denial of diagnosis or prognosis.

2) "Shopping around" for medical opinions, including trips to distant medical meccas.

3) Manipulating the members of the medical-care team to produce an illusion of disagreement with the prognosis, which thereby justifies either unrealistic hope or despair.

4) Willingness to expend money beyond reason to effect a cure.

5) Overprotective sheltering and permissive overindulgence of the child.

6) Failure to permit the child to be independent.

7) Overemphasis on health concerns, such as diet, adequate rest, and too frequent inquiry as to the child's state of health.

8) Realignment of the family to revolve around the patient, often to the detriment of the child's siblings.

9) Adamant refusal to let the child know the nature of his problem and prognosis.

10) Desire for sympathetic or even maudlin publicity.

11) Attempts by parents to assign guilt for the illness to themselves or others.

12) Exaggerated concern over minutiae.

13) Concentration of attention on some facet of the clinical picture,

and letting hope rise and fall with it, for example, the platelet count or white blood count in acute leukemia.

14) Acting as if the child were already dead.

The foregoing unhealthy attitudes and activities are natural products of grief, fear, and frustration. They are not deliberate efforts to antagonize the physicians or other members of the team but must be regarded as signals that more intensive emotional support is needed. An awareness that these activities may ensue makes it possible for the physician to discuss them before they can actually occur. Often the physician's indication that they are contrary to the child's best interests will mitigate their effects or even prevent them from occurring. Most parents want to help their ill child and are grateful for any advice or suggestion on how to achieve this. Without being condescending, members of the medical-care team must keep in mind that people under severe stress do not function as they normally would, and that more support than one might consider proper is imperative. If parents are to be aided in their adjustment to their child's impending death, the physician and his team must be willing and able to provide all the support and understanding the family requires in order to live through the ordeal of life with a dying child.

19

Parents of Fatally Ill
Children in a Parents' Group *

Irving J. Borstein and
Annette Klein

Families of fatally ill leukemic children have responded and benefited from
the formation of a parents' group and a patients' group within a medical-
clinical structure. Experience indicates that such a parents' group, with professional leadership, can assume its own momentum and be a vehicle for anticipatory mourning, as well as provide support for day-to-day life situations
as they relate to the patient, parents, siblings, physicians, extended family,

* In 1964 Edward Futterman, M.D., Director of the Child Psychiatry Program of the University of Illinois, and Irwin Hoffman, a doctoral candidate in psychology, began a research
project on "Parental Anticipatory Mourning." This study was carried on with the cooperation
of the Pediatrics Department of the University of Illinois College of Medicine. The subjects
were leukemic children and their parents.

By 1967 the research had led to the formation of a play group for children in the
Oncology-Hematology Clinic under the supervision of an occupational therapist and a pediatric
social worker. Simultaneously, a parents' group was started by Irwin Hoffman and Annette
Klein, A.C.S.W., Associate Professor, and Assistant Director of the Child Psychiatry Program.

In 1970 the project was redefined as a service entity and the focus shifted to a more therapeutic orientation. Miss Klein was joined in leading the parents' group by Dr. Borstein, Director of the Family Systems Program at the Institute for Juvenile Research and Assistant Professor
at the University of Illinois. Miss Georgia Halverson, an occupational therapist, continued with
the children's group.

and hospital personnel. This group also serves as a resource for the prevention of emotional breakdown in the family, both during and following the loss of the child, and in fostering communication among all those involved with the child and the family in order to facilitate the coping process.

INITIAL CONSIDERATIONS AND PLANNING

The first step in the development of a parents' group is the approval and understanding of the medical staff. Without the sanction of the administration and the involvement of the treating physician, there is little hope for a successful program. Once this initial agreement has been reached, various organizational and human problems emerge.

Approximately thirty-two patients are registered with the clinic and involved in this particular program. The children come to the clinic on a designated morning from 9:30 A.M. until 12:00 noon. They come from urban and suburban communities within approximately two hours driving time from the treatment center. After initial diagnosis and hospitalization, the children are treated on an outpatient basis, unless their medical condition warrants hospitalization. Some patients attend clinic weekly, others biweekly or monthly. Therefore, the group composition changes each week.

The patients are usually accompanied by their mothers or at times by their fathers, siblings, friends, or relatives. The standard procedure for each visit includes a blood test and treatment by one of the hemotologists. While results of tests or an examination are evaluated, the parents, patients, and others wait in the clinic waiting room for about two hours. The population is lower to upper middle class (including black, white, and Mexican patients), with educational levels ranging from elementary school dropouts to university professors.

It was determined that the most appropriate time to meet with the parents would be during a portion of the clinic time, from 10:30 to 11:45 A.M. weekly, and that professional help was necessary for the parents' group. These decisions were based on the premises that the parents were too depressed to take the necessary initiative themselves and that the domination of the issue of separation and the tendency to utilize denial as a defense would make an additional visit difficult. There was also the feeling that providing an opportunity for separation at the clinic would be beneficial. A children's activity group was set up in the waiting room; and another room some distance away was set up as a meeting room for the parents.

STAFFING

Two professionals should be able to co-lead the parents' group. This assumption is based on the recapitulation of helplessness which the parents have transmitted to these leaders. Such feelings, the struggle with the issue of death, and the ultimate predictability of loss, make it important that there be a shared leadership responsibility.

Leaders should be experienced in working with groups; they should have some knowledge, objectivity, and flexibility, and be willing to deal with the shifting composition of the group as well as their own personal difficulty in coping with the issues of separation, loss, death, and helplessness. The leaders must decide the extent of their availability to members of the group outside of the formal meeting situation. This is particularly important when a child is hospitalized or following the death of a child.

It is important that the leaders of the parents' group and the children's group meet regularly with the physicians in order to share experiences and deal with issues as they arise.

GROUP STRUCTURE AND FUNCTION

During the initial diagnostic involvement with the child and the parents, the parents are advised by the physician of the existence of the parents' group and its availability for those who wish to participate in it. Before each parents' session begins, an announcement is made in the waiting room. Prior to the meeting, the leaders usually spend a few minutes with the parents in the waiting room, introducing themselves to new parents and talking to those parents who do not choose to attend the group meetings. Physicians are usually somewhat reluctant to introduce parents to leaders because they do not want to give parents the impression that they must attend the meetings as part of the treatment process.

As the group process begins to unfold, parents who attend the group invite new or reluctant parents to the meetings. These parents may "find each other" in the waiting room and discuss issues, or one parent may remain with the child while the other parent attends the meeting. Some parents attend regularly, others come in periodically. At times, stress keeps some from coming, while others attend when there is a stressful situation, such as that of a child in relapse. Parents are not viewed as pathological or as patients themselves, but as families coping with an extremely stressful problem. It is hoped that making contact with each other can help them deal with common issues.

The leaders' contact with the group begins with the premise that it is the parents' group, and that the leaders serve as conveners and facilitators of communication. It is understood that the leaders will share information unless they are told that it is not to be shared. The general format of each meeting is one of discussion, and a sharing of feelings and experiences when it is comfortable to do so.

The leaders initiate movement into stressful or painful areas, and urge the parents to help each other by sharing information, problems, possible solutions, and feelings. Talk can center about anything of interest to the parents, and include spouses, extended family, siblings, medical care, and the ultimate issues of loss, separation, death, and grief. An important issue that can be clarified with the group is the extent to which the leaders are available to the members of the group. It is made clear that the leaders' major responsibility is the group meeting, and that visits by them to the parents and children during hospitalization may or may not occur. If the program has a full-time worker, it would be desirable for this person to be available during periods of hospitalization.

Introduction of Hospital Personnel into the Group

Since the main function of the leaders is to facilitate communication, they constantly encourage parents who bring up issues concerning nurses or physicians to communicate directly with the medical and nursing staff. Parents are often reluctant to express themselves because they are afraid that the care of their child will be affected, or they fail to question the physician because they really don't want to know his answers. The nurses on the floor are encouraged to attend the parents' meetings, and many issues have been resolved in this way, with nursing staff and parents learning from each other. When there are complicated medical questions, one of the physicians is asked to attend a meeting to answer them.

GROUP PROCESS—THEMES AND EVENTS

Although individual parents in the group are at various stages, it appears that the group as a unit moves through specific stages of coping with impending death. Initially, the group deals with new parents and the issues of denial and guilt. Information about drugs is shared and parents compare the cases

of their children and their progress. Themes recur. "My child is different."
"His disease is progressing differently." "I can handle this." Information
about the illness is extremely important and the parents "pump" each other
for facts. Their initial reactions to learning of the diagnosis are discussed.
As the group progresses and parents become increasingly aware of the
deaths of children, parents begin to identify their child with another whose
progress is similar.

Denial begins to fade, and feelings of helplessness begin to emerge.
Parents become more frantic, and their helplessness leads to hostility which
may be directed toward the nurses, the hospital, and/or the physicians. As
they acquire more knowledge they begin to question treatment, and are
angry because they were not given more treatment options. At this stage it is
important to have parents deal with their hostility directly in confrontation
with those upon whom their anger has been displaced. While dealing with
the objects of their anger and concern, they feel that they are not helpless
and are doing something for their child.

The third phase is one in which many issues are discussed. The theme
is: How do we live with this fact? Siblings, family relationships, and the
issue of communication are discussed. What does the child know? What
should I tell him? How do I feel around people? The child's physical status
often determines the mood of a group member. There can be expression of
anger toward the child for upsetting family plans. Parents begin to help each
other more, and a cooperative spirit begins to emerge. There is ventilation of
feelings and a sharing of experiences. Communication with hospital personnel improves. Parents begin to realize how different each case is and do not
compare treatments as often.

In the fourth stage, parents have seen enough patients die and enough
children relapsing to deal with the issues of death directly. Funerals are discussed, and some parents express the wish that their children would die.
There is talk about how they would like to see the end come. Yet, although
most of the parents talk about death, there always remains a glimmer of
hope. Conversations take on a more therapeutic character and real issues are
discussed.

Individual Coping

Within the group, parents are at many stages in the anticipatory
mourning process. Parents who have been at previous levels try to help

others deal with issues. One of the crucial issues has been that of how to give information to family members and others. At one meeting a parent told of discussing death with her ten-year-old daughter who had discovered the prognosis of her illness, and how this sharing had improved their relationship. Others compared the results of telling siblings about a brother's or sister's illness.

The parents talk about loss, separation, and their fear for themselves and their remaining families. Fantasies, such as "I feel I will lose all my children," are expressed.

Outside the Group

One of the positive results of the group meetings has been the development of friendships among the parents. They call and help each other. When a child is hospitalized, one of the parents will take care of a younger sibling of the hospitalized patient. A depressed mother might call a friend from the group at 3:00 A.M. for comfort. The parents feel that they are really understood only by parents with a similar problem. The mourning process for the children of other parents appears to help parents come to grips with their own impending loss, and at the same time helps them with their own mourning process.

Following a Death

Parents are concerned about the way other parents react to the death of a child. It is reassuring to them that inner strengths allow the bereaved to continue. Several parents have returned to the group for a session following the loss of a child and have shared their experiences, bringing back information regarding former members of the group. The parents, as they are brought into contact with actual bereavement, begin to discuss how they will adjust to their loss.

CONCLUSION

Many parents who attend the parents' group develop a positive attitude about their experience. At times the group, as it moves through various stages of development, creates difficulties for hospital personnel, but it has improved communication between physicians and patients, parents and patients, nurses and parents, and among parents themselves. The experience of sharing has given everyone a chance to grow and learn from each other about living as well as about dying. It has provided a setting for dealing with fear and hope, anger and gratitude, helplessness and strength.

REFERENCES

Futterman, E. H., and I. Hoffman, "Transient School Phobia in a Leukemic Child," *Journal of the American Academy of Child Psychiatry, 9:*477, 1970.
Hoffman, I., and E. H. Futterman, "Coping with Waiting: Psychiatric Intervention and Study in the Waiting Room of a Pediatric Oncology Clinic," *Comprehensive Psychiatry, 12:*67, 1971.

20

I Know, Do You? A Study of Awareness, Communication, and Coping in Terminally Ill Children *

Myra Bluebond-Langner

Death is very much a part of the fantasy thoughts of children (Anthony, 1940; Piaget, 1952; Nagy, 1959). It is also a part of a child's everyday life—the games he plays, the stories he hears, the books he reads, the television programs he watches, the movies he sees. Yet, American parents today are more open with their children about sex than they are about death and dying. While conversations about sex are no longer taboo, conversations about death and dying are becoming increasingly so, and are avoided.

However, there is a time when death cannot be ignored by any parent or adult—in the case of the terminally ill child, and in the perspective of this study, specifically the child stricken with leukemia, this is the time when great efforts are expended to shield the child from such knowledge (Karon

* The field research for this paper was conducted at the University of Illinois Hospital on the General Pediatrics Unit from June 1971 to February 1972, with support from the NSF and the Department of Anthropology at the University of Illinois, Urbana.

I would like to thank the Pediatric hematologists (Dr. I. Schuman, Head of the Department of Pediatrics, Dr. H. Maurer, Dr. G. Honig, Dr. M. Hruby, and Dr. R. Choi), the Pediatric House Staff, the Nursing Staff, and the leaders of the Parents and Childrens group (Dr. I. Borstein, Miss A. Klein, and Miss G. Halverson) for their assistance and cooperation. But, most of all, gratitude and appreciation are extended to the parents and children who participated in the study. (Note: All names used are fictitious.)

and Vernick, 1968). In spite of these efforts, most of these children are aware of the seriousness and prognosis of their illness. Richmond and Weisman (1955) and others have postulated that this is not so, failing to recognize the many sources of information available to the child and the "symbolic" way in which this information and his awareness of it can be communicated.

How these children become aware—assimilate, integrate, and synthesize information—and what they are aware of at different stages in the illness are the central topics of this chapter. Because children's levels of awareness and processing of information have a direct bearing on their personal and social perceptions, their ability to cope with the facts of their mortality also warrants discussion.

SOURCES OF INFORMATION

All the leukemic children (up to fourteen years of age) observed knew that they had a very serious illness. Many of the older children knew that it would be fatal. All of them knew of other children who had gone to the same clinic, taken the same drugs, been subjected to the same kinds of medical tests (bone marrows, etc.), spent time in the hospital in reverse isolation, received blood, became bald, and bloated, and then died.

The question raised is: How much did they identify with these other children? Evidence indicates how these children identified with other children from the Oncology Clinic, and with those who eventually died.* On admission to the hospital, they often asked, "Who else is in from clinic?" Until a period when there was a rapid succession of deaths within a relatively short time (eight children died in a two-month span), the children would ask regularly in clinic, "Who is in the hospital?" or "Where is so-and-so?" After this period passed, some of the children did ask about other children who had died, and then how they had died. At this point they would often make reference to their own present condition, with special emphasis on the differences in their own symptomatology. For example: "Well, he had lots of nosebleeds in the hospital, too. I only had one nosebleed. It stopped."

---

* Examples are cited from conversations and observations in hospitals and clinics. At no time was a child asked: "Are you afraid to die?" or "Do you know what is wrong with you?" The author was interested in what was on the child's mind, not what had been put there. The interaction was the child's to manipulate.

They were also interested in the other children's progress. Many of the disease-related conversations in the clinic began by a child's calling attention to another patient's appearance and then comparing it to his own. "Tom gets his hair back real fast. I wish I did." "Did Gene have vincristine too? When I had vincristine again, I got bald."

They knew who had died, and the dead child's name and his belongings became taboo.* Any mention of the name was for information purposes only, and then the subject was quickly changed. For example, one child would not play with toys brought to him by the mother of a deceased child. Another child, when asked where a specific toy came from, said, "Steven's mother, the one, you know . . . the one that—you know. He doesn't come to the clinic any more."

To obtain information about their illness, the children not only observed but also questioned one another. Questioning took place either in the playgroup or in areas beyond the hearing range of the adults, such as bathrooms and corners. Two boys often discussed their respective chemotherapy and progress. Alan, who had been coming to the clinic longer than Seth, would tell Seth when to expect bone marrows and the names of drugs used for treatment. When Alan did not come to clinic one week, Seth asked for him: "Where is Alan? I want to know what a 'relapse' is."

How long it took children to accumulate various kinds of information and become aware of its relationship to their own illness could be related to their attendance at the clinic and their contact with other leukemic children.† While some were given information from their doctors and parents, a large number relied on their observations and conversations within the peer group, especially with respect to some of the more taboo areas.

Eavesdropping on adult conversations (parent to staff, parent to parent, staff to staff) was frequent. When the parents or doctors were outside the room, a child would often become strangely quiet or say to the other chil-

* In two cases, however, the dead children's names were not taboo. But in each case, the child had been dead for a while and the parents of the three children were friends. Further, in each of these two cases the children knew that they would die and expressed this knowledge openly.

† Much of this contact came through the playgroup. The playgroup was conducted in the Oncology Clinic waiting room by the occupational therapist. The children were not forced to participate. Many remained seated with their parents in the waiting room, or in some cases (children less than five years old) went with their parents to the parents' group (Hoffman and Futterman, 1971).

dren, "Shut up! I have to listen." One child tried to conceal a tape recorder in the doctor's conference room during rounds. These children were obviously eager for information and would go to great lengths to get it.

The mass media (commercials for the leukemia foundation, medical dramas, soap operas) also contributed to their general corpus of knowledge, though more vaguely and indirectly.

STAGES OF AWARENESS

The children passed through different stages of awareness about their illness and what was happening to them. These stages and the kinds of knowledge they reflected could be arranged along a continuum.

dx	1	2	3	4	5	6
	serious illness	names of drugs and side effects	treatments, procedures, their purpose	relapse/remission cycle ($-$death)	relapse/remission cycle ($+$death)	prognosis internalized

All the children, regardless of age, reached first stage of awareness within a few weeks after diagnosis. Even the youngest children realized the seriousness of their illness rather early in the disease process. During this time, the children also accumulated information about the names of the drugs used and their side effects. By the time they reached Stage 2, they were conversant in the major drugs (especially the induction agents) and their side effects. For example, "Prednisone makes me eat like a pig and act like a brat." "Don't," in response to someone stroking his hair, "I'm getting Cytoxan." *

The third stage of awareness was marked by an understanding of the various treatments and procedures and their purposes. "They are going to give me platelets today to try to stop the bleeding. I got blood for my anemia part. After Dr. Richards looks at my bone marrow, I might get a new medicine."

By the fourth stage the children had an idea of the overall disease process. For some, this was expressed in terms of, "There are good times and bad times, but you are always sick." Others called the good and bad times by names, "remissions and relapses." At this stage the children had not yet incorporated death into the cycle.

---

* Weight gain and mood swings are common side effects of Prednisone. Alopecia is a common side effect of Cytoxan.

Incorporation of death into the cycle came in Stage 5. By then, the children had some idea of how far along they were in the relapse/remission cycle and the relationship of the drugs to the cycle. They were aware that there was a finite number of drugs, and that when these ran out death would be imminent.

But it was not until Stage 6 that this information was internalized, as compared to Stage 5, when death was still regarded as the outcome for other children. At Stage 6, their suspicions (for example, that the drugs do not last forever, that there is a reason why people bring things to me and not to my brothers and sisters) were confirmed.

ASSIMILATION, INTEGRATION AND SYNTHESIZING OF INFORMATION

There was, as has been noted, a great deal of information about procedures, drugs, and deaths circulating around the hospital and the clinic at all times, but it was not always assimilated by the child. What information was assimilated, integrated, and synthesized, and when, depended on the stage the child had reached in the awareness process. As such, the processing of information should be discussed in relation to the same continuum as that plotted for the stages of awareness.

As reflected in the continuum, information was cumulative. What the child learned at one stage was a necessary foundation for interpreting new information that would bring him to the next stage. For example, if the child had not yet reached Stage 5, or at the very least Stage 4, the fact that another child from the clinic died did not bring him to Stage 6, at which he would realize that he too would die.

Once having reached Stage 6, some children tried to revert, to act as if they were still at Stage 5, or even Stage 2. But the fact that they were at Stage 6 generally revealed itself. For example, one child was quite knowledgeable about the names of the drugs available and their side effects. It was all that he would talk about, to the point where one wondered if he knew anything more. He did, of course, as reflected in such statements as, "There are more drugs. I just don't know them all. . . . All they have to do is give the right medicine, this way. They don't always do it right."

The process of assimilation, integration, and synthesizing of information varied with the child's experience with the disease (in the subculture, if you will), not by his age. Some three and four-year-olds were at Stage 6, while some nine-year-olds, still in their first remission with few clinic visits, hence less experience, were only at Stage 2.

Proportionately, the time-lapse between the stages was the same for all children, regardless of age and/or experience. Passage from Stage 1 to Stage 2 was rather rapid. Passage through Stages 2, 3, 4, and 5 was comparatively longer. Passage from Stage 5 to Stage 6 took place in a few words once the child heard of the death of another child. All knowledge from the previous stages was quickly synthesized, often following conversations that took place when news of another child's death was revealed. For example:

> *Edward:* "Leslie died last night. I have the same thing."
> *Nurse:* "But they are trying different medicines for you."
> *Edward:* "What happens when they run out?"
> *Nurse:* "Well, maybe they will find more by then."
> *Edward:* "Oh!" (The child turned over and buried his head in the

pillow.)

COMMUNICATION IN LEUKEMIC CHILDREN

While all the children passed through the same stages of awareness, assimilating, integrating, and synthesizing similar kinds of information, some were not as direct in their expression as others.* Lack of direct expression was not necessarily an indication of lack of awareness. For example, while Martha on occasion said, "I'm dying," or "I'm going to die, you know," Betty, on going home, "buried" her paper dolls (which on an earlier occasion she had said looked the way she used to before her hair fell out) in a tissue box and referred to it as "their grave." It should not be assumed that because Betty's expression was less direct than Martha's she knew less than Martha. Many reasons might account for Betty's lack of direct expression. Betty's illness was somewhat denied by her family; the word leukemia was never mentioned in the house. Betty's mother assumed that Betty knew nothing and should not be told anything. Betty rarely spoke in the clinic or in the hospital, while the converse was true of Martha, even though Martha did not always use direct expression.

Children such as Martha often used less direct forms on different occasions and in different contexts. A child who, when critically ill, might say, "I'm going to die this time," would often regain some hope upon

* The less direct forms are what Kübler-Ross (1969) has called "symbolic expression."

going into remission: "There are more medicines left to try and even some to try again."

Some children were more direct with certain individuals than they were with others, even when talking about the same thing. The following conversation took place between the researcher and the child shortly after the child had told a visitor that he was going to die "just like Sam (the visitor's son)."

Child: "Do you drive to the hospital?"
Res.: "No, I walk."
Child: "Do you walk at night?"
Res.: "Yes. (Noting the look on his face): You wouldn't?"
Child: "No, you would get shot."
Res.: (Silence)
Child: "An ambulance would come and take you to the funeral home. And then they would drain the blood out of you and wait three days and bury you."
Res.: "That's what happens?"
Child: "I saw them do it to my grandmother."
Res.: "To your grandmother? I thought that you told me that you were here when your grandmother died." (He was.)
Child: (Quickly) "It was my grandmother. They wait three days to see if you're alive. I mean they draw blood after they wait three days." (Note: The child had been in the hospital three days. They had drawn blood and done a bone marrow that day.)
Child: (Pause) "That's what happens when you die. I'm going to get a new medicine and blood put in me tonight."

One notes, among other things, the child's heavy use of death imagery, his view of what death might be like, when to expect it, and its association with the medical procedures and care significant in leukemia therapy.

The overall quality of the communication varied in regard to what was being communicated. Conversations and nonverbal play about one's own or another child's death were characterized by a "staccato-like" quality, with periods of silence before and after statements. A child might say, "I'm never going home" or "I want to play. Children play in heaven." Conversations or play about drugs and procedures, however, were characterized by a long and detailed "monologue-like" quality.

Communication on nondisease-related matters was also often affected by the child's awareness of what was happening to him, although this was not necessarily on purpose. For example, Sandy's father was talking to another parent following a visit with the doctor. Sandy wanted to leave. Pulling on his father's sleeve to get his attention, he said, "Don't waste time." The father replied: "I'm just talking," and Sandy, with some urgency, repeated "We can't waste time!" This is not the usual way that a five-year-old tries to get his father's attention. While his intent was not to communicate the fact that he knew he would soon die, even in such seemingly unrelated moments he was expressing some awareness of his condition and what it meant. Time had taken on a meaning not usually observed in children of this age.

This type of behavior—fear of wasting time, urgency to have and do things immediately—differed from that of a normal child. It was often mentioned by parents of terminally ill children and by the staff working with them. They claimed that it was most prevalent in the child's daily life after another child had died.

COPING BEHAVIOR

The leukemic child must cope with the information that he possesses as well as with "forces and events beyond his control"—the greatest of which is death itself (Hoffman and Futterman, 1971). He must cope with the procedures, the process, the prognosis, and his anticipation of his ultimate death.

There are two levels to consider in understanding how children cope with procedures: first, the procedures themselves; second, the implications of these procedures. The range of coping behaviors was great—from open weeping to intellectualization. A child might use one or a variety of them. Alex would cry through the entire procedure, bite the doctor, and then come out to the waiting room and either bite everyone he knew or else give them "shots." Some children tried to protect themselves before the procedure. Alice would guard her room, crying and cringing under the covers whenever anyone in white approached. An older child used a more active approach, running out the side door of the clinic when the doctor came to take him for a bone marrow.

Richard refused to cry. He intellectualized the situation. His anger was not concealed, and he devised an elaborate plan for disrupting the doctors while they were doing the bone marrow. Paul, who still cried during procedures, tried to convince himself that "shots tickle." When the doctor would come, he would say, "Oh, goodie. Let's go get a shot. Shots tickle," and drag the doctor back to the treatment room by her lab coat.

All the children had some means of coping besides just "taking it." Often these ways involved other children. Regardless of their age and verbal ability, they would all engage in conversations and play about the procedures.

But for the majority, there was more to be coped with than the procedure itself. There was evidence, for example, that while the pain from the bone marrow was great, something else was bothering the child. As one child stated, "Waiting for the results is the worst part." Others expressed this same feeling nonverbally. They were often unable to eat until they heard the results.

The disease process also involved coping with threats to self-image (for example, hair loss, weight changes, mutilation, incapacity); realization of one's difference from other children (inability to attend school regularly, especially in the terminal phases; frequent hospitalizations; "my other house," etc.); unpredictability (waking with uncontrollable nosebleeds requiring hospitalization, bone pain). "You never know when you will get real sick. It messes up your plans and then nobody likes you." The range of coping behaviors was the same as that for coping with procedures (from crying to intellectualization). While it was also an area that children talked about with each other or dramatized, they did not do so as freely and for as long periods of time as they did about procedures.

The most difficult aspect of all to cope with, to talk about, to think about, once it was realized, was death itself—whether in anticipation of another child's death or after the realization of one's own prognosis. The two cannot really be separated. Through the news of another child's death, children's own suspicions found confirmation, and their realizations expression. This is indicated in conversations among the children that immediately followed the news of another child's death, in which attention was given to how the child had died and how they were different from that child. What followed was often a refocusing on the drugs being used or, more commonly, periods of withdrawal from other people (parents included), either through expressions of anger and hostility or through silence. "Then she won't cry so much and be sad." There would be occasional statements that reflected the child's awareness that he was going to die. "I'm not going home." "I'm not going to school anymore." "I won't be here for your birthday.'' The subject of another's death often never came up again, nor did a direct participation-invited conversation about the child's own death.

CONCLUSION

Dying is difficult to do alone, and yet in so many ways it cannot be shared. If anyone is aware of this, it is the dying child. He knows and observes the restrictions against speaking about death. If he tries to break taboos, he rarely does so directly and then, perhaps, only in a highly symbolic manner. But this lack of direct expression and the infrequency of communication do not necessarily mean that he is unaware of his prognosis and of what is happening. He goes through what can often be a long and painful process to discover what it all means. In this process he assimilates, integrates, and synthesizes a great deal of information from a variety of sources. With his arrival at each new stage comes a greater understanding of the disease and its prognosis. This leaves him then with a great deal to cope with, and it is all a part of his anticipatory grief process.

For the most part the stricken child relies on his own resources, but he attempts also to enlist the support of others (including peers, parents, staff, and even the researcher). The researchers' and clinicians' task is to investigate by listening. The child is not always asking nor always talking about dying, even when he knows the prognosis. Much of his time is spent in becoming aware, putting together, and probing for more information. A child who is terminally ill seldom tells what he knows in ways easy to understand. But when one learns to listen and take cues from him, it is soon realized that the child does know the truth, and this is often more than can be borne.

REFERENCES

Agranoff, Arthur, and Arthur Mauer, "What Should the Child with Leukemia Be Told?" *American Journal of Diseases of Children, 110:*231, 1965.

Alexander, I. E., and A. M., Alderstein, "Affective Responses to the Concept of Death in a Population of Children and Early Adolescents," in R. Fulton, ed., *Death and Identity*. Chicago: Aldine Press, 1965.

Anthony, S., *The Child's Discovery of Death*. New York: Harcourt Brace, 1940.

Bard, M., "The Price of Survival," in A. L. Strauss, ed., *Where Medicine Fails*. Chicago: Aldine Press, 1970.

Binger, C. M., A. R. Albin, R. C. Feuerstein, J. H. Kushner, S. Zoger, and C. Mikkelsen, "Childhood Leukemia: Emotional Impact on Patient and Family," *New England Journal of Medicine, 280:*414, 1969.

Friedman, S. B., *et al.,* "Behavioral Observations on Parents Anticipating the Death of a Child," *Pediatrics, 32:*610, 1963.

Friedman, S. B., M. Karon, and G. Goldsmith, *Childhood Leukemia—A Pamphlet for Parents.* Washington, D.C.: U.S. Government Printing Office, 1969.

Futterman, E. H., and I. Hoffman, "Transient School Phobia in a Leukemic Child," *Journal of the American Academy of Child Psychiatry, 9:*477, 1970.

Gartley, W., and M. Bernasconi, "The Concept of Death in Children," *Journal of Genetic Psychology, 110:*71, 1967.

Glaser, B., and A. Strauss, *Awareness of Dying.* Chicago: Aldine Press, 1965.

—— *Time for Dying.* Chicago: Aldine Press, 1966.

Gorer, G., *Death, Grief, and Mourning.* New York: Doubleday, 1965.

Hoffman, I., and E. H. Futterman, "Coping with Waiting: Psychiatric Intervention and Study in the Waiting Room of a Pediatric Oncology Clinic," *Comprehensive Psychiatry, 12:*67, 1971.

Karon, M., and J. Vernick, "An Approach to Emotional Support of Fatally Ill Children," *"Clinical Pediatrics, 7:*274, 1968.

Knudson, A. G., and J. M. Natterson, "Participation of Parents in the Hospital Care of Fatally Ill Children," *Pediatrics, 26:*482, 1960.

Kübler-Ross, E., *On Death and Dying.* New York, Macmillan, 1969.

——Lecture to Center for the Continuing Education of the Ministry, and a personal conversation, Champaign, Ill., 1971.

Nagy, M., "The Child's View of Death," in H. Feifel, ed., *The Meaning of Death.* New York, McGraw-Hill, 1959.

Natterson, J. M., and A. G. Knudson, "Observations Concerning the Fear of Death in Fatally Ill Children and Their Parents," in R. Fulton, ed., *Death and Identity.* Chicago: Aldine Press, 1965.

Piaget, J., *The Language and Thought of the Child.* New York: Harcourt Brace, 1952.

Richmond, J. B., and H. A. Waisman, "Psychologic Aspects of Management of Children with Malignant Diseases," *American Journal of Diseases of Children, 89:*42, 1955.

Rosenblum, J., "How to Explain Death to a Child," *International Order of the Golden Rule.*

Solnit, A. J., and M. Green, "The Pediatric Management of the Dying Child. Part II: The Child's Reaction to the Fear of Dying," in A. Solnit and S. Provence, eds., *Modern Perspectives in Child Development.* New York: International Universities Press, 1963.

——"Psychological Considerations in the Management of Deaths on Pediatric Hospital Services. Part I," *Pediatrics, 24:*106, 1959.

Toch, R., "Management of the Child with a Fatal Disease," *Clinical Pediatrics, 3:*418, 1964.

Vernick, J., and M. Karon, "Who's Afraid of Death on a Leukemic Ward?" *American Journal of Diseases of Children, 109:*393, 1965.

Wahl, C. W., "The Fear of Death," in H. Feifel, ed., *The Meaning of Death.* New York: McGraw-Hill, 1959.

Wright, H., *Recording and Analyzing Child Behavior.* New York: Harper & Row, 1967.

21

Implications for Therapy in the Pediatric Patient

Martin I. Lorin

Although cystic fibrosis might be used as a general model for the study of anticipatory grief in a fatal childhood illness, various critical aspects of this disease are so unique that it is actually a more suitable model for the study of certain specific questions only. In this discussion, the focus is on a single question: How does anticipatory grief affect the pediatrician's ability to carry out a treatment program? Two peculiar characteristics of cystic fibrosis make it an especially pertinent model for this question: first, the genetic basis of cystic fibrosis often results in more than one afflicted child in a single family; second, the treatment program prescribed is especially difficult and demanding.

To understand the phenomenon of anticipatory grief, or for that matter, any psychological or emotional reactions in patients with cystic fibrosis or their families, one must have at least a fundamental concept of the disease itself. It is necessary, therefore, to introduce this discussion of anticipatory grief with a brief description of cystic fibrosis.

Cystic fibrosis is a genetically determined, chronic, potentially lethal disease, for which there is, at present, considerable palliative therapy, but no true cure. The disease is transmitted as an autosomal recessive, in which situation both parents are carriers, although they themselves are entirely free of clinical disease. On an average, one out of every four children born to such a marriage will be afflicted with cystic fibrosis. The disease itself affects all the exocrine glands of the body, with major clinical manifestations in the pulmonary and gastrointestinal systems. Cough, sputum production, diarrhea, and malnutrition are the most common symptoms. The usual cause of death is progressive pulmonary disability secondary to relentless pulmonary infection. Early in the disease the patient may feel relatively well, with only a mild, chronic cough as an indication of the underlying disease. Eventually, coughing increases and produces large amounts of foul sputum. The patient appears and feels chronically ill. Finally, respiratory insufficiency develops and the victim is unable to function normally, eventually dying of ventilatory failure. During the final phase, which may last weeks, or even years, the patient is debilitated, dyspneic, racked by painful, spasmodic coughing, and by feelings of asphyxia.

Throughout all this, there is the need for a unique treatment program—day after day, week after week, year after year. The patient sleeps in a mist tent at night. He receives aerosol treatments, two, three, or four times a day. Following each treatment, the parent performs postural drainage, positioning and clapping the child's chest to assist in the evacuation of sputum. Each aerosol treatment requires ten to fifteen minutes, and each postural drainage session fifteen to twenty minutes. The time required for these treatments, the obligatory physical contact, and the forced interdependency of parent and child, combine to make the treatment program a potential focus of tension, hostility, and frustration. Both the disease and the treatment are, each in its own right, major emotional stresses.

In the past, cystic fibrosis was almost always fatal within the first few years of life. Today, with proper therapy, the majority of patients survive early childhood, and more and more such patients are reaching adolescence and adulthood. Some are able to function reasonably well; others are respiratory cripples. For any, the chance of attaining the proverbial four score and ten is nil.

The two major factors in determing whether or not anticipatory grief will interfere with therapy are the premorbid family personality and the time of onset of the anticipatory grief reaction.

By premorbid family personality is meant the family structure, the individual personalities and interactions of family members, prior to the onset of the anticipatory grief reaction. As explained above, the treatment program is a focal point of stress. The stable, well-adjusted family may rise to the challenge with truly magnificent camaraderie, self-sacrifice, and love, while the marginally adjusted, unstable, hostile family may disintegrate into a mass of hate, guilt, self-incrimination, and despair, all focused around the treatments.

If the premorbid family structure is not charged with guilt and hostility, the anticipatory grief reaction can be expressed as sorrow and sadness, but need not be incompatible with normal function and the carrying out of a full therapeutic program. If, however, the family situation is loaded with hostility and resentment, the anticipatory grief reaction is likely to mobilize guilt feelings, with resultant depression and an inability to function. The parents are overwhelmed by guilt and depression, which prevent them from exercising proper control over the child, who then escapes from therapy, much as a normal child might avoid cleaning up his room. The parent cannot tolerate the child's discomforts, real or imagined, and superficial overindulgence alternates with outbursts of hostility. The treatment program is demolished as the parents realize that their failure to carry out the treatment program will hasten the end, and guilt becomes magnified. In such a situation, anticipatory grief becomes a destructive force, not only separating parent and child emotionally, but also interfering with therapy and permitting the disease to run its course unchecked.

For many families, the premorbid personality has been determined in part by previous experience with a child dying of cystic fibrosis. By virtue of the genetic nature of the disease, many parents have more than one child with cystic fibrosis. It is not uncommon to see families with three or four afflicted children, families in which the parents may ultimately witness the deaths of all their children. The onset of anticipatory grief is likely to be earlier with each subsequent child. Having seen the death of an earlier child with cystic fibrosis, the parents find it harder to deny that the same fate will overcome the presently ill child. They recall how they had hoped, in vain, that the first child would live to see the day when this disease would be curable. Hope is more difficult now. Escape from reality is harder and can be achieved only by extensive rationalization and a fragile patchwork of denial.

The earlier the onset of an anticipatory grief reaction, the more likely it is to interfere seriously with treatment. In the usual situation, a significant anticipatory grief reaction does not develop until the disease is advanced and the patient is either very ill or terminal. However, some parents may begin anticipatory grieving as soon as the diagnosis is first established. This is especially likely to occur in parents who are already emotionally insecure and in those who have lost other children to cystic fibrosis. An anticipatory grief reaction at this time may prevent the treatment program from getting off to a sound start. To the parents, the child is doomed or already dead, and treatment will be of no avail, only adding to and prolonging the child's misery. Usually the mother becomes more depressed. She cannot function, is slow, disorganized, uninterested, and tired. In this condition, she is easily overwhelmed by the demands of the treatment program. She feels unable both to stop the disease that will kill her child and to carry out the treatments that might postpone the inevitable. It is a true test of the physician's art to guide such a parent through this type of reaction to a realistic, yet not defeated, outlook. Although life will be short, the child is still very much alive. Much joy, love, and even hope is yet to come before the end. The parents must be helped to realize that although life will be limited it need not be empty; and that although treatment cannot promise a normal life span, it can extend the period of useful life and normal function. They must be helped to maintain a meaningful, active, and loving relationship with their afflicted child.

Anticipatory grief reactions occurring very late in the disease, when the patient is obviously terminal, are not inappropriate. Although they may, if excessive, deprive those involved of a meaningful relationship, they are not likely to interfere significantly with treatment. The patient is at this stage usually hospitalized, and treatment is not dependent upon active participation by the parents. In the final days or hours, the patient is often comatose. Vigorous therapy is discontinued and all efforts are directed specifically toward alleviating pain and discomfort.

Perhaps the most difficult time to handle a severe anticipatory grief reaction, and the time when it is most likely to interfere with treatment, is when the disease is advanced and the patient disabled but not terminal. For the parents, the sense of impending loss is heightened. They see before them the failure of treatment and cannot appreciate that therapy has prolonged the child's life. They can see only that now their child is dying. They may visualize the disabled, dying child as already dead, and ask what value therapy has for the dead. Only by helping the parents work through the anticipatory grief reaction and bringing it into proper perspective can the physician hope to reestablish an effective therapeutic program. It should be emphasized to the parents that properly conceived and properly executed treatment can actually keep the patient more comfortable, as well as possibly prolong life. (This is not true for all diseases, but is valid for cystic fibrosis.) It should also be explained to the parents that the professional staff is aware of and understands their point of view, and that a time may well come when it will be wisest to restrict or discontinue therapy. But such a time is not during a still effective therapeutic program.

In summary, anticipatory grief, if premature, excessive, inappropriate, or disorganized, can be an obstacle to proper therapy in patients with cystic fibrosis. This is heightened and accentuated by the difficulty and complexity of the treatment program in this disease. Such a phenomenon, however, must be viewed as part of the total psychosocial adjustment of the patient and his family, and cannot be examined as an isolated occurrence.

22

Anticipatory Grief and Going on the "Danger List" *

John E. Schowalter

Many hospitals have an official designation for patients who are believed to be in danger of dying. Various names are used, such as "the danger list," "the critically ill list," "the seriously ill list," and so on. This designation is manifested variously in different hospitals, sometimes overtly by putting the patients' names on a board for all to see outside the nursing stations, sometimes more privately. The author's position is that specifically labeling critically ill patients on pediatric wards is psychologically more damaging than helpful.

THE DANGER LIST

For purposes of this discussion the procedure followed on the pediatric wards at the Yale-New Haven Hospital will be described. The Administrative Nursing Manual on each floor outlines this procedure but does not define who should be placed on the Danger List (D.L.), only that they be "critically ill." Although often first suggested by a nurse, putting a child on the D.L. must be implemented by a physician's written order. Wards vary in how freely they use the designation. For example, on some floors all pa-

* This research was supported by the Children's Bureau, United States Department of Health, Education and Welfare, the Connecticut Department of Health and United States Public Health Service Grant 5T1 MH 5443-20.

tients are placed on the D.L. before undergoing open-heart surgery, while on other floors this is not routine. Once the physician's request is written and the parents have been notified, the ward secretary telephones the order to the hospital administration. This call initiates a number of communications: the parents are allowed unlimited visiting privileges; the hospital switchboard is told so that this designation can be given to those phoning in regard to the child's condition; and, if the patient is Roman Catholic, a priest is notified so that he can administer the Sacraments of the Sick. It is not at all routine to tell the child. On the ward the nurses paste a red star on the patient's metal chart cover, one on the name slip inserted in the hallway census board, on the doctors' order sheet, and on the patient's index card in the nursing "Kardex." If the patient is removed from the D.L., the administration is notified and a blue star is placed partially over each of the above-mentioned red stars.

Pediatric house officers are often vague about their reasons for placing a child on the D.L. The unlimited visiting privileges are often mentioned. Some erroneously believe that it is important legally to place a critically ill child on the D.L., and that the hospital is somehow more liable to possible legal action if the patient dies prior to being put on the D.L. Other house officers feel it is bad form professionally when a child dies when not on the D.L. They fear that such a death might possibly cause superiors to believe that the house officer was caught by surprise and was not sufficiently aware of the seriousness of the patient's condition. In rare cases, putting a patient on the D.L. is used as a relatively impersonal way to convey to parents the imminence of their child's death.

In order to learn the administrative reasoning behind having the D.L., the author questioned the hospital's Administrative Director for Pediatrics. He said that the two main reasons were to allow families unrestricted visiting privileges and to alert the switchboard so those inquiring about the patient's condition could be informed of its seriousness. He concluded that, as with so many hospital procedures, "probably the real why is lost in history."

REACTIONS TO PLACEMENT ON THE DANGER LIST

Although it is relatively unusual for a child or his parents to comment directly about being put on the D.L., it would be naive to assume that the red stars are not accompanied by changes in attitude and by an effect on the

process of anticipatory mourning. Examples of reactions to the pronounce-
ment of the patient's new status will now be discussed in terms of the patients, their parents, the staff, and the other patients on the ward.

Patients' Reactions

By the time a patient is placed on the D.L., he is almost always bedridden and he may be lethargic or semiconscious. All these children know they
are gravely ill, and a fairly large number, at least among the older ones,
probably fear that they will die. Nonetheless, most do notice the red star on
their chart or name tag and occasionally ask about it. This question, the
equivalent of asking whether they are going to die, is very embarrassing for
the staff members, who sometimes ignore the query or answer with a joking
euphemism.

A thirteen-year-old boy, dying of leukemia, was placed on the D.L. He
discovered the red star beside his name and asked what it meant. The author
said it meant that he was very ill and indicated to the staff that he required
special care and attention. The boy began to cry, saying he didn't want extra
care and attention, and wanted only to get well. This experience accentuated
the fact that while the Danger List acts as an alert for the hospital personnel,
it might also augment the fears of the patient. After all, the patient is not
primarily interested in care—he is receiving that. He is interested in positive
results, and being put on the Danger List only emphasizes that previous care
has not produced the desired results.

The greatest impact on the patient is, of course, not the presence or absence of red stars but the change in attitude exhibited by those who care for
and about him. For Catholic patients it also means the Sacraments of the
Sick, a ritual which for children is often fraught more with terror than with
comfort.

Parents' Reactions

The decision to place their child on the Danger List and the way this is
communicated often affect the parents' process of anticipatory mourning.
Parents are usually stunned by this palpable evidence of their child's impending death. Although occasionally the action is useful in breaking
through pathologic denial, more often the designation is experienced by the
parents as just one more of fate's insults which is out of their control.

Anticipatory mourning by parents for their dying child is marked by varying degrees of decathexis or withdrawal. While this withdrawal may be helpful to the mourner, it is often experienced as rejection by the patient. At times parental withdrawal is accelerated when a child is placed on the D.L. As one parent put it, he felt that his daughter was "tagged for death" and used this as an excuse ("after all the doctor did it and he must know") for giving up all hope and abbreviating his visiting times. Other parents have said that they visited less after their child was placed on the D.L. because they were embarrassed about what other patients' parents would think and how they would act toward them now that it was common knowledge that the child would probably die. This wish to keep the child's dying a private matter may extend to phone calls as well. Some parents resent the hospital's giving friends and relatives information that the patient is on the danger list. They assert that when a child's designation goes from "stable" or even "critical" to "Danger List," most people assume the outcome will be swift and fatal. Many parents feel that the dissemination of such information should be a parental prerogative.

The securing of unlimited visiting privileges for families of patients on the D.L. is of no advantage in pediatrics at the author's particular hospital, since visiting hours are already unlimited during the day and one parent is allowed to stay with each child during the night.

Staff Reactions

When asked, nurses and house officers say they do not usually give much thought to putting a patient on the D.L. The child's condition is deteriorating, and the action seems the right administrative thing to do to make this fact known. Occasionally, but fortunately not often, the "red star" is used to break the news of a fatal prognosis to the parents. Certainly, such news should be communicated in a more personal way.

In understaffed hospitals, a Danger List of those requiring special attention on each ward is used to alert those house officers who "float" on the night shift. This use is not necessary in hospitals with house staff sufficient to provide coverage by physicians who are familiar with all the patients under their care.

Comments from nurses and house officers, however, make it clear that placing a child on the D.L. does not necessarily mean that the staff will spend more time with the patient. Indeed, the opposite may occur. Nurses are especially aware that once a child is placed on the D.L. they often wish to avoid being assigned to that patient. This reaction seems to be a combination of feelings of impending defeat, plus a reluctance to be present and caring for a patient at the time of his death.

Reactions of Other Patients and Their Parents

The significance of the red stars is not lost on many of the other patients (especially the older ones) and their parents. Although at times the new designation causes peers and other parents to withdraw from the dying child and his parents, this is seldom a major problem. Usually at this time parents and patient draw closer together with other family members and friends and rely less on acquaintances made recently on the ward. A larger problem occurs when the red stars initiate a sudden outpouring of curiosity from other patients and their parents. Although such attention is usually well-meant, most families wish their child's dying to be a private matter and want their privacy respected. Unsolicited questions and concern can therefore complicate a parent's process of anticipatory mourning.

Some patients and their parents react in a different manner. The red star is a visible reminder that if death approaches one patient, it can overcome others as well. Children ask their parents the meaning of the star, and must be given an answer or an evasion. Parents, too, feel the impact of this proximity to death. As one of the more literate parents put it, "When I saw the star on Phillip's name tag, I couldn't help wondering if the bell wasn't tolling also for our little Steven."

CONCLUSIONS

Many hospitals have a list similar to the Yale-New Haven Hospital Danger List, an official designation for patients who are critically or terminally ill. From a psychological point of view, the author believes these lists to be more harmful than helpful. Taken as a signal for withdrawal or of defeat ("tagged for death"), and as a threat to the patient's and family's privacy, such a designation artificially and detrimentally impinges on the process of anticipatory mourning.

On the wards of hospitals with insufficient medical coverage some method may be necessary to acquaint a "floating" house officer with those patients most needing attention, and this information can be conveyed via the daily nursing report. In any case, the list should be as inconspicuous as possible. Names on hallway clipboards, red stars, and other obvious symbols of the patient's critical condition only make a tense and tragic time more difficult. Consideration should be given to dropping or modifying the use of the Danger List.

Finally, the relatively recent innovation of intensive care units in many hospitals makes a D.L. less necessary. If such units are available, patients can be transferred from the wards to these facilities when extraordinary care is required.

23

Cancer in Adolescents: The Symptom Is the Thing *

Marjorie M. Plumb and Jimmie Holland

Here, verbatim, are the words of some young people who have cancer:

"I don't worry about anything unless maybe I'm bleeding all over the place . . ."

". . . but when my hair started to fall out, that was *really* rotten . . ."

"The thing that got me the most was the wheelchair. I couldn't tolerate the idea of some kid pushing me around the block. I couldn't face it . . ."

And here are the words of some parents of young people with cancer:

"She looked so bad that I said, 'I'll take the morning off and drive you,' and she said, 'No, I'll take a bus.' *Physically* she would have been better off if I drove her, but not emotionally."

"For a while there, he couldn't button his shirt; he couldn't go to the bathroom—it really got bad, it was miserable then . . ."

Such words illustrate a major thesis of this chapter—that in the psychological course of cancer in adolescence and early adulthood (1) the specific symptom is above all the focal point around which the behaviors and feel-

* The authors gratefully acknowledge the assistance of Josephine Holmes, M.S.W., Department of Medicine "A," Roswell Park Memorial Institute, in carrying out this study. It was supported in part by U.S.P.H.S. Grant #5T21 MH 12194.

ings of patients and their significant others revolve at any given point in time, and (2) this is true regardless of whether the symptom is a disagreeable byproduct of treatment or brutally mirrors the disease process itself.

This report is based on observation of young patients of Medicine "A," Roswell Park Memorial Institute, the cancer facility for New York State in Buffalo. Thirty-nine patients were studied, twenty-six boys and thirteen girls, and twenty parents or, in a few instances, spouses of these patients. Over two-thirds of the patients were between fifteen and nineteen years of age when first admitted; the remainder were twenty. The observations are thus of late adolescents and young adults admitted to an adult ward, and no doubt differ from observations which might be made of an early adolescent group in a general hospital setting. The index diagnosis for the patient group was acute leukemia, in twenty cases. Seven patients carried a diagnosis of osteogenic sarcoma. The remaining cases represented a variety of solid tumors and Hodgkin's disease. Table 1 shows the distribution of sex, age at admission, and diagnosis.

Psychiatric interviews with these patients and their significant others were held both on the inpatient service and in the outpatient clinic (some patients were seen in both). Stages of disease ranged from very early, with diagnostic work-up in progress, to late, within a few days of death. Consent for the interviews was obtained in all cases from patients, parents, and staff. Self-ratings of depression, plus interviewer ratings of depression/anxiety,

TABLE 1. DIAGNOSIS, AGE, AND SEX OF ADOLESCENT PATIENTS

Diagnosis	Total	M	F	Age at Admission at RPMI					
				15	16	17	18	19	20
Acute leukemia	20	16	4		3	5	3	3	6
Osteogenic sarcoma	7	6	1		2	1	1	1	2
Hodgkin's disease	3		3		1	1			1
Lymphosarcoma	2	1	1	1			1		
Malignant melanoma	2		2						2
Neuroblastoma	1		1					1	
Reticulum cell sarcoma	1	1						1	
Embryonal phabdomyosarcoma	1	1		1					
Astrocytoma	1		1				1		
Embryonal cell carcinoma of the testicle	1	1					1		
Totals	39	26	13	2	6	9	5	6	11

obtained in another study, were made available for fourteen patients and for twenty parents or spouses. Finally, nurses' observations of patient behavior were available for six patients who had been placed in germ-free isolation units.

From a psychological point of view, the situation of these patients is a complex one to analyze. During adolescence, the common forms of cancer—acute leukemia, osteogenic sarcoma, Hodgkin's disease, melanoma, and ovarian and testicular tumors—are protean in manifestations. There is, then, a great biological diversity of possible abnormal change in patients' mental and physical functioning. In a particular patient, such abnormal changes will depend on the specific nature of the cancer, its site, its treatment, and its course. These will determine what the patient and his parents must adjust to. Some changes, of course, impinge more insistently on the patient's awareness than others, some implying a greater lethal threat and some posing a greater threat of violating self-esteem.

Since a symptom is a patient's subjective assessment of abnormal change, it is obvious that the same change may be interpreted by physician or parent in the same or in different ways. The interpretations made by each of the three will vary as a function of such factors as psychic needs, factual knowledge, and the presence or absence of other changes. Changes, in other words, can be endowed with different meanings by the same and different persons, and by any one person with several levels of meaning simultaneously. Thus, hair loss resulting from treatment may be seen as a blatant reminder that the patient has a life-threatening disease or as evidence that he is receiving a powerful therapeutic drug, or both. Psychically for the patient it may be easier to dwell on loss of hair than possible loss of life or, alternatively, it may in fact be more deeply troubling than some hazy image of a future state. What is talked about among physician, patient, and parent will depend also on how symptoms are interpreted. Thus, it may be acceptable to discuss the fact that the patient is in pain. If the pain is due to injection with a large needle, it may be easy to speak of the source of the pain. But if the pain suggests that the disease has spread, this may not be openly discussed. At all phases of the course of disease, the symptom pre-empts attention, and its interpretation molds and colors both private hopes and interpersonal exchange.

A second thesis of this chapter is that current conceptions of the psychological impact of cancer during adolescence tend to be oversimplified because so much interest has been invested in but one of the possible courses of the disease. *Love Story* (Segal, 1970) to the contrary, cancer is not always rapidly fatal in adolescence or young adulthood. But that cancer *can* kill is only too obvious. In fact, we know that in adolescence and early adulthood the group of diseases collectively called "cancer" is the most frequent cause of death by disease. Yet, swift death is not inevitable, and we need no longer automatically mark the adolescent with cancer as a dying person. Though parents and child alike must deal with this possible outcome, and anticipatory grief phenomena are present in both at the time of diagnosis, the average period of partial health and even full remission from disease is lengthening, in some instances dramatically so. As treatment measures improve, an interval we may characterize as uncertainty of outcome, shared by the physician as well as by adolescent and parent, is coming into sharper perspective.

The psychological management of this period of shared uncertainty of outcome demands special study. It is a time when the patient may be coming to the clinic and requiring brief hospitalizations for treatment. Often symptoms secondary to treatment occupy the psychological center stage; in other cases, symptoms may be absent and intermittently the patient seems completely normal. There is a powerful sense of having survived which often overrides lurking thoughts of doom. Given a period such as this, clinicians may be better advised to date the psychological dying process not from day of diagnosis but instead from a later time in the clinical course when the disease is uncontrolled and the outcome all too clear.

In general, and briefly, the cancer patient may be said to follow one of four possible clinical courses, each associated with its own characteristic psychological experience (see Figure 1). Clinical Course A is that in which early cancer yields to surgery, radiation, or chemotherapy. The patient is elated, while at the same time highly fearful that symptoms may reappear. When some interval of time has passed without recurrence (and the length of the required interval will depend on the nature of the particular cancer) we say that the patient is cured. Gradually the individual incorporates his frightening experience, and though left with nagging concern about his vulnerability, he basically resumes his previous life-style. Because our society is one which still places a stigma on cancer, the patient usually does not talk much about what has happened to him. As we come to stigmatize cancer less, such patients will be more ready to speak out, and public awareness of cancer deaths will be counterbalanced by known cures.

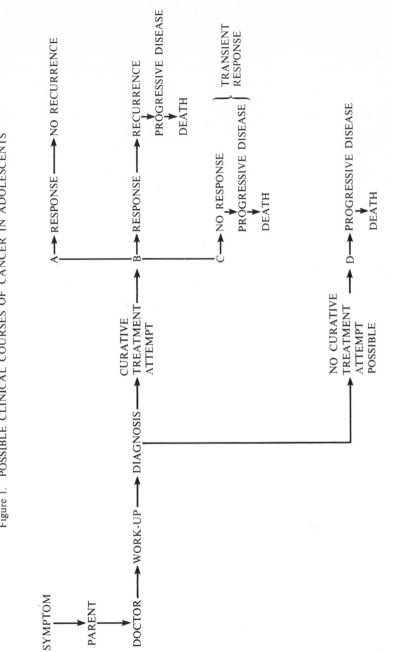

Figure 1. POSSIBLE CLINICAL COURSES OF CANCER IN ADOLESCENTS

In Clinical Course C, unlike A, diagnosis is followed by a curative attempt which achieves no significant positive results, and hopes are distressingly transient. Patients in Course C never experience the response indicative of possible cure. They may or may not acknowledge the inevitability of death. Some make their peace with it, others not.

Course D differs from C in that, at the time of diagnosis, the disease process is already so far advanced that no major curative attempt is possible. With at best a fleeting response to drugs, the course may be rapid, at times telescoped into a matter of weeks. In her conceptualization of the psychological stages of dying, Kübler-Ross (1969) seems to have addressed herself chiefly to these latter two unremitting courses, C and D, which are by no means the only or the most common courses.

We have left Clinical Course B for the final and most complete description because it is this course that is most conspicuous in adolescence, and the one followed or being followed by most of the patient group observed here. A definitive treatment is given, stressful though it may be. For a considerable time—especially in the beginning months or years of what we have called the period of shared uncertainty of outcome—response is good. The adolescent appears healthy and resumes normal activities. The watchful parents begin to breathe more easily again. Yet, this is a period of grace only, and metastatic or progressive disease soon becomes apparent. The recurrence is all the more devastating for the adolescent and his parents because it abruptly indicates that the prognosis is far poorer than they had hoped. Newer treatment procedures are tried, and new and experimental drugs used. Hope surges at the start of each regimen, but depression is severe when each fails. Patients may acquire a remarkable sophistication about available drugs. They will say, "Well, I've had X and Y and now all that's left is Z." They will know that so far there is no drug beyond Z. But some reprieves are won, and only gradually may it become apparent that outcome is no longer entirely uncertain but as certain as any prediction can be. Even then, few give up the fight altogether. Patients and parents say urgently, "Try anything, anything that has a glimmer of a chance." One father, for example, had brought his son 2,000 miles to the Institute after being told by a physician in another state, "Your son has tumors in both lungs and has fourteen weeks to live." He said, "Doctor, don't hand me that crap 'cause we're not going to do it that way." Though the patient in question was still alive many months later, there does come a day when all procedures have been exhausted. Koop (1969) has commented that the cancer patient dies twice, once at diagnosis and again at actual demise. But in Koop's sense, adolescents and their parents may indeed "die" each time there is a relapse from remission—and in acute leukemia today several remissions may be induced.

In the beginning of Course B, as in any other, is the symptom. Sometimes onset is insidiously slow, sometimes abrupt. Adolescent patients may describe their experiences in this way:

"I was short of breath, but I figured I was just out of shape for the winter. . . . I was working in this grocery store, and it seemed like for no reason my knees ached something awful. . . . I started having these headaches but otherwise I was fine. . . . I was healthy, normal, great all along, and all of a sudden this terrible cough hit."

Like the patients, the parents in speaking of this time over and again marvel at what had been the vigor of the adolescent before his illness, and often he is seen as special—he was the athlete, the one child in the family who didn't need glasses, the one always on the social go, the one who helped out most with chores, the bright one. Their words have a eulogizing quality, so perhaps this is anticipatory grief. Or a perceptual contrast effect may bias the retrospective account. Just as likely, all that is said is true.

The parents say that at the first sign of disease the adolescent comes to them with one symptom or another, an indication that something is wrong. From the parental perspective, the symptom may not seem serious enough at first to warrant fuss, but sooner or later a decision is made to see a doctor. Though the adolescent may now be acutely ill, few families suspect that what is wrong is so dire as cancer. They still may not suspect, even when the doctor calls urgently for X-rays or special blood tests in a hospital. Later, looking back, parents often blame themselves for not detecting symptoms sooner. Many times in the course of the adolescent's illness they will blame themselves for errors of judgment and seek ways to undo the past.

Depending on how physically debilitated he is, the adolescent at this time of diagnostic work-up will feel emotions ranging from mild bewilderment to utter confusion and terror. The suddenness of having to go to the hospital for tests is itself a shock. One fifteen-year-old boy reported that his mother had telephoned him at a dance to say that the next day he would be hospitalized. He thought this was "weird, but I still didn't think it was anything big." There is an aura of unreality around what happens so fast. For many adolescents, this can be their first hospital experience.

What doctors say or should say when a cancer diagnosis has been confirmed has been much discussed (Glaser, 1966; Vernick and Karon, 1965; Hoerr, 1963; Oken, 1961; Litin, 1960). Current consensus seems to be that the patient, in general, should be told the truth, though perhaps not the whole truth. In the case of an adolescent, the communication problem is especially delicate. Medical ethics assure that someone in the family is told, typically the parent. The adolescent is not a young child to be diverted while doctor talks to Mommy; nor is he an independent adult. He is thought to be vulnerable, but known to be sensitive to cues. Then, too, while the physician may be persuaded of the merits of frankness, parents may not. For the parent, deciding whether or not to send an adolescent to a specialized cancer facility may revolve in part around the fact that such a move will tell the adolescent he has cancer. The parent may feel that although he has failed to shield the child from having cancer, at least he can spare him knowledge of it.

The should-we-tell-him question is but one of many with which the parent will face the physician at this juncture. There will be also the couldn't-it-be-a-mistake question, the why-is-it-happening-to-us question, the what-do-we-do-now question, and above all, the will-he-die question. All of these involve requests for far more than factual information, and the physician must be prepared for symptoms of emotional and mental disorganization in the parents if he is to aid them and thus the patient. By clarifying gently that for the moment what-do-we-do-now is the central question, the physician may both expedite treatment and enable parents to cope with their emotions. A useful position to take is that, although the situation is difficult, the parents can and will rise to it. They will not disintegrate in crisis. All that is done at this time is vital spadework, preparation for the formation of the therapeutic alliance of physician, patient, and adolescent which is so crucial throughout the course of illness.

The physician who conveys the diagnosis is typically the one most familiar to the family. Although he is the first physician to feel this particular family's pain, in all probability it will in time be experienced by several. The conveying of the diagnosis is prototypic of many encounters to follow as the disease continues. The same agonizing questions will be heard again and again. At a time of relapse, a parent asks, "How can I tell her she still has things to face?" Or, "Was it something I did or something in my blood stream that did this? Is it your own blood or your own line or what?"

So the parents are told and, in one manner or another, the adolescent.

Rarely does telling the adolescent patient appear to be what might be called a managed revelation. Parents may tell one part, the physician another. The adolescent is becoming increasingly aware of a charged atmosphere, if nothing else, and extraneous factors enter in. A sixteen-year-old, sent to the hospital for tests, discovered his diagnosis traumatically when he walked out of his room to a nursing station. The station happened to be empty but his chart was on the desk. He read that he had "probable leukemia." Starting to shake, he telephoned his mother, who told him absolutely that he had no such thing as leukemia. He thought 'that's a lot of bull, I've got cancer.' It is of course a possibility that the adolescent, however he is told, will reject the diagnosis. An eighteen-year-old girl said, "I figured the doctor had to be wrong because I thought only little kids got leukemia." And a younger girl who had just come through a severe episode of illness with acute leukemia remarked, "Wow, that was really bad there. I *might* have had leukemia." It is important to note that these patients were in a large cancer facility surrounded by others with similar disease. The young patient hospitalized in a general hospital may have far less confrontation with the nature of his illness.

By and large, the psychological stress for parents at the time of diagnosis appears to be greater than for the adolescent, perhaps because the parent has both a more realistic comprehension of its possible implications and also because the probability is much greater that he has seen death at firsthand before. For example, the biological mother of a young girl had died in her twenties of cancer. Although the father had been long since happily remarried, the diagnosis of leukemia in the daughter not only precipitated new stress but also reactivated old tensions. The daughter, who did not remember her mother, did not seem disturbed per se by having the same disease since "it was a completely different kind of cancer." The father, however, was incapacitated for several days, and barely able to enter his daughter's hospital room.

Crucial to morale is the decision the family makes of how to share the terrible emotional burden of the illness. One sixteen-year-old's account of this is graphic but not atypical: "We kind of looked at each other and knew we had to stick together. Nobody could fall apart. We decided we'd have faith in the doctors and we'd stick together." Repeatedly throughout the course of the illness one hears expressions of the meaningfulness of this mutual support. "I never knew parents could be such a help until I had this."

"That kid has so much guts! If he'd given up, I might have given up, too."
Although parents may at times be inept, oversolicitous, tongue-tied, or irritable, if there is this fundamental sense of "sticking together" cancer can be
borne.

Mutual support does not necessarily require that life expectancy and
death be openly or fully discussed. Some adolescents and their parents are
able to do this. Whether or not it is done appears to be a function of the
parent's tolerance as well as the adolescent's. It may be observed that the
parent with this capacity is more often the father than the mother. If this is
true, it may be because opportunities for escape into outside distraction (job,
etc.) are often more frequent for the father. He often feels guilty about this,
but his emotional reserves may become greater as a result. Temperament
and self-confidence rather than sex of parent are, however, much more powerful determinants of willingness to discuss the outlook.

Once a remission is induced, the adolescent's major concern shifts from
fear of death to an acute sense of being different, different from his former
self and different from his peers. He may, in fact, be visibly, conspicuously
different from his former self because of amputation or alopecia. Even apart
from such drastic changes, a boy may be sensitive to weight loss which has
shrunken a formerly athletic physique, so important to self-esteem in the
high-school world. Weakness and fatigue are felt as humiliating; and the
hovering protectiveness of parents may only gall the patient. Word of the
adolescent's condition has doubtless spread, and it seems to him as though
everyone in the world knows and is either sorry for him (and thus somehow
entitled to lord it over him) or does not know what to do about him. Part of
his feeling may be shame that in the past he, too, failed to empathize with
others. While there may be some gratifications from his special status, there
is no question but that wherever he was in the social pecking order before,
he is someplace different now. Nor is he being unreasonably paranoid when
he feels this, especially if there is any lengthy period during which his activities remain restricted, and friends who rallied round earlier begin to fade
from the scene. Intellectually he and his parents may not blame the friends,
but emotionally the increasing infrequency of their visits is not easy to accept. And when the adolescent returns to the classroom during remission, a
hush may actually fall. If the patient is male and fifteen or sixteen years old,
someone may shout across the cafeteria or down the hall, "Hey, you with
the cancer!" To be set apart at any age can cause distress, but adolescence is

notoriously a time when both sexes feel emotionally at the mercy of their peers, and mutual scrutiny of physical and other idiosyncrasies is intense.

A major psychological turning point may come when the adolescent is able to demonstrate to himself that he can still function like others. For one girl, this point came when she was able to be a bridesmaid in a wedding party. She put it this way: "People were really looking at me when I went down the aisle, but I felt proud to do it. I held out better than the other bridesmaids."

The sense of being different is not confined to patients only, but is suffered by parents also, both for themselves and for their child. While all speak of their gratitude to truly helpful friends, neighbors, and relatives, few escape some such affliction as, for example, a ghoulish phone message from a near stranger reporting that some other cancer-stricken adolescent has just died. In general, though, there is much feeling of support.

Over a span of time, confidence grows that an initial remission is a stable state of affairs. Patients and parents habituate to the state of relatively good health or controlled disease. It comes to be accepted that survival has been paid for by, for example, amputation of a limb, and that routine clinic visits must continue. Even the exhilaration associated with having passed through an acute crisis subsides, and family life takes on a more ordinary cast. No longer troubled so much by thoughts of being different, the adolescent sometimes is even able to help others with their embarrassment. He has by now some favorites among physicians and staff, and especially likes those who know when to joke and when to be serious. His parents have stopped mediating so much between him and the physicians. Communication has become more direct, and from some incidents it appears that the parents may even be excluded. The adolescent may also acquire a certain expertise in managing new physicians. An eighteen-year-old explained what one does with doctors who have "this physical roughness and very business-like attitude." What one does is "help them loosen up, talk to them, ask them questions so there gets to be a more personal relationship there," and with this the seemingly cold roughness will disappear.

None of this should be construed to mean, however, that in the family equanimity is complete or that anxieties are rarely stirred. "I find myself automatically checking to see if he has his coat on," says the mother; or "I know how much sleep she is getting"; or "If he starts to sweat, I'm scared." And the adolescent says, "I'm always shook up on the way to clinic." Still, with each satisfactory report, with each well day that passes, the promise implicit in the treatment appears more likely to be fulfilled. "It's been so long now everybody forgets it," is one patient's summary.

Imagine how it is when this structure, built only on hope and the experience of remission, tumbles down. "To think," the parent says bitterly, "that we really thought the worst thing that could happen was that he lost his leg!" And the patient says, "I'm depressed, and I think I've got a right. They tell me not to cry, but I guess you'd cry too." The patient may not cry, but literally pounds the wall until exhausted.

Conspicuous at this time is the adolescent's sense of growing entrapment. "I can't be committed to anything. I can't do anything. I have no boy friends, no fiancé, no husband, no school, no job, no way to plan anything, and now I can't concentrate and it's driving me insane. This is the first time I feel the leukemia." Another patient, however, protests that she really isn't worried about her disease because, after all, she's "had it right along." However, she admits that she is bothered because "Now I wash my hands all the time with bleach and I can't stop it, and I can't carry out the garbage when I'm home, and I can't clean the bathroom and I worry when I clean something if I did it right. I know it's crazy, but it just seems like there's a wall of dirt and garbage all around me." While this latter patient is rare in exhibiting the development of a clear-cut neurotic syndrome, in general, as levels of discomfort and tension rise, characteristic behaviors take on more exaggerated forms. A nineteen-year-old, always direct and outspoken, may become at times belligerent and profane. Another, always rather daring, now takes more defiant risks.

Parents, too, become less certain how they should respond to excesses, whether to hold old lines of discipline or to indulge the adolescent, who may not be sure himself which he would prefer.

Times of relapse are often times of anger, anger with self, with parents, with staff, and with other patients. Of staff, such comments are heard as, "So she calls me up and tells me I have to come into clinic. I think if I ever ran into her that day I would of killed her." And, "They've been shitting around with these drugs since November and nothing works—they've wasted weeks." There is withdrawal often combined with a sense of taint from other patients. "That jerk—he's Mr. Depressed America. I don't want him around me. . . ." "You hear so many things, that Mrs. So-and-So doesn't have long to live and stuff like that, and I don't want to be one of them.'' At this phase, patients whom the adolescent has known fairly well will in fact have died. The adolescent is badly shaken by the loss of certain patients who had become good friends, battling a similar adversary. But he may also say coldly, ''Yeah, the death shock deal. I'm getting resigned to other people's deaths. Those are the breaks.''

This is an equally hard time for parents. When the child was in remission, it seemed that there was some justice in the world, some reward for effort. This is no longer so, but even now the effort is not given up. The parent may take the position that although the drug which produced alopecia is no longer working, at least with some new drug the child's hair will grow back again. It is destroying to a parent not to be able to shelter his own, and thus it is difficult to comfort the father who says that when he tried to donate blood ''they told me my blood wouldn't separate, and there was my boy, waiting for my blood . . . and that hurt!''

As belief in medical remedies pales more and more, a desperate faith in the power of attitude sometimes appears in its place. What cannot be accomplished through drugs or surgery may yet be accomplished through the power of the will. A twenty-year-old says of others, ''They died because they worried about it too much . . . you should just go on like you didn't have it.'' A father gives himself a pep talk: ''The mind is a tremendous force. I've seen people with nothing the matter with them get sick from the way they were thinking. You don't go into battle with a bunch of soldiers who think that they can't win.''

While faith in the will emerges as a dominant theme for many, religious faith in the conventional sense is a mighty fortress for certain families who have previously depended on faith to meet crises. Often religious attitudes diverge within a family. In one case, for example, a father and son conspired together to let a deeply religious mother believe that the son was regularly attending Mass. Certain young patients expressed the feeling that it is wrong to ask God to save a loved one. Sometimes the implication seemed to be that it is better not to ask, because to ask and be refused would be unbearable. One girl said that her mother had told her, ''You, of all people, should go to church!'' She then replied, ''Why me, of all people? I don't believe that just because you go to church you won't die. God knows what He is doing.'' Another patient said that he believed in reincarnation, and that he would come back as ''a slightly better person.''

Although responses were mixed, most of those interviewed did not feel that sickness had altered their basic religious beliefs. One father said he had come to realize that all along he never believed in Communion and prayer because "what does this do for you? Physically nothing happens." No one spoke of strengthened faith, but several told of continued faith and deeply meaningful prayers.

Not surprisingly, many interviews indicated a close relationship between thoughts of death and acuteness and severity of symptoms. As one father put it, "When my son was so weak, all I could think of was the funeral home, the black dress." Yet at the same time it seemed that patients and parents could talk more easily of death when not immediately threatened by it.

It is true that some cannot at anytime bring themselves to speak the words "death" or "die." Sentences may trail off to silence when these could have been the only words in mind. When feeling fairly well, adolescents will sometimes say briskly, "Let's face it, the life expectancy isn't all that great" or "Sooner or later, it's gonna catch up with you." Denial appears during serious relapse: "I know I can't have more than five or six more years." Or, "I know I'm going to get remission. It's just an inch away. I'll figure out something." The compulsively hand-washing patient mentioned earlier provided the clearest statement of denial of all those interviewed when she said, "I have what I want in my head, and I don't want anything else to get up there."

It must be acknowledged that in the late-adolescent/early-adult group there is little evidence of bland acceptance of death, that period "almost void of feelings" observed by Kübler-Ross (1969), when the individual has worked through his grief for his own loss of himself and has largely dissolved emotional ties with others. Such a state of quiescence may sometimes be difficult to differentiate from the organic effects of advancing critical disease. It may also be that such a peaceful acceptance is far more difficult for young patients than for older ones to achieve. A kind of adaptation, although not peaceful acceptance, may sometimes occur when it is possible that to die may become, for many, far easier than to live.

Parents, even though they rarely give up hope, sometimes may prepare for the inevitable death. Thus, one mother whose child was very debilitated and near death began to speak of her father, who had passed away some months earlier. She had felt little about her father at the time because she had been so preoccupied with her son. Now, she said, it seemed to her that her father's death was a good thing because he had reached the point where he "couldn't do everything he wanted, and he would only suffer." It seemed clear that she was seeking a rationale for the impending death of her son.

Given cancer in adolescence, a course marked by hopeful intervals and intermittently effective treatment, and in which outcome is for a long time uncertain although a bitter ending always comes, what psychological support can the physician offer? Here, as always, the truisms are true. The adolescent needs to trust his doctor, which means among other things that the patient should be prepared as much as possible for the side effects which result from treatment. The patient should know not only that his doctor can be reached, but also that his doctor will reach out to him when he needs it.

The importance of flexibility in responding to the young patient's yearnings for both reassurance and self-respect should be stressed. If the emotional capabilities of the relatively stable adult patient fluctuate and alter throughout illness, it is apparent that among adolescents who are changing inwardly the fluctuations will be even greater. As the adolescent is trying to move into the broader world, his illness may confine him more and more to a narrow one, frustrating his attempts to deal with the developmental tasks of this period of life.

Also, small differences in age can make large differences in the needs and aspirations of adolescents. Where "it's at" at fifteen isn't where "it's at" at eighteen, and thus the implications of specific symptoms at these ages may vary markedly. Many eighteen-year-old girls and some eighteen-year-old boys, for example, are thinking seriously about wanting to marry. Most fifteen- and sixteen-year-olds are not. The more perceptive the physician is of the particular patient's frame of reference, the more responsive he will be. Parents especially may need help in understanding that the adolescent, although ill, is still growing up emotionally and physically.

Although uncertainty of outcome allows for hope, to be kept in suspense for a long while is stressful in itself. One patient in particular expressed this vividly when he said, "The last time I went in for treatment I was almost sort of hoping that it wouldn't work . . . 'cause I wanted something definite. I either wanted to be definitely alive or definitely dead." How to manage the anxiety and irritation resulting from prolonged uncertainty is a problem physicians face more and more with cancer patients, and one which demands greater attention than it has as yet received in studies of the psychological problems of cancer. That the patient receive some temporary relief when he is allowed to air his feelings is only a partial solution to a problem for which there is no answer beyond the obvious.

In summary, it is suggested, first, that it is inappropriate to equate the psychology of cancer in adolescence with that of dying in adolescence, even though at times the two may merge.

Second, it has been argued that discrete symptoms rather than foreshortened life expectancy as such are largely central in the adolescent patient's consciousness throughout the course of disease. Efforts to understand the psychology of dying and the phenomena of anticipatory grief must take into account the power of symptoms and their day-by-day fluctuations to dictate mood and hope. Two seventeen-year-olds may both be a month and a half away from death due to cancer. Yet, the concerns of each on this D-Day minus forty-five may differ greatly because specific symptoms that day differ, not because one adolescent more than the other has come to accept or even be aware of the nearness of his death. Too many conclusions about terminal behavior are retrospectively biased by knowledge of the date of death. Observations made with proper prospective, and without benefit of such information, may lead to an enhanced understanding of the final period of life.

Both immediate physical symptoms and the individual's private and shifting interpretation of these symptoms determine the psychological reaction of adolescent patients and their parents. Symptoms remain central for a variety of reasons whose interactions are by no means fully delineated. Such reasons may include the inherent compelling character of the symptom, its external visibility, its salience to self-esteem, and the ease with which it can be utilized to meet defensive needs.

REFERENCES

Glaser, B. C., "Disclosure of Terminal Illness," *Journal of Health and Human Behavior, 7:*83, 1966.
Hoerr, S. C., "Thoughts on What to Tell the Patient with Cancer," *Cleveland Clinic Quarterly, 30:*11, 1963.

Koop, C. E., "The Seriously Ill or Dying Child: Supporting the Patient and the Family," *Pediatric Clinics of North America, 16:*555, 1969.

Kübler-Ross, E., *On Death and Dying*. New York: Macmillan, 1969.

Litin, E. M., "Should the Cancer Patient Be Told?", *Postgraduate Medicine, 28:*470, 1960.

Oken, D., "What to Tell Cancer Patients: A Study of Medical Attitudes," *Journal of the American Medical Association, 175:*1120, 1961.

Plumb, M. M., S. K. Park, J. J. Holmes, L. J. Dykstra, and J. C. B. Holland, "Comparative Study of Depression in Patients Facing Death by Suicide or Fatal Disease," paper presented at the Annual Meeting of the American Association of Suicidology, Washington, D.C., March 19, 1971.

Segal, E., *Love Story*. New York: Harper & Row, 1970.

Vernick, J., and M. Karon, "Who's Afraid of Death on a Leukemia Ward?", *American Journal of the Diseases of Children, 109:*393, 1965.

PART *4*

THE HEALTH
PROFESSIONS

24

Medical School Curriculum and Anticipatory Grief: Faculty Attitudes

Austin H. Kutscher and
Austin H. Kutscher, Jr.

Until recent years open discussion of death and dying has been treated as taboo, not only by the laity but also by practicing professional health personnel. Loss and grief, if not taboo topics, have been scantily researched, probably as a reflection of the restraints imposed on the discussion of the phenomena preceding them. Both deficiencies in the art as well as in the science of medical practice are evident from the limited literature dealing with these subjects. Such a situation accentuates the apparent lack of preparation of the health personnel charged with the emotional care of the dying patient, the members of his family, and the health teams themselves.

A series of studies undertaken under the auspices of the Foundation of Thanatology surveyed the educational content of the curricula of various allied health disciplines to discern where curriculum changes and additions might prove helpful to the health care disciplines in rendering care to the "community" they serve as well as for their own psychological support.

A previous report (Schoenberg and Carr, 1972) on the general subject of medical education in this area, including faculty attitudes and the dying patient, was based in part on a survey in this series. This chapter is a sequel drawing upon information derived from the same survey. It reveals faculty attitudes regarding the medical school curriculum dealing with anticipatory grief as extrapolated from replies dealing with education of students in dealing with the bereaved-to-be.

In this chapter, therefore, the authors have focused on the larger subject area of the anticipatory grief of the involved family members rather than the anticipatory grief of the patient himself.

METHODS

After consultation with a multidisciplinary group of academically oriented (medical school faculty, etc.) members of the Foundation's Professional Advisory Board, the authors decided to undertake a comprehensive survey of current activities and programs in medical school curricula to determine the preparation of the medical student to deal with various areas related to death and bereavement, of which anticipatory grief was one area particularly singled out.

The services of a sociologist were obtained to supplement the traditional "general-medical-psychological-psychiatric" approach to the survey. The survey questionnaire was then: edited; referred out for suggestions and comments to a small group of multidisciplinary, academically oriented allied health sciences personnel; use-tested on a small scale; and re-edited prior to mailing.

A personally typed letter, requesting the respondent's assistance in the completion of the survey, was thereafter sent to the chairmen of the departments of psychiatry, medicine, surgery and pediatrics as well as to the dean of every medical school in the United States.

RESULTS

The following represents the tabulated findings related exclusively to faculty attitudes on medical education in the care of anticipatory grief (of the bereaved-to-be rather than that of the patient). The 121 respondents included: 34 replies from departments of psychiatry; 22 replies from departments of medicine; 24 replies from departments of surgery; 27 replies from departments of pediatrics; and 14 gratuitous replies from deans.

SUMMARY AND CONCLUSIONS

In order to understand further the nature of the problems of thanatology in the allied health professions in general and, specifically, in regard to the teaching in medical schools, a questionnaire was prepared for distribution to the dean of each medical school in the United States and to the chairman of four departments of the medical faculty. The departments surveyed included surgery, medicine, pediatrics, and psychiatry.

Described in this report are the responses associated with their approach to anticipatory grief. It is the authors' hope that these measurements concerning this specific academic situation will make available to the total medical community data on current curricula in this area and will provide a stimulus to remedy such curriculum defects deemed worthy of added effort.

It is noteworthy that a high percentage of responses was obtained, considering the taboo nature of the topic and the length of the longer questionnaire itself (from which these cited replies were excerpted).

On the whole, the results seemed to indicate: the need for improved and greater curriculum coverage of the area of anticipatory grief; a general awareness of this need; and small evidences of intention or capability to make curriculum changes to affect such improvement in relation to the dying patient suffering anticipatory grief, let alone the bereaved-to-be under the same stress (the latter being the specific subjects emphasized herein).

The survey results suggest the need for further curriculum effort and time in the area of anticipatory grief as well as a vital and viable interest among medical educators to proceed with such efforts. The results follow.

1) Is the physician's responsibility in regard to the care of the dying patient or his family included in the medical student's curriculum?

The dying patient	Yes 69%;	No 28%;	N.A. 3%
The "bereaved-to-be" *	Yes 57%;	No 35%;	N.A. 8%
The bereaved	Yes 56%;	No 35%;	N.A. 9%

2) Has the subject of the teaching of the care of the dying patient and the family been discussed in department meetings during the past year?

The family	Yes 41%;	No 55%;	N.A. 4%

* The family of the dying patient—prior to the patient's death.

If yes,

	Dying patient	Family
Frequently	8%	9%
Occasionally	24%	23%
Seldom	10%	8%
No Answer	58%	60%

3) Does your department specifically prepare medical students to understand and deal with:

		Yes	No	N.A.
a.	The patient's emotional response to dying	63%	32%	5%
b.	The use of denial by the dying patient	56%	37%	7%
c.	The process of the patient's separation or disengagement from others	45%	44%	11%
d.	The dying patient's grief	52%	38%	10%
e.	The family's anticipatory grief and mourning	56%	37%	7%
f.	The hospital personnel's emotional reaction to the patient	57%	36%	7%

4) Does your department discuss with students controversial issues that are currently connected with the care of dying patients, that is, euthanasia, definitions of death, ethics of organ transplantation, etc.?

Yes 73%;   No 22%;   N. A. 5%

5) In treating the dying patient, which of the following activities are students encouraged to pursue?

		Yes	No	N.A.
a.	Talking with the chaplain	29%	48%	23%
b.	Talking with the social worker	60%	21%	19%

		Yes	No	N.A.
c.	Talking with the nurse	52%	31%	17%
d.	Talking with the family	80%	12%	8%
e.	Discussing social, financial, and family problems with the patient	43%	40%	17%

6) With regard to the following statement that "students are *not* adequately prepared to care for the dying patient's family," would the *majority* of your faculty members:

Strongly agree	35%
Mildly agree	54%
Strongly disagree	2%
No answer	9%

REFERENCES

Schoenberg, B. and A. C. Carr, "Educating the Health Professional," chapter in B. Schoenberg *et al.,* eds., *Psychosocial Aspects of Terminal Care.* New York: Columbia University Press, 1972.

25

Anticipatory Grief in Physicians and Nurses *

Jeanne Quint Benoliel

Some years ago Lindemann (1944) chose the phrase "anticipatory grief" to refer to the absence of overt manifestations of grief at the actual time of death in survivors who had experienced already the phases of normal grief, and who had emancipated themselves from their emotional ties with the deceased person. Fulton and Fulton (1972) have noted the rising incidence of anticipatory grief in families where members experience prolonged separation for reasons other than forthcoming death—such as military service, incarceration in prison, or lengthy hospitalization for chronic disease. They also examine some of the functional and dysfunctional consequences of anticipatory grief for the dying patient, his family, and the medical and nursing personnel providing services to them.

The isolation of the dying patient by his family and by health-care workers has been described and discussed in many publications in recent years. The evidence available in the literature suggests that health-care workers, no less than laymen, respond to forthcoming death with reactions and responses that reflect the primary values of the society. In the case of children with life-threatening disease, the inability of medical and nursing personnel to remain emotionally uninvolved has been documented in several ar-

* This chapter is based, in part, on research supported by a National Institutes of Health, Division of Nursing, Grant NU 00047, at the University of California, San Francisco.

ticles. Where the elderly are concerned, the opposite extreme of emotional detachment and withdrawal from social interaction has been reported.

There is much to suggest that the variety of behaviors reported for doctors and nurses reflects a lay response to death and points to a lack of appropriate and consistent norms for professional behavior in the face of death. This chapter considers the possibility that certain patterns of behavior observed in medical and nursing personnel might be viewed as manifestations of anticipatory grief having their origins in various combinations of professional and personal loss.

The sources providing the data that led to this analysis are several: interviews with some sixty or more student nurses about their experiences with death and dying (Quint, 1967); a clinical investigation to identify problems that nurses encounter with death in a university medical center; the experience of teaching a graduate seminar centered on the threat of death in clinical practice; and interviews and ongoing contacts with physicians and nurses who have chosen clinical work with certain life-threatening diseases—cystic fibrosis, cancer, coronary heart disease, and diabetes mellitus. Information and ideas reported in other publications have also been used.

LOSS AND GRIEF

In the United States, according to Volkart (1957), the small-family system provides for an intense emotional attachment to a few select people and thereby causes survivors to experience the death of another person (especially a member of the family) as a serious form of loss. He makes the point that vulnerability to loss through death is lessened in cultural systems where emotional ties are diffused among many persons rather than restricted to a few. Discussing the dynamics of grief, Switzer (1970) differentiates between bereavement as the actual state of deprivation or loss and grief as the emotional-physiological pain experienced in response to the loss.

The state of being without something one has once possessed is common in human experience, yet not all losses result in a response of grief. In the lives of human beings, Peretz (1970) suggests that loss appears in four forms: loss of a valued person; loss of some aspect of the ''self''; loss of external objects; and developmental loss associated with the process of growth and its concomitant physical, psychological, emotional, and social changes.

Using a sociological orientation, Weiss (1969) proposes that human beings have needs that can be met only through relationships with other people, and loss of a significant relationship produces two outcomes. The individual experiences a sense of personal trauma and psychological disorganization. He also experiences a deficit in living due to the continuing absence of the functions that were provided by the relationship that has been lost. According to Weiss, the psychological impact of a lost relationship depends on the relative significance of that relationship to the individual concerned and not on the type of relationship per se.

The ultimate effects of a lost relationship depend on the opportunities available for finding replacements to fill the gap that is present. In this regard, the loss of a significant person through death carries the double threat of severe psychological pain coupled with a relational deficit that often cannot be filled by new relationships. In an investigation of reactions to death among the British, Gorer (1965) found that the most distressing and long-lasting grief occurred following the loss of a grown child.

The high vulnerability of the young and the old to the effects of loss through death has been the subject of discussion in many publications. Concerning the former group, some recent investigations have attempted to identify the long-term effects of childhood bereavement on personality development (Moriarty, 1967) and on behavior disorders in later life (Markusen and Fulton, 1971). Discussing three forms of catastrophic loss, Benoliel (1971) points to the high vulnerability of the aged tied to the reality that they are people faced with multiple losses at a time when many of them lack the social, personal, and economic resources for coping with these realities.

The difficulties that death and dying pose for health-care professionals and other workers are increasingly being described and discussed in the literature. There is reason to think that some of the reactions experienced by doctors and nurses have their origins in loss of significant relationships associated with professional identity and professional performance.

SOURCES OF PROFESSIONAL LOSS

Given that the medical and nursing subcultures attach primary value to life-saving activity and secondary value to palliation and symptomatic therapy, the performance of tasks associated with the preservation of life carries greater weight in the allocation of professional and social rewards than does the provision of comfort. Weiss (1969) has suggested that one of the five relationships necessary for achievement of well-being as a person is that which provides reassurance of worth through experience attesting to an individual's competence in a given role. Translating this conceptualization to the meaning of professional work for physicians and nurses, one can conjecture that any activity or situation which negates the capacity to save lives can be conceived (and experienced) as a loss of an important relationship—professional competence. Research findings and reports by others suggest that the dying patient provides opportunity for several kinds of professional loss which can be analytically distinguished from personal and social loss shared in common with the society at large.

The inability to prevent or forestall a patient's death represents to the physician (more so than to the nurse) loss of power and ability to control. This form of loss for members of the medical community is experienced most acutely when inability to prevent death is compounded by a prolonged, downhill course during which physical complications increase and medical management becomes more precarious and delicate. Patients with cancer, advanced kidney disease, and other chronic conditions create situations which maximize the chances for physicians to experience a sense of professional failure associated with loss of power and control. Writing about cancer, Adelman (1971) commented: "It defeats my whole picture of the world, in which I am all-powerful, defying disease, knowing more than the layman, initiate into the secrets of disease, immune to old fears and superstitions."

A second form of professional loss is that produced by decisions and actions which result in negligent behavior in the performance of professional work. For any practitioner, a wrong decision or the omission of an important act affecting the life of a patient can have far-reaching personal and social consequences. Because clinical judgment is a critical component of professional competence, a mistaken diagnosis or an error in treatment can be deeply felt as a loss of one's own "best judgment." For student nurses, mistakes in practice are serious and disturbing events that threaten the individual's self-perception as a competent nurse (Quint, 1967). In addition, unexpected deaths are reported by nurses in general to cause them to ponder whether or not their actions may have been contributing or precipitating factors in causing a death to take place. Typical of the incidents described by nurses is the following:

I was supervising a house at night and had nothing but students on the floor, and we were busy. She [a patient] had a convulsion and seizure. We called the doctor, who was a neurosurgeon. At that time neurosurgery was relatively new at the hospital. There were some differences in opinion as to what she had—there was no definite diagnosis. After the surgery, we gave Demerol. Suddenly the picture changed remarkably—the pupils fixed and very comatose. I didn't get any satisfaction from the intern, and she died all of a sudden in spite of everything we could do. Calling everybody, and I remember the doctor being very upset—why didn't we call him? It was a conglomeration of many factors, and I blamed myself for the fact that this woman had died.

Negligent behaviors or errors in judgment on the part of any practitioner can also lead to another form of loss—that of peer respect for competence. Coser and Rokoff (1971) note that one of the elements that distinguishes a professional from a craftsman is a strong commitment to his colleagues in addition to his commitment to his work. Fox (1959) describes the critical supportive function of group interaction for physicians when they are faced with decisions in situations marked by uncertainty and life-threatening potential. In an opposite direction, Rabin (1970) has indicated that evidence of persistent or suspected incompetence in medical performance can lead to serious difficulties in maintaining a practice. In an extreme case, loss of peer respect can result in the severest of professional and social penalties—namely, loss of the privilege to practice medicine (or nursing).

A fourth way by which death and dying contribute to professional loss is through the creation of situations which cause the practitioner to engage in modes of behavior that violate the norms of established professional demeanor. In both medical and nursing practice, high value is attached to behaviors that emphasize composure, control, and competence. Situations most likely to cause practioners to experience loss of professional demeanor are those which place a heavy stress and strain on the person's ability to maintain control over the situation, to be and feel competent, and to retain composure.

There are at least three types of situations which carry a high potential for loss of professional demeanor. An incident in which unexpected and/or shocking death takes place puts a heavy strain on the capacities of doctors and nurses to remain composed. Work settings where the medical and nursing staffs are under almost constant exposure to patients facing death are also high in stress. A third and always difficult situation occurs when a child or adolescent is dying or has died.

Another type of professional loss is that which comes with the death of a "significant" patient. From the perspective of medical practice, a patient becomes significant when the practitioner has invested a good deal of time, energy, and clinical effort into making a diagnosis and effecting a treatment. When patient and physician together have shared the ups and downs of illness over a prolonged period of time, as for example in chronic dialysis (Short and Wilson, 1969), the significance is intensified. For nurses, the professional significance of a patient can be tied to a heavy investment in life-saving activity—especially when the patient's life has been prolonged by the nurses' actions on more than one occasion, as can happen on coronary care and intensive care wards. The significance of a patient can also be tied to a heavy investment in comfort-oriented care, such as happens with a cancer patient whom the nursing staff gets to know over a prolonged period of time before he dies.

Weiss (1969) postulates that one of the basic human relationships contributing to personal well-being provides for social integration—meaning opportunities to share with others in common goals and objectives. To judge from the observed reactions of doctors and nurses to the death of a significant patient, such a death means the loss of a socially integrating relationship of some importance in their professional lives.

MODES OF RESPONSE TO PROFESSIONAL LOSS

According to Peretz (1970), the extent to which a state of bereavement or loss produces grief and the type of grief-response elicited depend on a combination of circumstances: the personality of the bereaved person, the relationship between the bereaved and the object that has been lost, and the values of the society of which he is a member. The previous section has identified several types of situations which carry a high-grief potential for physicians and nurses because they provide opportunities for the loss of relationships that have significant professional meanings. This section will consider the reactions experienced by nursing practitioners in response to professional loss, and describe some observed modes of behavior used by nurses for coping with grief-producing situations.

Interviews with student nurses provide data which are helpful for understanding how nurses are socialized to define and to cope with grief-producing situations in nursing practice. In the first place, educational preparation for nursing places a heavy emphasis on the maintenance of professional demeanor—composure, control and competence—especially in the presence of patients. To reinforce this perspective on proper nursing performance, positive sanctions are bestowed by teachers and other nurses when students conform to these highly valued modes of behavior. Conversely, negative sanctions come into play when the opposite modes of behavior appear. The students are usually introduced to nursing in the hospital where they are exposed to institutionalized methods used by doctors and nurses for routinizing the irrational aspects of clientele behavior. In a very real sense, students of nursing are socialized to manage or prevent emotional displays by patients and families through the use of sedatives and tranquilizers, maintenance of control over activities on the ward, and referral of special cases (difficult problems) to special agents—clergymen, social workers, and psychiatrists.

At the same time, however, the students are learning through direct experience that the work they have chosen can thrust them abruptly and unexpectedly into a state of bereavement accompanied by intense feelings of grief. These somewhat devastating and often unexpected reactions appear in response to events in which professional loss takes place. One such event involves nursing performance in which a serious mistake in practice is made. Another comes with failure to recognize the possibility of forthcoming death and with lack of preparation for feelings of loss when that patient dies. Yet another type of incident is that in which loss of composure takes place under conditions in which the student believes maintenance of professional composure was important. Finally, there is the loss that comes when a significant patient dies.

The problem for many of these students is not so much that they encounter grief-producing situations but rather that the structural conditions under which the incidents occur tend to block the expression of grief and to encourage postponement of reaction, called by Lindemann (1944) "morbid grief reactions." The extent to which many nurses are living with unresolved or uncompleted grief reactions associated with experiences as students has perhaps not been recognized. The crippling effects of these unresolved reactions may well be at play in some of the tightly controlling, aggressive, and stereotyped behaviors that some nurses use in their transactions with patients, families, physicians, and other nurses.

Fortunately, not all students experience professional loss under conditions which prevent them from doing the "grief work" that is necessary for finding resolution. Students can have the fortunate experience of being in contact with an understanding and supporting instructor, head nurse, or supervisor at a time when the psychological impact of loss makes them much in need of someone who essentially "gives them permission" to grieve as nurses. Students who have the opportunity to express the grief produced by these early and intense experiences with loss seem better able to retain a compassionate approach toward patients than do their counterparts in nursing who have been prevented from coping constructively with the reality of their own professional losses.

Even though some nurses have the opportunity to "work through" the grief of these early and important professional losses, the fact remains that resolution of professional loss can never be complete. The work of nursing—in some fields more so than in others—involves nurses in ongoing contacts with potential and actual losses of many kinds. Frequent contacts with persons who have cancer or assignment to intensive care settings or pediatric wards for life-threatening illness are examples of nursing work that can be classed as high in risk as far as exposure to professional loss is concerned. In contrast, work as a school nurse or in the office of an obstetrician can be viewed as low in risk in terms of its grief-potential.

ANTICIPATORY GRIEF AND SOCIAL DISTANCE

The author's conversations with nurses over the past seven to eight years provide relatively clear evidence that many of them choose fields of work that minimize their chances for contacts with people who are dying or with situations where professional loss is likely to be frequent. Other nurses appear to cope with the stresses of nursing work (especially in hospitals) by moving from job to job or by transferring from one ward to another to ease the strain. In regard to choice of work site, interviews with nurses suggest that fair numbers of them attempt to avoid contact with grief-producing situations as much as is possible.

It is also clear that many nurses do not deliberately seek settings where the threat of death is infrequent. There are some who purposefully choose intensive care settings where they can share the excitement and challenge of active involvement in recovery-oriented activity. There are others who choose work with a high grief-potential, for example, in leukemia or kidney dialysis clinics, because there are compensatory rewards in the shared responsibility of membership on a medical team. In two such situations, the head nurse was the functional key to success in the team's efforts to combine cure efforts and care efforts into a coordinated and client-centered service. Despite the high exposure to grief-producing situations central to the work itself, the nurse in each case functioned quietly behind the scenes in much the same sense that the executive-secretary in a business office coordinates a variety of diverse activities and selectively brings certain matters to the attention of the executive (in this case a physician) for information or action.

Observation of nurses in various types of settings indicates that many of them employ a general stance of maintaining considerable social distance in interaction with their clientele, and markedly so where the threat of death is readily apparent. Glaser and Strauss (1965) have described in some detail the protective strategies used individually and collectively by nurses in the hospital for coping with the stresses of dying under different sets of structural conditions. Menzies (1960) postulated that nursing services in hospitals evolve a particular kind of social structure that serves to protect the nursing staff from many of the anxiety-producing aspects of patient care.

One might also speculate that this mode of behavior has origins in the psychological realm, that is, remnants of contact with grief at earlier periods of time. Is it possible that this mode of distancing behavior is a generalized application of the syndrome of anticipatory grief by individuals who early in their careers as nurses experienced intense reactions of grief in response to combinations of professional and personal loss and learned to guard themselves against the possibility of similar experiences in the future? It seems not unlikely that the need for psychological protection from a replay of emotionally traumatizing experience might well facilitate the use of a socially distancing approach that allows the nurse to avoid or minimize new involvements that are potentially grief-producing. In the same way that anticipatory grief serves to emotionally emancipate survivors from the family member who is dying (Fulton and Fulton, 1972), the phenomenon of anticipatory grief in nurses may function to keep them emotionally detached from situations which are high in risk in matters of professional and personal loss.

DISCUSSION

The importance of loss and grief in the ongoing professional lives of doctors and nurses has perhaps not been given the attention it deserves. Although the literature admonishes both groups about their responsibilities in the realm of psychosocial care, there is little direction given for offering this kind of assistance when the professionals themselves are caught up in their own reactions of loss and grief. A recent effort to institute improvements in psychosocial care for cancer patients produced all kinds of role conflicts and strains, altered relationships among the many health-care workers involved, and even active opposition from some segments of the hospital in which the experiment was tried (Ryser, Sheldon, and Schwartz, 1971).

The extent to which improvements in psychosocial care for patients and families can be initiated without concomitant attention to the psychosocial needs of doctors, nurses, and other health-care workers seems limited. More than that, the creation of services geared to the concept of care must take account of the reality that present structural arrangements for health care and its delivery are organized around the primacy of the cure-goal. If care is to become operationalized as successfully as has been cure, the reality of professional and personal loss in the lives of the deliverers of services cannot be ignored.

REFERENCES

Adelman, S. E., "The Dying Patient: An Unspoken Dialogue," *The New Physician, 20:*707, 1971.

Benoliel, J. Q., "Assessments of Loss and Grief," *Journal of Thanatology, 1:*182, 1971.

Coser, R. L., and G. Rokoff, "Women in the Occupational World: Social Disruption and Conflict," *Social Problems, 18:*535, 1971.

Fox, R. C., *Experiment Perilous.* Glencoe, Ill.: Free Press, 1959.

Fulton, R., and J. Fulton, "Anticipatory Grief: A Psychosocial Aspect of Terminal Care," in B. Schoenberg *et al.,* eds., *Psychosocial Aspects of Terminal Care.* New York: Columbia University Press, 1972.

Glaser, B. G., and A. L. Strauss, *Awareness of Dying.* Chicago: Aldine, 1965.

Gorer, G., *Death, Grief, and Mourning,* Garden City, N.Y.: Doubleday Anchor, 1965.

Lindemann, E., "Symptomatology and Management of Acute Grief," *American Journal of Psychiatry, 101:*141, 1944.

Markusen, E., and R. Fulton, "Childhood Bereavement and Behavior Disorders: A Critical Review," *Omega, 2:*107, 1971.

Menzies, I. E. P., "A Case Study in the Functioning of Social Systems as a Defense Against Anxiety: A Report of a Study of the Nursing Services of a General Hospital," *Human Relations, 13:*95, 1960.

Moriarty, E. M., *The Loss of Loved Ones,* Springfield, Ill.: Charles C Thomas, 1967.

Peretz, D., "Development, Object-Relationships, and Loss," in B. Schoenberg *et al.,* eds., *Loss and Grief: Psychological Management in Medical Practice.* New York: Columbia University Press, 1970.

—— "Reaction to Loss," in B. Schoenberg *et al.,* eds., *Loss and Grief: Psychological Management in Medical Practice.* New York: Columbia University Press, 1970.

Quint, J., *The Nurse and the Dying Patient.* New York: Macmillan, 1967.

Rabin, D. L., with L. H. Rabin, "Consequences of Death for Physicians, Nurses, and Hospitals," in O. G. Brim *et al.,* eds., *The Dying Patient.* New York: Russell Sage Foundation, 1970.

Ryser, E. P., A. Sheldon, and C. G. Schwartz, "Problems with Change: The Vicissitudes of a Pilot Comprehensive Cancer Care Program," *Journal of Thanatology, 1:*145, 1971.

Short, M. J., and W. P. Wilson, "Roles of Denial in Chronic Dialysis," *Archives of General Psychiatry, 20:*433, 1969.

Switzer, D. K., *The Dynamics of Grief.* New York: Abingdon Press, 1970.

Volkart, E. H., with S. T. Michael, "Bereavement and Mental Health," in A. H. Leighton, A. Clausen, and R. N. Wilson, eds., *Explorations in Social Psychiatry.* New York: Basic Books, 1957.

Weiss, R. S., "The Fund of Sociability," *Trans-Action, 6:*36, 1969.

26

Anticipatory Grief and the Disciplined Professions

James O. Carpenter and
Georgia Hall

On one of her increasingly frequent visits to the hospital for diabetic complications, an elderly lady began to discuss clothes and the forthcoming occasion of her granddaughter's wedding. "Why haven't you been wearing
your pretty blue dress lately, Mrs. Smith? Are you going to wear it to your
granddaughter's wedding?" inquired a staff member.

The lady indicated that she was reserving that dress for another special
occasion. She had neatly put it away and was to be "laid out" in the blue
dress.

Another staff member, catching bits and pieces of the conversation,
overheard "blue dress" and "wedding" and immediately asked which
shoes Mrs. Smith planned to wear. "Shoes?" exclaimed the lady. "Why do
I need shoes to be laid out in a coffin?"

This situation indicates the great social and psychological complexities
revolving about that which is termed anticipatory grief. The subjective definition by the patient of her condition, her conception of the future, and her
preparation intersect with the views, conceptions, and attitudes of health
practitioners in a complex intersection of cultures. These concerns comprise
the focus of our attention in examining anticipatory grief and the disciplined
professions.

ANTICIPATORY GRIEF IN PATIENT AND FAMILY

Anticipatory grief entailing a process of anticipatory socialization to the loss of a love-object is a cognitive and affective process occurring within the existing social environment. It is a process which does not occur in a vacuum, but often within the social parameters of the routinized practices of the disciplined professions. Both the family members and the dying family member are involved, over time, in anticipatory grieving which parallels and interacts with the dying trajectory of the patient, entailing the intersection of the patient with practitioners and others over time.

Anticipatory grief, in this case, involves both patient and family in the process of anticipatory socialization to the loss. The patient was involved in numerous social roles and affective relationships. The person may have been husband, father, and breadwinner; with the recognition of his condition he enters another role, that of the dying patient. A number of institutionalized expectations influence his definition of the situation as well as that of others. Socialization to the role of the dying patient entails cognizance of the impending loss of life roles and loved ones. The family also undergoes a process of socialization to the loss of the family member. This process of anticipatory socialization on the part of both patient and family is encompassed in our conceptualization of anticipatory grief. Anticipatory grief entails grieving prior to the expected occurrence of death. It also has applicability to other situations in life entailing the loss of an object of cathectic import. It is generally considered that anticipatory grief prior to the time of loss will serve to mitigate the emotional onslaught of the actual event. Premature grieving, however, especially when it occurs in front of the patient, creates a very difficult situation for the dying person, who may be working through his own grief and awareness of the impending event. Too early a resolution of grief on the part of family members may also be detrimental to the emotional well-being of the patient, possibly eventuating in the social death of the dying patient. The time element implied in anticipatory grief also embodies the supposition that adequate foreknowledge of the impending event is at hand. Needless to say, in the case of short or virtually nonexistent dying trajectories, little or no time is available for psychological and emotional preparation or anticipatory grief. Accordingly, the shock and ensuing emotional crisis may be heightened. This is seen in cases of "sudden death."

Such grieving, which entails a unique experience for both patient and family, occurs frequently within institutional walls and is subject to the routinized activity of staff in carrying out organizational goals. The great increase in specialization and advances in technology have eventuated in institutionalized death for many dying patients. Anticipatory grieving is thus more likely to take place within a hospital, nursing home, medical care facility, or other organizational context than it did in earlier times. Anticipatory grieving on the part of relatives and friends, involving working through the expressive and instrumental difficulties associated with the dying patient as well as the process by which the patient interprets his condition, is tied into an existing organizational framework or social structure.

SOCIAL-MEDICAL FRAMEWORK

The process of anticipatory grieving on the part of patient and family is indelibly stamped by the social parameters within which death and dying occur. This social locus has increasingly been that of an institution oriented toward treatment and cure of illness and disease. Advances in technology, the location of modern, complex life-saving equipment in major hospitals, and the wide variety of specialties designed to deliver medical care have entailed a shift from treatment in the home to curative endeavors within the institutional context. Moreover, insurance mechanisms frequently cover medical expenses only when incurred within a treatment facility such as a hospital. There has also been a remarkable growth in recent years in the number of paraprofessional health practitioners.

While in earlier times the general practitioner might have followed the patient through over a considerable period of time as both medical practitioner and friend, the dying patient and his family in the institutional framework discover that they are seeing a wide variety of different faces and specialties coping not with a single patient per se but also with the broader organizational demands imposed upon them by other patients requiring treatment. Within such a framework less attention may be allocated to meeting the individual emotional needs of patient and relatives. Thus, in earlier times, when the physician tended to most of the medical care needs of the patient at home, his orders were carried out by a close member of the family. His role encompassed some of the diverse services carried out by different people in the modern hospital. They included feeding, bathing, and administration of medications. Care was continuous, and if the patient expe-

rienced a sleepless night, a concerned member of the family was available to
comfort him. Claudill (1961) notes the comparable role of the *Tsukisoi* in
Japan, who meets the emotional needs of the patient and acts as the representative of the family in the hospital.

The medical care facility encompasses a much wider range of services
than could ever be provided in the home. But care is often fragmented and
lacking in continuity. The nature of the hospital as an organization entails
compartmentalization, role specificity, and fragmentation. Not only will the
patient himself be affected, but the family as well. This detracts significantly
from the capacity of the organization to meet the emotional and psychological needs of the patient and the family. The paucity of emotional support
may be detrimental to the well-being of the patient and his family engaged
in the process of anticipatory grief. Let us consider for a moment that in
order for a hospital to operate twenty-four hours a day every day of the year,
three eight-hour shifts of personnel are necessary each day, that is, three
groups of people performing comparable tasks. Schedules are staggered and
various staff members have various "days off" during different weeks. The
long nights often spent by terminal patients may well be lonely, and a fearful patient may have no one to confide in. The evening and late-night staff
are often overworked for lack of enough personnel. To complicate matters
further, those who perform most of the tasks related to direct patient care are
likely to have the highest job mobility. Labor turnover can have a profound
effect on patients. An extended relationship between a patient and a staff
member can be discontinued abruptly when that staff member resigns, and
the patient may feel deserted.

Thus, dying and anticipatory grief which, at earlier times, may have
occurred more frequently within the familial context of the home, have
shifted more in the direction of institutionalized dying; wherein anticipatory
grief and the perception of dynamics of a unique event to family and patient
occur within a social structure organized to deal with medical problems in a
routinized manner. A complex coping dialogue ensues between practitioners, patient, and family. The element of people processing within a routinized organizational context which makes great demands upon limited
resources is seen, in its extreme, in the wrapping of the body prior to the patient's death and in attempts of a nurse to close the eyes of the dying patient
prior to the onset of death (Sudnow, 1967; 1967a). Thus, that which is
regarded as a unique event to patient and family is likely to be visualized in
a seemingly impersonal manner by staff members, who are coping with the

heavy demands imposed upon them within the social system. Various social values also enter the picture with respect to the allocation of scarce resources to the dying patient. Sudnow suggests, for example, that if one enters the emergency ward of a hospital as a possible DOA, he had best be young, wearing a shirt and tie, and have clean breath. With respect to the age differential, he notes that "the older the patient, the more likely is his tentative death taken to constitute pronouncible death" (Sudnow, 1967).

A number of coping mechanisms are employed by practitioners to deal with the great emotional crises engendered by the fact of a dying family member while maintaining the objectivity and time to deal with the demands of other patients. Fox (1957), for example, in discussing medical education, notes that there is a socialization to "detached concern" on the part of the medical practitioner as he moves through medical school. In another context, Davis (1966) points out the use of two types of uncertainty by practitioners in dealing with the emotional crisis of parents of children with an unfavorable prognosis. Real uncertainty is uncertainty about a prognosis associated with the factual clinical picture. Parents may be told that "we don't really have the clinical evidence required for an accurate prognosis." Functional uncertainty, on the other hand, involves the conveyance of uncertainty regarding prognosis to parents despite the availability of clinical evidence as to the actual prognosis. Such uncertainty is deemed functional in avoiding entanglement in the highly charged emotional atmosphere of parents with a very ill child. It is, again, one of the ways in which the disciplined professional attempts to deal with the many demands competing for his time and energy. Comparable mechanisms may be operative within the context of the dying patient. It is voiced in the query, "When should the patient be told?" The decision reached holds significant implications for the interactional system between patient, family, and staff. This interactional context as it evolves about levels of awareness of dying on the part of the patient and his significant others has been called the "awareness context."

Anticipatory grief on the part of family members harbors clear implications for the emergent interactional context. Attitudes toward staff and the dying family member are of clear importance. Their willingness to relinquish the affective and instrumental tasks associated with the dying patient to the institutional staff and the staff's reaction to the forthcoming event are all part and parcel of the social environment of the dying patient. The awareness context is of importance with respect to anticipatory grief and the ways in which grieving is handled. Some level of awareness is a basic element in the initiation of anticipatory grief. Glaser and Strauss (1965) note the different meanings of awareness for interpersonal relationships in the presence of a dying family member. They delineate four forms of awareness context: closed awareness, suspected awareness, mutual pretense, and open awareness. "Closed awareness" entails the interactional context in which the patient is not aware that he is dying even though others are. "Suspected awareness" is when the patient suspects that those around him know and tries either to confirm or invalidate his suspicion. Particularly trying for patient and family is "mutual pretense awareness," in which both the patient and others know, but pretend to be unaware. Finally, with "open awareness," both patient and others are aware that the patient is dying and act openly on this awareness. If one simply cross-tabulates subjective awareness of impending death on the part of family members and the patient, the complexities of interaction are further elaborated. More specifically, this procedure indicates the stages in awareness of the impending loss of love object and, accordingly, suggests various points for the initiation of anticipatory grief. The first stage would entail the lack of awareness of the impending loss on the part of both patient and family. The situation may also occur in which the family knows but the patient does not or, conversely, when the patient is aware and family members may be unaware.

If the patient is unaware, too early visible grieving on the part of the family may carry over to him. The final category would entail the situation in which both family and patient are aware of the impending loss. The level of awareness influences the interactional context and is reflected in the awareness contexts. Awareness, in turn, initiates the process of anticipatory grief or anticipatory socialization to the impending event on the part of both patient and family members. "I fell into the equivalent of a postpartem depression, feeling myself a dry husk, already harvested to wither quietly away . . ."

The patient, when faced with this knowledge, attempts to cope in diverse ways. An element of anticipatory grief clearly permeates the thoughts and concerns of the patient. Kübler-Ross (1969) has found a general theme running through the patient's mind following knowledge of the impending death. She notes that, over time, in the dying trajectory, patients move through different stages in attempting to cope with the great weight of their plight. Initially, the patient reacts with shock or denial. "No, not me. There must be some mistake." Indeed, they and their families may "shop around" for a more favorable prognosis. This stage is followed by anger and rage, in which the patient asks, "why me?" Bargaining follows, in which the patient in essence says, "yes, me, but. . . ." Depression is the next stage. Finally, it is hoped, the patient attains a state of acceptance of the situation.

Comparable stages may be manifested by family members. All of the stages may be said to be part and parcel of anticipatory grief, for they entail socialization to an impending event and attempts to cope with that great crisis. The crucial intersection of familial grieving and patient coping must be of vital concern to the providers of care. If, for example, the patient has come to accept his condition but the family is unable to do so, difficulties may emerge. Similarly, if the family members have become resigned and have accepted the impending loss, and this is reflected in their interaction with a patient who is still attempting to cope with his awareness of the situation, their reaction may be harmful to the emotional well-being of the patient. The attempts of the family to cope with the great loss of a family member and the intersection of these attempts with the role of the practitioner in the medical setting is documented in the following case:

An eighty-six-year-old woman was admitted to a nursing home with a diagnosis of cerebral and generalized arteriosclerosis. She was a terminal patient and was receiving a liquid and soft diet. She was visited daily by her daughter, a widowed schoolteacher, who had lived with her mother for many years. Days passed and the daughter continued to hope for sufficient improvement in her mother to allow her to eat solid food. She expressed great concern about her mother's dentures which had not been worn for many weeks. She felt that new dentures would permit her mother to consume more solid foods, and, thus, lead to improvement in her condition. The daughter's concern was seen as disruptive by staff members, who informed her that nothing could be done for her mother. To impress this fact upon the daughter, a member of the dental staff was called in.

The dental staff member found the daughter standing by the patient's bed. The daughter told the staff member of her close relationship with her mother and of her inability to accept her mother's impending death. They talked for some time. Evening approached, and the nursing home assumed a different atmosphere. The daughter began to cry and the staff member listened as she voiced her many concerns about her mother. When the time came to consider the dentures, the daughter was in agreement that any dental changes would be more harmful than helpful in her mother's present state. Indeed, what the daughter really wanted was someone to talk to.

In this case, the importance of extending concern to the family member as well as the patient is clearly highlighted. The concern with dentures was but one element in the daughter's attempt to cope with the impending loss of her mother. Factual knowledge provided by professional staff was not sufficient in meeting the complex affective needs of the daughter.

SUMMARY AND CONCLUSIONS

Examination of anticipatory grief or the process of anticipatory socialization to the impending loss of a love object has been attempted within the organizational constraints of the medical institution and the disciplined practitioner. The shift from the home to institutionalized dying on the part of many patients entails a variety of complex interaction between patient and family in coping with the enormous burden of impending loss and the organizational structure designed to cope with continuous demands upon available resources. The role specificity of staff and organizational demands may serve to fragment the care provided the dying patient and his family. Moreover, professional socialization frequently entails a de-emphasis on the great emotional correlates of the dying trajectory and the crucial elements involved in the management of the dying patient, including anticipatory grief. The need for professional concern not only with the dying patient but with the family as well is of vital importance. Training of the disciplined professions to an enhanced awareness of these complex issues of coping and interaction must receive increasing attention.

REFERENCES

Claudill, W. "Around the Clock Care in Japanese Psychiatric Hospitals: The Role of the Tsukisoi," *American Sociological Review, 26:*204, 1961.

Davis, F., "Uncertainty in Medical Prognosis, Clinical and Functional," in W. R. Scott and E. H. Volkart, eds., *Medical Care.* New York: Wiley, 1966.

Fox, R. C. "Training for Uncertainty," in R. K. Merton, G. Reader, and P. Kendall, eds., *The Student Physician.* Cambridge: Harvard University Press, 1957.

Glaser, B. G., and A. L. Strauss. *Awareness of Dying,* Chicago: Aldine, 1965.

Kübler-Ross, E., *On Death and Dying.* New York: Macmillan, 1969.

Sudnow, D., "Dead on Arrival," *Trans-Action, 5:*36, 1967.

—— *Passing On: The Social Organization of Dying.* Englewood Cliffs, N.J.: Prentice Hall, 1967.

27

The Social Worker's Responsibility

Elizabeth R. Prichard

Social work is concerned with human needs, needs affecting relationships, emotional and economic deprivations, environmental stresses, man's interaction with others, and his striving for a stabilized and fulfilled life. There are inevitable life situations which place a greater strain on the individual's coping patterns than others, and it is at the time of crisis within the family that the social worker has a contribution to make. Family and children's agencies, courts, child guidance workers, psychiatric clinics, and hospital social workers can cite their involvement in innumerable cases of helping individuals and families with problems of adjustment as the result of the death of a mother or a father, a spouse or a child. These problems might have been alleviated on a preventive basis if they had been handled at the time of the immediate crisis, the period during which death had been anticipated.

The social worker's responsibility for the dying patient and the patient's family and the assumption of this role as a caregiving professional are not new. As noted recently, next to the nurse the hospital social worker has the most continuously close relationship with the patient and is the person in whom the patient can most readily confide (Phillips, 1972). Since the social worker is not involved with medical treatment, the relationship may in certain aspects be a freer one, with the anger and frustrations which a patient may feel at being subjected to painful procedures being directed toward the nurse and physician. On the other hand, these experiences may bring the patient closer to the nurse and create a chasm between the patient and the social worker. The social worker must establish relationships with both the patient and the family, although in many situations it is preferable that the relationship be primarily with the family. The patient's relationship with the physician and the nurse, a hospital chaplain or the patient's own spiritual advisor, are determining factors.

Hospital social workers have often taken their role in helping patients and their families prepare for death so much for granted that they have tended not to record this aspect of their work on charts and, like many others in the helping professions, have appeared to shy away from discussions of the topic. Lack of recognition of this area as one which requires guidelines,* the formulation of basic principles, and a careful review of practices has, until recently, resulted in relatively little being written by social workers.

When is grief or bereavement anticipatory? For the patient, grief starts when he first becomes aware that his life will end, or that at least it is threatened. He may recover and live for many years, but he will always remember this shattering moment of first awareness. The experience may add new dimensions to the meaning of life for such an individual. For the patient who is very ill, the shattering moment may imply a release from pain and from the problems of everyday living with which he can no longer cope. This does not necessarily mean that any patient is ready to accept fully the idea that as an individual he will no longer exist. Philosophical concepts of the meaning of death and the nonacceptance of nonbeing have received too little emphasis in helping patients through their last crisis. A life which has been fulfilled makes acceptance of the end more easy and graceful. Each individual has his own ideas of fulfillment, and the biological, psychological, and philosophical programming differs for each individual. In attempting to help the dying patient, too often all of these differences are not recognized or accepted either by his family or those who want to help.

When the individual is aware that he is dying, pretensions or denial of the fact by a spouse or close relative are demeaning to the relationship and place a greater strain on the patient. This should be a time for eking out as many satisfactions as possible in the remaining days and reinforcing a mean-

---

* It is worthy to note that a recent issue of *Social Work* included an excellent article, "Social Work and the Mourning Parent," which did formulate needed guidelines (McCollum and Schwartz, 1972).

ingful relationship, a time for planning the family's future and recognizing the patient's right to participate in decision-making. How better to ensure a peaceful death for the patient and an enriching and sustaining force for the future of the bereaved?

These goals are not easy to realize, and may not be achieved to any significant degree. However, their achievement is possible. Many steps must be taken, the first of which is for someone to establish a very intimate relationship with the patient. This person may be a member of the professional staff, a husband, a wife, or some relative or friend close to the patient. Death can come with great sadness and loneliness when the patient does not have family and friends "rooting" for his recovery. And patients generally have hope, even when they talk openly about dying. As Dr. Kübler-Ross mentions in her discussion of hope and patients' attitudes, "They did not regard their discussions of death and dying as either premature or contraindicated in view of their 'comeback' '' (Kübler-Ross, 1969).

Critical illness is a threat to one's functioning, relationships and to life itself, and with it comes the beginning of grief for the patient. Unfortunately, all too often it marks the start of abandonment for the patient. The fact remains that in order to help the patient, someone must know him and sustain a relationship with him. It is the experience of the social work staff of the author's hospital that the patients with whom they have had a relationship over the years through several admissions or have followed in clinic, and those for whom plans are made for care at home and with whom the social worker has remained in close contact, gradually are able to express their fears and concerns and involve themselves actively in planning. Time is an important factor in giving the patient the opportunity to become aware of his situation gradually and make his adjustments to the inevitable. Time and meaningful relationships which can sensitively pick up the clues from the patient are the major factors for any intervention.

Whether or not the social worker has a working relationship with the patient, the social worker is usually and correctly viewed as working with the family. It is the social worker who has an understanding of the needs of individual and family relationships and an extensive knowledge of community resources—understanding and knowledge which can be brought to bear to help the family members cope and to make plans for the patient and family as necessary.

In the beginning of the relationship with the family, the social worker must make a sound clinical evaluation. What are the existing relationships? If it be a husband or wife who is dying, has it been a satisfying marriage? Have the needs of each been met? Is the dying patient the dominant person in the relationship? What responsibilities did the patient carry which must now be borne by others, how well prepared are these others to assume the responsibilities, and what are their capacities to do this? Are there children? Is it a stable family? Relationships, ages, financial concerns—all must be evaluated. Are there in-laws who will want to take over caring for children? Are there difficult financial and business matters to be arranged? Emotional reactions can cause an immobilization of mind and body, and sensitive guidance into positive action with continued support is the social worker's responsibility. In addition, all who bear any professional responsibility for the chronically ill and dying patient and his family must be fully knowledgeable about the cultural factors and spiritual beliefs involved.

Social workers are often called upon to make plans for the patient and/or the family, and it is through the making of these plans together that a helping relationship starts. Social work, although problem-oriented and reality-focused, is always based on social and emotional factors without which there can be no reality. Recognition must be given to the fact that living patterns within the family have been seriously affected, relationships threatened, and that the family must go through the various stages of shock and disbelief, anger, hope, depression and, finally, acceptance.

It is not unusual for an anticipatory period to start early. Mrs. D., a thirty-five-year-old woman, the mother of two young children and married to a man twice her age, has been treated for depression in a psychiatry clinic, with the social worker carrying primary treatment responsibility. Previous struggles in the patient's life situation had seemed to be stabilized by her marriage to a man who had lived a full life, and whose job on a passenger ship had taken him all over the world. His outgoing personality and ease in relating to people had brought new spirit into the patient's life. The patient's depression developed when her husband became seriously ill with emphysema, and the recurring attacks and poor prognosis resulted in a threat to the patient she could not handle. With the help of the social worker, she has been able to develop some feeling of self-esteem and plan constructively for the future and the care of her children. She has finally been able to take a part-time job, but undoubtedly will need continuing support for an indefinite period of time.

The anticipatory grief period is one in which a husband, a wife, children, parents, and all involved members of a family need as much support as possible. The strain can be very great, for while they may be preoccupied with their own sense of grief, they must also be supportive to the patient. The emotional investment involved in a close relationship and the feelings of abandonment if the patient dies create a shattering impact. How much can and should a husband and father tell his children if their mother is dying? The uncertainties of the future for a wife and mother when a husband and father is dying can be appallingly great. At this particular time help is needed, and the social worker's knowledge of the meaning of loss and separation and their impact on later years can be used effectively.

The emergence in recent years of the use of groups to help families, particularly parents of critically ill children, has been an extremely effective method to ventilate with others needs, anxieties and experiences, and to discuss what must be faced and how to accomplish this. "Most parents gain emotional support from verbalizing their frightening thoughts as well as from a knowledge that these thoughts are prevalent among mourning parents" (McCollum and Schwartz, 1972). At Babies Hospital (Columbia-Presbyterian Medical Center, New York, New York), social workers participate with physicians and psychiatrists in conducting groups for parents of children with leukemia, with serious urological disturbances, and with cystic fibrosis.

Work with parents of the critically ill child or the dying child presents unique challenges, and supportive help is usually required over a long period of time. Close collaboration with the physician, the nurse, and the chaplain is essential for a full understanding of the child's reaction and parental attitudes. There are some families who withdraw from the dying child, and others who become so totally preoccupied with him that they neglect other family members. A sound psychosocial evaluation and sharing of this with all members of the helping team, on an interdisciplinary basis, can provide guidelines as to how far to encourage the parents' participation and intervention in the various tormenting aspects of the situation. Differences in attitude and readiness of the mother and father are particular challenges. Premature mourning by parents is not uncommon, and the lack of understanding of one parent toward the other who becomes totally grief-stricken may have an adverse effect on their future relationship and, therefore, on other children in the family.

The psychosocial evaluation is of benefit not only in the medical and social treatment process, but also as an effective means of gently involving the parents in preparing themselves for the future during the anticipatory period. It provides an opportunity to examine attitudes and can, as a result, modify these attitudes when necessary so that coping defenses can be established, and the period following death need not be one of total anguish and regret. As stated by McCollum and Schwartz, ''An issue of comparable importance is that of maintaining a supportive structure of activity and gratifying function. That is, it is crucial to direct attention to the quality of the child's remaining life. Without such attention, the extension of life is little more than an extension of death'' (McCollum and Schwartz, 1972). This is of particular importance when the illness may be a continuing one, although the final outcome is known or suspected. The child may have several admissions to the hospital, and the demands on the family members may be a tremendous drain on their emotional resources. But life for the family must continue: the father has his work responsibilities; the mother her home responsibilities; other children require attention.

Recently parents' need for help during the anticipatory period has been receiving increased emphasis. ''There is no more devastating experience in the life of a family than the fatal illness and death of a child. It tears into the family's life as a functioning unit and confronts each family member with a crisis in coping with loss and grief'' (Wiener, 1970). The most serious aspect is how the reaction of parents, especially that of the mother, affects other children in the family. The parents' preoccupation with their own grief may exclude adequate recognition of the feelings of the other children in the family. Lifetime scars can be inflicted. All members of the interdisciplinary team must be aware of this—and especially the social worker, for the social worker has the responsibility during this period for helping the family develop coping mechanisms for a stablilized future.

It is this writer's contention that the death of a parent, particularly of a mother, can be the most catastrophic experience in the life of a family where there are young or adolescent children. A husband facing the possible death of his wife is preoccupied with his own sense of impending loss and often finds he has little emotional reserve for his children. Children, especially younger ones, have a certain resiliency, but their reactions will vary in accordance with their years and stage of development. They have not yet learned to cope with life, they are dependent upon parents for emotional support and, through identity with the parent, for their future development. The death of a parent can result in marked personality impairment. If children are not helped at the time of crisis, difficulties and adjustment problems in later life are clearly predictable.

Much more can be stated on the various aspects of anticipatory grief or, in effect, on preparations for bereaved individuals' lives after the death of a family member. However, the author has stressed the fact that social workers have had a more extensive role in these preparations than has been fully recognized either by themselves or others. The social worker's contribution during the period of anticipation has not always been fully appreciated because all members of the caring team until recently have not given due value to this crucial period of people's lives.

Social workers are concerned professionals trained to handle the problems of everyday living. Most of their time is spent picking up the pieces of people's lives when problems arise, but many of these problems could have been averted at the time of crisis. Knowing the results, social workers have a responsibility to speak out more forcefully on how to prevent problems. Their knowledge must be put to use.

In the process of growth, it is important that we learn that life is uncertain, that it has vicissitudes and that we need to invest as much interest in as many people and in as many things as we reasonably can. Samuel Johnson said that we must work at making friends and "we must keep our friendships constantly in repair." In other words we should be prepared for loss, not necessarily dwell upon it or brood about it but be emotionally and ideationally prepared for it. There is no reason at all why we should not accomplish this attitude of mind with the proper training (English and Pearson, 1945).

Also, as Dr. Kübler-Ross states, "It might be helpful if more people would talk about death and dying as an intrinsic part of life just as they do not hesitate to mention when someone is expecting a new baby. If this were done more often, we would not have to ask ourselves if we ought to bring this topic up with a patient, or if we should wait for the last admission. Since we are not infallible and can never be sure which is the last admission, it may just be another rationalization which allows us to avoid the issue" (Kübler-Ross, 1969).

If we are not aware of our own feelings about death and cannot comfortably do a sound social evaluation, we will always avoid the issue or pass it by. Our own feelings about death or the ending of a life seem unreal when we are healthy. They are also contingent upon our age. These facts cannot be confused with responsibilities to those who will survive us. If they were, no one would make a will, or designate trusts and other benefits for survivors.

The living must go on living, and it is this philosophy to which the social worker addresses himself, with full knowledge and awareness of the result if preparations are not made during the anticipatory period. Countless case histories could be presented—of the depressed mother, the depressed wife or husband, the individual with psychosomatic complaints, the drug-addicted child, the unwanted pregnancy, the adolescent who steals, the alcoholic husband—all because incipient problems were not handled at the time of crisis.

Much more must be known and facts gathered about the relationships of the wanted, loved child who develops normally into adolescence, young adulthood, the responsibilities of adulthood, how he prepares for his family and how he faces the end of his life. Relationships are the core of life. Sorrow and sadness are personal matters and with time can be dealt with. The healthy person replaces the lost love object. The unhealthy person, according to Freud, takes a long period to reinvest his interest in the world and in other people and things. The period of anticipatory loss is the period for gradual preparation. It is not the time to transfer one's interest, but the time to prepare for the loss. During this period, the social worker can help in terms of understanding a family. Experienced in dealing with problems, the social worker is basically concerned with the stabilization of life; understanding the various steps which must be taken to achieve stabilization, the social worker is ready and prepared to support the patient and the family during this period and the family after the patient's death. The social worker—of all members of the interdisciplinary team—is more free to follow the patient and his family within the hospital walls and into the home and community. And, further, the social worker is concerned with the problems of everyday living and understands family dynamics, the stresses and strains of daily living, and the results when relationships are thrown off course. The complexities of this must be fully understood if the social worker can really be of help to the patient and the family during the period of anticipatory grief or, more pertinently, anticipatory bereavement.

REFERENCES

English, O. S., and G. H. J. Pearson, "Reactions to Inevitable Life Situations," in *Emotional Problems of Living*. New York: Norton, 1945.

Kübler-Ross, E., *On Death and Dying*. New York: Macmillan, 1969.

Lang, P. A., and J. Oppenheimer, "The Influence of Social Work When Parents Are Faced with Fatal Illness of a Child," *Social Casework,* Vol. XLIV:3, March 1968.

McCollum, A. T., and A. H. Schwartz, "Social Work and the Mourning Parent," *Social Work, 17:*1, 1972.

Phillips, D. F., "The Hospital and the Dying Patient," *Hospitals, Journal of the American Hospital Association, 46:*4, February 16, 1972.

Wiener, J. M., "Reaction of the Family to the Fatal Illness of a Child," in B. Schoenberg *et al.,* eds., *Loss and Grief: Psychological Management in Medical Practice.* New York: Columbia University Press, 1970.

28

Selected Tasks for the Dying Patient and Family Members

Mary T. Ramshorn

"We live each day of our lives with the fact of our death. Yet, none of us wants to know the time or the circumstances—and woe to the messenger who must carry the news to us."

Such was the response of a patient with leukemia, after hearing that the second program of intensive chemotherapy had failed to produce a remission of his disease. His philosophical mode of dealing with death, that is, in the abstract, as part of the human condition and as separate from himself, continued practically to the point of his death, four weeks later. Experiences with this patient and others facing terminal illness and death raise a number of questions about the nature and work of anticipatory grief and mourning (Ramshorn, 1971).

"Anticipation is prior imagination, and the extent of one's capacity to imagine a profound event has important bearing upon the way in which one responds" (McGrath, 1970). Much of life is spent in anticipating personal events and their meaning, new roles and relationships, and all the changes that are part of living; imagining our responses to moments of great joy, as well as to times of tragedy and loss. Yet, faced with the profound reality of our own personal death, the capacity to imagine changes, and, at times, fails us. Our own death, Lifton maintains, ". . . is not unimaginable but can be imagined only with a considerable degree of distance, blurring, and denial";

and further, ". . . we are not absolutely convinced of our own immortality, but rather have a need to maintain a sense of immortality in the face of inevitable biological death" (Lifton, 1971).

Within such a framework, and recognizing the personal limitations inherent in discussing grief and loss, it does seem possible to describe some of the experiences and the tasks both the patient and his or her significant partner share and attempt to complete in anticipatory grief.

Formulating the Personal and Social Meaning of an Anticipated Death. This requires not only confronting the perennial questions: "Why me?" "Why now?" but also dealing with the ambiguity of the experience and the feelings generated by it. Few, if any, have realized their self-ideal or completed their life's work. In anticipating death, however, one must find significance and value in the life lived, in a sense embracing it fully, knowing it personally as uniquely one's own before letting go.

Significance in life comes from many sources: intimate and enduring relationships; one's creative influences and the impact of one's work on coming generations of mankind; one's children who maintain the continuity with the future; and the transcendental values, including but not limited to the theological ones, which have guided and given meaning to personal experiences in life. All these must be sifted and weighed—the wheat separated from the chaff, as it were, for the final harvest. It is a dynamic process, at one and the same time offering hope and the sense of immortality, and yet generating feelings of profound sorrow at the approaching final separation. It is a difficult experience not only for the patient but also for the family members and professional caregivers, who at different times and to varying degrees are asked to give validation and support, who at the patient's behest are challenged themselves to seek final answers.

For the spouse or other significant partner in the relationship, formulating meaning during the anticipatory grief period has some dimensions which are complementary to the patient and others which are quite separate. While there is a mutuality between partners as they consolidate the significant events of the past, share the present in a heightened awareness of each other, and mourn the loss of the future, there are points of differentiation and noncomplementarity in the grief experience and work. For example, the spouse must deal with the feelings of anger at the prospect of being abandoned, guilt for the spontaneous feelings of anger, as well as for his or her perceived omissions and failures in the relationship. Additionally, he or she must work though any of the elements of "survivor guilt," that is, any of the needs to justify his or her own continued existence in the face of the other's impending death. Many times only minimal support is given to the partner in this experience of anticipatory grief.

Personal Time-Space Dimension. Anticipatory grief involves a profound sense of the loss of the future. This is paradoxical, indeed, since none of us possesses the future. And yet we do define and experience ourselves as possessing, if not even controlling, time ahead—time for completion of life work, time for using the options, time for closer approximation to the ideal self. Faced with the certainty and finality of approaching death, we grieve the loss of "becoming" either in ourselves, our spouse, our parent, or our child. What were once infinite possibilities in life now have finite boundaries. Consequently, the time-space axis shifts, with a greater emphasis on the past and present: the history of having been and the experience of being. Nor is it suggested that this occurs in an absolute and irreversible sense. Rather, a dynamic tension exists between what one has experienced and what one tries to anticipate: the finality of death. A patient described it in this way: "No man can take in his own death—his own mortality. After all, how can an individual deal with the fact of oblivion? But, it seems to me, as long as a man is remembered, is a memory to his family—even to one person—he lives."

It is critical for professional nurses and other caregivers closely involved in the experience of a patient's anticipatory grief to understand this change in being in time-space. For the patient and family members, the present is intense; the moments and experiences not to be relived; the work still to be completed—however that work is defined—so that the patient comes to a relative point of closure, or of being able to let go and withdraw.

Of equal importance is recognition that to anticipate and discuss the future need not be denial of impending death, but rather a means of holding on to "the sense of immortality," of maintaining hope even though it generates feelings of intense sorrow and loss. A parent looking ahead to the continued growth and maturity of his children gains a sense of hope and comfort in the thought of the generations that will follow him. At the same time, he experiences the sadness and loss of no longer being an integral part of that future. It is not enough to have known one grandchild; a person grieves for the grandchildren he will never know. It is not enough to know and love a son or daughter through his or her childhood; a parent longs to know the man or woman the child will become.

This change in the experience of time and self must be recognized and understood by professional caregivers if they are to relate effectively to patients and families in anticipatory grief. They must be sensitive to how the patient is experiencing himself, and to the coping behaviors of a lifetime that are being marshaled now for the task at hand.

In managing the anticipatory grief of the patient and the significant family members involved, the following suggestions come to mind:

1) An anticipatory grief period does not allow the patient and his family to work out all the perceived failures, hurts, and disappointments of a lifetime, nor to change significantly the established patterns of relating and caring. Indeed, these very long-established patterns help the patient to find a sense of meaning and should be recognized and supported. During the terminal period, Shneidman maintains, ". . . the individual displays behaviors and attitudes which contain great fealty to his lifelong orientations and beliefs. . . . dying behaviors . . . are an integral part of the life style of the individual" (Shneidman, 1964). Difficulties arise in care settings when the patient's habitual, preferred coping style and his value orientations do not meet the expectations and demands of the treatment environment and its professional inhabitants.

2) Anticipatory grief is a period of intense involvement, which requires suspension of normal roles within the family, work, and community systems. In treatment settings, this requires more flexibility in visiting hours, much sensitivity to needs of the family, and greater attempts at individualization of care. For the patient and his family, anticipatory grief is a period of time given only once. Not done "well," not fully lived, it can never be replayed. At the very least, the tasks of the period of anticipatory grief require that professionals define in a rational and humane way the role of the significant partner in the treatment setting. Without such role definition, the grieving partner can be experienced by the staff as an "outsider," just another visitor, a "querulous" family member, particularly as he or she attempts to maintain prolonged closeness with the dying patient, or to gain a sense of some control over the experience. In addition, the demands placed on a family member to support and comfort the patient at this time can be overwhelming and quite unrealistic.

3) Finally, professional staff in treatment settings will need support if they are to maintain such an orientation toward the needs of patients and families during the period of anticipatory grief. Nurses in the high-risk care areas are particularly aware of this, since they are involved in prolonged and

intimate relationships with dying patients. In a very real sense, as nurses care for individuals and families going through the period of anticipatory grief, they themselves anticipate the experience personally. They must develop ways of coping with the ambiguity and pain of loss, and attempt to find answers and meaning in the experience, not only for their patients, but also for themselves.

REFERENCES

Bakan, D., *Disease, Pain, and Sacrifice*. Chicago: University of Chicago Press, 1968.

Lewis, C. S., *The Problem of Pain*. New York: Macmillan, 1962.

Lifton, R. J., *Death in Life: Survivors of Hiroshima*. New York: Vintage Books, 1969.

—— *History and Human Survival*. New York: Random House (Vintage Edition), 1971.

McGrath, J. E., ed., *Social and Psychological Factors in Stress*. New York: Holt, Rinehart and Winston, 1970.

Ramshorn, M. T., "Patient Adaptation in Extreme Treatment Environments," unpublished doctoral dissertation, Teachers College, Columbia University, New York, 1971.

Shneidman, E. S., "Orientations Toward Death," in R. W. White, ed., *The Study of Lives*. New York: Atherton Press, 1964.

29

Social Work: Its Institutional Role

Phyllis Caroff and
Rose Dobrof *

꧁꧂

One of the "givens" for most of those who are involved in the care of
the terminally ill and their families is that a salient characteristic of the
American culture is its worship of youth and the resulting fear and avoidance of the subject of death or the dying person. There is one implication of
the recognition of this cultural characteristic which tells something about the
nature of the task of those interested in the developing discipline of thanatology. If a dominant note in the American ethos is this fear of death, then
those who work with the terminally ill and their families, who study and talk
and write about subjects like "the psychosocial aspects of terminal care" or
"anticipating grief and the bereaved family," constitute a kind of "counter-
culture." Such a counter-culture is neither so colorful as that of the young
people in the communes in Vermont, nor so threatening to deeply cherished
American values. It is, nonetheless, a counter-culture designed to question
certain components of the prevailing culture, to challenge individuals, pro-

* The authors wish to acknowledge the assistance given by Jacob Reingold, Executive
Director, Anastasia Cunningham, Director of Nursing Services, Marcia F. Jacobs, Director of
Social Services, and Jeanne Elster, Director of Group Activities, all of The Hebrew Home for
the Aged at Riverdale, New York; and the helpful advice of Harold Lewis, D.S.W., Dean,
Hunter College School of Social Work, City University of New York.

fessions, and institutions to reassess their rules and to develop new ways of doing things and new institutional arrangements which will provide the context for the doing.

This concept of counter-culture provides a pertinent backdrop against which to assess where we are now and to define the tasks which lie ahead. The point of vantage here is that of the profession of social work which, since that day in the early 1900s when Dr. Richard Cabot employed a young social worker named Ida Cannon to work with the families of the Massachusetts General Hospital patients, has had work with bereaved-to-be families as one of its salient professional tasks.

Within this context, we are limiting ourselves primarily to the anticipatory grief process which occurs in families in which the terminally ill person is aged, in which the cause of death is an insidious, chronic, long-term illness, and in which the death itself takes place outside the home in a hospital or extended-care facility. Several reasons impel us to select these as the limiting guidelines. These are increasingly the person, the trajectory and the locus of the dying process in the United States (Fulton and Fulton, 1972). These are the specialized areas of the authors' own professional experience and practical knowledge. Finally, this selected population group, the aging person and his family, because of its clear-cut process of anticipatory grieving, provides a particularly fruitful line of inquiry from which it should be possible to derive generalizations useful to the study of and work with other groups of the terminally ill and their families.

Certain factors concerning the nature of the task definition and institutional assignment are obvious. First, the unit to be served must be defined as the family, which includes the patient. Such a definition most nearly describes the reality context in which anticipatory grief work is done and death experienced. Moreover, such a definition saves us from the often insoluable dilemma and immoral act of choosing between the needs of other family members and the needs of the dying person.

Second, services to the family in which a member is dying must be organized to guarantee continuity of care from the beginning of the illness beyond the death of the member, to the point where surviving family members have successfully completed their grief work. The organizational implication of this is clear: that definition of the family as the unit of service and provision of service begins at the point at which medical service to the patient begins; that hospitalization represents only one episode and one kind of service; that service is extended into the community; and that the death of the terminally ill patient is not the signal for closure but rather that service continue until the family and the accountable professional or institution mutually agree that maximum benefit has been derived, or that service is no longer required.

And third, the guarantee of this continuity of care carries with it a system of accountability in which tasks are assigned and professions and institutions held accountable for performance of these tasks from the beginning to the end of the process.

One more set of assumptions must be explicated, a set which is part value assumptions and part theory about human behavior and family life. As we work with families and patients who are going through a process of anticipatory grief, we question the true definition of a successful grieving process. When Dr. Avery Weisman discusses the task of the hospital and its staff in the care of the terminally ill, he quotes the words of one of the early superintendents of Massachusetts General Hospital, written when that institution was still part almshouse and part hospital for the poor, the aged, and the ill of Boston. When all hope of recovery had gone, when everything curative had been done that could be done, the superintendent wrote that the task of Massachusetts General was to provide "safe-passage" for the dying patient.

In this era of the jet airplane, it may take us a moment to recapture what the words "safe-passage" meant in time past; to think about weeks and months in a vast and still largely uncharted ocean, at the mercy of the elements of wind and rain, with the destination only dimly known or understood. Safe-passage then might have been from the Old World to the New; safe-passage now for the dying person may be from this world to the unknown; and safe-passage for the grieving and bereaved family is certainly from the pain and anguish of a traumatic life experience to years that remain to be lived and tasks that remain to be done. (It is noteworthy that many thanatologists have also established this as their goal—whether or not they have expressed it so succinctly.)

Further, with respect to the families, we define the goals of the institutions and helping professions as providing them with the needed supports so that each member is able to play his appropriate role during the process of grieving and bereavement in order that the family, as a system, and the individual actors within it, may emerge from this process depleted * and with a

* We use this word in the sociological, not psychodynamic sense, as Shanas, et al. (1968) use it to describe the family depleted by the deaths of members.

changed configuration, but intact, with the dead family member now occupying his rightful place in the annals of his family's history and in the memories of those still living, and with each survivor able, in Erikson's words, "to accept the historical inevitability of what has happened," including the life, the dying and the death which has occurred.

As essays and studies proliferate in the areas of death, grief, and bereavement, written from the perspective of the doctor, the nurse, the man of the cloth, the social worker, and so forth, a number of variables can be identified which seem to influence the way dying and death is experienced and managed. These include the norms and values of the larger society and the particular subculture of which the family is a member, the idiosyncratic norms and values of the particular family, its own coping patterns and life style; the role and status of the dying member in the family system; and the career of the dying person, by which we mean the duration of the process of dying, the pain attendant to it, bodily changes and mental impairment which may be associated with the process.

From the perspective of social work, we must include the institutional arrangements which will facilitate the realization of articulated values: that death will be managed with dignity for the patient, and the family members will have coped well within their own expectations and those of the larger social system.

To recapitulate, the focus of attention here is primarily on the chronically ill aged who are confronted with the task of living out the end of their lives in a medical institution and who have experienced periodic and prolonged separations. Their families, who in some measure have been party to this situation, have, by virtue of these separations, begun the preparation for the ultimate separation. A series of studies, generated by the reality of increasing numbers of aged and chronically ill persons who live out their last years or weeks in institutions ideally designed to insure maximum well-being, have served to throw light on such important dynamics as the interaction between hospital staff and these patients (Glaser and Strauss, 1965, 1968); the differentials between private and public hospitals in care of dying and dead patients (Quint, 1967); and the many issues and questions which confront the patient facing imminent death (Kübler-Ross, 1969).

Blauner (1966) suggests that the limited systematic study of the families which survive the deaths of their elderly relatives may be explained by a series of variables which reduces the impact of death on those who survive.

One among these is the sense that when death occurs in old age it is as it should be, as God intended, or as it must inevitably be, and, therefore, both the dying person and his family can accept the death. Neither has cause to rail against a cruel or unfair fate.

Also, changing social and familial structural arrangements have retired the elderly from the labor market and social activities, thus diminishing the importance of their functions within the family. The separations created by institutional care dilute friendship and familial contacts, weaken social and emotional commitments, and reduce the effect of death on the life of the family. Thus, according to Blauner, the death of an elderly person may not evoke the responses traditionally expected of the bereaved.

Fulton and Fulton (1972) have added clarity to the differences observed, for example, in the grief reactions to the death of an elderly parent or relative and that experienced by the family at the sudden, unexpected death of a family member carrying a key instrumental or expressive role. Their conceptualization of a "high grief potential" death or a "low grief potential" death points out "that the degree or intensity of one's grief at the time of death is a function of the kind of death experienced."

Lindemann's seminal work, "Symptomatology and Management of Acute Grief" (1944) and the subsequent studies under the rubric of "crisis intervention," have served to familiarize us with the series of intense reactions characterized as "normal grief" following the sudden and unexpected death of a significant family member. Similarly, we are familiar with the importance of what Lindemann described as "grief work" as a necessary process to working through traumatic loss successfully. We have less understanding of the reactions of patients and families where the process of dying is protracted, and the circumstances of dying appear to affect behaviors in a direction which seems to violate our expectations of how families should behave in relation to what we perceive as most functional for the dying patient, the family and, we suggest, the institutional caregivers.

At this juncture, a caveat should be introduced: the essential work being done in observing and ordering reactions and behaviors of all the important parties involved in this process has the potential to stereotype expectations of how death and dying should be managed, exacerbating strains which may well be termed normal in the complex interactions between the institution and its caregivers, the family and the dying patient. This is not to obviate our norms, values and goals for intervention, but should serve to underscore the importance of understanding, appreciating, and accepting the range of possible behaviors that may be functional in coping with what is culturally the most frightening of all tasks, dying.

For social workers, the principle of individualization, incorporating concepts of need and capacity, must obtain. As an institutionalized profession, social work has long existed with both the supports and constraints of organization. However, social workers perceive their tasks as those of facilitating and enhancing, to mediate and negotiate between the needs of the patient, the needs and capacities of the family, and, similarly, of the institution to enhance the functioning of the three. However, social work's value position which, together with knowledge informs its principles of practice, asserts that such individualization be concerned within the broader conception of socialization, which implies the strengthening and loosening of human ties as appropriate at given points in the life cycle, decrying the isolation and alienation which can easily become the scourge of our era.

Returning to a consideration of the concept of "anticipatory grief" as it applies to patients and families, we perceive its salutory effects and some of the consequences and dilemmas which, at this time, appear counterproductive. Social workers operate on the assumption that with institutional and caregiving supports the opportunity to prepare for death enables patients and their families, as interdependent, interacting elements of one system, to cope successfully with the tasks with which each is confronted. For the patient, ideally, it is the acceptance of his ceasing to be by virtue of having been, the affirmation of self through the ability to relinquish, the final acceptance of life and of man's fate. Experience suggests that, where desired, encouraging the patient to participate in the planning around his death enhances the integrity of the self. The degree to which this can be facilitated for patients depends in significant measure on improved medical technology to make pain manageable, the caring ministrations of the staff which affirm and value the patient's being, and the opportunity and ability of the members of the patient's family, particularly children, to demonstrate the value of his being through their caring, support, and affection as a measure of the patient's immortality.

For the family, this "lead time" can be an opportunity to become more conversant with death as a part of life, to prepare for the inevitability of death through accomplishing in part the "grief work" which may involve experiencing depression, anger, guilt, and anxiety, heightened preoccupation

with and concern for the patient, a rehearsal of the actual death, and preparation for the necessary adaptations that may be required because of it.
Our own evidence supports other reports that such preparation does diminish
the impact of the actual death and the intensity of the grief which follows. It
is important to note, however, that many family members, prior to the death
of the relative, continue to express their anxiety about how they will react
when the death actually does occur.

Disturbing consequences can arise when the process of anticipatory
grieving results in family members being emotionally and even physically
unavailable at a time when the dying patient is most in need of interest, caring, affection, and support. An additional complication and strain is the critical attitude on the part of staff members to what they perceive as inappropriate, indifferent, or calloused behavior on the part of the family at a point
when the staff members are investing heavily in their ministrations to the
dying patient but also struggling with their own conflicts and ambivalences.
The dysfunctional consequences of these concomitant occurrences, for both
the patient and the family, are evident. In our experience, however, many
families consciously want to ''do everything they can possibly do'' because
of inner need, responsiveness to perceived external expectations, and the
hope that they will provide appropriate models for their own children.

Most families ascribe power, authority, and expertise about death and
dying to the institutions and their caretaking personnel. If they experience
the staff as helpful, staff members may well be asked, ''What should I do?''
This can open the door to a process for understanding the needs which under-
lie the question, as well as the coping capacities of the family. At times, it
may be an informational question based simply on no prior experience with
the dying or knowledge of what is perceived as helpful to the patient. To
the staff of a home for the aged, for example, informational questions were
frequently posed by those who had never before had to assume the role of a
responsible family member at a time of impending death. Typically, these
individuals were the patients' middle-aged children whose experience had
been limited to the deaths of their grandparents in the remote past. Their
responses and behaviors had been limited to providing emotional support for
their own bereaved parents. Consequently, their ''what should I do?'' covered a range of questions. ''What does Mother need?'' ''Whom does she
need?'' ''Who needs to see her?'' ''What arrangements need to be made?''
''What do you, the institution staff, expect of me?'' As questions are asked

and responses given, there may be every indication of emotional and physical resources to meet the needs of the patient and to deal adequately with the grief processes of all concerned.

At other times, the questions may bespeak heightened conflictual feelings about the patient which impede the ability to deal with these feelings vis-à-vis the dying patient, and thus interfere with the family members' own expectations for their behavior. For these individual family members, the question is more accurately, "Can I do it?" Not too infrequently, the question may also reflect intrafamilial conflict: with a spouse because of too much time spent away from home, or strains created by the demand to spend time with the patient and the demand of children who are at home needing supervision. In such situations, when there are strong pulls to be with the patient, there is need to understand, with the patient and family member, what is a reasonable expectation, and to support those behavior patterns which maintain a viable balance in the total family network.

Sometimes, the "what should I do?" reflects the inability to act on felt need because of system requirements. An example is the single daughter who must spend all day, every day, with her dying mother because of the threat to self-equilibrium created by anticipation of the ultimate separation.

Finally, if available and accepting of individual needs, capacities, and styles, the social worker may be able to help those family members whose question "what should I do?" reflects their own shock and dismay at an absence of grief and their wish to be free of the burden of being supportive in a process which exacerbates their discomfort. Understanding their unique experience may help to assess whether indeed they have done their "grief work" too well, or whether there are psychological blocks to the process of working through. In either case, with support behaviors can be encouraged which can be helpful to the family members, as well as to the dying patient, in bringing their expectations more in line with what is possible for them to do and feel and, thus, to mitigate against the potentially destructive effects of guilt and shame.

Those who staff extended-care facilities face a professional dilemma of particular poignance, a dilemma which has its origins in the historic societal task assignment of such facilities, and which is played out today in the particularities of some of the families of patients. Erving Goffman (1961), in his prescient analysis of the total institution of which the extended-care facility is but one type, writes that ". . . most total institutions, most of the time, seem to function merely as storage dumps for inmates. . . ." The historic and sociological analysis of the precursor for today's extended-care facilities—the almshouses, the municipal hospitals for the chronically ill or incurables, the poorhouses, or the county farm—all testify to the origin of these institutions as "the storage dump" for the frail, the mentally impaired, the chronically ill old person for whom neither family nor community could make any other provision.

However, social work professionals cannot live with so bleak a definition of their task, one which dehumanizes staff no less than patient. Moreover, social workers know, intellectually and emotionally as they subject their institutional task assignment to functional analysis and spend days involved with lives and deaths of their patients, that the extended-care facility is an integral necessity in the health care delivery system. Its presence does not testify to the failure of the unit of the family, nor to the weakening or destruction of bonds of love and responsibility among family members but, rather, to changes in the dying process.

We must now deal with a penumbra of the reality of the extended-care facility system and the variety of actors within it. There are among the families encountered those who *do* use the institution as a "storage dump" for the mother or father who long ago had lost the love and respect of their children, and whose entry into the institution signaled, but did not cause, exclusion from the members of the family group, and their children's reconstruction of their own lives without their parents. Such behaviors may be reinforced by the appropriate valuing in our society of being in touch with real feelings and being able to accept them. The daughter may say, "My mother was a selfish, bitter woman who never gave us the love and care we needed but expected us to do everything for her. I've made my peace with this and I've got a good life now. I don't love her and you can't expect me to pretend I do."

We must ask ourselves whether the value placed on awareness and acceptance of a person's own feelings carries with it the freedom to act on these feelings without consideration of the consequences of so doing. This is doubtful, and the final event of the death of a family member is rarely free of any ambivalent feelings about the role the family, as survivors, played in the process. For, in our culture, we do perceive death as a loss and still expect that survivors exhibit some expression of grief and show respect for the human struggle of life, of which death is the ultimate expression. It is within the context of such notions that there is a role for social work professionals, "as carriers of the cultural norms," to reach out, to explore the reasons for absence of involvement, and to support that side of the ambivalence which will encourage a new interaction in relatively neutral areas.

In one instance, a fierce old lady was dying in an extended-care facility. She had, in the words of her sons, always been a "taker," never a "giver." She had fought hard against her sons' marriages and then against their wives, always referring to each daughter-in-law, not by name, but as "she." This patient demanded a dominant position in her sons' lives, and when the demand was not met she fought back. She was brought, fighting every step of the way, to the institution, when her declining health status prevented her from living alone and her sons and their wives, fearful for the survival of their marriages and family life, could not accept her presence in their homes. Nor could they visit her at the institution except in a ritualistic fashion, on Mother's Day, her birthday, the anniversary of their father's death.

When it became clear that she did not have much longer to live, the staff telephoned her family. "It is a matter of days or weeks at the most. We thought you should know." (There is a routine procedure in hospitals and extended-care facilities of notifying the family when death seems imminent. It serves the needs of institution, patient, and family. For the institution, it is, at least in part, protective. If death seems to occur unexpectedly "without warning," questions may be raised by the family about the quality of medical and nursing care. Staff members also say that the advance warning gives the family members a chance to prepare for the death which, in professional terms, permits them to do anticipatory grief work. In the institutional lexicon, this means that the family will be able to cope with the death better, with minimal strain on the institution. Finally, such notification may provide the family with the opportunity to call together the important family members and friends to become part of the dying process and to help provide "safe-passage" for the dying patient.)

The sons and their families did come, and although there was in this case no apparent deathbed reconciliation, the head nurse did observe that "Mrs. X's family visited this afternoon. She seemed in a better frame of mind after they left."

There is an opposite familial response to the death of an aged parent—that of many middle-aged children, themselves parents and not infrequently grandparents, who are racked by the grief they are experiencing, and whose honorable grief is tarnished by their fear that it is somehow excessive, self-ish, childish. To use the terminology of Fulton and Fulton (1972), these people are suffering "high grief" in a "low grief potential" situation, and their grief at the loss is heightened further by their perception that the grief they feel may not be viewed by others as altogether appropriate. The social worker's principle of individualization demands acceptance of the reality of these grief-stricken feelings and providing comfort to the family member during the preparatory, anticipatory period and through the bereavement.

The focus here has necessarily been on the family of the dying patient. But it should be clear that helping families during the period of anticipatory grief can mean that patients' needs are better served also. In essence, we are saying that the social worker's facilitating, enabling role does not encompass the prerogatives of judging critically the "correctness" of the feelings experienced in the process of preparing for death. For here each will manage in his own way, hopefully with professional support and acceptance. Professional behaviors are informed by knowledge and values, and demonstrate that there are benefits to patients and families to maintain a connectedness. Family members can be helped through this process when they are clear about their expectations for themselves and clear about what the institution perceives as helpful, which is based ideally on genuine regard for the families' needs and capacities as well as those of the patient.

If maximizing possibilities for coping with dying and death involves interaction between the patient and family, and the anticipatory grieving of the family potentially attenuates emotional bonds, it must be asked whether institutional arrangements offer the necessary supports to encourage family involvement. Simple, yet financially costly questions must be answered. Are family lounges readily accessible on each floor, as well as acceptable eating facilities? Is there sufficient staff to allow more flexibility in visiting and greater availability of staff members to the families of patients? Are there in-service educational opportunities for medical and paramedical personnel to learn more about the special psychosocial needs of patients and families as well as the research being done in thanatology? Are there resources available to provide the necessary emotional supports for staff members to deal with stressful feelings occasioned by the nature of their tasks? Is there sufficient social work staff available to offer counseling or consultation to patients, families, and staff as needed? Does the institution recognize its continuing responsibility to the family after the death of the patient? Is there the collective potential for staff and administration to press for the necessary funding to provide needed resources? These are basic questions which must be persistently asked.

In summary, it is our contention that the social worker's interprofessional endeavor in the new discipline of thanatology represents a kind of "counter-culture" to the prevailing notions of Western thought and culture, notions which perceive death and dying as failure and, consequently, repugnant. We perceive the social worker's tasks as affirming the dignity of life through becoming conversant with death; as enhancing and enabling the process by facilitating relationships between the dying patient, family members, and the institutions which exist for the purpose of supporting endings and beginnings as these reflect life in its continuum. As professionals, we welcome the important and necessary attempts to order observations, to provide the guidelines for assessing and intervening, to achieve "safe-passage" for the patient and "safe-passage" for the family members so that they may continue to live, having come to terms with the death of one of their own. We are concerned, however, that the concept of individualization continues to be regarded as essential to understanding and accepting the processes through which patients and families master this most difficult of tasks. The value of individualization exists within a broader conception, that death and dying is a social process which values connectedness within the parameters of need and capacity of the individuals and institutions involved. Consequently, we perceive our interventions as individuals and as caregivers in institutions as supporting this connectedness—between the dying patient and his family, between the patient and the caregivers in the institution, and between the institution and the family. We have recognized the salutory effects for both patient and family in the process of anticipatory grief work, have identified some potentially dysfunctional counsequences, and have taken a position for initiative on the part of the professional to understand the reasons for inability to maintain connectedness and, where necessary, to work actively for enhancing opportunities to re-establish connectedness on more mutual ground.

The demand on the institution and its staff, if the guarantee of safe-passage for both patient and family is taken seriously, is not an easy one to meet, nor does the acceptance of the task carry with it the guarantee of success. Yet, in the end, the words of the *Talmud* seem particularly appropriate in defining the task: "You are not called upon to complete the work," according to Rabbi Tarfon. "Yet you are not free to evade beginning it."

REFERENCES

Blauner, R., "Death and Social Structure," *Psychiatry, 25:*378, 1966.

Fulton, R., and J. Fulton, "Anticipatory Grief: A Psychosocial Aspect of Terminal Care," in B. Schoenberg, *et al.,* eds., *Psychosocial Aspects of Terminal Care.* New York: Columbia University Press, 1972.

Glaser, B., and A. Strauss, *Awareness of Dying.* Chicago: Aldine Press, 1965.

—— *Time for Dying.* Chicago: Aldine Press, 1968.

Goffman, E., *Asylum.* New York: Doubleday, 1961.

Kübler-Ross, E., *On Death and Dying.* New York: Macmillan, 1969.

Lindemann, E., "Symptomatology and Management of Acute Grief," *American Journal of Psychiatry, 101:*141, 1944.

Quint, J., *The Nurse and the Dying Patient.* New York: Macmillan, 1967.

Shanas, E., P. Townsend *et. al., Old People in Three Industrial Societies.* New York: Atherton Press, 1968.

PART *5*
THE MANAGEMENT OF ANTICIPATORY GRIEF

30

The Vectors and Vital Signs in Grief Synchronization

Carl A. Nighswonger

Anticipatory grief, as a creative process, has become a growing concern for the professional who works with the families of the terminally ill. That experience through which family members must pass as they anticipate the death of a loved one precedes bereavement grief in that it occurs while the loved one is still alive but terminally ill. It is, therefore, an experience which occurs simultaneously with the dying person's own experience of preparatory grief.

Effective anticipatory grief work does not prevent the necessity of experiencing bereavement grief, but the successful resolution of the conflict arising in anticipatory grief can do much to decrease the likelihood of morbid, unhealthy, or abnormal bereavement grief following the actual death of the loved one.

Studies in the "Death and Dying Program" at the University of Chicago hospitals and clinics reflect the necessity of dealing effectively with the family's anticipatory grief concurrently with the dying person's own preparatory grief experience. This simultaneous intervention contributes significantly to the dying person's ability to experience death with dignity, equanimity, and a sense of "appropriateness."

The author refers to this total process of facilitating the congruency of the preparatory and anticipatory grief experiences as grief synchronization.

One's professional concern is to enable the dying person and the family to "mesh" their grief "gears" in such a way that they are able to move toward a mutal acceptance of the appropriateness of death at this moment in the shared experience of their lives together. Reference to the meshing of gears in no way implies that this is a mechanical experience; nor is it inferred that the experience is without pain and suffering. Rather, it is a tribute to the capacity of the human spirit to respond to life's crucial encounters with dignity, meaning, and purpose.

Unfortunately, the real tragedy often lies in professional insensitivity to the vectors inherent in the grief synchronization process, and unresponsiveness to the vital signs of anticipatory grief.

THE VECTORS IN GRIEF SYNCHRONIZATION

Vectors refer to the contextual factors which affect the intensity of and give direction to the preparatory and anticipatory grief processes. One might diagram the contextual relationship as follows:

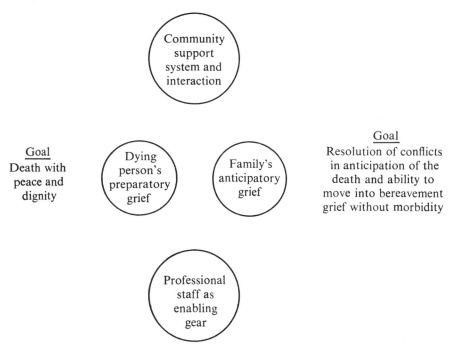

Vector One: The Community Support System

The community support system ''gear'' may facilitate or inhibit the dynamic quality of the grief processes for the dying person and/or the family. Cultural attitudes and social practices which seek to disguise and avoid the reality of death as a natural part of life create barriers for the family and may prevent the dynamic quality of the anticipatory grief process. Similarly, they may also adversely affect the dying person's preparatory grief. (However, this concern is beyond the scope of this chapter.)

Although much has been written in recent years concerning these barriers, the more significant factors should be noted:

1) *Encouragement to panic.* Failure of the support system to respond may cause the family to turn to magic, medical quacks, or other means which might allow them to avoid the reality of the terminal illness of a loved one. In contrast, a sensitive support system within the community may provide the family with the support needed to cushion the shock and to allow them time to muster their forces in response to the crisis.

2) *Reinforcement of denial.* May result from the community's need to pretend that death is not real. Consequently, although the family may be ready to move on in their grief, they are encouraged not to do so by those around them.

3) *External control of feelings.* Social patterns frequently make it difficult for families to ventilate their feelings. The reinforcement of denial keeps their feelings submerged. Taboos against the expression of anger, and popular attitudes that strong emotions should not be expressed, may inhibit both the positive and negative feelings which then remain unexpressed and unresolved.

4) *Irrelevant and inadequate life perspectives.* As to the meaning of death, these may contribute to the feelings of absurdity and emptiness that are so frequently felt by the family. (The statement that one's daughter is dying because God is short of little girls in Heaven is unlikely to provide any meaning to a father.)

Such responses of support are more likely to arrest the grief process than facilitate the movement of the family through the anticipatory experience.

Vector Two: The Professional Staff

With almost two-thirds of all deaths in this country occurring in institutions, the majority of families experience anticipatory grief in relationship to some type of professional personnel. The attitudes and practices of professionals may, in themselves, provide further barriers which limit the intensity of and direct the family away from creative anticipatory grief.

Although attempts are being made in professional education to prepare institutional personnel to deal more sensitively with the dying person and his family, all too often death and dying are still dealt with objectively and impersonally by the professional.

It is difficult for the professional to shift his focus of concern from healing to a concern for helping a family cope with their anticipation of the loss of a loved one. Such a shift in focus need not represent failure on the part of the professional, but rather an awareness of the reality of the situation. It need not mean the sacrifice of clinical skills or medical competence; but rather the redirection of professional energies to the sensitive care of the dying person, and to the reassurance of the family that the loved one will be permitted to experience a "good death."

Frequently, the fear of the process by which a loved one may die is a major barrier in the anticipatory grief experience; and, when remembered as such, it contributes significantly to the morbidity of bereavement grief. Yet, a preliminary study conducted by the College of Chaplains in 1971 indicated that in almost half of the 112 deaths which occurred in 35 medical centers during a one-month period, the family was not consulted as to whether they desired prolongation-of-life procedures to be performed on their loved ones.

Routine staff procedures often indicate little sensitivity to the needs of the family's preparatory grief. For example, few, if any, families are able to cycle their grief to the visitation schedule of the intensive care unit. Yet, all too often the patient is kept in intensive care until his death, even though the staff has acknowledged that the situation is "hopeless," and that nothing more can be done to "heal" the patient.

Studies indicate how frequently the hazards of grief identification inhibit the staff's ability to respond to the needs of the family. Often, unknowingly, such identification leads the staff to focus on their own feelings rather than to remain sensitive to the dynamics of the family's grief.

The professional staff can function as a vital vector in facilitating the anticipatory grief of the family, and, as a mediating gear, can assist in synchronizing the family with the grief experience of the dying person. It has been our experience that professionals are becoming increasingly aware of their responsibility, and are concerned about becoming more sensitive to their role as facilitators in the anticipatory grief process.

Vector Three: The Dying Person's Preparatory Grief

Next to the family itself, the dying person's own preparatory grief process is the strongest vector in grief synchronization. As the dying person goes through the process of preparing to give up the "I" in the "I-thou" relationship, he is experiencing intrapersonal death, and his response has a direct effect upon the family's ability to cope with their anticipation of the interpersonal loss of the "thou" in the relationship.

Arrested preparatory grief confronts the family with the dying person's inability to cope with the crisis confronting him. His pain and anguish intensify their own, and a process may emerge which, without intervention, may lead to the destruction of the dignity of the experience, thus contributing to the patient's sense of resignation and forlornness while increasing the family's likelihood of later morbid bereavement grief.

In contrast, the dying person, who is able to move through the dramatic process of his own preparatory grief toward the completion of his life with a sense of acceptance of the "appropriateness" of the timing of his death and the fulfillment of his life, may himself facilitate the family anticipatory grief by enabling both to share their "walk through the valley of the shadow" together, embracing the presence of each other as they struggle with the effects of the stings of death. Their ability to share in the resolution of the conflict and in the realistic hope for the completion of life in a "good death" encourages the family to remain open to each other and to the conflicts which are produced in their own anticipation of what life will be without the loved one.

Vector Four: The Family

The resources the family brings to the anticipatory grief process provide the fourth vector, which determines the intensity and direction of their experience. The professional who is concerned about the needs of the family's anticipatory loss experience must be sensitive to the unique and dynamic nature of the family's encounter with the forthcoming death of a loved one.

There are certain vital signs which are just as essential to the assessment of the point a family has reached in the anticipatory grief process as are the physical vital signs to the physician who is concerned with the medical condition of his patient. One's sensitivity to the readings of these vital signs illuminates the dimensions of conflict, the areas needing therapeutic intervention, and the prospects for enabling the family to cope creatively with their anticipatory grief experience. In short, the vital signs let one know where a family is and provide clues as to why they are there.

FAMILY VITAL SIGNS IN ANTICIPATORY GRIEF

Focus of Concern

In crisis situations such as grief, families tend to direct their psychic (emotional and spiritual) energies toward a common focus of concern. Although there may be other concerns, one issue tends to remain dominant as they attempt to come to grips with the situation and to resolve the conflicts produced by the situation. When a family cannot share in a common focus of concern, it is not responding as a unit, and the multiple focii to which family members are directing their energies become indicators of the family's need for assistance with their fragmentation.

Since grief is a dynamic process, it is appropriate that the family's focus of concern will shift as new issues and conflicts arise in their experience. The failure of a shift in focus may be an indicator that the family's anticipatory grief process has been arrested. The professional must them assist the family in helping themselves overcome the obstacle or remove the barriers which are inhibiting the movement of the grief experience.

The initial focus of concern for the family in anticipatory grief is the shock which results from the disclosure that they must face the prospect of living without the loved one. The conflicts produced by this disclosure may be dealt with by denial, panic, or other measures which seek to reduce the conflict for them. The focus of concern tends to indicate the drama in which the family is involved. It frequently shifts from the shock of disclosure to the release of emotions to negotiation as the family progresses through the anticipatory grief experience.

The most significant shift in the family's focus of concern is the transition of the meaning of hope. Initially, in anticipatory grief, hope equals cure, and the family's energies are directed toward attempts to deal with their feelings and frustrations which emerge from the concern that death should not, and perhaps even the feeling that it will not, occur.

If permitted by the vectors described above, however, the family's hope will shift to a concern for the meaningfulness or purposefulness of death as a means of coming to accept the appropriateness of the loss of a loved one. Such hope may be expressed in the desire that the loved one not linger on in a prolonged illness of pain and suffering, or loss of dignity. Or, it may be reflected in a concern that the person is prepared or has had a chance to take care of his unfinished business. Frequently, however, the family will seek assurance that they will be able to get along, or even survive, after the loved one is gone.

It is unfortunate that professionals often miss the signals that the family's focus of concern has shifted to the experience of dying as they continue to respond to their own focus of concern that hope still means cure, or that something more must be done to prolong the patient's existence. Such insensitivity often creates in the family a sense of isolation both from the patient and the staff and provides a further barrier to grief synchronization, with the subsequent potential for morbid bereavement reactions.

Circumstances

The resources available to the family for coping with anticipatory grief are largely determined by the circumstances in which the death of the loved one is experienced. One needs to be aware of how the family's equilibrium is affected by the terminal illness. If the loved one played a dominant social role in the family, the equilibrium is likely to be affected quite severely, and the family may be paralyzed in their attempts to function effectively in their imbalance.

The family will also be affected by the type of illness, its intensity, and duration. Hereditary illnesses often intensify the guilt felt by the parents. Families with a history of deaths from cancer will often react more severely than those for whom cancer does not have such strong fatal connotations. Similarly, families who have experienced previous losses from illness in unfortunate or unusually difficult circumstances will tend to anticipate the loss of this loved one in a similar manner.

And, as previously indicated, the vectors of community and staff support may provide additional circumstantial stress which will further inhibit the anticipatory grief process.

Coping Patterns

A family's previous experiences of crises may have enabled them to develop creative coping patterns for dealing with loss, and thus they are able to respond to this anticipated loss with resources which have been hammered from the anvil of experience. Often, however, families have been weakened by such losses, and have been unable to develop effective patterns for coping with such crises.

Effective coping patterns reflect the family's ability to accept reality without distortion or avoidance. They can realistically perceive their responsibility in the situation without feeling the need to take too much, or too little, responsibility for what has happened to them and to their loved one.

Creative coping patterns include a family's ability to deal with conflict and to express their feelings about the crisis experience appropriately. Families who have faced previous crises by ignoring them and pretending that they will go away are likely to find such denial mechanisms of little value in anticipatory grief. Families who are unable to sanction the expression of emotion, either negative or positive, may need assistance in developing ways of expressing their feelings in constructive ways which do not produce further conflict for other family members, or for the dying loved one.

Grief synchronization reflects the ability of the family and the loved one to have coping patterns which allow them to share their feelings, frustrations, hopes, and concerns with each other as part of the experience of walking together in death's shadow.

Congruence of Meaning

The human spirit has an amazing capacity to cope with loss when the individual is able to make some sense and meaning out of the experience. Families able to find meaning and purpose in the anticipated loss of a loved one constantly confirm confidence in the integrity and beauty of the human spirit to cope with tragedy, hurt, and loss.

The family's ability to find meaning within their shared experience can make the difference between fulfillment and frustration, acceptance and resignation. Effective grief synchronization implies the family and loved one's experiencing of congruence of meaning as they encounter death together.

Realistic hope, which is essential to acceptance, implies that something purposeful and meaningful can come out of the experience being shared by the family and the loved one. It is unfortunate when families are denied the opportunity to search for meaning by vectors of professional or community interaction which inhibit or prevent such exploration.

Experience, in and of itself, is without meaning; death as a human phenomenon is as empty of meaning as is life itself. The meaning which is to be found in life experiences is the meaning which we choose to give to those experiences. One's endowment of meaning to his experience always reflects some life perspective or point of view from which he examines his experience and determines the meaning of that experience.

The family that has shared a common perspective about the meaning and purpose of life and death prior to anticipatory grief is more likely to experience a congruence of meaning in the approaching death of the loved one. Such shared meaning enhances their understanding of each other's reactions and responses to the situation as well as providing a common base of support in a stable equilibrium.

The pluralistic perspectives in contemporary society often thwart a family's ability to endow death and dying with meaning. Death reminds man of the finitude which he has often attempted to avoid, disguise, or evade in his attempts to pattern his life and determine his destiny.

The maintenance of relevant rituals which are congruent with adequate meaning concerning the nature of birth and death has ceased in this transitional period of contemporary culture. Present studies of death and dying indicate, however, that we are critically examining our death rituals and grief practices, which will more meaningfully reflect the values and rights of human life and dignity. It is quite possible, therefore, that we shall soon experience more stable and creative community and professional vectors which will lend themselves more effectively as facilitators of grief synchronization for the preparatory grief of the dying person and the anticipatory grief of his family.

31

Anticipatory Grief and Mourning

H. Robert Blank

The complex problems of anticipatory grief are pertinent to three frequent situations:

1) Anticipation of the death of the loved one by the soon, or not-so-soon-to-be-bereaved.

2) Anticipation of one's own death.

3) Anticipation of the loss of a major body part or function.

In each of these situations, age, health, productivity, and emotional stability are vital factors.

The author's clinical and personal experience in psychiatry has led to certain convictions:

1) The longer the bereaved-to-be "knows" in advance, the greater the opportunity to accomplish a good deal, if not most, of the painful job of mourning in advance, and to reduce the intensity and duration of the acute-grief reaction.

2) The favorable outcome of mourning in advance is dependent largely on the physician's honest communication with and emotional support to the dying patient and his family from the time treatment begins.

3) Pari passu, in the case of loss of a major body part or function (for example, amputation, blindness), successful rehabilitation and acceptance of one's different self- and body-image are dependent largely on the primary

physician's psychological handling of the patient and his family during the illness leading to the loss.

Psychologic preparation of patient and family for the loss is the primary responsibility of the physician in charge, the one who has to make major medical or surgical decisions. The psychiatrist can provide this physician with insight and guidance on the timing and technique for such preparation. He can provide the necessary psychotherapy that is indicated frequently, even with the best preparation. But the psychiatrist, psychologist, or case worker should not be expected to take over the primary interpretation to child and parent of the medical problem, the indicated treatment, and what results may be anticipated. Too often this preparation is evaded, the need for it denied and rationalized away, with serious psychologic consequences. Many subsequent complications and failures, in education and rehabilitation, are attributable to grossly inadequate psychologic preparation for loss. The patient is left anxiously confused, distrustful, and hostile to all physicians and anyone or anything associated with hospitals, agencies, and other institutions.

If the physician has reason to suspect in a given case that child or parent is predisposed to pathologic reactions to loss, it is all the more important not to evade the issue, but to advise a consultation with a psychiatrist. Such consultation will be not only of immediate assistance but can also provide in advance the means of coping with anticipated and unanticipated pathologic reactions.

At worst, honest and considerate preparation of patient and family will produce fewer serious emotional and physical complications than the too common policy of "evade now, try to pick up the pieces later." At times, the practice of evasion and denial by physician and parents would appear ridiculous if it were not so tragic. The leukemic child whose physician and parents persist anxiously in keeping secret the nature and name of his illness from him after he has been told bluntly and cynically by fellow patients in the hospital that he has leukemia and that he will die from it may be cited as an example of this. The anxiety and guilt-laden disturbances of communication that characterize such secrecy create a vacuum which inevitably becomes filled with the child's most distressing fantasies.

It cannot be overemphasized that the child's worst fear is the fear of abandonment, not the fear of death which, to the extent that it can be conceptualized, tends to be reacted to in terms of abandonment. What is more difficult for parent and physician to understand is that disturbed communication between parent and child and between physician and child constitutes a form of abandonment to which the child is very vulnerable, in spite of their physical presence.

A colleague consulted the author about a thirteen-year-old boy with a six-year history of treatment by an internist for ulcerative colitis. After the latest and almost fatal recurrence and subsidence of colitis, the findings seemed to indicate resection of the bowel, and the physician was preparing the boy physically, but not psychologically, for the surgery. The psychiatrist was called in "to get the child's agitated mother off the internist's neck."

The author suggested that it was essential for the internist to give the boy and the parents a simple and direct anatomic and physiologic interpretation of the illness. And, if surgery was decided upon, both parents and patient should know *what* was going to be done and its net result, an ileostomy. It was clear that the mother would need prolonged psychotherapy, but it appeared that the internist would be able to handle the emotional repercussions in the boy.

The suggestion was followed. The undersized boy had establish a passively dependent and compliant relationship with his doctor and the hospital staff. Outwardly he was depressed and asocial, subtly provoking his mother's agitated, anxious, and hostile demands on the internist. Medical frankness with patient and family and psychotherapy for the mother resulted in marked improvement in the emotional climate of the home and in the boy's total functioning. He became more active, alert, and sociable, and his physical condition improved markedly. Even though he was prepared for surgery, the operation proved to be unnecessary. This continued to be the status one year after the initial consultation.

It is no more than suggested that the sustained physical improvement was related to the improved psychologic handling of child and family. What is emphasized is that, with or without surgery, honest interpretation is far more likely to produce a cooperating patient and family than evasiveness and false reassurance.

What has been said here about handling a pediatric patient and his family applies as well to the older patient:

A fifty-eight-year-old diabetic man, blind for four years, with a preceding six-year history of retinitis, was brought by his wife and son for consultation because of a

chronic, severe depression and angry, resentful intolerance of any attempts at rehabilitation. He had been a successful businessman and more than adequate as husband
and father, until visual impairment made it impossible for him to work. His internist
and ophthalmologist had never honestly interpreted to the patient or family the nature
of the illness and the possibility of permanent visual impairment. Rather, they handled the situation with a Pollyannish optimism until the man was almost totally blind;
whereupon patient and family were told rather abruptly that it was unlikely his vision
would improve and the man was referred to a rehabilitation agency. This produced a
severe state of shock followed by a depression, with the patient refusing angrily to
see his doctors. Aided and abetted by his family, who believed that blindness was
obvious reason enough for dependency, he embarked on years of medical shopping
all over the United States for a magical cure for blindness, rationalizing that he was
not really blind because of his variable (but not very useful) light perception. When
he was finally convinced that the quest was hopeless, he was taken to a rehabilitation
agency where his hostile, depressed, and demoralized state made psychiatric consultation imperative. Prognosis for rehabilitation was poor.

Often in consultations and seminars, the author hears, "What do you
tell them? " When blindness is anticipated, an amputation has to be performed, or a fatal illness has been diagnosed, this question covers an unconscious demand: "Give us the magic formula with which we can preclude the
intolerable reaction that the dreadful news will produce." No one wants to
be the bearer of sad tidings, especially the physician whose job it is to cure
and relieve suffering. If, however, the physician clearly understands that a
grief reaction, a manifest depression, is the normal reaction to loss of a body
part or function (as it is to loss of a loved one), and that he can materially
help the patient through the painful and frequently prolonged period of
mourning, he will have less difficulty in finding the appropriate words with
which he can honestly and supportively convey the sad news.

There are, of course, situations in which the physician's "honest interpretation" has to be confined to the family of the patient with a fatal illness, and the patient's denial mechanisms supported. Here, it is the family's
anticipatory grief and mourning that merit the physician's attention.

One of the most difficult cases observed by the author involved a forty-
five-year-old physician with an inoperable abdominal malignancy. His wife
insisted that he not be told the truth about his "diverticulitis," despite no
evidence of his having any personality fragility and his plans for major ex-
penditures that eventually almost obliterated his estate. It was not surprising
that the wife showed little overt grief before or after her husband's death,

and six months later herself developed a chronic, recurrently disabling physical illness.

In the typical case of a fatal illness, anticipatory grief and mourning are desirable for patient and family; evasion and denial are contraindicated; and the physician can provide the honest interpretation and emotional support that will facilitate healthy mourning.

32

Reflections on Two
False Expectations

Robert B. Reeves, Jr.

In a pilot study at the Columbia-Presbyterian Medical Center, New York City, in the summer of 1971, designed to explore ways of helping relatives of terminal patients in their anticipatory grief, it was found that after the first interview few of the relatives responded to invitations to return for further conversation. The investigators were surprised, because the gratitude expressed by the relatives had led them to expect that the opportunity to come back and talk some more would be welcomed.

Similar surprise and disappointment have frequently been expressed by theological students in training at the center when patients or members of their families have openly talked about death once or twice, and then never referred to it again. In nursing staff conferences similar behavior on the part of patients or their relatives has often been reported, with the same kind of surprise and disappointment expressed by the staff. Both the theologs and the nurses are sometimes more than disappointed. They are often chagrined and angry at what they think is either a relapse into denial by the patient or relative, or a failure on their own part to maintain communication.

Sometimes the chagrin is expressed by members of the staff who have heard that a patient has talked about dying to a particular nurse or social worker or chaplain, but have found that he will not talk to them about it.

Doctors sometimes tell of similar experiences, and they almost always interpret them as evidence that patients cannot face the prospect of dying and must take refuge in denial.

In all these cases, two expectations seem to be at work, and both of them are false. One is that, if the prospect of death is faced and dealt with, it is faced and dealt with once and for all. The other is that, if a patient or relative has in any degree come to terms with the prospect, he will want to talk about it repeatedly and with everyone.

The first expectation, that anticipatory grief can be worked through once and for all, has probably been fostered by the schematizations of the process that have appeared in print in the last few years. In spite of repeated warnings by their authors that the process is hardly ever seen in the five or six neat stages of the schema, readers take on a mind-set which imposes an outline or chart of the stages on every manifestation of grief that they encounter. A nurse, who had attended a conference on death and dying, said, for example, "Mr. J. seemed to be doing so well. He was no longer denying and was beginning to express some anger. Now, he's right back where he started, pretending the whole thing isn't so." In another case, an intern complained that a patient's wife, who had at one point talked freely about her husband's impending death, appearing to accept it, had during the final week plunged into angry questioning of the ways of God, and desperate insistence that the doctors do anything to gain more time. And the intern said, "According to this thanatology crap, that shouldn't have happened! "

This does not mean that the schematizations are irrelevant or false. They do accurately differentiate the elements of anticipatory grief and provide a broad overview of the dynamics of the process. But like statistical averages, the schemata are rarely exemplified precisely in any particular case. The concept of "stages" may sometimes be useful to the degree that it can be set aside.

The fact is that most people in their grieving follow an erratic course: back and forth, this way and that, reversing themselves from day to day, if not from hour to hour. But while this is erratic, it is not meaningless. It means that the realization of impending loss strikes at deeper and deeper levels as the time draws near, and at each deeper level the process, which seemed earlier to have been accomplished, must be worked through again.

Intellectual acceptance of loss is one thing; acceptance of loss at the gut level is another. Reason may be reconciled; but then old memories start coming back, slumbering emotions begin to stir again, and the pain may be so acute as to force again the cry, "No—it isn't so!" Or anger because "it isn't fair," or guilt because "it is my fault." And this can happen many times, as strata after strata of memories and feelings are uncovered. Each time, the prospect of death must be faced and dealt with again. Never is it finally dealt with, once and for all, until we ourselves are dead. Acceptance is always relative to the level at which we have been stirred. Stir deeper, and the cry goes up again.

A dying woman in her last waking moments seemed to be at peace. But as she lapsed into what appeared to be coma, her lips and lower jaw began to move, she frowned and twisted her head, and clenched her fists, as if at a hidden level of awareness she was doing battle all over again. After a while she was calmer, seeming once more to be at peace. And then she died. The point is that, as much as she appeared to have arrived at the stage of peace in her last moments of awareness, she still "had work to do," as she was reduced to deeper, subconscious levels of feeling.

In trying to help people at any level of anticipatory grief, it is important to support and facilitate the expression of whatever feelings have been aroused, at whatever stage, in the hope that as the level deepens the repetition of the stages will come more freely. If a person has found that he can deal with his grief and move through the stages at one level, chances are that he will be able to deal with his grief at a deeper level, too. But if he has had no help, and has been unable to move through the stages of his early grief, when his feelings at deeper levels are at last aroused he may be almost irretrievably in trouble. Learning how to grieve is essential to learning how to live. People can be helped to learn how to grieve, but it must be remembered that it is a never-ending task.

The other expectation, that a person who has in any degree come to terms with the prospect of death will want to talk about it repeatedly and with everyone, reflects perhaps the emphasis placed today on openness of expression. Much good has come of this openness. But it can become a fetish. To "get it all hung out" is not always desirable or possible. People have their reticences; each of us has a distance he must keep; time and place and the identity of the person we are talking to—all set limits to the degree to which we can comfortably be open. These limits should be respected, especially in one who is facing loss. He is sustaining damage enough already, without being forced to endure the further damage of invasion of his privacy.

If he needs to talk, he will give some kind of signal. Ambiguities, ambivalences, trailing sentences, discrepancies between what is verbally and nonverbally communicated are usually a tip-off that he needs a listening ear. If the signals are picked up gently, he may talk. When, in spite of giving such signals, he will not talk, it may mean sometimes that the listener has either failed to give an answering signal, or responded too strongly, crowding him or pinning him to the wall.

But many people do not give such signals. They have worked through their grief to a stage of acceptance, at a deep enough level of memory and emotion, at least for the time being, not to need to talk. The big question has been answered; the most accessible feelings have been expressed; expectations have been redefined—and life goes on. Secondary matters—comfort, the easing of pain, the little pleasures a day may bring, making arrangements, tidying up unfinished business, setting right things that were wrong, bidding farewells—these now become the primary concern. When dying patients and their families have worked through their grief together, these closing-out activities are not likely to be "heavy." They are usually dealt with rather blithely, almost as if they had nothing to do with death.

It is possible that such behavior represents merely a deeper level of denial, and that more grief will come as death draws nearer. In view of what has been presented in the previous section of this chapter, this is almost inevitably the case. Ultimate grief work is never done. How far acceptance really goes is a relative matter. Maybe, at its best, it is still a cover for deep denial. How can a living being really "accept" his own not-being?

But there is a valid distinction to be made between acceptance/denial which brings some observable degree of repose, and that which sets up observable distress; between the patient whose signals are easy and consistent, and the patient whose signals are heavy and discrepant; between the person who has come to terms with death at a deep enough level not to need to talk, and the person who is still fighting his way through the stages of anticipatory grief and desperately needs a listening ear.

In the former case, where some degree of repose has been achieved, it is unlikely that the person will say much about dying; or if he does, it will be perhaps only to the one or two people with whom he feels most comfortable. To all others he may present a "business-as-usual" aspect. As long as his signals are consistent, we should be content simply to be with him on his own terms.

33

Psychotherapy and Pharmacotherapy as Enablers in the Anticipatory Grief of a Dying Patient: A Case Study

Eda G. Goldstein and
Sidney Malitz

Death leaves mourners behind. Growth leaves stages of our lives in the past. Blows to self-esteem bring a sense of loss. Physical separations from those we love generate grief. These are not pathological states, but experiences which have potential for growth if resolved successfully.

Does someone dying also experience a nonpathological grief process? In terminal illness a person is a victim of multiple losses: increasing loss of bodily functioning and integrity; loss of independent functioning; loss of a future; knowledge of the impending final separation from all loved ones; and often loss of human companionship and intimacy because of the mutual withdrawal of the dying person and those around him. In face of this, how can anyone not experience grief? But the time for mourning is in advance of death—as reaction to the current moment and in anticipation of the final one.

Dying patients may need as much help in doing this grief work as those who are left behind. The task for the dying person is to prepare for death.

One aspect of the task may require that the dying person be able to share his or her angers, hopes, pains, nostalgia, and intimacy with someone. Paradoxically, those who are closest to a dying person are often least able to tolerate the demands of this task because of their own needs, including their anticipatory grief.

A second and crucial aspect of this task is that in order to achieve the working through of the grief process a person has to feel well enough emotionally and physically to remain positively involved in the experience. The expert use of tranquilizers, antidepressants, and sedating medication may play a vital role along with a therapeutic relationship in easing the grief process. But this enabling role should not be confused with using medication to keep a person from experiencing feelings.

The maintaining of the highest level of functioning in those faced with death can result in being able to fulfill some of the tasks of life, or in coming to terms with not being able to, before the final "sleep."

The following case description is not meant to be a model of what the treatment of a dying patient should be. Rather, it represents how one patient responded. Although some generalizations about the dying patient are made, the more important focus is on the need for a family member, friend, counselor, or professional person to be aware of and attuned to the patient's individual emotional needs.

THE CASE OF MRS. P.

Mrs. P. did not originally come to our attention because of a terminal illness. She was referred to us because of a functional depression. The patient, a thirty-six-year-old housewife and mother of a six-year-old son, had a history of previous depressive episodes in 1960 and 1965, both times responding successfully to conventional psychiatric treatment. She was admitted to a psychiatric hospital in April 1969. It was not until twenty-one months later, in January 1971, after continuous psychotherapy and pharmacotherapy by the same psychiatric social worker and psychoanalyst respectively, that a collaborative effort originally aimed at helping Mrs. P. live a fuller life was changed to help her die.

Mrs. P. was born into a Russian, Protestant family. Her grandmother raised her because her mother, a physician, worked long hours. The patient was sickly during infancy and childhood. When she was nine, in 1942, the family left Russia for Poland, where they met even more unexpected and severe hardship than in Russia. The years from age nine to age sixteen were lonely and frightening for Mrs. P. There was the constant threat of actual danger, frequent exposure to death, the stark realities of displaced persons' camps, and the arrest and presumed death of Mrs. P's father when she was twelve. Mrs. P. always felt different from her peers. Her feelings of rejection and isolation were epitomized by the statement, "Mother had no time for me because she had to keep us alive."

One year after her mother's remarriage in 1950, Mrs. P. married her English tutor. She and her husband came to the United States in 1952, following her mother by several months. Soon after, the mother began a relentless crusade to break up the marriage. When Mr. P. accepted a teaching position in the Midwest in 1959, the patient's mother prevailed upon Mrs. P. not to accompany him. By the time Mrs. P. joined her husband (after many months) in what she described as "an act of independence," she was already severely depressed. She was hospitalized with her first depression in 1960, shortly after arriving in the Midwest. Except for a brief depressive episode in 1965, Mrs. P. described the years away from New York as the happiest in her life. When she, her husband, and their son moved back in late 1967, intense family conflict ensued, leading the patient to seek psychiatric help in the summer of 1968 and to hospitalization in April 1969.

In the hospital, Mrs. P. was given high doses of Tofranil, an antidepressant, and treated with supportive psychotherapy. She made a rapid recovery. Following discharge in August 1969 the patient was seen in weekly psychotherapy by one of the authors, a psychiatric social worker. The patient was kept on a maintenance dose of another antidepressant, Aventyl. Medication was administered and the case supervised by the other author of this chapter. It was felt that psychotherapy on a long-term basis might help the patient with her chronic family problems, specifically centering about her hostile-dependent relationship with her mother.

Until March 1970 the patient sustained her improvement, but it was difficult to engage her in therapy. In January 1970, in response to family pressure, the patient had stopped taking her medication. In February she was in bed for a week with a high fever. Immediately following this episode, in March, she became acutely depressed and became subject to crying spells, anorexia, insomnia, and feelings of worthlessness. Aventyl was restarted, sleep medication introduced, and psychotherapeutic sessions increased to three times a week. Within five days there was some improvement. Until June 1970 the patient continued to be seen three times a week, and medication was increased. But there were many ups and downs. Family friction increased, and the patient's mother began taking her to a variety of doctors, unbeknown to the therapist. After one visit, during which one of the doctors stressed the childhood origins of her difficulties, the patient screamed at her mother, blaming her for all her problems. Her mother responded by striking the patient and vowing she would never speak to her again. The next day the patient slashed her wrists. She was readmitted to the psychiatric hospital on June 20, 1970.

Medication, the therapist, and the number of sessions remained the same. However, it was discovered that the patient was severely anemic. Medical consultation recommended treatment with ferrous sulfate, and there was immediate symptomatic improvement. The patient again seemingly made a rapid recovery, and went home on pass in early August. She was discharged in September 1970 and began seeing her therapist twice a week as an outpatient. She continued on the same antidepressant medication with the addition of the ferrous sulfate. She did not feel the need of anything to induce sleep.

September to December of 1970 were happy months for the patient. She welcomed her therapy sessions, took her medication, talked openly and in depth about herself, and began asserting herself with her mother and husband. She weathered the arguments that ensued, and felt a sense of mastery in being more independent. She had more time for, and seemed more sensitive to, her son and his needs. She resumed playing the piano, made a new friend, and convinced her husband that she should look for a job.

On January 11, 1971, Mrs. P. was hospitalized at a city hospital dealing mainly with malignant disease after a weekend of abdominal pain and rectal bleeding. Within two weeks, a malignant tumor of the colon was removed. Metastases to the liver were observed at operation. The patient was given six months to a year to live. The medical staff told Mrs. P. about the malignancy but not about the metastases nor her prognosis. She was told that the operation had been successful. Her family was told the truth.

Repercussions were immediate. Mrs. P. was shocked and terrified to learn of her malignancy. She wept and expressed anger at ''the double curse'' of having both a psychiatric and physical illness. ''I want to live. I don't know how I could have tried to kill myself.'' Mrs. P's mother, in addition to blaming Mr. P. for his wife's condition, berated the therapist. She exclaimed, ''Why didn't you stop them from telling her she had cancer? Why didn't you keep this from happening? Your medications are to blame.'' Mr. P. was stricken by his wife's prognosis but proceeded to deny the inevitability of her death, refusing to discuss the situation. Mother and husband competed with each other about the best way to help Mrs. P.

The goals of psychotherapy were altered to help the patient face whatever problems she now felt she had, and to aid her in adapting to the increasing reality pressures that would inevitably develop. Ideally the family would have rallied to help Mrs. P., or the therapist might have helped the family system deal with this tragedy. However, the therapist had observed prior to the medical illness the negative attitudes of both the patient's mother and husband toward psychiatric treatment. They had consistently advised the patient not to attend sessions, nor take medication, and had refused to attend conferences and joint sessions.

When the patient became physically ill, the mother and husband escalated their chronic battle. Both the therapist and supervisor felt that, although the therapist and family would need to have access to each other, it would be futile to try to mobilize the family to help Mrs. P. in a way they had never been able to do before. Mrs. P. had a lonely road to travel, and it was decided that she remain the focus of treatment. Was Mrs. P. aware she had a terminal illness? Treatment proceeded on the basis that she knew or would know she was dying because of clues from the family, hospital, therapist, and from her own body.

In the hospital, Mrs. P. was seen three times a week for about thirty minutes. She remained in the hospital until later March 1971 because of the necessity for a second, almost fatal, operation performed in late February. The surgery was for treatment of a pelvic abscess. Mrs. P. was aware of what had happened and seemed genuinely grateful that she was still alive. The word "cancer" loomed very large in her thoughts, and Mrs. P. became preoccupied with her chances for living a long time. She wanted to see her son reach manhood, and "bargained" for enough years to accomplish this. It was about this subject that Mrs. P. was always most depressed. Sharing the future with him as well as carrying out her responsibility as a mother was uppermost in her thoughts. However, in early discussions about her son Mrs. P. made no reference to the impending separation from him. It was not long before she even laughed about having given herself a "death sentence."

Mrs. P. began reassuring herself by talking about the great strides made in medical science. At the same time, she questioned the inconsistencies she was perceiving around her. For example, although she knew she was to receive chemotherapy she couldn't reconcile this with her reportedly "favorable" prognosis. She then wished for the chemotherapy to be truly experimental because she knew there was no known cure for cancer and hoped what she was getting would be a new cure. At the same time she denied that the chemotherapy was more than a precautionary measure. Mrs. P. remarked on the change in her husband, saying, "he finally realizes I'm sick." Yet the support he was able to give initially made her uneasy because "it's not like him." She became annoyed at her mother for taking the news "like such a child," but said, "I guess a mother is always a mother." She constantly sought answers to questions related to her diagnosis, but never asked if she had been told the truth. She actually stated that she didn't think doctors should tell patients the whole truth, citing her mother, a physician, as an example. She boasted with pride that she was being strong and handling the crisis "normally" and "not like a mental patient." She often asked her therapist if her other patients were as strong. The patient's courage seemed very important to her. She recounted that prior to her hospitalization and after she had been a "coward" all her life. The patient strove for a bravery and independence she felt she had missed, asking the therapist to help her be independent. As for the constant cues Mrs. P. was getting from her environment about her illness, the therapist tried to give the patient every opportunity to talk about her fears of death and tried to answer both direct and indirect questions with candor and honesty.

Although Mrs. P's increasing physical strength made her feel more hopeful, one of the strains was the drawn-out recovery process following the second, near-fatal operation. Mrs. P., though much stronger was still not ready for discharge. She began to feel she would never get home. Other patients around her were dying, and her defenses seemed to dissolve, resulting in overwhelming anxiety. In mid-March she became withdrawn and tearful, increasingly anxious, helpless, and hopeless. For a few days she would hardly talk to the therapist. She asked for sleep medication and tranquilizers from staff, then complained of headaches and double vision in the morning, probably resulting from the barbiturates. These symptoms upset her further, and the medical staff called for neurological consultations. It was only when these proved negative that the medical staff reluctantly agreed that psychotropic medication be resumed. Mrs. P. was restarted on Aventyl, Valium, a tranquilizer, and

Dalmane, a nonbarbiturate sedative, for sleep. Within two days the patient was sleeping better, with no side effects from the medication. She was more relaxed during the day and experienced a lessening of diffuse anxiety. She was able to talk openly about the frequent anxiety attacks she experienced when she looked in the mirror. She talked about the change in her physical appearance, her loss of weight and her scars. She didn't connect this with apprehension about the future except in an offhand way. "Will I ever be the same?" She did describe anger at her body "not working right." "I'm too young to look and feel like an old woman." At about this same time the patient was told she would be discharged. She left the hospital at the end of March.

The patient's mood remained improved after she went home. For someone who was so physically weakened, her energy was often remarkable, as was the look of alertness in her eyes. At times she felt elated and was actually hyperactive. This state continued for nearly four months until readmission to the city hospital in early August 1971. While out of the hospital, Mrs. P. was seen in therapy twice weekly for a forty-five minute session. She reported for medical follow-up once a week, but during the month of April was too weak to come to the therapist's office. Home visits were then arranged. The therapist also saw the patient while she was waiting to be seen by the medical clinic. Mrs. P. developed sleep difficulty and increased anxiety the night before her medical appointments. At other times she slept without the need of sleep medication or increased tranquilizers. The therapist, after consultation with her supervisor, strongly recommended to the patient that she take an extra dose of Valium, and use the sleep medication the night before her clinic visits. The patient did so and experienced a diminution in her anxiety and insomnia, although the clinic appointments remained a source of some discomfort.

In addition to the clinic appointments being a constant reminder of illness, Mrs. P.'s mother accompanied her on these visits, and was often of physical help to the patient as well as taking care of Mrs. P.'s son. This aid was counterbalanced by the mother's taking doctors aside in front of the patient and then lying to her about what had been said. The mother continued to berate the therapist, often in front of the patient, who remained in the middle. In spite of the opportunity to ventilate given her by the therapist the mother continued her accusations, and no amount of logical discussion by the therapist altered her viewpoint.

An espisode in late April was pivotal in many ways. Mrs. P. had begun feeling stronger. She found herself more able to assume the responsibilities of wife and mother. She outlined a plan for self-improvement, for better family relations and more pleasure. Sessions dealt with her current functioning or with careful exploration of her recurrent fears. Mrs. P. appeared relieved at being able to talk openly. However, she still did not feel strong enough to visit the therapist in her office, although she had planned to. The day before the scheduled session, she called, in tears, saying in despair that she just couldn't accomplish all she wanted to. She was apologetic about calling. "You're a busy person. I know you have other patients." She seemed relieved when the therapist told her she would again visit her at home the following day. The therapist visited the patient, expecting that she would require an increase in her Aventyl and Valium. Instead, she found Mrs. P. in good spirits and well-groomed. She had acquired a new hair-do and a brightly colored new dress with matching shoes. The latter were both bought the afternoon following the telephone call. She modeled her new outfit for the therapist, saying she wanted to look nice even if her mother and husband might object to her extravagance. When asked how she felt, she commented on the beautiful spring day, saying it made her feel new. She added, "Today let's not talk of anything bad." She served her therapist tea in the living room, refusing to serve it anywhere else. She also gave her a necklace and earrings, saying, "I just want you to wear these when you go places." With some mild prodding, which she seemed to expect, she proceeded to sing and play the piano. She invited her therapist to sing along with her. For over an hour, Mrs. P. sang of the countries in which she grew up, about time passing, people parting and flowers dying. The patient seemed to be choosing to communicate the true awareness of her impending death through indirect means which she told the therapist not to undermine. Not to talk of anything bad, to entertain, to give a present to the therapist to be worn in the future, and to happily sing songs involving the pain of separation were the patient's way of dealing with death—her attempt to merge with the therapist and have the therapist live on. Several days later Mrs. P., again in a new outfit, appeared for her "comeback" appointment at the therapist's office after an absence of four months. She brought a huge bouquet of flowers, saying she wanted to express her thanks for all the kindness shown her when she was ill. Her euphoric mood broke at one point when she cried about the constant pain which wouldn't go away and which frightened her. After much serious talk she began animatedly describing her plans for getting out more and paying more attention to her son. As she left, she encountered several staff members who asked how she was. She replied, "I'm better now, thank God. I hope to stay this way."

Mrs. P. improved in terms of functioning, but experienced more pain and weight loss. She spent a great deal of time with her son, visiting his teachers and going to P. T. A. meetings. She reviewed some friendships and joined a choir composed of mothers of school children. Mrs. P. got some of her "rights" back at home in terms of allowance and budgeting. She showed a sensitivity to her son's needs which had previously been absent, and often seemed compelled to make up for lost time with him. However, she couldn't bring herself to talk about what would happen. Curiously, she asked for advice about a minor problem he had, and seemed reassured that he would receive emotional support if he needed it. She revived her interest in improving her family relationships. To this end she discussed the same familial conflicts that existed prior to her physical illness, except that now the content of the conflicts centered about her illness.

Mother and husband continued to openly blame the other for the medical problems. Mrs. P.'s mother became both more protective and dominating. Mr. P., depressed and working long hours, left Mrs. P. alone a great deal, and when he came home went directly to bed. Mrs. P. felt almost completely abandoned. She could not express herself to her family because it only led to their withdrawal, attempts to cheer her up, or becoming hopeless along with her. She alternated in sessions between being angry at or feeling sorry for both of them. She asked the therapist to call her husband to see if a problem could be resolved about the son. When the therapist was able to be helpful the patient didn't question the surprising result. Rather, she attributed it to the therapist's power. The therapist had been able to establish a small degree of alliance with the husband. Although not able to reach out actively for help, he would accept regular calls from the therapist and talk at length. He was very troubled but managed to function at work, not admitting that he was walking on a tightrope. His defenses were antithetical to achieving closeness with his wife.

Toward the end of May, Mrs. P. complained of increasing pain which kept her from going out. For two weeks she rarely left the house except for medical or psychiatric appointments. She did not want to talk about anything other than her pain. She chastised the therapist for suggesting that emotional pain might be intensifying her suffering. She had developed more difficulty in sleeping. Sessions seemed blocked. The medical people could find no specific explanation for her increasing pain since there was no apparent increase in the physical progression of her disease at that point. They continued her pain medication at the same dosage level. In consultation with her supervisor, the therapist raised the patient's dosage of Valium and asked Mrs. P. to resume the sleeping medication. The dosage of Dalmane was increased also, since she complained of waking up because of pain. Relief from anxiety and insomnia ensued. Depression, as measured by mood, did not increase, but there was the constant complaint of pain plus anger at everyone. The patient seemed relieved of the pain temporarily when she became angry.

One evening Mrs. P. called, quite hysterical, after an argument with her husband. When she came to session, in pain, she related her anger and despair about feeling that Mr. P. no longer found her attractive. She described feelings that she thought he had about the ugliness of her body, and then realized she felt this way about herself. She felt he rebuffed her sexually but, at the same time, stated that she cried when they were intimate and would become angry because she couldn't stand the pain of their usual sexual activity. During this ninety-minute session, Mrs. P. experienced no physical pain. She was actively grieving for her body. Several days later she reported that she was sleeping without a night sedative, although she remained on the increased Valium. She fatigued easily when she left the house, but her complaints of pain receded.

Until mid-July Mrs. P. steadily lost weight. However, she dressed meticulously, was energetic, showed a sense of humor, and was relaxed. There was always underlying tension which surfaced at least once a week during a session, with talk of not being able to go on. After, as she put it, "talking her heart out," she laughed at her own basic life-long pessimism. Mrs. P. was still not talking about impending separations from people. An artifact was introduced when the therapist had to be away for two weeks in August and stumbled on a way of handling Mrs. P.'s anxiety about a final separation by means of using the temporary separation from the therapist. Three things happened when the patient learned, many weeks beforehand, that the therapist was to be away. First, she began talking less about the present and more about relationships in the past that had been lost, going back to childhood, including fond memories of her life in Russia. She actually renewed correspondence with her real father in Russia. She told anecdotes about her upbringing, and said she had never been able to share them with anyone before. She had always wanted a sister, saying that she felt she had found one in the therapist, although she wondered if this was "all right." She asked more questions about the therapist's own life, particularly about her future plans. She was most interested in the therapist's intention to go back to school. "Maybe you'll be a famous social worker and write about me, when my case is finished." She couldn't explain clearly what she meant by "finished," and tried to laugh it off. But at the same time she said she'd like her therapist to write of her bravery. She didn't want her therapist to marry for a long time, because she felt that she had married too young and didn't want her therapist to make the same mistake.

Second, there was almost no denial about how she felt about the therapist's going away. Mrs. P. mobilized more anger than in the whole previous period. She expressed her wishes for the future, her despair that she would not have one, and her jealousy of her therapist's having one. She didn't actually say she was going to die, but the discussions were dominated by that awareness. As she mourned her lost future she seemed to feel she was sharing it with someone.

One of her greatest fears—of being forgotten—could be discussed now, and when she realized that the therapist would write to her and the patient could do the same there was a sense of relief seeming to go beyond the immediate. This was also true of the arrangement made for the Director of Social Work to be in face-to-face contact with Mrs. P. She would not be abandoned completely.

These discussions about death were not shared with Mrs. P.'s family. In fact, she withdrew even more from them because she said when she tried to talk to them it upset them too much. This, in turn, upset her even more. With increasing discomfort, Mrs. P. ceased to ask questions about her condition. She stopped planning for the future. She stated that she thought she didn't have much longer, perhaps only a few months, but could never explain what led her to this conclusion. Nor did she press anyone to tell her whether or not she was right. While logically deducing the results of her metastases from the original tumor, surmising that her liver was really the organ to worry about, she continued to talk about raising her son and did not lose hope. In late July Mrs. P. called the therapist to say she was jaundiced and frightened. Her therapist visited her. Many things were talked about, and the therapist asked her what would be most important to her if she really were dying. Mrs. P. replied that she wanted to be left with hope and that she did not want to suffer extreme pain. She again said she did not want to be forgotten, nor did she want her son to have a new mother. The last two issues were the focus of the remaining weeks of psychotherapy.

The patient was readmitted to the city hospital several days later. All medications were reduced. She was again seen three times a week, except for the therapist's absence, when the Director of Social Work saw her and read the therapist's letters to her. When she was able to converse with the therapist she related intense self-recriminations about being a bad mother. She felt that her son would only remember her illnesses. She wept as she spoke of never being able to see her son as an adult, and was afraid that he would be damaged emotionally by not having two parents. "I know what it's like to lose a parent," she stated. However, she was able to begin talking of the pleasure her son had given her, of his accomplishments and assets, and of her ambitions for him. She said, "Maybe he won't be so bad off after all." At one point she joked about her smart son, saying, "He certainly didn't get his brains from me." This was the last time the therapist saw Mrs. P. laugh. She was coming to terms with separation from her son, forgiving herself for what she considered her misdeeds, and giving her son a healthy prognosis, implying that she had not been a "bad mother." Soon thereafter, the injections of opiates began. The injection of strong and frequent pain medications and limitations on physical mobility confused the picture. There was intermittent disorientation and behavioral regression, as evidenced by pleading with the therapist to be taken out of bed to the bathroom and demands to be fed when this was not possible.

Just before Mrs. P. became inundated by medication for her pain she flung her arms around her therapist and cried uncontrollably. Nothing was said. Finally she lay back, exhausted. As she was slipping off into sleep, she whispered "I know you'll look after my son." Two weeks later she awoke to find her therapist sitting by the bed and immediately smiled. She was not able to talk, but struggled to show the therapist a get-well card written and signed by her son. She was not forgotten by him. Seventy-two hours later, Mrs. P. was dead.

DISCUSSION

The process of anticipatory grief is real. It can be touched. It is always felt. It is rarely talked about or shared among those immediately concerned in the experience. This case highlights the need for laymen and professionals to be aware of this human process. Dying requires active, positive preparation rather than passive despondency or helplessness on the part of those involved.

One of the tragedies is the inability of the patient's family to find roles for themselves and for the patient that would ease the burden for everyone, or even transcend it. Yet, it is not because Mrs. P. and her family were so unique, although they did present special problems. Families are not prepared for or supported in viewing themselves as effective helpers in the dying process. Not only does this rob a family of what can be a growth experience, but it often results in emotional withdrawal from a loved one who desperately needs companionship but cannot reach out for it.

It is true that in this case certain roles were not allocated to the family. The therapist took on the role of "enabler." But this was a choice, not the result of a sense of helplessness concerning the problem. In most situations there can be no choice because professionals themselves do not see what they can accomplish through working with a family or patient or because there is no family. They must carefully examine what tasks can be allocated among themselves, to family members, and examine innovative uses of those who are in positions to be helpful to the dying patient.

How can the nature of this helping process be translated into practice? The kinds of losses involved in dying and the way anticipatory grief may manifest itself have been suggested. But they cannot provide a manual of techniques. However, certain elements are essential. A helping person should be able to identify a specific task that would guide his work with a dying person, such as taking care of a child. This will decrease helplessness and promote involvement. Coupled with this task should be an understanding that the task may have symbolic, concrete, and emotionally charged meanings to a patient who might find relief in sharing feelings verbally. Therefore, a third element is to be able to be in tune to the need to talk about or listen to the meaning a task has to a dying patient. For a dying mother to share with the person looking after her child how she feels about the child is essential. This should not be forced but rather should stem from cues from the patient. How much better it must be for a mother to talk about her fear of being replaced than to watch the process in silence.

This is not to argue that psychotherapy and pharmacotherapy are the ultimate means for handling anticipatory grief. To the contrary, it would be better in our view had there been no role for psychotherapy and pharmacotherapy. Similarly, psychiatry does not have all the answers even though this particular case required psychiatric management. What was found seems to apply to any dying patient. The positive resolution of anticipatory grief can make the difference as to whether or not a person dies in peace and dignity.

34

LSD Therapy: A Case Study

Charles Clay Dahlberg

Sufficient resource material supports the use of LSD in terminal cancer patients (Kurland *et al.,* 1973). My reasons for using LSD are based essentially on the same thesis: LSD breaks through defenses and heightens emotionality. This can mean that conflict areas are brought to the fore and under the special circumstances of a crisis such as death have a good chance of being resolved.

However, no attempt was made to induce a psychedelic experience. The use of LSD in a more traditional psychotherapy setting seemed to be more fitting in this particular situation. Excerpts from the session with the patient that follow are highly emotional, and demonstrate the highlighting of the conflict in the patient's life. Abreaction occurred. Conflict resolution is demonstrated by the results.

It might seem that the time and understanding necessarily given to a dying person are consistent with this patient's experience. Certainly her husband gave her a great deal of attention, even if some of the doctors did not. The point that this case demonstrates is that she couldn't accept what was given her. This particular woman had been in psychotherapy for serious emotional problems. Does this mean that LSD is useful only for dying people with emotional problems? I believe not, since very few people are without conflicts. On the other hand, it does seem likely that people with some experience in psychotherapy are better equipped for the kind of problem-solving that psychotherapy involves, and possibly even for that which involves LSD-facilitated psychotherapy.

It has been said that if drugs can do anything in psychiatry, they can alter a person's mode of relating so that he may be effected for the better in an interpersonal relationship (Sullivan, 1934). The following case, a brief history of the patient as given to me, starts with and demonstrates the truth of this observation.

A thirty-two year-old mother of a five-year-old child was referred to me by a colleague who had treated her analytically for five years, but had ceased treatment five years ago. Before that she had seen a number of other psychotherapists. She had a Schwannoma in the mediastinum, was hysterical and panicky, but never disorganized, and no contraindications were seen for the use of LSD. Psychoanalysis had not been especially successful, but by no means a total loss. The patient was a complainer, hypochondriacal, and the past therapy had consisted of trying to get her to recognize her gross dependence and her responding in terms of massive denial of this.

I saw the patient four or five times before giving her LSD. First contact was on the telephone when she called and asked about LSD. Told that regulations forebade administering the drug to fertile females, she said that this was no problem since she was dying of cancer.

When she first appeared at my office she had just been to see her physician, who had told her that the tumor had resumed growth. She said that following discovery of the tumor she had undergone surgery in August 1970. She also had had chemotherapy and radiation treatments. Assured at this time that the tumor had been removed and that she was cured, she immediately became pregnant. A persistent cough developed and her physician found that the cancer had returned. An abortion was performed. She has had chemotherapy and radiation since then.

Her main stated reason for wanting LSD was to be able to "talk straight" to someone. She said she had three fears. One was of a long, painful terminal hospitalization and that she hoped she could kill herself before that. The second fear was that she wouldn't be decisive enough to kill herself in time. The third was that she would fall apart emotionally before her death. Her daily life was miserable, and although she kept herself very busy, it was getting more difficult because of her waning strength.

She said she thought she had a few months of life left, that she had maintained a fairly normal facade for about five months, but that now it was getting to be too much of a strain to do so.

She described herself as a fairly unhappy person who kept herself busy with work and school. But now she had too much time on her hands and realized that she was stubborn, obsessional, and indecisive. She knew now that she had dominated her husband to whom she had been married for twelve years. She said her marriage was a fairly unhappy one but that it had improved after her daughter's birth. Her husband was kind and supportive. She depended upon him but didn't like this role.

She wanted her husband to attend the LSD session, or at least part of it, if it was decided upon. Because of difficulties in scheduling the date was set for a Sunday, six days hence and I made several special appointments to be able to get to know her better before beginning the sessions.

I learned that she had had some Orthodox Jewish training as a child, but no longer went to synagogue, although she did have some ill-defined sense of the meaning of religion in her life. She said she was obsessed with religion as an adolescent but didn't think about it now.

Her parents she described as domineering. Her dislike of her mother was mutual, but she was mildly fond of her father who was by now fairly senile. She had an older unmarried brother who lived with her and her husband. He was described as obese, dependent, and neurotic.

A release from her and her husband and a letter from her physician confirming the diagnosis and prognosis indicated no reason not to try anything that might make her more comfortable since there was no hope for her. This is mentioned because it comes up in the first segment of the recorded excerpts where the patient expressed surprise at her physician's consenting to the LSD procedure since she considered him "square."

In a later interview, when asked what it was that was especially hard for her to express, she replied "positive emotion" and that she was most comfortable with hostility. The point of this and the questions about religious background were to find out what it would be most important to try to get to under the LSD.

She said that she could remember three or four times when she was very happy. One was when her baby was born by natural childbirth. This procedure also changed her sex life, as she had been frigid before the baby's birth but not after. She said she had always been uncomfortable with her body but gave a very good description of the childbirth. The patient was not very sexually oriented (since arousal for her meant being bothered) and so she tended to turn her husband away.

Eight days after the first phone call I gave her 100 mcg of LSD at 11 A.M. Her husband was with her for about an hour while the drug was taking effect. I was out of the room for a part of this time. She vomited a good deal, which was an exaggeration of the usual nausea and vomiting caused by the radiation and chemotherapy. It didn't seem to bother her especially.

The following excerpts are presented from the five-and-one-half hours of taped LSD session which started roughly one hour after the LSD was injected intramuscularly. Throughout the session there was a good deal of silence, much of which was consumed by tears, either silent or loud sobbing. Early in the session she said she had visions of Egyptian gods which she said were nonhuman. They were part human and part animal, and this was taken to mean you cannot communicate with them. These were frightening to her and so as the visions and fantasies went on she usually caricatured them in the florid manner of de Mille movies.

Certain things came through:

1) She wanted some hope—2 percent she said.

2) She was almost completely wrapped up in herself.

3) She was observing herself and testing me to see if I respected her.

4) She had no interest in my comments except insofar as they *concretely* applied to her.

5) She was to some degree histrionic—probably to minimize her feelings.

6) She wanted to express her feelings and now had a setting and a drug which helped her to do so.

Excerpt, 12:30 P.M. (The transcript is edited slightly to increase readability by deleting repetitions and numerous expressions, such as "you know" and "like".)

PT: I had wondered today what the people who were very old, lying dying, if there's the same, if the process changes at any point, like saying, you know, "Oh God, not today," or is it going to be today. You know ninety-two or whatever. I'm not interested in explaining.
CCD: You're not being very clear.
PT: No, I lost the train of thought, Anyway I sort of went into this shriveled up, old chicken babi yaga thing. I sort of felt like, I was convinced I wasn't going to get any better. Did it?
CCD: Did it what?
PT: I was faking it, I was waiting to see if you were going to say "Yes, yes it, it has to get better." I still haven't recuperated from your saying, "they told me there was no hope."

CCD: You didn't have to believe it.
PT: You didn't have to tell me.
CCD: You told me.
PT: I didn't tell you. Did I phrase it quite that way?
CCD: I don't know how you phrased it.
PT: If I did I didn't believe it. No, I would never say "no hope." I'm faking when I say it now. I'm torn. I feel like I ought to say I ought to give up.
CCD: I don't see why. . . .
PT: I thought that would be sort of a healthy thing to come out of this experience. Lie down and die quietly. I didn't want to believe it then. I had to be a fighter. I didn't want to be. My brother didn't. They just destroyed him. My father never held my hand crossing the street when I didn't pull away. Those first conscious remembrances—pulling away.

Excerpt 2, 2:00 P.M.
PT: You can't really control. I'm trying to reconstruct it. And I'm always getting this big pink Easter egg and bunnies. Sort of pink Easter egg, bunny. Maybe I had too many of them. I always like that tinsel. I've cut out tin figures, very pretty, like all children's picture books. Hansel and Gretel, Bavarian forestry. It's all very sugar tinselly. I didn't have very many. I always sort of liked that, like I liked street fairs. We went to one today, we went yesterday, yesterday, Saturday. Like I know they're corny and I have this clever distinction of corn—higher class corn versus low class.
CCD: Lots of people like them.
PT: I'm a connoisseur. A Good Humor truck, a park, they let the kids pull the bell. My brother took us to the circus. It was my idea but it wasn't really what I wanted to do. I don't like the circus. It's much too violent. Why should people have to do terrible and dangerous things like hanging in the air, mean things to other people. Like hanging in the air. Mean to themselves. Why?
CCD: It's frightening?
PT: Yeah, sure it's frightening hanging up there. I'm watching myself go through all these processes when I see them.
CCD: Are you afraid of heights?
PT: No. By processes I meant identification with them.
CCD: I understood what you meant.
PT: Once upon a midnight weary I was a psych graduate student. The greatest pity is when I lost the intellectual curiosity. I don't really give a shit now about like you know Buddha can be lecturing on Broadway—I wouldn't go hear him. And I came to Brandeis just athirst for knowledge. Somehow like I had been living in a desert and here I was going to hear wisdom and I went to everything, you wouldn't believe the lectures I went to. Seven o'clock in the morning on Hindu music and four people there including me. And 10 o'clock at night in Cambridge, eight buses. I'd listen to anybody on anything and wrote it all down. Never digested any of it. I didn't know how. I didn't know how to digest it.
CCD: When did you lose your curiosity?

PT: Well, I think, I can't make a logical case. My associations are: When I was at Barnard and I worked at Payne Whitney Psychiatric Clinic which was a miserable experience. We didn't know what to do. We just were horribly conspicuous in our white lab coats. We wanted to burn it down or open it up. [Softly] No, I don't want to burn anything down, just open it up. Tell them the truth. There's really no substantial difference between the people in and out. [Excited] It certainly at Payne Whitney is true, God knows. There was this adolescent boy there who would wait for me every week and talk to me. I started to say, I keep wanting to say, we played chess though we really couldn't have played chess; I'm an atrocious chess player—I barely know how to play, but it's possible. And I was so delighted to have something to do instead of sitting there like a complete idiot. Conspicuous. It was written "manipulative" all over the kid's record, in large psychiatric hand, bold. Not mine, God knows. So I mean at the time I think I was very shocked by it because I realized—I guess I didn't realize.

I think I was shocked by it because I've always been frightened by my dependency business and I realized that I really did want to be dominated by somebody or other. It's hard to figure out—you can't really figure anything out though. Everything is too diffuse. Not that I could ever figure anything out. I must have. I wrote real logical papers. Neat and wow! Tightly reasoned. It just came out. I was unaware of the reasoning process. That's funny. I mean tight reasoning has been like. . . . The only thing I've done incessantly in my life. Incredibly tight reasoning.

Not that it's done a lot of good. I'm simply bored with myself. I don't care for all these esthetic things.

CCD: Do you see the leaves out there. They are just starting to come out. [LSD frequently enhances esthetic experiences. Later I asked her husband to get a flower. She could appreciate this briefly.]

PT: Without my glasses I can't make it to the wall. No, I can see them. 0/200 vision is what I have. I'm trying to think of my garden; I have five tulips, and I really didn't look at them. I guess I should have. I don't know if I even. . . . Cliches! God I wish I would stop doing that. This cliche monitor in my head. I think I've done that all my life.

CCD: You're doing in *excess* what you've done all your life. And you noticed it.

PT: I've always noticed it. Like the Diamond crystal shaker salt thing; a picture of a girl looking at a picture of a girl looking at a picture of a girl. I wish I could stop for about fifteen minutes. [She means, stop the LSD.]

CCD: No chance.

PT: I don't feel bad enough to want to get off it but . . .

CCD: Yeah.

PT: Just like a rest. So tired, very tired. I feel like I'm not marshaling my resources or utilizing. I ought to start . . .

CCD: Take your time.

PT: I have a feeling you're going to keep saying that till I walk out the door. Is that one of the things you keep saying until people walk out the door?

CCD: No. I say, "good-bye."

PT: No, but really I can't stand being conned. My God I feel like I'm drowning in con. Actually it's not true. When you said to me "You're definitely going to die, lady," I don't like that either, so 2 percent con I like, applied well, like mustard.

CCD: There's no point in my conning you about anything.

PT: Yes, there is a point because I'm going to feel very anxious about like all these things I'm not going to deal with. Like I ought to have an agenda of dealing with life, death, my daughter, cancer, my husband, you know, the state of the U.S. economy, and how to get out of Vietnam. . . . [Typical of the patient. Starts seriously, and then mocks herself.]

CCD: I'm afraid that you cannot program this. There have been great efforts made to program these LSD experiences and it just doesn't work.

PT: Bullshit. I'm joking, you know, I've very stubborn. I challenge. I'm stubborn; I'm unsuccessful, incredibly. My God. Anyhow, I don't know, I spend my whole life—I'm getting sort of echo, echo effects. It sort of goes with the scene now. My mother's famous story is of how I entered a swimming contest. I went to a swimming pool when I was very young and I couldn't swim and I jumped in, absolutely determined, and sank like a stone. Determined that I could have won.

CCD: That's a marvelous story. How old were you?

PT: I was just very embarrassed; I knew I wasn't going to win. I was just very humiliated.

CCD: Are you still like that?

PT: What?

CCD: Like that story.

PT: No, no I'm not at all. I wasn't like that story even then. I just was probably, I don't know why.

CCD: I mean entering something like that . . .

PT: Oh, entering.

CCD: That wild impulsiveness, without knowing what you're doing.

PT: Oh, I was convinced I was going to win. I knew I couldn't swim.

CCD: I know. I'm sure you were.

PT: I thought all it took was strong determination.

CCD: Right.

PT: I don't know. I entered this! Brave deed of the week. So far it isn't so bad all things considered.

CCD: Would you say it's good?

PT: Yeah. I'm frightened it's not going to stay this way. I always feel like I've got to pay. You know, it's only act two, or something.

CCD: Well, you're getting something for nothing. I don't think you'll have to pay.

PT: I've worked very hard and it's zero I have to show for it. It's an incredible number of . . . . I mean to turn out 80 million trillion shitty papers, good papers, 'A' papers, lovely, charming papers—all the nights you really wanted to go to sleep. You sit there you know, clunk, clunk. The 80 million compositions that I didn't really want to read. Thank God I never signed up to write a life of Dickens. This time slowing up bit is very very strong, I don't like it any more. I'm not going with things enough. I'm very frightened I'm running out of time. I'd like to come back tomorrow, calmer, better prepared, to do a better job and that's . . . that's why I want so desperately to have a second child because I would enjoy it much more because I'd know what to look for. You know, watch here carefully, closely for that. You don't know what to pay attention to the first time.

Excerpt 3, 2:40 P.M.
PT: Now there were times that seemed very frightening. Why don't I ever write anything down, even things like this unfortunate business that I was very upset about? Why don't I ever. . . . Why can't I find. . . . I have so much energy supposedly for other things. . . . To ever take it out on myself, to make a statement about myself.
CCD: I don't know you very well but I would guess that if you wrote it down you would have to take yourself seriously.
PT: Yeah! I'm afraid to. *My God, if I took this thing seriously I'd really be upset.* I wonder how I strike people. We went out to dinner last night and it even struck *me* as bizarre. In between the soup and French pastry we went from my imminent death to my kid's getting his finger caught in the door and she has contemporary furniture in the dining room and she's inviting a lot of people to dinner next week and is going to get special meat. And it all struck even me as being a little bit bizarre.

Excerpt 4, 3:50 P.M. [Long compulsive monologue on how hard it is for the patient to make decisions.]

CCD: What decisions are you speaking about?
PT: I don't know. You know I've gone through a great deal of my life with this feeling that at four o'clock on June 23rd you're going to have to make a decision when most of the time, not all of the time, June 23rd came and went and the decision didn't get made. A little red light just went on over there. It indicates. . . .
CCD: It means the telephone is ringing. It flashes.
PT: You should have it at four o'clock though. What a pity because I've used such tremendous anxiety, building up to June 23rd, when I knew I wasn't going to make a decision anyway about whatever the hell it was. I always listed two or three options—going to move to California, going to move to Israel, going to do this, do that kind of thing. I don't know; seems like I never did any of them. I must have done some of them.
CCD: [Interrupting.] Let me ask you a question. What do you want to do? Speak from your guts.
PT: [Softly.] I want to have another baby. I can't do it. What do I want another baby for? [Shrieking] Why isn't one enough? Why do I have to always spoil everything?

Excerpt 5, 4:20 P.M.
PT: What I would like to do is get a few good laughs in.
CCD: I don't think that's the purpose of LSD.
PT: What, get a few laughs in?

CCD: Yeah.

PT: Does anybody laugh anymore; I can't remember the last time people really did. TV stuff. Does anybody laugh? Kids laugh I guess. I can't imagine myself laughing. Smiling maybe but I can't remember anyone actually laughing.

CCD: Depressed people can't.

PT: I remember reading something in the literature on how LSD shouldn't be given to people who are depressed. Like this guy screening his psychiatric therapy patient; what other kind of therapy patients are there besides depressed ones. I mean, is there really anybody else? I understand that depression supposedly has some narrower meaning, but really does it?

CCD: Not really. The question of depression and LSD is one of degree.

PT: Like someone who is very depressed? I take it, I wasn't very depressed.

CCD: You're not suicidal. That's the point.

PT: That seems to be my problem. I ought to be. I'm trying, you know really that's true—I'm not. It seems, it's really a thing I've been trying to work on. I know I'm not. I'm a fake. [Sardonic.] That's funny. Why not? People who are suicidal, it comes out in some way? Why did you think I wasn't suicidal?

CCD: Because you came to me. Because of the way you act. Because you are so unhappy. You show all the signs and symptoms of a person who wants to live very, very badly.

PT: I'm embarrassed about it. [Voice cracked.]

CCD: Really?

PT: Yeah. When you said that, I felt so embarrassed. As if I had been caught out in a shameful secret. You caught me. Actually it's one of the things I've been trying to tell you, tell doctors, "I accept my death." I had to say that. Because they would all fall to pieces at the concept that the patients know what's wrong with them.

CCD: Hmn. . . .

PT: I can't understand that. [Incredulity.] What do they think these people think they have? A common cold?

CCD: Could be.

PT: My radiologist just told my husband that I'm the first patient in twenty years of practice who ever knew what was wrong with him. He does not believe in telling patients anything, etc., etc., etc. What do these people think, don't they know what's going on?

CCD: I don't know. How did you happen to know?

PT: Had they tried to lie to me, they could've very easily. Much more easily than I made them think. I would have bought! I bought the original surgery; they told me everything was fine. I didn't ask question one. I should've asked and my chances of survival might have been better today if I had asked then. I didn't. They said "You are fine." Fine. Pregnant immediately! I never asked. In fact all the coughing I started to do two weeks later. I never made the connection between cough two and cough one. I never said there was a recurrence. It never occurred to me. I kept saying I must have bronchitis, I must have an allergy. I must have a cold. The most obvious, obvious thing that it may be a recurrence never crossed my mind. Because they said to me, "You're fine" and I accepted it. If they had lied to me I suppose I would have resented it in a way. They couldn't win. If they had lied I would have resented it. If they hadn't lied, I would have resented it. But nobody tried.

CCD: Why?

PT: I don't know why they didn't try. When I asked what's happening. The radiologist said Charles [an old family friend and physician] would tell me and Charles said the radiologist would tell me. So somebody had to tell me, so I called up Charles. [Enraged.] And Charles one Sunday night says, "All right, you want to know, this is it. You got malignant Schwannoma. You'll probably last a couple of months blah, blah, blah." You know, flat out. A gem! Ten years of deep friendship and good. He couldn't manage to get his ass over to tell it to me in person. I was home alone yet. My husband came back in a little while. This is a legitimate grievance. He informed me. He lives all of twenty minutes away. He couldn't manage to give me this charming news in person. But nobody tried to lie. I mean, he didn't say to me, "Gee, we do feel you're seriously ill, you know you have, but he said . . ." I wrote down everything he said. "Three or four months—if it doesn't stop—the probabilities." I remember asking him what were the possibilities of, couldn't it go away? Couldn't some of the treatment? He would say, "Well if they can shrink it down you will last a little longer." I asked, "Well how about couldn't they shrink it down so it would go away." I think he said something like [bitterly] "not too likely" or some terribly helpful phrase like that. Nobody tried to lie. I would have bought a lie. I went to the New York Medical Library *last Friday*. I didn't even go there in December! People take me at my word, that's the problem.

CCD: Yeah.

PT: [Unintelligible] It was very spooky not knowing how much he knows. It would probably make it much easier for my husband if there weren't this whole web of lies there, and all things considered I wouldn't have wanted to be lied to. Just maybe 1 or 2 percent.

CCD: But you would have liked to have been told differently.

PT: That's true. But it doesn't really matter how. What difference does it make to tell things with a brass band?

CCD: It makes a difference.

PT: Not really. What I would have liked to be told is to an orchestration of (in fact I can still appreciate it now when I get it). Five years ago I would have said to a Hodgkin's disease patient, "You have two, three months, and now look, blah, blah, blah. You know, that people have reached X crossing lines and still they. . . ." I think somebody could say that to me, without lying.

CCD: I think so.

PT: Without going into this "Jesus is coming down to heal." This is not me. It would take a much more reasonable reassurance. But within this more garden-variety framework, I don't know. Maybe I'm lying to myself.

CCD: I think that you're right and I think that you should take what you're saying seriously.

PT: It'd be nice if once a week somebody would say that to you. My husband has this thing, that everything is going to be okay.

CCD: Nobody could convince you that a miracle was going to happen, but within the framework of history things might change. When I say you should take these things seriously, I mean that you might be able to teach doctors something about how to deal with people.

PT: I'm not going to be around long enough.

CCD: You've talked about writing. What you've just told me might be written for doctors.

PT: You know what it is? [shouting.] They're very angry at patients! Livid anger at patients who know the truth. Real anger. The radiologist would like to hit me when I made him say, "Yes." He had to look me in the eye. It wasn't as if I had this real live human confrontation. It was just that a patient passed him in the hall who knew his diagnosis and he was really angry.

CCD: You see, these people are dealing with an enormous problem, and they deal with it daily. It's very very hard on them. I'm not asking you to be sympathetic with them, but I am saying that they haven't worked out good answers because they are so involved in blocking out what they are dealing with all the time.

PT: Absolutely right.

CCD: A friend of mine died of cancer three or four years ago. A long drawn-out business. It was an entirely different sort of thing than yours. She'd had a breast cancer and the breast removed. Nothing happened for fifteen years and then it flared up. She described her experiences at ———— Hospital. She said the worst thing was that *nobody looks at you*. Meaning they can't afford to.

PT: The radiologist fortunately had very nice assistants in his office. Without them it would have been unbearable. I really looked forward to going to them. It's funny; I never realized how significant it was to what your friends said. You had to strip and put on this . . . I don't know why I'm crying while I'm describing this flowered smock job. They have the same one for you each time. When I first saw it I said, "Oh, they save on the laundry." But you know also it's yours, your identity. Somebody's looking at it, recognizes it, your specific body, private, you know. It's very helpful. They also count for you which is very nice—how much to go. They really personalize—humanize the operation. The radiologists themselves are madmen.

CCD: Well, I think they probably are to begin with, that's true.

PT: I think they get over exposed to X-rays because there were times that either he was crazy or I was and I don't think I am. He was absolutely, totally, paranoid, irrational.

CCD: Well, you see radiology is the speciality which deals less with people than any other specialty.

PT: Destruction. And also specializes in the destruction of cells. What he's doing is saying, "How much of you will I kill." I mean he creates nothing! Radiation never created anything and if it did it was by accident. And it never cured much.

CCD: But what they would like to do (all these people who deal with cancer and things like that) is to deal with the tumor.

PT: Oh, I know that [laughter]. The other day he asked the nurse, "Which room is the Schwannoma in?" No, I mean I accept this.

CCD: But that's very hard on the person who is carrying the Schwannoma.

PT: No, no it's [contemptuous rage]—the last thing I want him to do is treat me as a human being. I don't want to rub identities with this jerk. I don't want . . . I just want. . . .

CCD: What you're saying about his systems is another thing. It means something.

PT: I just want . . . if I ask him a rational question like "How many more weeks are you going to use that actinomycin?" "Is it working as well as you thought it would?" Either answer "I don't know," or something.

CCD: But you see. . . .

PT: Tumors don't talk, I guess.

CCD: Right, right. You shouldn't ask questions like that.

PT: I know he won't answer. He gets furious. In fact if he answers them he acts like he's performing some bizarre service. Like he said to me, "Most doctors wouldn't answer." Well, why not? Isn't it a question a normal person will ask? If someone jabs you nine weeks running in the arm wouldn't you say at one point in the nine weeks, "How many more weeks are you going to jab me?"

CCD: Right. But you see you're not supposed to be a person. You're supposed to be a tumor.

PT: I have to say something while I'm lying there being jabbed. In fact, this doctor I went to last week nearly drove me insane. He wouldn't answer anything. I said to him, "You just took the X-ray. Is the tumor bigger or smaller or the same?" The first time I asked him that he said to me, "I didn't know you went to medical school." Now I ask you, do you have to go to medical school to ask that question? Unless you were retarded you would ask that question. He didn't answer, and yet when I was lying there I said I didn't want to get the drug on Friday. I was going away. I didn't want to tell him I was coming here this weekend. He got very talkative. "Oh, where are you going?" I said like none of your business, first of all because I didn't have an answer. Second of all, if he wouldn't tell me whether my tumor was bigger or smaller, I didn't want to have this human relationship with him. It wasn't any of his business where I was going. I was intimidated for lying.

CCD: No, that's all right. You see, that question, "Where are you going" was fine.

PT: He'd love to make chitchat but I didn't want to have a human relationship with him. I just wanted him to answer big or small or the same. Hold up one finger. Tumor size.

CCD: But that's too much to the point.

PT: But why can't they do this?"

CCD: It's too painful.

PT: To who?

CCD: To them.

PT: You know what he said? Maybe it's true. [Appalled.] He said—I was so devastated—he stood over me and said (this is a guy I only saw once before) "I am more worried about you than you are yourself." It struck me as being one of the most bizarre statements from somebody who doesn't know somebody else at all. So I suppose it makes sense. It must have made some sense to him.

CCD: In some sort of general way, he's very worried about you and all the others.

PT: But it was an absolutely insane thing to say to somebody you don't know at all. In fact, to say to anybody you know very well it's a perfectly ridiculous remark. But in the context when he said it to me? That's why I was so upset on Friday. [The first day she saw me.] You know, one of us is crazy!

CCD: It makes exactly the same kind of sense as saying to a child you are spanking, "This hurts me more than it does you."

PT: I wouldn't do anything like that. [Softly.] Actually, I was never much of a hitter. The few times I did it, I was angry.

CCD: You may be able to see that the problem with the doctors—radiologists and people like that—is that they can't afford to think about the problem they're dealing with. So maybe you could tell them.

PT: I don't know. I always say, "I can't." What I have to figure out is simply how to protect myself in a situation so that I don't come out the way I did on Friday so utterly devastated. I think the tumor stayed the same, so I should have felt. . . . I came out. I was absolutely wiped out, hysterical. I was a combination of angry and, I think, just baffled, like I'd encountered this Martian and one of us was a Martian, and I wasn't sure which one.

CCD: That's the problem.

PT: They ought to hire a bunch of intermediaries or something; I don't know. Can I have some water?

CCD: Let me get some fresh.

The day after the LSD I saw the patient, and was told that she was very excited after she was taken home by her husband and spent a good deal of time on the telephone proselytizing a friend who had warned her against taking LSD. She found that people weren't very accepting of the procedure, and had some difficulty with her husband, who was disappointed in not being in the entire LSD procedure with her. She had brought him along because she was frightened, but she only used him during the period when the drug was coming on. She said she thought she would like to take it again in a month or two, but meanwhile would go to Mexico to see a "quack" who gave some sort of a medication for cancer. She was pleased following the LSD session to discover that she really wanted to live. The first thing she told her husband as she got into the car when he took her home was that she was happy to know she was not suicidal. She told me, however, that she felt rather bad knowing that she wanted to survive. She had made an implicit deal with her doctors to the effect that "You can talk to me about it because I don't mind dying." She was also pleased that she been able to have eight hours of freedom from pain, and said that she no longer had her normal gut anxiety.

Following her visit to the "quack" she got in touch with me in the middle of June and said she wanted to try LSD again. She said she had emerged from the LSD with the determination to fight, and that also when she got anxious she could remember how much better she had felt at times under LSD, and would try to recapture that feeling of diminished anxiety.

LSD was administered again on June 20. The patient had previously said that she had felt like a "specimen" by being taped, so it was decided not to tape her this time. But when she noticed that the tape recorder was not on, she said that her objections weren't serious and that she had hoped that she could hear played back what she had said to doctors. "Maybe they would learn something."

The fact is that there was nothing worth taping in the second session. There were a great many tears and a few sardonic jokes. It was early summer and toward the end she had become very passive, sitting in a chair eighteen hours a day. Attempts to encourage her to try to minimize her discomfort and enjoy her passivity were not successful. She said she wanted to go into a garden outside my office. She found it overwhelming, saying that she had avoided life so much in the last few weeks that she wasn't able to deal even with the garden. But she told her husband, now present, to not let her withdraw so much. Later she contradicted this, and said she wanted to withdraw.

The day after the LSD treatment she said that the session had relieved her depression. It had given her a chance to look at where she was and see that she didn't like it. It frightened her to see that she had become so withdrawn. She thought the whole experience had been worthwhile.

Soon after the session, she died.

Her husband told me that he was extremely enthusiastic about the LSD treatment. He said that although the second one had had little effect, the first had caused a remarkable change. Before LSD she had been resentful, bitter, and picked on him. She felt it was demeaning to have to be cared for, and resented him bitterly. For example, when they had to buy a new car she had said to him, "Now you'll have a shiny new car to go to the funeral in." Numerous times she had said to him, "You'll be glad when I'm dead."

Following the LSD treatment her first remark to him was, "I'm not suicidal." Apparently she had worried about this without saying so. Her hostility toward him rapidly died down and did not reappear. She was calmer, and could be appreciative and accepting of his help. Therefore, he could also be more helpful to her. Her death was a quiet one, the result of a last injection of the chemotherapeutic agent.

One reason this patient came was because she had read in the literature that LSD helped people accept death. She had tried to convince herself and her world that she did accept her death. *In fact she did not.* If LSD did not bring acceptance of death, it did bring an acceptance of the reality of serious illness and the necessity for help. This allowed her to maintain her dignity under circumstances that were extremely trying for about four months.

REFERENCES

Kurland, A. A., S. Grof, W. N. Pahnke, and L. E., Goodman, "Psychedelic Drug Assisted Psychotherapy in Patients with Terminal Cancer," in I. K. Goldberg, S. Malitz, and A. H. Kutscher, eds., *Psychopharmacologic Agents for the Terminally Ill and Bereaved.* New York: Columbia University Press (distributor), 1973.

Sullivan, H. S., discussion of E. Lindemann and E. Malamud, "Experimental Analysis of Psychopathological Effects of Intoxicant Drugs," *American Journal of Psychiatry, 90:*879–81, 1934.

35

Drug Ingestion and Suicide During Anticipatory Grief

Bruce L. Danto

During the period of anticipatory grief, both anxiety and depression may mount for those who will be bereaved (Danto, 1972). When insomnia is an associated symptom, the physician is often tempted to prescribe various types of tranquilizers and sedatives. These prescriptions may communicate to the "survivor patient" that the grief he is anticipating may be overwhelming and that suicide may provide the solution to his emotional problems. Prescription of such medication may suggest or provide a method of suicide for the person in distress. Since both the terminally ill patient and his immediate family may be receiving various kinds of oral medication and, for the most part, may be receiving both sedatives and tranquilizers, an unaware medical staff may witness the death of a grieving family member at or before the time of the terminal patient's death.

In the United States, one suicide out of three kills himself with a drug prescribed by a physician (Brophy, 1967). This individual is often an impulsive person whose success at suicide depends upon the amount he ingests, his health at the time of ingestion, and the type of agent he uses. Physicians cannot control efforts by their patients to accumulate a "suicide cache" of pills (Petty and Jensen, unpublished), but they can make the initial decision of whether or not the patient really needs such pills and how many should be dispensed at any given time (Brophy, 1967).

In an effort to place this problem in its proper perspective, Brophy pointed out that since 1954 approximately 400 tons of barbiturates have been produced annually. This would amount to about six billion 1-grain barbiturate tablets. The dollar value of these barbiturates has increased over a decade by one million dollars annually. Ettlinger and Flordh (1955) found that 73 percent of their group of 500 attempted suicides used barbiturates. With the tremendous increase in the use of tranquilizers it would not be unlikely to see this class of drugs used more frequently in suicide attempts and in successful suicides. Lending validity to the latter assumption is the U.S. Public Health report (Department of Health, Education and Welfare, 1966) which showed that the majority of 1968 attempted suicides with tranquilizers involved use of the minor ones. Other studies (Hinwich, 1965) reveal that most of the tranquilizer prescriptions, over 65 percent in this country, are for the minor tranquilizers.

It is commonly assumed that the massive dose (lethal dose) of a barbiturate is ten to fifteen times the average hypnotic dose (Brophy, 1967). As this has been fairly well borne out, it is apparent that a two-week supply could be lethal to the average patient, and is contraindicated if the patient is adjudged to be suicidally depressed. The massive dose of antidepressants may be found in the amount of a ten-day supply (Brophy, 1967). The major tranquilizers are fairly safe, as is documented by their involvement in the fewest reports of overdose deaths. However, a month's supply of minor tranquilizers, if consumed at one time, could be lethal (Brophy, 1967). Over all, what may be considered a massive dose may vary, depending upon such factors as the age of the person, his medical status, sex, the form and amount of the drug ingested, the time between ingestion and treatment, and the form of treatment.

Studies such as those of Sanborn, Casey, and Niswander (1971) reveal that both drug abusers and suicide attempters have much in common. MMPI scores reveal that both score high on the paranoid and schizophrenia scales. The researchers felt that both groups use different methods to manipulate their environment. In a study of 106 poisoning episodes, McHugh and Goodell (1971) found a third group of patients who ingested overdoses in reaction to disturbed life circumstances. Frequently in this group were those who were actively grieving the loss of a loved one. Further, the authors concluded that those who died or made the most serious attempt at self-destructure were depressed about a life circumstance rather than suffering from a personality disorder. These individuals obtain drugs from a physician by arousing his sympathy and his need to treat his own anxiety by quieting that which exists within his patient.

Thus a picture of the survivor-to-be begins to emerge. Here is a person who may develop a progressively worsening depression with or without anxiety. As he passes through the stages of anticipatory grief (Danto, 1972), he may find it necessary to deal with the affective aspects of his personal situation, often turning to his physician or a relative, either of whom may offer massive dose medications instead of verbal and emotional support. If he approaches enough friends and relatives, he can collect the necessary massive dose of medication without a prescription, like a squirrel gathering nuts for the winter. His friends, and possibly his physican, may register shock at the news of his serious suicide attempt or death, having been so skillfully manipulated by the patient that they did not see their role in his suicide. Without insight, they may proceed onward, supplying other survivors-to-be and depressed persons with massive doses of medication.

What can be done to deal with this problem? First and foremost, the medical community must lead an effort to change the belief that pills can solve all problems. Physicians and nurses must learn to talk to those experiencing anticipatory grief. Neglected in both psychiatry and medicine, in general, is that period when the family of a dying patient should be treated and assisted. When a baby is born, there is rejoicing. The obstetrician beams as he sees the family lighting cigars and calling friends to sound the clarion of good news. But where is the doctor when death is predictably near? What does he share with the family then? A prescription for tranquilizers and sedatives? He must be wary lest his pen become a scythe of death.

The physician, nurse, and possibly even the pharmacist might well talk to members of the dying person's family. If depression beyond that which can be normally anticipated during the terminal phase is observed, the medical staff must be cautious. If sedatives or tranquilizers are felt to be necessary, no more than a week's supply should be prescribed, with approval necessary for refill. Other family members should be advised to keep an eye on the overly depressed or suicidal survivor-to-be. If the pharmacist calls the physician for approval of a refill or authorization for an increase in the prescription amount, the physician must be cautious. He should schedule an appointment with the patient each time a new prescription is forthcoming, to ensure that his patient's depression and anxiety have not reached suicidal proportions. If a dramatic and sudden lifting of depression is noted in the patient, the physician should suspect that there is a possibility of his patient's suicide. That sudden lifting of depression before the medication can become effective should be a warning signal of an impending suicide attempt. The physician must maintain a discussion level of relationship, insuring that he can offer psychotherapeutic help either through his talks with the patient or through referral to a psychiatrist or mental health worker.

In summary, it should be acknowledged that both sedatives and all forms of tranquilizers are potentially lethal. Their unbelievable abundance makes them ready-made for those who wish to commit suicide. *Among those who may commit suicide are those who become intensely depressed during the stage of anticipatory grief.* Relatives must be cautioned about making such agents available to the survivors-to-be of a terminally ill person or the survivors of the deceased. The entire medical staff must prescribe for them cautiously and be on the alert for those who are manipulating their physicians into becoming a part of the suicide method itself.

REFERENCES

Brophy, J. J., "Suicide Attempts with Psychotherapeutic Drugs," *Archives of General Psychiatry, 17:*652, 1967.

Danto, B. L., "Anticipatory Grief," paper presented at Symposium of the Foundation of Thanatology, New York, April 14, 1972.

Department of Health, Education and Welfare, "Statistical Analysis of Accidental Poisoning Reported to the National Clearing House, 1965," *Bulletin of National Clearing House for Poison Control Centers,* May-June, 1966.

Ettlinger, R. W., and P. Flordh, "Attempted Suicide: Experience of Five Hundred Cases at a General Hospital," *Acta Psychiatrica et Neurologica Scandinavica, 103:*1, 1955.

Hinwich, H. E., "General Discussion," in J. Marks and C. M. B. Pare, eds., *The Scientific Basis of Drug Therapy in Psychiatry.* Oxford: Pergamon Press, Symposium Publications Division, 1965.

McHugh, P. R., and H. Goodell, "Suicidal Behavior: A Destruction in Patients with Sedative Poisoning Seen in a General Hospital," *Archives of General Psychiatry, 25:*456, 1971.

Petty, T., and V. Jensen, "Suicide Cache," unpublished paper.

Sanborn, D. E. III, T. M. Casey, and G. G. Niswander, "Drug Abusers, Suicide Attempters and the MMPI," *Diseases of the Nervous System, 32:*183, 1971.

36

The Ministry and a Parents' Sharing Group: * Preliminary Report

LeRoy G. Kerney

Much of the literature of thanatology focuses on the experience of patients and their families as they face the problem of death and dying. Included in this literature is the secondary aspect of the feelings, reactions, and insights of those who treat and minister to the terminally ill. But little has been written about methods of helping and sustaining dying patients and their families. This chapter is an account of one attempt to devise a method to help parents of children with leukemia cope with their life situation. Focusing on the methodology rather than the content of the group sessions, this preliminary report is divided into three parts: first, an examination of the needs of parents of children with leukemia; second, a description of the project; and third, an assessment of the methodology.

NEED OF PARENTS

A basic clue to the needs of parents of leukemic children is to be found in Toffler's well-known book, *Future Shock*. Anticipatory grief can be understood as a form of future shock, and the topics discussed regarded as the basic themes of the parents' anticipatory grief.

The initial confirmation of the diagnosis as leukemia brings with it an

* This particular group was established at the Clinical Center, National Institutes of Health, Bethesda, Maryland.

awareness of "the death of the permanence." Parents are caught in a time period of unknown duration, and move from a stable situation where the family is intact, through the death of a child, to (hopefully) a reorganized and stable family constellation. Those patterns of living which were taken for granted, the hopes and dreams surrounding the future of the child, the ongoing roles of the working father and the mothering parent, have been threatened. Change and adaptation become mandatory. Coping mechanisms, life styles, and individual social roles and relationships are also questioned, threatened, and often shattered.

The family becomes aware of "transience." What was once taken for granted crumbles. Daily routines of the home—children going to school, financial arrangements, working patterns, care of other children—are changed radically. Children and their parents (usually the mother, with the father visiting from time to time) are moved from the home to a hospital. When the child is in remission and returned home, trips to the hospital are still necessary for check-ups or visits to the outpatient clinic. Even during periods of health, there is the ever-present cloud of uncertainty.

In the midst of change, there appears "novelty." Children are faced with living in a strange place, sleeping in a strange bed, being cared for by strangers. There is the "novelty" of medical procedures, intravenous feedings, finger sticks, reaction to toxic drugs, oxygen tents and respirators, and the mingling with other children and parents whose children are in various stages of the ride on the "roller coaster of leukemic death." In the words of the Psalmist, "How shall we sing the Lord's song in a foreign land?"

In this foreign land there is a "diversity" of peoples, life styles, coping devices, medical opinions, and therapies. Moving from the familiar to the unfamiliar, there are divergent and disparate patterns of hopes and fears, meanings and methods, and personal feelings of hope and relief, rage, apathy, confusion. Life is no longer simple, if it ever was. It becomes even more complex, complicated, and confused. Parents begin to wonder how much they can take, what their "limits of adaptation" are. Often there is reversion to earlier patterns that were once effective but now seem inappropriate. Signs of the limits of adaptation are seen in mothers who become overweight; in tensions between parent and nurse over who is the "mothering one"; in anger at physicians for not treating their child appropriately; or in feelings of rage at the doctor for appearing to be cold-hearted and unconcerned. Parents wonder how long they can endure the burdens that each day brings.

In the last section of *Future Shock,* Toffler writes about strategies of adaptation. He suggests that, rather than focusing on "being" or "doing," attention should be given to "becoming." Are there ways to devise a methodology that can sustain and support, bringing out the strengths of people in need and helping them bridge the gap between one stable state and another?

Medical treatment by itself is basic—but in and of itself it is not enough. Most cancer research is focused on the "hardware" of the problem, and little if any attention has been given the "software" or support system for those afflicted. There is a variety of resources available in the attempt to meet these needs. These include the work of doctors, nurses, social workers, recreational and occupational therapists, chaplains, family members, and friends. The clinical center may include a "Mothers' Group" led by a pediatrician and social worker who discuss the medical problems that arise.

But neither a place nor a group exists for discussing questions of a philosophical, religious, and existential nature in a more formal and explicit fashion. When such a void is not filled, the parents' interest in medical quackery, "faith healing," and "faith healers" is often aroused.

The fact is often overlooked that these parents themselves are the "experts." They are experts in the sense that they have experienced and are experiencing existentially the problem of dealing with terminal illness and anticipatory grief. They have much to share and learn from each other.

Many of the forms of traditional hospital chaplaincy tend to fragment this temporary but very meaningful community of "fellow sufferers" into major faith groups. Leukemia, the common enemy, makes this group a cohesive unit.

DESCRIPTION OF THE PARENTS' SHARING GROUP

Briefly stated, the Parents' Sharing Group is a group process designed to help parents of children suffering from leukemia cope with some of the human threats that accompany the diagnosis, treatment, and hospitalization of the disease. It evolved out of an attempt by the Department of Spiritual Ministry in a research hospital setting to enhance the service dimension of the department's program for patients and their families and meet the need of chaplain trainees in a program of clinical pastoral education to develop their skills and insights in working with groups.

The Clinical Center is a research medical hospital in which patients are grouped by diseases in nursing units. The patients often come from homes that are geographically separated as well as emotionally removed from the

Clinical Center. The parents, generally mothers, often accompany their children to the Center, and remain with them most of the day. There is a short period of time after lunch, called "quiet time," when they can turn to their own needs. The group meets once a week during this time.

The group is composed of those parents who are in the hospital and voluntarily wish to participate in the group process. All religious faith groups, and persons with "no faith," are welcomed and encouraged to attend. Those who attend vary in number. A typical group is made up of three to eight mothers, and is fluid in nature, with new persons coming in and others dropping out. The group meets in a seminar room away from the nursing unit. The mothers welcome getting away from the nursing unit and the solarium, away from their children and their prying eyes.

The leaders of the group are two trainee chaplains who bring with them mature experience gained from working in churches and military posts. They have had extensive experience in working with study groups, fellowship groups, and in religious counseling. They are familiar with questions of faith, of religion, and of the use of symbols and rituals. They bring with them a personal warmth and concern as parents in their own right.

The agenda is wide open. Any topic or concern can and is encouraged to be shared. There are no right or wrong answers, and although various aspects of religion are discussed there is no attempt to impose an explicit value or religious system on the group. Of course, the general values of health as against illness, openness vs. closedness, support vs care-less-ness, and sharing vs denial, are encouraged and supported. Permission is secured from the group members to tape the sessions, and the tapes and transcripts are often reviewed by the staff, and other disciplines, including a psychiatrist.

Although the major focus of this report is on the methodology, a few final comments on the content of the discussions may be helpful. In "Some Parents' Concerns About Death: A Partial Report of Group Work with Parents of Leukemic Children," written by Chaplain (LTC) David W. Polhemus for a course in the program on religion and medical care, held at George Washington University, Chaplain Polhemus, a cofounder of the group, stated that "nearly 50 percent of our time has been concerned with death and ten closely related subtopics surrounding it."

In a recent session, the two leaders asked the parents to tear pictures from a stack of magazines and make a collage that would say something about themselves as a means of communicating to each other about their dilemmas and concerns. Through this technique, an easing of communication about the "unspeakable" in consequent sessions and in individual visits by the chaplains appeared. These collages were reviewed by an art therapist with the staff and the leaders of the group. At this stage of the project, this technique appears to be a very useful and helpful method of communication.

AN ASSESSMENT

Although this is a preliminary report on one of the many methods of helping people cope with anticipatory grief, some basic questions emerge.

With the leadership representing only one discipline, what are the advantages and disadvantages of this fact? Discussion opens up issues and feelings. Other than the usual follow-up and referral endeavors, does the process leave too many "loose ends" of ideas, concepts, feelings, social and medical planning unattended? Although the leaders and the members of the group are aware that beneath the conscious expression of feelings and concern there lies the unconscious mooring of thoughts and feelings, these are not programmed into the function and purpose of the group. What are the implications of this fact? Although it is called a group for parents, there are very few, if any, fathers and husbands involved.

FINAL COMMENT

This chapter concludes with comments made by Chaplain Polhemus, in his paper cited above:

"Speaking for myself, I find I have fewer answers to give—whatever they are using to cope capably with the disease is too necessary. We try to offer an open, understanding pair of chaplains. As the child becomes more ill, and death more certain, the parents get to the place, they pray for death."

By virtue of the fact that we've been with them as they enter the valley, we can stay with them until they come out of the other side. That is our ministry.

37

Anticipatory Grief from the Perspective of Widowhood

Phyllis R. Silverman *

THE WIDOW-TO-WIDOW PROGRAM †

The Widow-to-Widow Program, an experiment in preventive intervention, reached out to the bereaved woman shortly after the demise of her spouse. The reaching out was done by a small group of other widowed women (Silverman, 1970) who offered their condolences and the opportunity to share their own experiences in coping with widowhood to every newly widowed woman (under age sixty) in a particular section of Boston. The "aides" visited people of racial and religious backgrounds similar to their own.

The program evolved from a pilot study (Silverman, 1967), which

* The author thanks Dorothy MacKenzie, Mary Pettipas, and Elizabeth Wilson, who were widow aides in the original program, and who are now program coordinators for the Program's current activities. The author has been greatly helped by the reality that comes from the willingness of these women to share their personal experience, as well as the experience they have gained from helping widowed people over the last five years.

† The Laboratory of Community Psychiatry, Department of Psychiatry, Harvard Medical School, established the Widow-to-Widow Program under the auspices of the Preventive Intervention Unit. The Widow-to-Widow Program received the death certificate from the Boston Health Department. An aide, herself a widow, then sent an informal note to the surviving spouse, establishing her own widowhood and suggesting a time when she would come by to visit. She gave her home phone number in case the widow did not want her to visit or wanted to change the time.

had indicated that most people tend to withdraw from someone in mourning, that the assistance they do offer is superficial and full of platitudes, and without any real comprehension of what is needed for successful coping with widowhood (Silverman, 1971).

It is the purpose of this chapter to explore the impact of a wife's knowledge of her husband's terminal illness and her anticipation of his impending death on her subsequent grief. Differences in their reactions to the program's offer of help and the responses of women whose husbands died suddenly will also be examined.

Fulton (1972) has pointed out that a consequence of grieving in advance of the ill person's actual death can be a spouse's premature withdrawal from the patient before his death. Yet, according to data derived from the Widow-to-Widow Program, many women, although aware of their husbands' terminal state, did not grieve in advance. Indeed, it can be extrapolated from this data that it would have been dysfunctional for them to have done so. They had learned to live with the illness and modified their lives to accommodate to the changes brought about by it. Only when the door was finally closed did they in fact begin to mourn—and the trajectory of this grief was not dissimilar to that of any other new widow. This involved the acceptance of themselves as widows and adaptation to changes in their style of life to accommodate to this role change.

The data presented in this chapter are from the original experiment, in which over 450 women were contacted within three weeks after their husbands' deaths. An extensive analysis was conducted on the first 300 women, including follow-up interviews with both those people who had refused the offer of help and those worked with most closely over a period of three years. In this group of 300, there were 39 women whose husbands had suffered from a long-term illness; that is, a condition which involved more than a year's illness before the ultimate death.

THE SAMPLE

Thirty of the men in this sample were over fifty, several over sixty, and the oldest sixty-four. One was only twenty-five, another thirty-eight, and the others in their middle forties at the time of death. These men were primarily members of the working class (including bus drivers and policemen); the most educated (two years of college) was an electronic technician. Some of the widows worked as sales girls, several were registered nurses, and one woman was an executive secretary. Many had to turn to welfare to support themselves and their families during the terminal stage of the illness; and some women went to work doing housework for others to supplement their incomes. None were women who would be financially independent after her husband's death. In all, illness created both economic and emotional hardships for the entire family.

Causes of death varied. In one instance, death was the result of excessive drinking, in spite of a physician's warning of a fatal outcome. Another man was an assault victim, and sustained such severe brain damage that he was a vegatable case in the hospital for one year and a day. (The length of this period prevented his assailant from being charged with murder.) The other men died primarily from cancer, emphysema, or complications of coronary illness.

Their widows acknowledged that they knew what was going to happen, but in retrospect none of them thought that they had accepted the reality of the situation until the actual moment of death. As one woman said: "I knew he was dying, but I couldn't believe it would happen."

A very intelligent woman in her late forties said: "We never talked about it. I think he knew, but we kept fooling ourselves that he was going to beat it. If he kept eating, he would regain the weight he lost and get better."

Only one or two women tried to keep the prognosis from their husbands—and to accomplish this they became involved in complex conspiracies. In one instance, the husband had been ill for eight years: "We always found an excuse for his difficulties until we ran out of them. It was a continuous struggle." Family behavior seems to typify an inability to cope effectively. It may also be symptomatic of a poor marital relationship, one in which the man never had charge of his own life.

There is an important difference in meaning between lying about what is happening and simply not talking about it. And this has a strong impact on family relationships. In only one instance did the husband take the initiative and discuss his condition openly. His wife remained a reluctant participant in such talks, preferring to cling to any false hope. She later felt, however, that this frank talking had helped some and made her better able to handle the funeral details. Yet, she was still shocked that her husband had really died. For more than a year afterward, she could not refer to herself as a widow or say that her husband was dead.

The youngest widow, age twenty-three, felt that she was not in shock, as she might have been had the death happened suddenly: "Even though I was grateful when it happened, he was so sick, and in such pain, I was still very depressed. I had to face a complete change in my life and rebuild. Like my in-laws seem to act as if it doesn't mean as much to me and my baby as it means to them. But they don't have to shift gears as much.''

Those women who had cared for their husbands during the illness experienced a great sense of relief when the end came. But this was usually temporary and in reaction to their own fatigue, a response to the fact that the deceased was no longer suffering and the family no longer living with false hopes and frustrations typical of a hopeless situation.

One woman whose husband had died from emphysema said: ''His attacks were so bad, he would almost choke to death. It's the worst thing that can happen to anyone, and you have to live with it to realize it.''

Another woman said that a state of depression sets in from the strain of caring for the patient. ''We were worn out from caring for him. We couldn't get any sleep.''

The woman whose husband's drinking led to his death said that his death was a relief: ''The problems he created from his drinking were worse than those created by his death.''

Except for this particular situation, relief was transitory. Once physically recovered, the surviving spouse still had to deal with her grief, the reality of her loss, and the need to build a new life. None of this could have been done appropriately in advance.

Only one of the men, formerly a truck driver, found alternate employment when he became ill. When the other men could work no longer, they fell back on their wives' earnings, disability pensions, or some type of welfare assistance. Several of these men spent a good deal of time at home and—if there were children—assumed some responsibilities for their care while the wife worked. This kind of care brought them closer to their families than ever before. On the other hand, as their disability increased, their nursing needs so taxed the family that the wife's total life was wrapped around her husband. In some instances there was complete withdrawal from any social life. This was especially true when there were no children or the children were grown. Thus, when there was no large, extended family, some women found themselves completely isolated when death occurred. One women said, ''My husband lost all his hair and didn't want anyone to see him. People stopped coming. When he died, I couldn't simply pick up and see the people we had once known as a couple.''

In other instances, the ill man drew closer to members of his family, and satisfying his needs became the focal point of all their energies. Most of these people, exhausted by this effort and the constant exposure to a loved one's suffering, were relieved by the death. However, in some ways, at the time of death there is a greater shock than if the man had died suddenly while the family members were investing themselves in other interests and relationships, as they would do in the normal course of family life.

THE OFFER OF HELP

The Widow-to-Widow Program tried to reach an entire population at risk by trying to contact every potential "client." * These findings, then, reflect the reactions of a broader population than those normally seen by other agencies. There was no selection process such as occurs when an individual takes the initiative to seek out and ask for help from a local doctor, a clergyman, a mental health facility, or the like. The willingness to develop a relationship with the aide was not necessarily an indication of the existence of serious problems or a reflection of great need.

What were these women's reactions to the aides' offers of assistance? Of the women contacted, 25 percent refused and 75 percent accepted (Silverman, 1971). This is a slightly larger population of acceptance than in the larger original sample of 300. However, defining acceptance or refusal is not a simple matter. As a friend and neighbor, it was possible for the aide to call back in six months or so to see how things were, and there were additional opportunities available to become involved as things changed and new needs emerged for the widow.

Only five women persisted in denying their need for any help, not meeting the aide or talking with her at any length on the telephone. Five other women had very friendly meetings with the aide or talked at length on the telephone, but basically felt no need for further contact. Twenty-one women were accepting of and responsive to the aide, and maintained continuing contact with her for from three months to several years. Eight women had refused the aide's invitation at first but accepted it at a later date. Their initial behavior seems in part to be related to the husband's lengthy illness and to their exhaustion when the ordeal had ended.

Certain information is available concerning the women who refused the offer because they agreed later to participate in the follow-up study directed

* This word is used advisedly. These people were not clients or patients, and these terms were deliberately avoided in the Program. They imply a subordinate-superordinate relationship which was alien to the kind of helping the aide provided.

at determining why they had felt no need for the aide. Only one woman could not be located. She did not respond to letters and was not at home when the aide visited. The aide knew members of her family and learned that her husband had been in a nursing home for eight years, essentially a vegetable; and she had built a new life without him before he died. In such a situation, where it was impossible for a relationship with the ill person to be maintained, this behavior pattern might be regarded as the only appropriate alternative.

Findings indicate that the women had assessed their situation correctly and, indeed, had no need for this additional resource. The women who refused shared several qualities: they were all active, independent women who had worked before their husbands' deaths; they seemed able to accept the reality of their situation; they could mobilize any additional resources that they might need; and they could cope with the problems presented by widowhood. There was a dimension to their independence which may suggest that they were afraid to become involved because they were unaccustomed to seeing themselves in the role of "being helped." For example, the only woman with small children who refused the offer of help said: "I would think that it might be nice and it might not. It might confuse you more because they have their own problems. . . . I like to think by myself and make my own decisions."

To be helped in some way implied for these women that it was necessary for them to subscribe to any advice offered. They seemed to have difficulty accepting that this did not necessarily follow. In their view, under these circumstances, to become involved also meant being burdened with other people's problems as well as their advice. In addition, all of these women had many people living in their homes—parents, children, grandchildren—and they were used to taking care of people rather than themselves being in a dependent position. Their own assessment of need was accurate. They did agree to be interviewed in the follow-up study, and they have all made new lives. It is possible to arrive at some general evaluations concerning their awareness of their husbands' impending deaths and their reactions to it. None of these women had discussed death with their husbands. But, as one said: "He had so many heart attacks. The last one, I think, we both knew it was the end, but you're never prepared for it emotionally." The trajectory of their grief was no different from that of any other widow who had contact with the Widow-to-Widow Program (Silverman, 1971).

The other group of five women who refused help did so after lengthy face-to-face or telephone contact with the aide. They saw no need for additional assistance, but were willing to tell the aide about themselves and to find out about her. These were women in their late forties and fifties, and all had other identities in addition to that of wife (Silverman, 1971). The woman who can define other satisfactory roles for herself, beside that of wife, has more resources available to her to enable her to learn to live as a widow.

These women live alone, they work full-time, their children are grown. They are friendly, busy people, with many friends to talk with, including other widows. They have no need for another confidant or for additional support to help them learn to live as widows. Like the first group of women discussed, during the period of their husbands' illnesses, each of these five women focused her energies on living with her husband at whatever stage he was at, emphasizing to the end his involvement in their life as a couple. Death brought the same relief, the same shock, the same despair, and the same confusion about what it means to be a widow, as it did for most women in this sample. However, while not afraid of accepting help, these women had no immediate need for it.

From the twenty-one women who accepted help from the aide, two groups emerged. The first group could be called "chronic noncopers." Nothing seems to change things for them. The way they deal with grief is the way they deal with everything—poorly. The aide, in spite of great effort, for the most part made little impact on their lives, nor could she help them fully with the vast number of social, emotional, and economic problems at hand, most of which had nothing to do with their grief.

There were five women in this group. One had left her husband before and during his illness, so that he was burdened with the care of their small children for up to six months at a time. After his death, she left the children periodically with neighbors and babysitters. One woman, an alcoholic, had managed to alienate everyone in her family many years before and, after her husband's death, alienated those who befriended her out of pity. Another woman developed a serious depression and requested electrotherapy. The aide could not intervene to prevent the illness. This woman had responded to stress in the past in this way—and, almost inevitably, broke down again. The aide was more successful in helping her deal with the details of her daily life, and in providing concrete guidance about what to do. (When this involved interacting with other members of the family, the effect of the

helping broke down. Here, the widow felt frustrated, receiving little appro-
bation; the family members constantly criticized her, and demanded what she
realistically tried to do for them. The entire family was evidently disturbed.)
It is not clear whether in some families the husband had been a buffer between his wife and the rest of the world, keeping the family together, or
whether he had been as inept as his wife. As might be expected, this type of
woman was an unreliable informant. It is difficult to know if the presenting
problems were exaggerated by the lengthy illness.

The second group that accepted help was composed of sixteen women
who could be termed "copers," some coping more adequately than others.
They became involved with the aide to varying degrees, and seemed to build
on the relationship in order to help themselves. Three years after their husbands' deaths, all had made some accommodation to their changed circumstances. The problems they presented after the deaths were as varied as
those found in the entire population of new widows. The youngest widow,
since remarried and with another child, needed someone who could talk with
her about what she was feeling, what her baby's needs were, how to handle
her in-laws, someone to call at midnight when she couldn't sleep and was
consumed by loneliness. The aide introduced her to another woman with
small children whose husband had died the year before, and they were able
to help each other.

Sometimes the widow and the aide talked without any focus. It was
hard to connect any subsequent move the widow made with these encounters. In retrospect, however, some women have said that they got the moral
support they needed. In part, this came as a result of their not feeling so
alone anymore. Several women eventually admitted to the aide that they had
had poor marriages and were feeling better now than they had ever felt
before about themselves as people. They got direction from the aide about
finding jobs, and the aide introduced them to other widows in their community, thus expanding their social network and the kind of activities they
could become involved with.

There were several women who turned to the aide for advice and guidance on anything they did. In a sense, the aide was literally functioning as a
husband. She was a transition person to whom the widow could turn until
learning to act for herself on her own behalf. One woman in this group had
lied to her husband for eight years. A chronic complainer, she seems to
characterize a way of dealing with the world. It is hard to evaluate her real-

ity. She seems committed to this stance, no matter how her reality has changed to her advantage. This is a difficult person to work with. It is easy to feel discouraged. Nothing seems to improve. It is necessary to constantly make an independent assessment of her situation to see whether help is being accepted or not. The author's role as professional consultant to the aide was often to help the aide get some perspective so that she didn't feel discouraged by the complaining.

Several women were isolated with few, if any, surviving relatives. In one woman's words, the aide's visit was "like a piece of heaven coming into my home." The aide's friendship helped in finding new friends, and she helped with other details, like taking the widow to the welfare office and arranging for a tombstone for the grave. Isolation here was not a consequence of the husband's illness, but of the woman's basic shyness and the fact that she had no family (not even children, in one instance).

As stated above, there were eight women who at first refused but later accepted the offer of help. Their behavior was clearly tied to what they had been going through during the last months of their husbands' life. This may be the group with problems most clearly related to the husband's death, but also the group having fewer clearer solutions. There appear to be two kinds of women in this group: those exhausted in the extreme by the illness, and those most afraid of confronting widowhood.

The group suffering from exhaustion was offered help too soon, and regarded the aide's offer of help as an additional social burden. These women incorrectly defined the offer of help as involvement in a social network, an obligation to entertain the aide if she came to visit. The value of talking, of giving vent to their feelings, was not clear to them. As they became aware of their needs they thought of calling, but worried about "not wanting to impose or bother the aide."

These are very independent women who solve many of their problems by themselves. However, they are people who need people, who need to feel needed. Six months or a year after their bereavement, they were floundering, lonely, not recovered as they thought they would be. They needed to talk, needed new social contacts, to find out how to live widowed. At that point, the aide could give help—even if simply giving information about a group for widowed people where a widow could meet people with similar interests.

In the second group of this subsample were those women who had difficulty accepting the aide because she was a widow, and were thus reluctant to acknowledge that they too were widowed. The woman whose husband had talked frankly about his impending death was in this group. This frankness had not helped her accept her new role as a widow. In an extreme situation, one woman's daughter did not want her mother involved because she thought that the aide would introduce her mother to other men. Still depressed, still spending a good deal of time talking about the past, she is difficult to help because the daughter is unwilling to talk with the aide, and discourages and interferes with her mother's efforts to be involved. These widows needed help to accept their widowhood and to find a new direction for living. The aide helped not only by talking, but also by the example she set in her own life, and through other widows she has introduced to the new widow—thus repeopling her life and making it possible to find new alternatives.

The common factor in these eight situations may be timing. In the author's opinion, even after three weeks (which was when the aide generally made contact), these women were too confused to relate in any way to another human being. They all had sufficient resources to manage adequately with their situations at that time. But, at a later date, they came to a realistic confrontation with the facts of widowhood, their lack of experience in this role, and the accompanying difficulties that follow. They were willing to talk with the aide, but they never took the initiative. The need was there. But it was met only because the aide called again.

DISCUSSION AND CONCLUSION

Grief is a complex phenomenon. From the data presented, it is possible to see that wives prefer to remain related and involved with a terminally ill husband. Confronting the reality of his death is possible only after the death has occurred. If there is a difference between this population and those women whose husbands died suddenly or as a result of a shorter illness, it is that the former group did not experience the sense of total shock that the suddenly bereaved talk about. Many, however, were exhausted as a result of caring for their husbands. The numbness all widowed people talk of that sets in immediately after the death may be compounded by this exhaustion and by its relation to the state of tension that may have existed during the period immediately prior to the death.

These women were all involved with large medical centers and their staffs. However, none of them were involved in any efforts to help them understand what was happening to their husbands or to help them or their husbands cope with the many problems the illness and ultimate death were causing. To have helped them grieve in advance would have been inappropriate. Some of the denial, some of the false hope, and the surprise in the face of reality when death finally comes may be normal. The shock, the emptiness, the reluctance to face the fact of being a widow, and the loneliness that develops are part of a process that cannot be met until they occur.

What are the appropriate issues to deal with during the terminal stages of illness? It may be possible to establish an atmosphere in which people can be open about their feelings, or can be taught to accept these feelings, seeing them as the consequences of the various acts of a drama. It may be possible to prevent total social isolation from developing for both the patient and his family. It may be possible to help make some long-range economic plans for the needs of the surviving spouse and children. However, it may not be appropriate to aim for open discussions about the impending death. The goal must be to maximize the possibility for whatever living is possible during this period.

Real grieving and coming to terms with the changes death makes in a wife's life can come only after the husband has died. While he lives, it is her reality to care for him. Some people even talk about the coming death, but this is not grieving in advance. Engagements are not marriages. Neither is a rehearsal for widowhood the real thing. This happens only when the other person is no longer there to interact with.

REFERENCES

Fulton, R., and J. Fulton, "Anticipatory Grief: A Psychosocial Aspect of Terminal Care," in B. Schoenberg *et al.,* eds., *Psychosocial Aspects of Terminal Care.* New York: Columbia University Press, 1972.

Silverman, P., "Facts Involved in Accepting an Offer of Help," *Archives of the Foundation of Thanatology, 3:*3, 1971.

―― "Services to the Widowed: First Steps in a Program of Preventive Intervention," *Community Mental Health Journal, 3:*37, 1967.

―― "The Widow as a Caregiver," *Mental Hygiene, 54:*540, 1970.

―― "Widowhood and Preventive Intervention," *Family Coordinator, 1:*95, 1972.

Silverman, P., *et al.,* eds., *Helping Each Other in Widowhood.* New York: Health Sciences, 1974.

PART **6**

PASTORAL
ASPECTS

38

Initiatory Grief
Robert E. Neale

To live is to wonder about life. And life includes death and dying. So it has been said: "Death is a truth made profound by the size of our wonder." Unfortunately, the size of man's wonder about death tends to remain pitifully minute. Great wonder would include grief. To wonder about death is to grieve.

Grief can occur after or before death occurs. The latter, anticipatory grief, can refer to the death of another or to the death of oneself. And anticipatory grief over one's own death can be divided heuristically into four types. In the first, death is perceived as near and certain. The terminal cancer patient may be well aware that death will occur within weeks, days, or even hours. In the second type of anticipatory grief, death is perceived as near but uncertain. Some heart patients know that death is not inevitable but surely an immediate possibility. Those participating in such dangerous work as mining or soldiering may also see their own deaths in this fashion. In the third type, death is perceived as distant and certain. Death surely will occur, but probably not for a long time to come. This is a prevalent theme of philosophers, and perceived by anyone who actually acknowledges that the fact of death, along with taxes, is the one thing man knows for sure. In the fourth type of anticipatory grief, death is perceived as distant but uncertain. This is the awareness that death will not occur for a long time, and perhaps not even then. Examination of observable human behavior, and not so observable human fantasy, suggests that this type of awareness is exceedingly prevalent. Man may lead lives of quiet desperation in which anticipatory grief is covert and open wonder about death negligible.

The focus of this chapter is on anticipatory grief when death is perceived as distant and certain. It is assumed that this type is preferable to the view of death as distant and uncertain, and that it can play a significant role in modifying responses to death as near. Within this type, there are a variety of responses. The following remarks consider only a religious response, which can be labeled initiatory grief. It is visible in contemporary religious practices, but is most clearly manifest in primitive religion. So the discussion will examine very removed and somewhat extreme behavior in order to highlight a basic religious perception.

DEATH AS AN ISSUE

Theologians tend to become defensive when it is suggested that religion is born out of fear—specifically, fear of death. This is an unnecessary reaction for many reasons. First, it is not the only category of human behavior to originate from fear. So also do philosophy and science. Second, there is no need to subscribe to the reductive fallacy that the nature of the source determines the value of the product. Clearly, fear is a useful response which assists survival of the species. The positive results of such fear are apparent in modern medicine. Third, it is not true that religion arises only out of fear. A case can be made for the role of anxiety-free elements of curiosity, mastery, creativeness, love and joy as well. And fourth, it should be noted that fear of death is a basic attribute of human existence. That religion directly concerns itself with this human awareness is a sign of its responsiveness to the facts of life. Religion is overtly preoccupied with death for the good reason that human beings are covertly preoccupied with it.

Given the above understanding, it can be stated simply that death is an issue for primitive man. His basic tool for dealing with it is religion. The anthropologist, Clifford Geertz (1965), defines religion as follows:

(1) A system of symbols which acts to (2) establish powerful, pervasive and long-lasting moods and motivations in men by (3) formulating conceptions of a general order of existence and (4) clothing these conceptions with such an aura of factuality that (5) the moods and motivations seem uniquely realistic.

To this comprehensive and abstract definition, Geertz appends a lengthy and concrete interpretation. Of pertinence is his understanding of man's need for "conceptions of a general order of existence." As has been noted by historians of religion, the problem for primitive man is chaos. The solution to the problem is the sacred. The sacred is powerful form. It is what has the power to bring order out of chaos. Whereas the profane is powerless and chaotic, the sacred is powerful and orderly. In brief, the profane is death and the sacred is life (Neale, 1969).

Geertz specifies three types of chaos that make primitive man anxious. The first focuses on the limits of man's analytic capacities. Man is baffled in the face of his limited analytic ability to explain anomalous events. He cannot leave these to themselves but must discover some hypothesis about dreams, volcanic eruptions, and death. The second focuses on the limits of man's powers of endurance. Man suffers in the face of his limited ability to make suffering endurable. He cannot ignore suffering, but must come to some conclusions about illness and mourning. The third type of chaos focuses on the limits of man's moral insight. He has to cope with ethical paradox, his inability to discover working criteria for ethical action in the face of evil. There is a discrepancy between moral advice and material rewards. Survival appears unconnected with right and wrong. It is noteworthy that all three types of chaos involve death. More than any other event, death is both beyond and yet requiring interpretation. The problem of chaos is the problem of death.

Geertz has defined religion as a set of symbols which creates moods and motivations by offering conceptions of order. More specifically, he concludes that religion is ". . . a matter of affirming, or at least recognizing, the inescapability of ignorance, pain and injustice on the human plane while simultaneously denying that these irrationalities are characteristic of the world as a whole." So it is useful to suggest that religion is born out of fear. It is an issue for primitive man. Just how he achieves both the assertion and the justification of the inescapability of death is revealed by his images of death.

DEATH AS AN IMAGE

It may be that death has always had an image to human beings. If not, primitive man would have experienced total chaos and responded with total horror. His behavior, if any, would have been flight. There is a group of people in northeast India so primitive that they do not have domestic animals, not even dogs. When a member of the tribe dies, the rest simply run away in panic, never to return if it can be avoided. This is not typical, however, as images of death abound among most primitive peoples (Herzog, 1967). Because of them, something more than flight is possible.

Death may be seen as a corpse or as a group of corpses, a body in which breathing does not occur and blood does not flow, a body which is decomposing, a skeleton, a ghost. Death is pinned down by images. Consequently, man can do more than flee. He can dispose of the corpse. Fear remains, but it is confined to corpses, burial grounds, and nighttime.

Death may also be seen as the devourer. In stumbling upon an abandoned corpse, it appears as though the earth were swallowing it up. The image is of jaws. Earth is like a beast of prey. It is a hugh carnivore which will suddenly open its jaws to tear apart and devour the living. The tearing away at the flesh and bones by earth's emissaries—dogs, wolves, and hyenas—increases the vividness of the image. Concerning the Greek hound of hell, it was said: "Cerberus is the earth and devours all living things." Primitive man had this perception. Fear of death remains, but burial of the corpse or throwing it to the dogs becomes meaningful behavior.

It can be speculated that the negativism of such images is overcome partially when death is viewed anthropomorphically. The inescapability of death becomes justified when death is perceived as mother and father.

Primitive man saw earth as a mother who created and sustained him. But if the earth is also the jaws of death, then death is a mother. Earth is the womb of the mother and the jaws of the wolf. The womb and the jaws are put together in a single image, and death is seen as the fertile and yet fatal mother. What creates also devours. This is illustrated by an ancient Chinese bronze of a tiger with wide-open jaws and a human figure in its paws. An anthropologist affirms that the tiger is both a demon of death and an earth-divinity. He argues that the demon gave birth to the man and is about to devour him. Through this image, the fundamental opposites of human experience are brought together. The most familiar and the most unfamiliar, life and death, become related. Therefore, there is a possibility of something more than flight or passive acceptance. Birth and death have the same source, and one can be interpreted in terms of the other. Death can bring birth.

The image of death as a father is linked to images of corpses and ghosts—the dead. The dead are to be feared. They are inclined to linger around a village causing destruction and death until final rites are held. At that time the souls take up their new abode with the community of ancestors.

This group of long-deceased fathers possesses great wisdom which the living need. Man often consults them over their graves for advice on important matters. The fathers remain death-dealing butchers who carry off the living. But they possess wisdom which they are somewhat willing to share with those heroic human beings who dare confront them and humbly request their aid. Of course, the heroes must be suitably armed with magical defenses, for the fathers cannot be fully trusted. And with luck, the hero can even outwit the dead and receive more wisdom than the fathers desire. Through this image of death as father, wisdom and death become related. Again, there is a possibility of something more than flight or passive acceptance. Wisdom and death have the same source, and one can be interpreted in terms of the others. Death can bring wisdom.

The conclusion is that these images of death as mother and father enable primitive man to do more than assert the inescapability of death. They allow him to justify death as that which offers the gifts of rebirth and wisdom. This justification is an experiential one of death as initiation.

DEATH AS INITIATION

An initiation is a group of rites and teachings which produces significant change in an individual. This change is caused by death. The one fundamental and irreplaceable insight of primitive religion is that death is initiation and initiation is death. This is made abundantly clear by historians and phenomenologists of religion. According to Eliade (1965):

All the rites of rebirth or resurrection, and the symbols that they imply, indicate that the novice has attained to another mode of existence, inaccessible to those who have not undergone the initiatory ordeals, who have not tasted death. We must note this characteristic of the archaic mentality: the belief that a state cannot be changed without first being *annihilated*.

What such a death does for the individual is indicated by the following review of the rites of puberty and the rites of the shaman.

Imagine a boy of about ten years of age who is a member of a primitive tribe in Australia. He is about to pass through a puberty rite. The rite has three stages: death, gestation, and rebirth (Eliade, 1965).

After the older men have prepared a sacred space in the bush, the mother brings her son to the edge of the village. She does not know the content of the rite. She has heard only rumors about death and manhood. She does know that occasionally a child fails to return. The boy knows the same.

Both are filled with excitement and pride, but also with anxiety. The men rush forward and tear the boy away from his mother. She weeps over his possible forthcoming death. The boy is taken to a hut where he lies down on his back with his arms crossed over his chest. He is covered with a mat and told not to utter a sound. During the coming days he may be symbolically burned by a fire, buried in a shallow pit, or ritually dismembered. All these things—separation from mother, darkness, silence, physical danger—are experiences of death. The boy is told that the god or gods are killing him. He does not know for sure whether he will survive or not. Occasionally, the dangerous rite does kill a child. So this first stage of the puberty rite is one of death. The child's self and the child's world are destroyed.

The second part of the ritual takes place over an extended period of time. The boy meets his god and receives his name. After this he may be fed by a guardian for as long as six months. Newborn infants cannot feed themselves. During this time, he is instructed and trained to meditate on his experience. By means of dance, pantomime, and myth, he is introduced to the gods, the history of the tribe, and to the way he is to live. This second stage of the puberty rite is one of gestation. A new self and new world have been impregnated and nourished.

In the final part of the rite, the boy is returned to the community to take his place as a new person in a new world. The boy and his mother do not acknowledge each other for some time to come. Her son has died. It is a strange man who has entered the village. And the boy does not know his mother. He does know the ways of adults and the ways of the gods. The old self and the old world have been transformed.

The experience of the primitive would-be clergyman is essentially the same as that of the pubescent boy (Eliade, 1964). A shaman is called upon only in severe crises, such as to divine both the future and the appropriate action when his community is threatened, to find and return the wayward soul of someone who is sick, or to guide the soul to its final abode in another world when an individual dies. The shaman accomplishes these feats by dying and being reborn himself on each occasion. It is an arduous life which requires lengthy and arduous training. For as long as nine years the shaman experiences repeatedly the drama of death, gestation, and rebirth. Whereas the boy passing through a puberty rite experiences mother death and father death only minimally, the shaman tastes the full force of these images. When fully trained, he can travel up the cosmic pillar to the heavens, where the fathers initiate him into the mysterious wisdom of life and death. And he can travel down the cosmic pillar into the bowels of the earth for restoration of life by the mother. So, in India there are still tales of both the Hindu rope trick and the Hindu basket trick. The coil of rope is thrown into the air and remains suspended, pointing toward the heavenly fathers. The boy or man climbs the rope and disappears. But, in the course of receiving wisdom, his body is dismembered. From nowhere, from that invisible realm above the sky, the parts of the body fall to the ground. They are placed in the large basket (mother earth) and covered. Then the body is marvelously reunited and the person springs out of the basket alive. These two tricks, still performed by stage magicians, originate from primitive initiation rites for clergymen.

Primitive man's justification of death, then, is not an academic exercise wrought by other-wordly philosophers, but a rigorous experience of death, gestation, and rebirth. It may well be that the images of death must be ambivalent ones for the theme of death as initiation and initiation as death to occur. Not only are negative images of death ultimately destructive, so also are purely positive ones. When mother and father gods become totally beneficent, the trials and tribulations of man are no longer necessary. Life and wisdom are simply handed to man on a platter; at least, so he thinks. But what may really happen to the all-good and all-powerful gods is that they no longer rule as gods of death. Death is given over to some lesser god such as Satan or ignored altogether. When this happens, death is either unrelated to life or is not really death at all. An example may be modern man with his "nice-guy" god and his tendency to see death as unrelated to life or as unreal. The development from ambivalent images of death to more completely positive ones is not a sign of progress. Indeed, it leads to the opposite image. A god of life only is being replaced by a god of death only. Modern man passes from denial of death to worship of death and back to denial again. This path is the path of suicide for the individual and the society. He who must be met in contemporary times must be a god of both life and death.

INITIATORY GRIEF

The assumption here is that a participant in a primitive rite of initiation experiences grief. It seems reasonable to suggest that the symptomatology of normal grief mentioned by Lindemann as somatic distress, preoccupation with the image of the deceased (to be), guilt, hostile reactions, and loss of patterns of conduct, will occur in the child who undergoes a puberty rite or the adult who undertakes shamanistic training (Lindemann, 1944). And those who experience initiation would just as obviously experience the elements of anticipatory grief which Lindemann outlines as "depression, heightened preoccupation with the departed, a review of all the forms of death which might befall him, and anticipation of the modes of readjustment which might be necessitated by it." Such grief experienced in religious rites can be designated initiatory grief. Thus far, it has been argued that this unique type of grief is a product of both primitive man's perception of death as distant and certain and his justification of death as the mother-father which leads man into new life and wisdom through death, gestation, and rebirth. It remains to suggest two implications of initiatory grief.

The first implication concerns the nature of anticipatory grief. Major religious rites are responses to the crises of life. A crisis is that event which raises the issue of survival. Birth, coming of age, marriage, and death are such crises. They are met by rites of initiation. The religious response is that man must die. The natural threat of death is met by a spiritual demand for death.

So what is the task for those who anticipate death? It is to die. What is anticipatory grief? It is the process of death, gestation, and rebirth. And, all grief is anticipatory grief. Grief is not a healthy human response to death merely because it allows the individual to overcome negative symptoms. It does not occur to return one from anxiety, meaninglessness, hate, and guilt to only the banal. Grief is healthy because it allows the individual to gestate and be reborn. It occurs to move one from the banal to new life. Grief is the anticipation of life as well as of death. Whenever awareness of death appears, either before or after the fact of death, man responds with a dual negative. He says "No" to death and "No" to life. The dual response is contradictory: "Nothing happened," and "I can't go on." This is a primitive flight from both death and life. Nothing is anticipated. But, if the grief process occurs and is completed, the dual negative becomes positive. Man says "Yes" to death and "Yes" to life. "Something did happen," and "I will continue to happen." Everything is anticipated. So experiencing initiatory grief involves perceiving all grief as the process of death, gestation, and rebirth. By this means, primitive man both asserts and justifies the inescapability of death.

The second implication of initiatory grief concerns the timing of grief.

Primitive man did see death as distant and certain. When this perception is genuine, the time for grief is always "Now." It is always now when man is to die, gestate, and be reborn. Religion is what transforms man's covert and chronic grief into grief that is overt and occasional. Initiatory grief is for every man in every condition.

Consider the puberty rite. Undoubtedly, it had something to do with the stage of adolescence. But it was not conceived by the primitives primarily as a tool for fostering maturity, which is a modern interpretation. Lying in a grave is not the same as reclining on a psychoanalyst's couch. The puberty rite existed to create a human being. Before the rite took place the boy was not human. He was only an animal that might become a human being someday. A primitive tale makes the identical point. History began, so the story goes, when all the people were required to pass through a narrow gate and to touch the corpse of a goddess on the other side. Those who passed through the gate and touched "death" became what are now known as human beings. Those who refused and did not touch "death" became what are now known as animals and vegetables. The puberty rite and the tale illustrate what happens in contemporary hospitals—discarded opportunity to become human in the nearly visible forms of animals and vegetables. But it is illustrated also that initiatory grief is for all men in all conditions.

So the time for grief is always the present. It has been said that man, when he does not grieve, almost ceases to exist. Primitive man understood the situation differently. Man, when he does not grieve, has not begun to exist.

To wonder about death is to grieve. Religious wonder is initiatory grief. The mystery remains. Death is not a puzzle to be solved, any more than is life. But the mystery of initiatory grief links the mysteries of death and life. Therefore, religious man can be both amazed and at home with death. This is the meaning of wonder. For religious man, death is a truth made profound by wonder.

REFERENCES

Eliade, M., *Rites and Symbols of Initiation: The Mysteries of Birth and Rebirth.* New York: Harper & Row, 1965.

—— *Shamanism: Archaic Techniques of Ecstasy.* London: Routledge and Kegan Paul, 1964.

Geertz, C., "Religion as a Cultural System," in M. Banton, ed., *Anthropological Approaches to the Study of Religion.* London: Tavistock, 1965.

Herzog, E., *Psyche and Death.* New York: Putnam, for the C. G. Jung Foundation for Analytical Psychology, 1967.

Lindemann, E., "Symptomatology and Management of Acute Grief," *American Journal of Psychiatry, 101:*141, 1944.

Neale, R. E., *In Praise of Play: Toward a Psychology of Religion.* New York: Harper & Row, 1969.

39

Anticipatory Grief

Irwin M. Blank

Many clergymen have observed that after the death of a loved one (following an extended illness during which the awareness develops that the illness will, indeed, be fatal) members of the immediate family, who within most religious communities are expected to observe particular mourning rituals, will do so without any real feeling of mourning, returning to their normal pursuits in what may appear to be an inordinately brief time. The concept of anticipatory grief offers an explanation for this: the bereaved have already done their mourning prior to the death and, therefore, are prepared to resume the normal pace of their lives.

An example is found in 2 Samuel, Chapter 12 (verses 20–23), in which the child born of the adulterous relationship between David and Bathsheba becomes very sick and dies. During the illness David fasts, lies on the earth, and practices all the other culturally-established mourning procedures of his day. When the child's death is announced to him, the Bible records,

Then David arose from the earth, and washed and anointed *himself,* and changed his apparel; and he came into the House of the LORD, and worshipped: then he came to his own house; and when he required, they set bread before him, and he did eat.

Then said his servants unto him, "What thing *is* this that thou has done? Thou didst fast and weep for the child *while it was alive;* but when the child was dead, thou didst rise and eat bread."

And he said, While the child was yet alive I fasted and wept: for I said Who can tell *whether* God will be gracious to me, that the child may live?

But now he is dead wherefore should I fast? can I bring him back again? I shall go to him, but he shall not return to me.

Thus, David sees his behavior as anticipatory grief, which also serves as a petition to God to have mercy upon him. There is something in this which suggests that an important aspect of grief is not so much sorrow over the fact that the beloved person has died, but rather sorrow over the loss sustained by the living and possibly sorrow brought on by the heightened awareness of one's own mortality.

It is this last attitude which is most clearly expressed in Ecclesiastes and traditionally attributed to Solomon in his old age. Ecclesiastes is read in the Synagogue during the festival of Sukkah. Sukkah celebrates the harvest and the journey from the slavery of Egypt to the Promised Land. A primary symbol of the Sukkot festival is a frail shelter decorated with fall fruits, vegetables, and leaves. A specific quality of the Sukkah is that the roof should not be completely covered over so that the inhabitants of the booth may gaze up to the heavens. Traditionally, this is understood both as an expression of appreciation to God as the source of nature's bounty and as an act of recognition that life is frail, (the Sukkah) and that man's eternal relationship is with God. Ecclesiastes is read during this festival because it tells us of a person of royal lineage with all the prerogatives of a royal personage who is now approaching the reality of his own death. He wonders what, if anything, in his life has meaning since everything ends in death. The mood is somber and the focal point is the awareness of man's finiteness. Here we have an example of existential anticipatory grief.

In a sermonic interpretation of why men and women sit separately in an Orthodox Synagogue, Rabbi Joseph B. Soleveitchik has suggested that this is an expression of awareness that all human relationships, no matter how intimate, as for example that between husband and wife, must be recognized as finite. Therefore, husband and wife take leave of each other when they enter the Synagogue so that they may establish their relationship with the transcendent, infinite God.

In his discussion of Job, Robert L. Katz (1958) suggests that Job's expression, "For the thing which I did fear is come upon me. And that which I was afraid of hath overtaken me," may express moral masochism and Job's "need for punishment." Katz sees the possibility that Job may be one of those "who are wrecked by success." He continues, "A successful person might be troubled unconsciously by the thought that his success has been won only at the cost of depriving someone else, perhaps a brother who was less fortunate.'' It may be that an aspect of anticipatory grief has to do with the feeling that things are going too well. Hence, there is a sense of anxiety which is relieved when the actual death occurs preceded by a period of mourning, the totality of which is felt as an atonement experience for having succeeded too well. It would be interesting to examine the extent to which those who manifest anticipatory grief and return to normal activities following the death in what seems to be an unusually brief time do experience at some later date a recurrence of anxiety.

Relevant to our discussion, perhaps, is the traditional practice of saying the memorial prayer ''El Mole Rachamim'' for the deceased parents of the bride and groom at the wedding ceremony. There is something in this practice which suggests that this is not only an act of filial reverence, but also a recognition that this is the goal toward which all of us are tending. Even in our moments of great joy we should be mindful of that.

It becomes the clergyman's function to help the mourner who has already done his mourning prior to the death of his dear one to understand the meaning of his behavior when he returns to his normal pursuits in what conventionally might be considered as inappropriate haste. It is also the function of the clergyman to help the community understand the nature of anticipatory grief so that the community will know what it is experiencing when the bereaved find it possible to return to the pursuit of life—very much as David did.

REFERENCE

Katz, R. L., "A Psychoanalytic Comment on Job 3:25," *Hebrew Union College Annual, 29:*377, 1958.

40

Anticipatory Grief Work

Allan W. Reed

Grief is most often associated with death, but a broader frame of reference is necessary. Throughout this chapter, the discussion will be based interchangeably on losses incurred through the death of a person and losses stemming from other forms of separation, that is, divorce, moving to a new place of residence, or sending children off to school. All the relevant data about the techniques or dynamics involved in anticipatory grief work cannot be covered here, but what is offered may serve as a refresher or stimulant to further study and practice.

THE HISTORICAL

Dr. Erich Lindemann and his associates made pioneer observations following the Coconut Grove fire in Boston of how we do our grief work (Lindemann, 1944). Their study has served as a resource to deal effectively with grief. However, graduate schools continue to turn out so-called helping persons who have little awareness of the processes involved in bereavement and grief work, and little awareness of the possibility of shaping individual experience and social systems and rituals. Grief work is thus hindered and not fostered.

Grief work is a normal function of being. To not engage in grief work when it is appropriate, although common, is not normal. Failure to grieve may be more indicative of abnormality than the embarrassing and dramatic displays sometimes seen at wakes and funerals. But our society often prefers controlled behavior in the face of loss. The praise given the apparently stoic behavior of the widows of three nationally-known slain men demonstrates our preference for order. Our population seemed to respond to those tragic funerals as if the few moments of public control which the widows showed were signs of the right American spirit, of mature response to loss, of undefiled religion. In the face of such pressures and opinions, any outward signs of grieving could be viewed as treason, as childishness, and as atheism.

Lindemann (1944) noted how some of his patients tried to avoid facing their losses. Such responses can be found, but most people are eager to talk about their losses and to do their grief work if they find that they can talk to someone who will not try to hurry them through the process or make them feel guilty, foolish, or unfaithful when they express honest pain, doubts, fears, anger, or other responses. The clergyman is often felt to be the appropriate person to turn to, for religion claims to be concerned with failures, losses, death—with the frailties of our being as well as with its strength.

DEFINITIONS

Bereavement is the loss of something—we are bereft of an object, a person, thing, body part, ideal, model, or a relationship in which dependency has played an important part. Generally speaking, the greater the dependency, the more the loss will be felt.

Grief is the emotional state which usually occurs when a person is bereft. Its psychological and somatic expressions are stated in the literature (Lindemann, 1944; Benda, 1962). We experience grief as a response to our loss.

Grief work is the inner process of working through, managing, coming to terms with, developing and growing through, acknowledging, making peace with—a bereavement. Grief work can be helped or hindered by a person's own emotional status; by the nature of the relationship he had with the lost person; by the ability of those around him to allow the expression of grief; by a person's awareness of the fact that grief is all about him—that the funeral is, indeed, for the mourner.

Anticipatory grief work is the grief work we do as we try to prepare ourselves ahead of time for a loss. It is putting our house in order. It is setting the stage for a moving and perhaps difficult event. It is a forewarning of a condition which will demand energy and effort. It is working through the impact of an event ahead of time.

THE PROCESS OF GRIEVING

The content of grief work has been described as the ". . . emancipation from the bondage to the deceased, readjustment to the environment in which the deceased is missing, formation of new relationships" (Lindemann, 1944). Talking is the usual tool for undertaking such a task. The author's experiences have demonstrated the ease with which grieving people will talk about their loss and the person who was lost, quite naturally, with moments of ebbing which seem to be times of rest, and with renewed momentum if the listener is interested. Such a flow of data can make us uncomfortable, and many people demand that the griever behave more "maturely," or get over it, or plan for the future.

The counselor has the opportunity to ask about the loss, and must resist the temptation to move the griever into the more comfortable future by such cues as "Now you must make funeral plans"; or "What will you do with the house?" "He is in God's hands, you need not worry." Recorded interviews and experiences with other staff members show that even the most enlightened person can get trapped into saying stupid things. However, if such remarks do not make up the major content of the conversation, the griever's own momentum will often allow mistakes to slip by without affecting the relationship.

The griever is full of the past and wants to share it. He may feel guilty, sad, angry, remorseful, happy, relieved—a variety of emotions stemming from relationships in the past. The present death (or loss) is too fresh to deal with. He must be started in the near past, be brought up to the unbearable future, and come to the point where he may say, "I'm here because. . . ." Then he must be brought back into the past again, perhaps further in time and psychological distance. As the past is relived in these brief but meaningful excursions, the person practices facing the loss. He might repeat over and over again, "I'm here because. . . ." Finally, in a breakthrough which may be highly emotional or quite controlled, he may state in his own way, "I am here . . . because she is dead."

Such a process can accomplish more when it takes place in the area in which the loss occurred (for example, the hospital). An hour spent with the relatives of a dying person at the time of dying seems to be worth four hours spent later when the change of setting, time and, perhaps, medication have dulled the sense of loss.

This recounting of what has proven to be a valuable process is too brief to stand on its own as presented. Benda (1962) offers a more complete account of the task of grief work. He also helpfully describes some of the cultural, religious, philosophical, and age factors which affect the ongoing process. Others also have noted the importance of leaving the past behind in order to be creative in the present and future, and how anxieties about separation seem to keep us from leaving this past behind. In the author's own experience, the process of grieving can best be described at the blackboard with diagrams of interaction, or in role play for simulation of events that actually took place. However, no amount of teaching or description can take the place of "sticking it out" with a grieving person as close to the time of loss as possible, with a tolerance for repetition, and an ability to guide the conversation when that tolerance weakens.

ANTICIPATORY GRIEF

The foregoing presents a broad base needed for understanding the structure of the grieving process, and for moving into a consideration of anticipatory grief work. The following is an extension of the concept of anticipatory grief work, an illustration of two contemporary problem areas which make this type of work necessary and suggestions and examples of how we ourselves might live most consciously and conscientiously for our own benefit and that of anyone who is bereaved.

Anticipatory Grief Work

This is the work we do as we try to accomplish, before the fact, an understanding about the place that a loss has in our personal economy. Anticipatory grief work is as natural as any grief work. It is an ability to face facts and to do the work that the circumstances demand. In spite of its futuristic orientation, it is being anxious about today and not tomorrow. That is, it deals with the anticipation that exists today, so that tomorrow we may deal with tomorrow's anticipation or fulfillment.

"Being anxious about tomorrow" may be mistaken for anticipatory grief work. If it is connected at all, it may be a pathological manifestation of it, much as pathological grief reactions may point to the same fact as real grief work, but actually impede resolution. The apparently neurotic and insecure person who is always worried about the future is hard to get along with. We should not confuse that person, and our feelings about him, with the person who is engaged in anticipatory grief work.

Anticipatory grief work is done in the same manner in which grief work is done: recollections, looking at, measuring, bringing ourselves up-to-date, taking stock of, coming to terms with. Then the griever may be able to present himself with his future, for he has been in the process of unhooking ties to the past. Sometimes people grieve for a person who does not die. The counselor needs to be alert to keep the person at the point of turning over the page into a separated future. If the grief work turns out to have been premature, a process of reattaching the person to the object can take place. Here the counselor should quite pointedly and consciously direct the person's attention to the facts of the case. "Harry was gone there for a while, but now he is still with us. . . ." "You were prepared for the worst. . . ." "It looks as if she will have to suffer some more. . . ." "The kids decided to come back home right when you were ready to have them leave. . . ."

Reasons for Understanding Anticipatory Grief Work

MOBILITY

We live in a mobile age, as a mobile population, with ideals and social and economic pressures which tend to produce even more mobility and separation. Not only are people moving, but they are doing it in smaller family units. Grandmother wants to remain in her home; or the children want her to remain there and not crowd in with them. Either way, the "primary family" has come to mean not three or four but two generations. With some families, the children rush out or are pushed out of the primary family at a very early age. Earlier schooling for toddlers, extended schooling for young adults, the draft for young men, early marriage and the setting up of a new primary family—all these factors lead us to see that the stationary family and person may very well be in a minority.

Frequently, children from supposedly "fine" families and "fine" schools can show very little warmth for others, and have a very weak sense of their own identity. Often, these children are found to be movers— children of fathers "on the way up in the corporation."

Churches and synagogues with traditions of large membership, active programs and generous support for outside charitable giving are now experiencing very high turn-over rates. Their programs for years have been geared to the long-term family—baptizing, confirming, marrying, and then baptizing the children of individuals who are members. Clergymen find that they enter into the life of a family in the middle of a life crisis, no longer able to take an active part in the developmental aspect of a family's living, but often called in to "put out the fires." There is too little time to build up trust. And it is no wonder that many people decide not to join a series of churches or temples, where they would most likely feel like strangers. Religious institutions are weakened as the older and generous contributors of money die, and the financial support of the church or temple is dependent upon "newcomers" who usually start in at a somewhat low level of support and only begin to share their money more generously as their hearts are won by the institution. Mobility calls for more professional manpower, but produces less money to support it. Mobility helps produce alienation and aimlessness, but it also reduces the resources which could support people who are trained in dealing with such existential states of being.

Another phenomenon, which is somewhat related to the mobility problem, is that which can be found in many large apartment houses. This phenomenon can best be described as an attempt to "get away from it all." Some people seem to welcome the anonymity which large buildings create. Energetic and resourceful clergy once tried to create a ministry to these apartment dwellers, even giving up the traditional church building complex and moving into massive apartment buildings with those people in whom they were interested. These clergy now report that their "neighbors" did not want their ministry or significant human relationships. Little imagination is required to view these alienated apartment dwellers as exhibiting most of the characteristics of persons undergoing a pathological grief reaction (Lindemann, 1944).

With such an abundance of problems resulting from our mobility, some technique is needed to permit ourselves to come to terms with constant separation and constant attempts at building trust. The Welcome Wagons and the Newcomers' Clubs are either too commercial or too superficial to do the task, although any contact is welcomed by some separated persons.

The use of techniques involved in anticipatory grief work has proven helpful to many people. The quite natural and graceful ways of saying goodbye at teas, dinner parties, block parties, and over-the-back-fence work well in many neighborhoods. The informal "talking it over" that occurs in the

midst of coffee breaks, during phone calls about babysitters, or in brief recollections with the supermarket cashier, can help us get ready to leave. But
these encounters must be utilized, along with additional and more definitive
activities, which direct energy at the specific task of looking back at past experiences, facing the present moment of loss, and looking forward to new
relationships.

EARLY RETIREMENT AND EXTENDED AGE

Early retirement and extended age make separation and loss an important experience for many people who a few years ago would have remained
productively at work or would have died before such issues arose. Early retirement can be very difficult.

A clergyman decided to retire early in order to work at a special project which had
become dear to him. His constant need to keep busy had once enabled him to administer and help create an active and influential congregation. After retirement,
however, he became a gadfly as he pushed his pet project. He was unable to see that
he was behaving in an irrational manner. His peers and friends could not communicate with him about the effect his behavior had on others, and how he was un-
dermining his own goals. He had been encouraged (by his own drive as well as by
his friends) to switch his passion from his past, effective ministry to an area in which
different behavior was called for. He was still the "old man." He had not come to
terms with what the impact of retirement can be. A judicious and noncrisis-centered
program of preparation for retirement for all clergymen in his community might have
enabled him to detach himself from formerly appropriate modes of working, enabling
him to attach himself to a new form of behavior which would have served his own
ends.

Extended age presents many problems, some of which are so overwhelming that no amount of programming seems to help. Perhaps here the
real anticipatory grief work needs to be enacted by politicians and social
leaders—by the nation—before it can be effective with individual old people. However, there are still people who live longer than they had planned
to. Their shrinking financial resources may seem to be the biggest problem
(and it often is), but anticipating an extended age could be helpful.

One retired man continued to look at his life insurance program, retirement resources, and real estate holdings as if they were existing in earlier years when he had
achieved his greatest business success. His attachment to the meaning of what his
possessions once had for him kept him from realizing that his plans were unrealistic,
and that a different manner of investing his resources could extend the useful life of
his investments.

This man could be called a victim of circumstances, but such a label dismisses too quickly the possibility that federal or local governments, fraternal or religious, or educational institutions, the mass media and other opinion-setting groups could exercise tremendous influence on people who feel that they are planning ahead, but may be using outdated information or ineffective means for meeting problems of our times.

One man neared his retirement age with full and extensive plans for his and his wife's future. He invested in a power boat, fishing equipment, sports gear, and recreational vehicles. He planned to make his retirement like the series of weekends which had satisfied him so much when he was well and active. Shortly before his retirement he had a stroke, which left him unable to engage in the outdoor physical activities which he had loved. His depression was severe, for his life had been wrapped up in a program of constant activity and continuous vacations. He had, quite unrealistically, assumed that he always would have the energy he felt at age sixty. This man measured the future only by the present, and discovered that this was not adequate. Some preparation for older age might have let him see that he might better invest in a variety of ways of spending his time, including some activities which would allow him to exercise his mind more than his muscles.

Resources for Furthering Anticipatory Grief Work

DREAMS AND APPARENTLY CHANCE ASSOCIATIONS

One young man was struggling with his identity and the need to find his autonomy and independence. In a supervisory session, he mentioned that he had dreamed that his mother had appeared to him, her image becoming smaller and smaller, until it finally disappeared. When his supervisor repeated "smaller and smaller," the young man quickly realized that he was preparing himself for a time when she would not exist at all as a barrier to his own fulfillment.

The mother of a high-school age son commented on the newspaper's reports of what life in a modern college dorm was like. Her interest in coed arrangements and rebellious students remained academic until her husband noted that their son was soon to go away to college. Both parents then shared with each other their own feelings—both hopeful and apprehensive—about the loss that they would experience when their son would not be living with them and would not be under their direct supervision.

A middle-aged man with terminal cancer kept his room darkened and the door closed. The chaplain noticed this, and told the patient that he seemed to be cutting off relationships earlier than his physical condition called for. The patient grasped this opening and talked for many minutes about how he would miss his survivors. His loss was not that of his life, but rather all the relationships which were meaningful to him. The loss of the life (dying and death) was relatively unimportant for him.

Each of these three examples demonstrates that the process of anticipatory grief work was set into motion because someone was listening and was able to respond to the feeling content of the remarks or of the situation. Each person grasped the opportunity for sharing the emotional content of his particular situation. Each example also contained the possibility that the emotional content might keep a listener from responding to the feeling, and thus might use any means available to escape talking about a bereavement.

RITUALS AND CEREMONY

Primitive cultures provide us with many examples of rites of passage which allow a person to let go of one stage of development and social organization and attach himself to a more advanced stage of behavior, responsibility, and understanding. Our own culture contains many less exotic but equally important rituals.

Those of the churches (of all faiths) tend to speak most directly to bereavement, and are often the best resources for giving support to anticipatory grief work. However, even the institutions most interested in life and death may tend to be "death-denying" rather than "life-affirming." They are death-denying when they stress the overcoming of death, the victory over death, the steadfastness of a person in the face of loss, the existence of all that negates death rather than the stressing of all that gives meaning to life. Death-denying arises out of our fears and doubts. Life-affirmation arises out of our belief that we matter enough to have meaning (and perhaps existence), no matter what happens to us (Reed, 1968). Although funeral rituals and their ceremony need to be looked at critically in order to ask what they say about those of us who live, other rituals are as important as funerals.

One eminent professional man remarked at a retirement party given for him that he, being a simple man, had in the past looked down on the celebration of anniversaries and other important events which had their own rituals. He now noted that as he faced retirement himself, the act of getting together with his friends and co-workers took on meaning for him. The ritual was a way to move from one world to another—helpful to all concerned.

A man refused to say "good-bye" to people, and discouraged others who wanted to say that word to him. His acquaintances decided that he was still affected by the "good-byes" that he had experienced in a concentration camp. He had not finished saying good-bye to his murdered friends and did not want to be reminded by others. His renunciation of a common ritual which prepares us for a loss kept alive whatever pleasure he obtained from the memory of his friends to whom he still granted life.

SMALL LOSSES IN LIFE'S ORDINARY PROCESSES

Weisman and Hackett (1967) noted, "One factor mitigating the fear of death in the aged is that incapacity and waning powers are already familiar to them." A series of small losses can let us know what it is like to be bereft. Unfortunately, many people go through life without much conscious appreciation of the fact that they learn not by having experiences but by analyzing their experiences. Discussion groups in nursing homes and retirement centers can foster a sharing of the meaning of experiences which may help people prepare to lose a loved one, or their own life.

A couple whose children have grown and left home may use their moving into a smaller apartment as an opportunity for saying good-bye to many events of the past which will not be repeated, and of saying hello to new experiences and limitations which actually foretell their own reduced energy and responsibilities.

A sixty-five-year-old woman was dying of cancer in the hospital. She told the chaplain that she had never had a relative or close friend die, and that both her parents and all her relatives with whom she had been acquainted were still living! She and the chaplain decided that she had never learned any experience of death, and that perhaps she ought to practice dying. Through a gathering of the past, looking at it, evaluating various parts of it, hanging on to some especially meaningful memories, discarding (in imagination) parts of the past which did not seem worthy of dealing with in the limited time left, she utilized small losses and handled them to devise a pattern which she would be likely to use as she said her last good-byes. She was true to her practice and died peacefully, surrounded by relatives and staff members who felt at ease about her dying.

SELF-CONSCIOUS LIVING

This resource may be too idealistic for many to achieve. It is the conscious participation in meaningful relationships in the present that can be lived in, evaluated, and appreciated for themselves at the moment of experience, rather than only by hindsight. This self-conscious living may allow us to appreciate what John Dorsey calls our "inviolable-individuality" (Dorsey and Seegers, 1959) so that we can recognize the illusionary character of what we call "relationships." With an appreciation of the unique individuality of each person, and with seeing the universality of that uniqueness, we may come to see that we were never separated because we were never joined together in the first place. This highly developed religious appreciation of the oneness of all mankind is experienced by many people, although it can very seldom be verbalized.

The sensitivity training movement is another a possible resource for helping anticipatory grief work when it is called for. The less that we leave unattended to in relationships, the less we will have blocking our grieving. At the same time, we have a more meaningful relationship to "lose."

CONCLUSION

In the author's experience, people can handle grief work and anticipatory grief with relative ease and great benefit as long as they "keep their wits" about them. There are pathological cases or, rather, situations in which the people do not grieve as the chaplain would like to have them do. But when a period of several days to several weeks is available for follow-up, the average minister, physician, social worker, neighbor, friend, or teacher can engage in facilitating grieving for most people who suffer loss. The universality of the experience of separation and the experience of "coming to terms with" it seem to indicate that we are talking about a process that does not belong in the hands of a few professional do-gooders, but a process that needs to be recognized for its naturalness, its productiveness, and its ability to bind us together in a common situation which reminds us of our universal selfhood.

REFERENCES

C. E. Benda, "Bereavement and Grief Work," *The Journal of Pastoral Care,* Vol. XVI, No. 1, Spring, 1962.

J.M. Dorsey, *Illness or Allness.* Detroit: Wayne State University Press, 1965.

Dorsey, J. M., and W. H. Seegers, *Living Consciously: The Science of Self.* Detroit: Wayne State University Press, 1959.

Lindemann, E., "Symptomatology and Management of Acute Grief," *American Journal of Psychiatry, 101:*141, 1944. (Reprinted in R. Fulton, ed., *Death and Identity.* New York: Wiley, 1965).

Reed, A. W., "Problems of Impending Death—The Concerns of the Dying Patient," *Journal of the American Physicial Therapy Association, 48:*, 7, July, 1968.

Weisman, A. D., and T. P. Hackett, "Denial as a Social Act," in S. Levin and R. Kahana, eds., *Psychodynamic Studies on Aging*. New York: International Universities Press, 1967.

Ritual and Therapy

Thomas Nolan

The purpose of this chapter is to demonstrate how religious ritual can be employed effectively with psychiatric therapy as an intervention in the process of anticipatory grief. A summary of the dynamics of anticipatory grief, and the place of ritual in maturational crises, especially grief, will form the background for a case history. A discussion on the significance of the combined use of ritual and therapy in the anticipatory grief process will follow.

DYNAMICS OF ANTICIPATORY GRIEF

Grief is commonly understood only in one of its aspects, namely, the reaction of a person to the loss through death of a loved one or friend. Actually, grief can be a reaction to any significant loss. Indeed, the dying person himself grieves. As he consciously or unconsciously anticipates death, he fears separation from the significant persons and things in his world. The dying patient also experiences acute or gradual loss of various capacities and functions: cognitive skills, motor skills, and capacity for pleasure.

Anticipatory grief begins before loss actually occurs. The person faced with his own declining health may grieve for himself in much the same way he would grieve when an actual loss is sustained. In nearly all instances in which loss is imminent, those concerned experience the beginnings of grief, ranging from quiet periods of sadness and tears to those symptoms usually associated with grief over actual loss (Peretz, 1970).

Individual differences in response to the threat of illness, helplessness, disability, pain, and separation are based on differences in personality patterns which are derived from past experiences. Kübler-Ross (1969) has identified five general stages through which most terminal patients pass.

Denial, used by almost all patients, functions as a buffer after unexpected shocking news, allowing the patient to collect himself and, with time, to mobilize other, less radical defenses. Denial is usually temporary, to be replaced by partial acceptance.

When the first stage of denial cannot be maintained any longer, it is replaced by feelings of anger, rage, envy, and resentment. In the dependent patient, anger often stimulates feelings of guilt and fear of retaliation. It is frightening for a patient in a dependent position to express anger to a physician, nurse, clergyman, or family member upon whom he feels dependent for survival. To control or hide anger, he may withdraw from all self-assertive behavior and become emotionally inaccessible.

The patient may feel guilt over hostile thoughts and feelings, as well as overtly angry behavior. An ill patient may view his disease as a punishment visited upon him for past sins, although he usually cannot identify what he has done that is so bad (Schoenberg and Senescu, 1970).

The third stage, of bargaining, is helpful to the patient for brief periods of time. Bargaining is actually an attempt to postpone pain or death. It offers a prize for good behavior, sets a self-imposed deadline, and includes an implicit promise that the patient will not ask for more if this postponement is granted. Most bargains are made with God, and they are usually kept secret, or mentioned only implicitly. Psychologically, promises may be associated with quiet guilt for not attending church more regularly, or for deeper, unconscious hostile wishes.

When the terminally ill patient can no longer deny his illness and begins to have more symptoms, his numbness, stoicism, anger, and rage are replaced with a sense of great loss and a feeling of deep depression. Actually there are two kinds of depression: reactive and preparatory. Reactive depression may be secondary to loss of body image, or to financial burdens, or to inability to function and loss of a job. Preparatory depression is secondary to impending loss, and is necessary to facilitate acceptance. The patient is in the process of losing everything and everybody he loves. This kind of depression is more silent than the first, during which the patient had much to share and required many verbal interactions.

If a patient has had enough time and has been given some help in working through the above stages, he will reach a stage during which he is neither depressed nor angry about his "fate." Acceptance should not be mistaken for a happy stage. It is almost void of feelings. When the dying patient has found some peace and acceptance, his circle of interest diminishes. He wishes to be left alone, or at least to have shorter visits. He is no longer in a talkative mood, and communication becomes more nonverbal than verbal. However, even the most accepting and realistic patients usually leave the possibility open for some cure. It is this glimpse of hope, a form of temporary denial, which sustains them through long periods of suffering.

The patient's family significantly influences the patient's response to his illness by their reactions. Families experience parallel stages of anticipatory grief. The dying patient's problems come to an end, but the family's problems go on. The tendency is to hide feelings from the patient in an attempt to keep a smiling face, a front of make-believe cheerfulness.

RITUAL IN CRISIS

People in every culture seek effective means of dealing with the inevitable crises of life. These are the biological crises of birth, growth, aging, death, and environmental crises, such as retirement or loss of one's role partner. These stressful life situations pose coping tasks for the individuals involved. Every instance is critical because it causes the person to move from a state of relative security to the uncomfortable unknown.

In short, crises are precipitated by actual or threatened loss of need satisfaction, or loss of self-esteem because of an overwhelming challenge to one's abilities. Crisis presents both danger and opportunity: danger that the person will be unable to cope with the crisis, or opportunity for increased growth and ability to cope successfully with future crises.

Religion traditionally has made one of its main concerns the management of loss. Each step in life that was marked by a rite of passage was in some sense a dying and rebirth, the loss of an old and taking on of a new identity. At each of the critical steps in life the individual was sustained in the passage by rituals that performed three functions: (1) support in the expression of grief at the loss; (2) approval of the renunciation of what was lost; and (3) guidance in redefinition and reinvestment of self. An example of this function of religious ritual is the funeral wake, which supports the bereaved in their grieving through socialized rituals of mourning, thereby preparing the way for subsequent renunciation, redefinition, and reinvestment (Reeves, 1970).

Birth rites, puberty rites, wedding ceremonies, and burial rites are other examples of community action executed within the framework of cultural tradition. In the Catholic ritual there are seven sacraments: baptism, confirmation, eucharist, penance, orders, matrimony, and anointing of the sick.

When properly performed, these religious rituals include the essential aspects of crisis intervention. They provide someone, in the persons of the relatives, friends, and priest, who cares to help. They offer psychological supports, thus maintaining the person near the reality situation, offering minimal possible escape. Keeping an explicit focus on the crisis, they assist with cognitive mastery of the situation by minimizing feelings of guilt and inadequacy. Using familiar, concrete symbols and words, they involve the participants in organized activity, such as praying, singing, and gestures.

For the bereaved, the institutionalization of the mourning experience in terms of the various rites and rituals of the funeral helps to initiate the recovery process. It involves a gathering together of family and friends who mutually share the loss. At the same time there is acknowledgment of the need for support of the more stricken survivors, whose regression is accepted. Many of the rituals of the funeral emphasize clearly the reality of the death, the denial of which cannot be allowed to continue if recovery from the loss is to take place. This experience takes place in a group, permitting ordinarily guarded feelings to be shared and expressed more readily. In addition, individual religious and spiritual beliefs offer recourse in various ways to the help and support of a more powerful, beneficent figure (God) and provide the basis for the expectation of some kind of union after death. The funeral ceremony includes a symbolic expression of triumph over death. Frequently, mourners gather after the funeral for a feast symbolizing an attempt to return to life and living (Engel, 1962).

The sacrament of the sick serves a similar purpose. Today, when the Church's ritual allows more flexibility in the manner and form in which sacraments are celebrated, it is possible to ritualize in a therapeutic way the process of anticipatory grief. Family and friends gather with their priest around the patient and mutually support each other. It is possible for feelings to be shared and expressed. Recourse is sought in God's help. Guilt is assuaged in the sacrament of penance. By sharing the bread of the Eucharist, union with each other is symbolically maintained, and hope for continued life and triumph over sickness and death is expressed.

A CASE HISTORY

The following case history illustrates how ritual and therapy were combined to help a patient and his wife through the period of anticipatory grief.

Mrs. R. called the rectory for a priest to visit her husband, aged fifty-four, at home with terminal cancer. The priest answering the call was also a professional nursing student. Mrs. R. cautioned him at the door that the patient did not know his diagnosis. She did not want him informed, because "He would not be able to stand it." The priest suggested that Mr. R. might already realize the seriousness of his condition and might even welcome an opportunity to talk about it.

Mrs. R. and the priest went into the sickroom together. Mr. R. said he felt alone with his illness, as though people were avoiding him, even his wife. He said he could understand why people become bitter when they are so sick, and that he himself sometimes felt this way because they were not as sick as he was. He said that he even felt angry at God at times for allowing this to happen when he didn't think he deserved it. He described his situation as a "lonely journey," one that he had "to travel all alone." He complained that no one talked to him or would listen to his feelings about it.

In successive interviews the patient and his wife were able to openly discuss their feelings about each other and about his impending death. Even though Mr. R. was able to use the word "cancer" only once, when asked what he thought was happening to him he was able to speak about his future in the third person. "I'm not eating well these days. I know that people need nourishment; if they don't eat, they won't last." Mrs. R. discussed with her husband her plans for the future and what it would mean for her to live alone.

Arrangements were made for Mr. R.'s children and other relatives to be present for the sacrament of the sick. Everyone spoke together part of David's Psalm 18, acknowledging God as a source of strength and protection. Then each member prayed silently, placing hands one by one on Mr. R.'s forehead. This gesture brought all of the members to a confrontation with Mr. R.'s illness and gave them an opportunity to cry, without having to rely on words to express their deeper feelings. Those who, prior to this experience, were afraid of "breaking down" or "going to pieces" were allowed to share these feelings in a way in which they could face. Forgiveness of sins was proclaimed, and the Eucharist was shared. The concluding prayer composed for the occasion summarized the reality of the situation:

O God, you know well Your servant Mr. R. who grows weak as his body fails. If it is Your will, give him back his strength and full health. But if in Your loving wisdom you have decided not to make him well again, give him strength to face Your will with courage and to accept it in peace. Look kindly, O Lord, upon Mr. R.'s wife and children as they stand here before you in humble prayer. Protect them and guide them in the days ahead. Give them true peace and understanding; give them love and encouragement.

There were twelve weekly interviews with the patient, and each one concluded with sharing the Eucharist. The patient felt "great relief to know he was living so close to God." He felt reconciled not only with God, but also with his family, for having expressed his anger and bitterness earlier in his illness. He believed the sacrament to be a promise of future life, his triumph over death.

On the last visit, the sick man said "Good-bye" with a kind of finality indicating he knew he would not see the priest again. His wife confided that he was anticipating his birthday two days hence with some enthusiasm, and had asked about his cake. The cake had always had two candles in the past, "one for the year gone by and one for the coming year." This time when Mrs. R. brought it to her husband, he blew out only one of the candles. The next morning he died peacefully with his wife and son at his bedside.

Because of the ongoing relationship the priest had established with Mr. R.'s family, he was able to employ the ritualized wake and funeral to provide them with an opportunity to grieve and to facilitate closure.

DISCUSSION

Combining the role of priest with that of nurse, while not common today, is not a new idea. Historically, the care of the sick was in the hands of those who controlled the religious life of men, namely the priests. Early in the Christian era special orders of monks and nuns performed nursing tasks. Later, responsibility for the practice of medicine and nursing shifted from religious to secular groups.

It is the author's opinion that Mr. R. and his family would not have been as effectively cared for by a priest or nurse alone. Nursing knowledge gained from the concept of the therapeutic relationship's specific interviewing techniques, and understanding the dynamics of the human personality under stress, have contributed to a more intense and effective priestly ministry. Furthermore, supervision by a psychiatric nurse specialist assured more insight and objectivity in the therapeutic relationship with Mr. R. As a result, the employment of rituals during the crisis of anticipatory grief became fuller and richer experiences for the patient, his family, and the priest.

In this post-Second Vatican Council era, when the traditional role and identity of the priesthood are re-examined, fresh new forms of ministry are being explored. The combination of the complementary services of priest and nurse is one satisfying way of responding to the gospel challenge to "Go forth to all peoples."

REFERENCES

Engel, G. L., *Psychological Development in Health and Disease*. Philadelphia: W. B. Saunders, 1962.

Kübler-Ross, E., *On Death and Dying*. New York: Macmillan, 1969.

Lindemann, E., "The Medical Psychological Dynamics of the Gamut of Normal Experiences of the Normal Individual," in I. Gladston, ed., *Ministry and Medicine in Human Relations*. New York: International Universities Press, 1955.

Parad, H. J., *Crisis Intervention: Selected Readings*. New York: Family Service Association of America, 1965.

Peretz, D., "Reaction to Loss," in B. Schoenberg *et al.*, eds., *Loss and Grief: Psychological Management in Medical Practice*. New York: Columbia University Press, 1970.

Reeves, R. B., "The Hospital Chaplain Looks at Grief," in B. Schoenberg *et al.*, eds., *Loss and Grief: Psychological Management in Medical Practice*. New York: Columbia University Press, 1970.

Schoenberg, B., and R. A. Senescu, "The Patient's Reaction to Fatal Illness," in B. Schoenberg *et al.*, eds., *Loss and Grief: Psychological Management in Medical Practice*. New York: Columbia University Press, 1970.

Schnaper, N., "Care of the Dying Person," in D. L. Farnsworth and F. J. Braceland, eds., *Psychiatry, the Clergy and Pastoral Counseling*. Collegeville: St. John's University Press, 1969.

APPENDIX

Anticipatory Grief: Terminology, Meaning, Usage, and Connotations in Thanatology

Austin H. Kutscher, Ivan K. Goldberg, and Elsa Poslusny

Few studies of the phenomenon of anticipatory grief in the bereaved-to-be and in the patient himself have been reported in the scientific literature. More recently, as other areas of thanatology have been studied, this phase of grief has begun to receive more attention, particularly as a potentially important point of intervention to mitigate the effects of stress on the ultimate recovery of the bereaved following his loss.

Various members of the Professional Advisory Board of the Foundation of Thanatology suggested that an opinionnaire be circulated among a randomly selected but significant number of the multidisciplinary members of the Board regarding the term, its definition, and context in the absence of a standardized dictionary definition.

It has become apparent that many of the major terms used by thanatologists should at this juncture be exposed to finer semantic observation and definition. Dictionary editors and other authorities have not delineated clearcut definitions of some of these terms, nor have they revised outdated ones. The information assembled by this study is proposed as a base for the selection of one or several definitions to be submitted for examination by the edi-

tors of the most generally used medical and other dictionaries, with the hope
that the definitions currently in print can be amended or revised. Where no
definition appears, it was hoped that this material would be of value in the
creation of one. Refinement in the definition of the term "anticipatory grief"
will add a more useful and effective word to the vocabulary utilized in multidisciplinary deliberations.

In approaching this task, we were mindful of the fact that the concept
of an allied health team approach to patient care requires definitions that cut
across disciplines for effective interchange among practitioners. As they
communicate with each other, either verbally or in print, it is obvious that
meanings should be shared, appreciated, and understood. It is imperative
that commonly agreed-on definitions be utilized within the periodicals of
medicine, its allied fields and the humanities, as well as in such reference
works as medical and standard dictionaries. Envisioned as a result of this
survey is a general definition for anticipatory grief of the dying patient for
himself and that of the bereaved-to-be. Potentially, the phenomenon could
affect many persons. To set up controlled studies it is necessary to explore
acceptable working definitions for this concept. The following statement was
submitted to sixty-four thanatologists:

In setting up a controlled study of "anticipatory grief" we have come to realize that
we need an accepted working definition for this concept, which is nowhere spelled
out as such in our dictionaries. What is your definition of anticipatory grief, both for
the dying patient and for his survivors—spouse, family, etc.?

Set forth below, categorized by discipline only, is a selection of replies
received from the responding thanatologist recipients. The rate of response,
40 percent, is regarded as high, since the recipients of the survey were not
chosen in general from among those participating in the "Anticipatory
Grief" Symposium held in April, 1972.

DEFINITIONS OF ANTICIPATORY GRIEF

Medicine

HEMATOLOGIST: See Kübler-Ross's book for an excellent definition.

Nursing

NURSE: Anticipatory grief is the developing awareness on the part of the patient or the family of all that will be forever lost when the impending death

actually comes. The behavior of those so aware becomes altered into a grieving pattern, basically one of desolation, helplessness, and rage. Because of the reality of the situation, comforting words of cheer should never be given at this time. Subsequently, death may be viewed as a relief since the depths of anguish have already been experienced.

Pediatrics

PEDIATRICIAN 1: Feelings or experiences of loss or grief for a dying patient felt before death has actually occurred. They must be distinguished from feelings related to the patient's illness or suffering rather than his expected death.

PEDIATRICIAN 2: This would require a ''paper'' to describe fully, inasmuch as there are distinctive stages or degrees in addition to the variations described. Most physicians do not allow the development of anticipatory grief soon enough in most relatives and even friends of the dying. Preterminal information is needed especially in the cases of siblings who may have guilt feelings that require erasing ''by the patient.''

Anticipatory grief, therefore, is that period of sorrow that should be allowed to develop slowly around the dying patient to assuage the crises of death and separation.

Psychiatry

PSYCHIATRIST 1: Simply a grief process initiated in advance of (in anticipation of) loss, as a result of awareness of, or conviction of, imminent loss. The term was first used in 1955 (Aldrich, C. K., *Psychiatry for the Family Physician,* New York: McGraw-Hill, 1955, p. 10), although it was not indexed as such until a revision was published under the title *An Introduction to Dynamic Psychiatry* in 1966.

PSYCHIATRIST 2: (1) The reactions seen in people, usually spouses or primary relatives, coping with the expected or inevitable death of someone close. (2) Less satisfactory (after Lindemann) the reaction seen in people, usually spouses or primary relatives, coping with the potential death of someone close. Theoretically the term refers to people involved in acute life-threatening situations, such as war. However, because it is a broader definition, it could include people involved in dangerous occupations—firemen, policemen, etc. (3) Unacceptable—the reaction seen in people coping with the loss of an object (for example, departure of a person, separation from a person, fantasied loss of a person, loss of a limb).

PSYCHIATRIST 3: A specialized psychological reaction to an anticipated (but not actual or realized) loss. Perhaps one could even extend—or when it is better understood—necessarily extend this definition to focus on a process of self-induced grief reaction aimed at object detachment (or decathexis). This should also proceed according to stages, which must be identified and defined. The work of anticipatory grief might be better called anticipatory mourning.

PSYCHIATRIST 4: Anticipatory grief is that effective reaction experienced and displayed by survivors from the time they learn of the terminal state of a loved one. Such grief can be looked upon in terms of low- and high-type grief potentials. Such circumstances reflect the situational influence which helps determine the quality and intensity of the anticipated grief reaction.

PSYCHIATRIST 5: Anticipatory grief is the normal response preceding an expected loss. The expected loss of a person, life, culture, or concept is accompanied by a normal grieving period. The broad definition is the most useful.

PSYCHIATRIST 6: Anticipatory grief is a syndrome affecting the patient who is terminally ill, and all who come into contact with him—including the professional staff. It is characterized by the presence of denial, anxiety, and tension in the patient, and often more so in the surrounding group of family, friends, and staff. It is expressed in two separate entities—two parallel paths—that of the patient who follows the Kübler-Ross stages to some extent, and that of the relatives and friends whose path has not yet been charted, although it appears to be radically different from that of the patient. Anticipatory grief of the staff is the third as yet unrecognized and undefined phenomenon.

PSYCHIATRIST 7: Anticipatory grief is that feeling of sadness, despondency, and loss which an individual feels in expectation of the impending death of a love object or himself.

PSYCHIATRIST 8: Anticipatory grief is the beginning of the process of separation and loss, a period of "trial-action" concerning the event for the purposes of constructing defenses against intolerable pain; a means of avoiding a gross stress reaction by reducing the unexpectedness of a situation, experimenting with coping mechanisms, and resolving unfinished aspects in the relationship.

PSYCHIATRIST 9: Anticipatory grief is a profound emotional response to impending, irreversible loss, which may be experienced by both the dying patient and his loved ones. The dying patient may feel the pain of parting from those he has loved and cared for (a spouse, children, close friends), and anxiety over whether they will be able to manage life without him. Also, there may be frustration because he has not finished his life-work or fulfilled his ambitions, or a bitter sense of failure because he has not been allowed time to utilize his potentials and, therefore, feels he has wasted his life. In addition a cold fear of death may be interjected, and grief about the cruel reality of having to die. But there can also be a desire for death when the daily battle for survival becomes too painful to be endured and when a longing for final peace outweighs all other affects.

For the family and friends of the dying patient, facing the impending loss and the absolute finality of death, anticipatory grief involves a heightened sense of anxiety, pain, remorse, and depression, the intensity of which depends on the meaning and intimacy of the threatened relationship. In addition, their anticipatory grief may be exacerbated by fears of losing a source of security, protection, or a cherished companionship.

Psychology

PSYCHOLOGIST 1: Undoing before the fact. Beginning process of separation. Distantiation. Experiencing the anger, resentments, frustration, loss before the fact of loss, ahead of the time. Process of making new attachments, new relationships involving feeling concerns or reshuffling of old relationships so that they now provide structure for support. "It's rough, but we're all together" kind of mood state.

For the patient: inept attempt to come to grips with the fact of loneliness, being left, being alone, being valued less and less. The tears of wanting to be close yet finding no one caring to be close. The terror and fright of not death qua death but of the intense loneliness. Anticipatory grief, modes of preparation for coping with the later assault when defenses are less than well organized; through tears, anger, silence and withdrawal.

PSYCHOLOGIST 2: The definition of "grief" should include a statement indicating that such reactions may come prior to the actual loss, as a function of expectations.

PSYCHOLOGIST 3: Systems continuously reassess costs, payoffs, and trendline—investing accordingly. Anticipatory grief is a subclass of patterned desocialization or the culturally peculiar ways of undoing interdependency networks, that is, behaviors which reduce the cognitive and/or effective aspects of previously established relationships (where) minimizing the assumed disruptive effects of dissolution are a focal concern.

Definitions of processes should strive for the most common elements of applicability, not only the unique elements of the immediate situation.

Social Work

SOCIAL WORKER 1: *Crisis Intervention: Selected Readings,* Howard I. Parad, ed., published by Family Service Association of America, 44 East 23d Street, New York, N.Y. 10010, 1965, is a valuable source. Both Caplan and Lindemann have spelled out much data describing "anticipatory grief," and there is an excellent bibliography.

To define this concept as it applies to the dying or the life-threatened individual and to the bereaved-to-be is a difficult but important task.

SOCIAL WORKER 2: Definition is difficult, and this writer does not particularly like the term "anticipatory grief." One usually associates the word "anticipate" with a joyful or pleasant event, one to which one is looking forward. To do otherwise is morbid and unhealthy. One individual might well anticipate and experience feelings of grief when the situation does not fully warrant it, because of his own inner needs.

When it is known that a dear one is going to die, and that there is no possible reversal of the situation, then grief already has started. It is no longer a matter which can be considered purely anticipatory, but rather the beginning of grief, the start of grief, or the beginning and culmination of grief. It is the beginning and climax of grief, or beginning, sustaining, and climax of grief.

The term anticipatory grief is not directly pertinent to the dying patient, although it is frequently so. Patients very often have to help their already grief-stricken families and friends so that they themselves can die at peace. One would hope that the patient, with help of family and friends, can derive comfort, solace, and help with unfinished business and realization of a life completed with satisfactions and peace of mind. It must also be recognized that this is a period of sustained grief for the dying patient and those for whom he has meaning and mean much to him. This is both accepted and satisfying. Sorrow and sadness are understandable, and to totally hide this from the patient even if he knows only that he is very ill certainly lowers his feeling of self-esteem. To feel that no one cares enough to grieve is indeed the saddest of all deaths.

Surgery

SURGEON 1: There is agreement with the Foundation on the opinionnaire you sent out.

SURGEON 2: Anticipatory grief implies the response of a patient or those close to a patient to an expected loss. The expected event may be loss of life but the emotion may be elicited by anticipation of lesser losses, such as amputation, loss of voice, loss of sight, etc.

Theology

THEOLOGIAN 1: Suffering is due to anticipation of undesirable loss.

THEOLOGIAN 2: The emotion of "feeling a loss" before that loss has in fact taken place is a preparatory function of the total person for what promises to be a loss of relationship to an object (person or thing or concept) in which dependency is an important factor. After accident or surgery, the loss may involve body parts or functions. In terminal illness or extreme injury, this threatened loss may be the loss of the person's own life and relationships.

Anticipatory grief work may be done consciously or unconsciously; it may be facilitated or hindered by the person's unconscious feelings, by influential people, by cultural pressures and tradition, by immediate needs to cope with the situation.

Anticipatory grief may give way to grief when the loss actually happens. It may give way to morbid grief reactions if the anticipatory stages of preparation have not been influential enough to make actual "grief" seem to be desirable; it may have to be replaced by a recommitment to the "object" if the loss does not take place. This recommitment itself involves a working through of the threat of loss, its accompanying feelings, and the new feelings brought about by the change in expectations.

Psychiatric writers usually state (often quoting a previous writer) that no human being ever really imagines himself as dying or as being dead. While the difficulty of doing this is apparent, anticipatory grief work is part of a person's actually being able to imagine himself as dead (that is, in the case of the dying person doing grief work for himself). As far as is known, the dead ''person'' is not thinking about himself as dead. However, many ''religious categories'' do enable people to come to terms quite realistically with the fact of death, and with the fact that this state will one day describe them.

KEY WORDS USED FOUR OR MORE TIMES

Coping: 4	Potential: 4
Cultural: 4	Process: 5
Emotion: 5	Reaction: 6
Expected: 6	Reality: 4
Experience: 5	Relationship: 5
Feeling: 6	Separation: 4
Grief: 5	Situation: 5
Loss: 12	Terminal: 4

''POSSIBLE'' KEY WORDS USED ONLY ONCE OR TWICE

Anger: 2	Impending: 2
Anguish: 1	Intensity: 2
Anxiety: 1	Loneliness: 1
Awareness: 2	Mourning: 1
Behavior: 2	Rage: 1
Comforting: 1	Relief: 1
Defense: 2	Resentment: 1
Denial: 1	Response: 2
Desolation: 1	Sadness: 2
Despondency: 2	Sorrow: 2
Detachment: 1	Suffering: 2
Frustration: 1	Tears: 1
Helplessness: 1	Tension: 1
Imminent: 1	Withdrawal: 1

Index

Lucia A. Bove
Elaine A. Finnberg